Colin Fredyks

H. d. Kah

Palo Alto 1979

TO ACQUIRE WISDOM
The Way of Wang Yang-ming

Faculty of Asian Studies
Australian National University
Oriental Monograph Series, Number 16

Studies in Oriental Culture, Number 11
Columbia University

This unusual portrait of Wang Yang-ming was painted by Tseng Ch'ing, famous portrait artist of late Ming times who allegedly combined Chinese and Western techniques. It passed into the possession of Miwa Shissai (1669–1744), a Japanese Yang-ming scholar. The reproduction here has been made possible through courtesy of Prof. Okada Takehiko, of Fukuoka.

TO ACQUIRE WISDOM
The Way of Wang Yang-ming

JULIA CHING

Columbia University Press
New York and London   1976

The Publications Committee of the Faculty of Asian Studies of the Australian National University has generously provided funds to assist in the publication of this work.

Julia Ching   taught at the Australian National University and Columbia University. She at present associate professor of Chinese Philosophy at Yale University. She is also associated with the Institute of Oriental Religions, Sophia University, Tokyo.

Library of Congress Cataloging in Publication Data

Ching, Julia.
　To acquire wisdom.
　(Studies in oriental culture; 11)
　Includes selected essays and poems by Wang Yang-ming in English translation.
　Bibliography: p.
　Includes index.
　1. Wang, Shou-jen, 1472-1529.　I. Wang, Shou-jen, 1472-1529.　Selected
works.　English.　1976.
II. Title.　III. Series.
B5234.W35C49　　181'.11　　75-20038
ISBN 0-231-03938-7

For my "families"

Studies in Oriental Culture
Edited at Columbia University

CONTENTS

ACKNOWLEDGMENTS

IT IS MY PLEASURE and privilege to acknowledge here the debt of gratitude which I have incurred in preparing this book for publication. As I think back to the days when I was writing the doctoral thesis, my thanks go especially to Liu Ts'un-yan, of the Australian National University, who also read through the revised version, which was to become the book. Others in Australia gave me much help and encouragement, in the direction and verification of my translations, as well as in regard to English expression and style. I think in particular of J. D. Frodsham, K. H. J. Gardiner, D. Leslie, and Wang Gung-wu. I think also of Anthony Ruhan, now at Port Moresby, who gave me valuable advice on methodology. I am also grateful to A. L. Basham, our famous Indologist, who gave me untiring encouragement. And I cannot forget others in Australia who, at the same time as myself, were preparing doctoral theses in the field of Chinese studies, with whom I had interesting discussions and exchanges.

During my visits to the Far East, while writing this book, I received the friendship, help, and critical advice of Okada Takehiko, of Kyūshū. I was also able to discuss certain problems with Ch'ien Mu, Mou Tsung-san, and T'ang Chün-i. And then, both while still in Australia and after coming to the United States, I received the help and encouragement of W. T. de Bary and Wing-tsit Chan. Their own works, as well as their examples, have been a source of strength. I have also been fortunate in the critical advice and encouragement I received from Fang Chao-ying, D. S. Nivison, and A. F. Wright. I have had some profitable discussions on comparative analysis with European philosophy with Thomas Berry, David Dilworth, Eugene

Kamenka, Hans Küng, and Anthony Ruhan. I remember also the encouragement of Anthony Johns.

In all my travels, I have benefited from the kind help given by library staffs attached to state or university libraries—in Canberra, Taipei, Hongkong, Tokyo, New York, and Washington, D. C. Thanks are due especially to the Australian National University Library and the Australian National Library, both of Canberra.

My thanks are extended particularly to the Faculty of Asian Studies, Australian National University, where I received my training and research and teaching experience, and whose Publications Committee allotted a generous grant toward the publication of this book. I thank also the staff at the Columbia University Press, who prepared this work for publication.

I will not forget the stimulus and encouragement given me by so many other friends, as well as by members of my own "extended families". My warm thanks go particularly to my sister Priscilla and her family whose hospitality I enjoyed during the final days of revising the manuscript.

It should be mentioned that certain parts of the book have appeared in modified forms in some scholarly journals. These include the introductory chapter, "Truth and Ideology: The Confucian Way and Its Transmission" (*Journal of the History of Ideas,* 1974); Chapter 1, on the life and spiritual evolution of Wang Yang-ming (*Papers on Far Eastern History,* Canberra, 1971); Chapter 5, on Yang-ming's teaching of the Unity of All Things (*Oriens Extremus,* 1973); and the Epilogue, which deals with the "Yang-ming controversy" (*Journal of Oriental Studies of Australia,* 1974).

JULIA CHING

Columbia University
September, 1974

PREFACE

ODAY, there is a definite need to examine more closely the philosophy of Wang Yang-ming (1472–1529), the Chinese thinker who has influenced the intellectual and political development of China, Japan, and Korea, and whose fifth birth-centenary is being marked in Japan by the publication of a 12-volume compendium.[1] Although, for the English-speaking world, there is the translation of Wang Yang-ming's *Ch'uan-hsi lu by* Professor Wing-tsit Chan,[2] there is not yet a full-length study of his thought. These considerations have led me to this present work. It is an attempt to see Wang's philosophy as a "way" of acquiring wisdom, against the background of the problem of "orthodoxy" with regard to such a way, in the light of the state-supported doctrines of Ch'eng Yi (1033–1107) and Chu Hsi (1130–1200).

I wish to point out first the ambiguity of the problem involved. By "orthodoxy" is usually meant, a right way of thinking. The debate in China has always been over a right way of living, that is, about the correctness of ideas regarding the good life. The issue is thus not so much one of the correctness of certain intellectual propositions, than of wisdom, which concerns insights into the whole of life, of man and his place in the universe, the knowledge of which must be accompanied by virtuous behaviour.

I believe also that a distinction should be made between the *content* of this message concerning the good life, and the *way* by which it has been transmitted. For the human mind attains truth by means of confronting problems. At one time, men might have conceived that the right way of thinking—such as about wisdom and the way of acquiring it—was contained in certain formulae. Later on, with the rise of new situations and new problems, others might have been obliged to devise new ways of thinking, but without discarding the old formulae. The problem of orthodoxy involves the study of continuities and discontinuities, in the use of terms and in their interpretations, which bring about eventual modifications in the thought-content itself.

My main objective being to see Yang-ming's philosophy as a departure from the Ch'eng-Chu norm, I have begun the investigation—after a short historical introduction and an outline-chronology of his life—by a discussion of the tension between truth and ideology, which reveals itself as a historical pattern through the development of Confucianism from a living body of thoughts into a state orthodoxy. I have concentrated on the new philosophical synthesis constructed by Chu Hsi with the help of earlier and contemporary thinkers, as a response to the metaphysical-ethical challenges posed by Buddhism and Taoism. Throughout the entire study, care is given to indicate similarities and differences between Yang-ming's insights and the teachings of the Ch'eng-Chu system, without discussing in detail the extent of Buddhist-Taoist influences on Yang-ming's thought, which is only of secondary interest to a work of this scope. I propose to pursue my objective by a discussion of the shifts of emphases made by Wang Yang-ming, first in moving away from the Ch'eng-Chu orthodoxy, and then within the orbit of thought which he himself constructed. I intend to analyze with some care certain key-words he used, indicating the nuances of meaning wherever possible, or, failing that, the ambiguities involved. As many of these nuances can only be understood when seen in the context of his entire thinking, with growth and development taking place more in depth of understanding than in extent of interest, this study will proceed in a "spiral" fashion, as a series of concentric circles, while following Yang-ming as he talked always about the same thing but in different words: wisdom or Tao, and how it could be acquired.

I consider my task to be mainly that of a textual exegete. I believe that the literary genres contained in Yang-ming's collected writings, as well as the principal tenets of his thought, lend themselves to such an approach, which gives its attention to the meaning of words and sentences as well as to the burden of his central message.[3]

Before setting out, it should be understood that Yang-ming's philosophy was at the same time ethics and metaphysics as well as mystical insight. Analysis will not be made with the view of separating one
from the other, but only to indicate the various ethical, metaphysical,
and mystical connotations of the same statements. This fact is true of
many other Chinese thinkers, being in great part the result of the
fluid nature of the Chinese language itself. But it is above all characteristic of the thought of Wang Yang-ming, which was highly integrated, and closely interwoven with his life and actions. For this
reason, I have translated key-words according to their contexts, without
attempting to "fix" their meanings in English. For example, I have
avoided rendering *liang-chih* as "innate knowledge," or "innate moral
intuition," not only on account of the Cartesian overtones involved,
but also because I prefer to interpret it according to the different
levels of contextual meaning. And I usually refer to *chih liang-chih* as
"extending" *liang-chih,* while taking some pains to explain how this
liang-chih is at the same time inborn and acquired, so that if usage of
the word "extension" connotes increase and development, it does so
without denying the need also of "realizing" that which is innate, of
"actualizing" the potential, of "making manifest" the latent. In the
case of the word *hsin,* which appears so often, I have rendered it sometimes as "mind" and sometimes as "mind-and-heart," keeping to the
shorter form nearly always in the selection of essays and poems in
translation, but doing so without usually intending any difference of
meaning. Lastly, on account of the difficulty of translating technical
terms accurately and comprehensively, I have made use of the romanized forms of these words even while venturing some English
equivalent or near-equivalent.[4]

On account of the method chosen, I have also, with few exceptions,
avoided using the more commonplace terms, including that of neo-
Confucianism itself, which may be susceptible of misunderstanding.
I have refrained from referring to the Ch'eng-Chu and Lu-Wang
movements as belonging to schools of "realism" and "idealism," although these terms are aften used by scholars, because they have been
taken over, out of context, from the history of European philosohy,
and remain useful to the student of Chinese thought only when carefully defined. And as this study is directed to specialists of Chinese

thought as well as to a more general reading public, I have sought to make use of a language that can be understood by both.

I have deliberately desisted from giving too much of my own judgment until the final, concluding chapter, in order that the critique itself may be based on an impartial analysis of his words, as examined in the light of their historical context, since, as we shall see, Yang-ming's doctrines were given expression largely in response to the questions addressed to him by others, so that his whole philosophy may be described as the product of a living dialogue. I have not, however, given any detail of his life, travel, or career except when such is relevant to the evolution of his teachings. I have also made no attempt to present the development of the Yang-ming school in late Ming times. But I have given, as Epilogue, a discussion of the so-called Yang-ming controversy which raged during and after his life.

I have deliberately limited myself to brief, footnoted indications of certain similarities or parallels between various aspects of Wang Yang-ming's thought and those of some well-known Western philosophers and religious thinkers.[5] I am of the opinion that much interesting comparative analysis can be made between many great Chinese thinkers and those of the Western European tradition who have followed certain Platonic and neo-Platonic insights regarding the relationship between man and himself and man and the world, from which an understanding of the Ultimate has been acquired—whether this be termed "creativity" according to A. N. Whitehead's suggestion, or the "absolute," which, he claims, is the tendency of monistic systems such as Spinoza's.* Such comparative analysis cannot be adequately given within the limited scope of this book, which offers a rather comprehensive presentation of Wang Yang-ming's philosophy, but remains in its own way an introductory study, since the very depth of subtlety and richness of content of Wang's thought is such as to require many more studies yet to be made. I have endeavored rather to

---

* *Process and Reality* (New York: Free Press, 1969), 10. May I note here that I realize the inadequacy of the term "absolute," which cannot yield itself to meaningful analysis, but I have made use of it in this book for lack of a better alternative. The Chinese *wu* (nothingness) cannot explain itself, or lend further meaning to the ultimate reality which it frequently signifies.

avoid making superficial comparisons between Wang Yang-ming and thinkers of other very different traditions, even when indicating the closeness of certain philosophical insights. For example, Wang Yang-ming's personal, interior evolution and his teaching of *chih liang-chih* might offer evidence of existentialist attitudes, such as those pertaining to the moral decision, so emphasized by S. Kierkegaard.[†] Yet Wang's central intuition of the oneness of all things recalls rather strikingly Hegel's vision of the Absolute as reality unfolding itself in a process of its own becoming, a process in which man partakes by transcending his own particularity.[‡] Taken each in its own context, Kierkegaard's teaching is a conscious reaction against the Hegelian system, which, according to him, negated the possibility of personal responsibility and authentic existence. In Wang Yang-ming, however, the interpenetration of such distinctions as particular and universal, subject and object, is always presupposed, and often clearly enunciated. In any case, it is my earnest hope that this *introductory* work of Wang Yang-ming's thought will provoke others to undertake more specialized studies, including those of comparative analysis.

I should like, however, to point out what seems to me an important historical parallel in the development of Ming thought and that of the recent West, which may contribute to a clearer understanding of certain problems and suggested solutions inherent in the Ming thinkers, especially Wang Yang-ming and his school. In regarding his philosophy as a search for wisdom, and particularly for a method by which this may be acquired, I have found that the later metaphysical heights to which Yang-ming and his disciple Wang Chi aspired, through their teaching of the absence of good and evil, tended in some ways to overlook the more practical aims of the original quest. This provoked a reaction which expressed itself diversely, whether in the efforts of the Tung-lin school, to modify Yang-ming's positions by reconciling them with those of Chu Hsi, or in the iconoclastic attitudes of Li Chih (1527-1602), whose disillusionment with the pretentious, would-be metaphysicians and sages of his time led him to deny the transcendent and the ultimate, and to return to a study of words and texts,

† See footnote on p. 112.
‡ See footnote on p. 176.

particularly the nonphilosophical. This return to textual exegesis was promoted also by another Yang-ming follower, Chiao Hung (1540–1620), and would eventually lead to the development of philological and textual studies during the Ch'ing dynasty (1644–1911). In a parallel way, the movement of thought in Western Europe following the appearance of Descartes (1596–1650) and Kant (1724–1804) and culminating in the metaphysical synthesis of Hegel (1770–1831), provoked also important reactions, of the iconoclast Nietzsche (1844–1900), with his insistence upon the need for the transvaluation of values, and of those recent and contemporary linguistic philosophers who also deny the validity of metaphysics and content themselves with the positivist analysis of words and sentences, and, by doing so, give expression sometimes to a conscious or unconscious sense of reverence for the unutterable.

Besides discussing the philosophy of Wang Yang-ming, which makes up Part I of this book, I am presenting in Part II a selection of his philosophical essays and poems in English translation,[6] including especially documents which are most relevant to the main thrust of this work. I have not tried to translate everything with philosophical value; I do not consider it so important, since I should wish that every serious student of Yang-ming tackle his thought in the original Chinese. Of the essays included, three have been done before, by F. Henke, in *The Philosophy of Wang Yang-ming* (1916). The selection, however, presents the first English translation of Yang-ming's poems.

Certain supplementary information is also presented in the Appendices. These include a brief survey of the Yang-ming school in Japan, which attempts to show how a different situation, arising, among other factors, from deeper Buddhist influences, has kept Japanese thinkers from being as much affected by criteria of doctrinal orthodoxy imposed on the Chinese themselves; a summary report of the Yang-ming school in Korea, of which so little is known; some charts outlining the schools of Ming thought, particularly those which stemmed from the teachings of Yang-ming and his disciples; and a suggested interpretation of certain selected terms of Yang-ming's philosophical vocabulary. The bibliography both of selected Chinese sources, their translations, and of secondary works relevant to the subject follows the notes. There are two glossaries—a glossary of technical terms and one of personal names, in romanized letters as well as in Chinese and Japanese scripts—and a general index.

A brief *history* of this book may also be appropriate in this Preface. It was originally completed in 1971 as a doctoral thesis at the Australian National University, revised during 1972, the year of the 500th anniversary of Wang Yang-ming's birth, which witnessed various symposia and publications in his honor, and revised again in 1973, mostly at Columbia University. As a final product, the book represents the result of work done on four continents—Asia and Europe as well as Australia and America—to which the necessities of research itself and the circumstances of my own life have led me.

The importance of my subject matter is such that I see little need for explaining how and why I became interested in the study of Wang Yang-ming's Way of Wisdom. But, writing as a woman—and hence with a more personal note—it may be useful for me to say that the figure of Wang Yang-ming, with his restless energy for activity and social commitment, and his irrepressible yearning for stillness and contemplation, held an attraction for me which has been powerful and enduring. I see his life, in appearance full of contradictions, yet developing in the direction of a dialectical reconciliation of these contradictions. He first resolved them on the existential level before proceeding to an articulation of his insights on the rational level— according to the Chinese life-view and world-view, the Chinese *rationale*. And I believe that the Chinese *rationale*, in particular Wang Yang-ming's, has much to say to today's world, where intellectual pursuits tend to favor technical specialization over creative and personal syntheses, and where the quest for the good is often set aside to give time to minute analyses into the meaning of "oughtness." As a Chinese from the fifteenth century, Wang Yang-ming cannot resolve our contemporary problems. But he has pointed out a way which is both human and relevant. He tells us how the manifold problems of human life may be grappled in their depths, and made to contribute to a fuller and more meaningful human existence. As any human vision, his too is limited. But his limitations only challenge us to discover wider horizons, to create our own personal universe without losing contact with the real, to seek for wisdom and enjoy its quest.

As this work is about to be sent to the printer (September, 1974), the "Anti-Confucius Movement" in the People's Republic of China appears to be waning, after a full twelve months of intensive and widely publicized political campaigns. It is not my task here to discuss the anti-Confucius campaign, except to point out that the recent outburst has been directed principally against Confucius himself, and not so much against his followers of the Sung and Ming periods.[7] But I have included, in the Epilogue to the book, some reference to criticisms of Wang Yang-ming made in mainland China at an earlier time. In publishing this book, I wish to invite the reader to assess for himself the richness and importance of Wang Yang-ming's thought, against the background of the entire Confucian tradition in China—as well as in Japan and Korea—and to do so in a dialectical manner, if he so wishes, by examining also for himself some of the criticisms which have been voiced against Wang Yang-ming or even Confucius. I should like to think that, while the reader may discern dimensions of thought in Confucius and Wang Yang-ming which were timebound or con-nected with the interests of particular social classes, he will also dis-cover other, more important dimensions which point to the lasting greatness of both Confucius and his disciple, Wang Yang-ming.

HISTORICAL SUMMARY[1]

THE MING DYNASTY (1368–1644) reached its zenith of glory and prosperity in the early fifteenth century with the development of a strongly centralized government, the promotion of successful maritime expeditions, and the publication under imperial sponsorship of several encyclopaedic compilations which have, among other purposes, that of systematizing and propagating the Confucian synthesis of the Sung dynasty (960–1279).[2] Soon afterward a period of gradual decline set in, as a succession of mediocre, pleasure-loving sovereigns replaced the earlier, vigorous emperors. They increased the abuses of total power with the assistance of a "secret police system" conducted by eunuchs, and maintained a "closed door" policy by the cessation of maritime efforts and by concentrating on the defense of the northern frontiers against Oirat and other raiders. An official orthodoxy was also enforced, through a rigid civil service examination system which regulated not merely the content of the syllabus, but also the form of expression of thought.[3]

In reaction to a government which was always despotic—and frequently in an unbenevolent manner—many intellectuals of the time manifested a reluctance to take part in official service, despite the Confucian tradition and its appeal to the social and civic conscience. The execution of Fang Hsiao-ju (1357–1402) with his entire clan and his disciples, for his steadfast refusal to shift loyalty to the usurping Emperor Ch'eng-tsu (r. 1403–24), shocked the scholarly circles, and the conditions of servility in which scholar-officials were held by the Court did not ameliorate the situation.[4] Many early Ming Confucians refused even to take part in the state examinations, preferring to spend their entire lives in semiretirement, devoting them-

selves to the cultivation of their moral characters[5] and to the quest
for an all-inclusive method of self-perfection.[6]

Wang Shou-jen [Wang Po-an], also known as Wang Yang-ming,
was born into such an atmosphere, marked by a conflict between the
concern for inner freedom and self-transcendence, and the traditional
Confucian teachings for service to the state and to the people.

His many achievements as a writer, statesman, soldier, and philosopher, could not conceal the underlying tensions he experienced
between an attraction for silence and contemplation and the call for
activity and service. He came from a distinguished *literati* family.
He was interested from childhood in Taoist and Buddhist methods
of cultivation.[7] He looked everywhere for a teacher of wisdom but
found none. A passing visit to the philosopher Lou Liang (1422–91)
made a strong impression upon him, and the later meeting with Chan
Jo-shui (1466–1560), a disciple of Ch'en Hsien-chang (1428–1500),
confirmed his desire to strive for the Confucian ideals of sagehood.[8]
But his courageous intervention in favor of certain officials unjustly
imprisoned, enraged the eunuchs in power and led him into exile in
Kweichow and an experience of inner enlightenment.[9] He discovered
in the midst of suffering and privations that the secret of wisdom lay
hidden in his own self-determining mind and heart (*hsin*). He grew
continually in this discovery, throughout his later years of active
military duties and the teaching of his disciples.

Yang-ming suffered a further setback in his political career after a
victorious campaign he had conducted against a powerful rebel, the
prince Ch'en-hao of Ning. Quite ironically, this success made him the
object of wrath and envy on the part of the playboy emperor, Wu-
tsung (r. 1506–21), and sent him once more into retirement.[10] It also
offered him the occasion for a further, final discovery in the nature of
wisdom, and the method for acquiring it, which he described as *chih
liang-chih*, extension and realization of the knowledge of the good.
This was his bequest to the world, which he left at the age of fifty-
seven, when he died of illness after successfully completing a last
military campaign in southern China (1529).[11]

Yang-ming was stripped of his honors posthumously on charges of
having left his post without proper permission during his final illness,
and for teaching a doctrine which was regarded as unorthodox. He

was reinstated only in 1567, and given a posthumous title, Wen-ch'eng. In 1584 his tablet was included in the Confucian temple as a special mark of honor and distinction.[12] This was a real vindication for his good name and an official judgment of the "orthodoxy" of his teachings. Had the man himself been alive to witness both the disgrace and the late reinstatement, he probably would not have considered either very important.

For Wang Yang-ming had frequently referred to the Confucian notion of "madness" or eccentricity (*k'uang*) as the characteristic of a man fired with a single desire for true greatness, who lived above all considerations of human respect.[13] Such a man was singled out by Confucius as a worthy disciple.[14] Such a man was compared by Chu Hsi and Yang-ming himself to a phoenix flying above ten thousand feet.[15] But Wang Yang-ming was not only eccentric. He went beyond that description. He was also a sage (*sheng*).

Indeed, as a philosopher and a wise man, the figure of Wang Yang-ming towered above those of all others of the Ming dynasty, while his teachings and insights provided direction to the later development of philosophy as well as social protest in late Ming China,[16] in seventeenth century Korea,[17] and in late Tokugawa Japan.[18] But he was also a sign of contradiction, during his own lifetime and after. He had been variously praised and blamed. His critics of the past regarded him as a heretic and a hypocrite, a Ch'an Buddhist in Confucian disguise, for his departures from the "orthodox" system of Ch'eng Yi and Chu Hsi. Although it has largely lost its relevance, this controversy has not completely ceased in our own days, while other criticisms of his doctrines, usually ideologically oriented, have arisen too.[19]

One well-known critic of Yang-ming's philosophy has written the following lines which indicate the importance of Wang Yang-ming's philosophical legacy to both his admirers and his critics. They say:

> One single man can change [the destiny of] the world [by his thought], and leave behind an influence that is felt for over one hundred years. [We know of] men who did so in the past: Wang Yi-fu by his "Pure Talk," and Wang Chieh-fu by his "New Laws". In recent times, Wang Po-an [Wang Yang-ming] did the same through his [teaching of] *liang-chih*.[20]

CHRONOLOGY

1517–8   Pacification of bandits and reorganization of local gov-
            ernment
1518   Publication of two works:
            "The Old Version of the Great Learning"
            "The Definitive Views of Chu Hsi, arrived at Late in
            Life"
            Hsüeh K'an, Wang Yang-ming's disciple, publishes the
            first collection of his recorded conversations, the *Ch'uan-
            hsi lu*
1519   Suppression of the rebellion of Prince Ch'en-hao
            Southern expedition of Emperor Wu-tsung (r. 1506–21)
1520   Emperor Wu-tsung returns to Peking
1521   Begins to speak of the "extension of *liang-chih*"
            Accession of Emperor Shih-tsung (r. 1522–66). Honours
            accorded to Yang-ming
1522   Death of Yang-ming's father
1522–27   Six years of teaching in retirement
1527   Recall to active service, to suppress rebellions in Kwangsi
            Teaching of "Four Maxims"
1528   Pacification and reorganization of Kwangsi
            Yang-ming's health deteriorates steadily
            Homebound journey
1529   Death of Yang-ming, on his way home, on January 9 at
            Nan-an, Kiangsi

TO ACQUIRE WISDOM
The Way of Wang Yang-ming

ABBREVIATIONS

BSOAS	*Bulletin of the School of Oriental and African Studies*
CSPSR	*Chinese Social and Political Science Review*
CTCS	*Chang-tzu ch'üan-shu*
CTYL	*Chu-tzu yü-lei*
CWWC	*Chu Wen-kung wen-chi*
CYTC	*Cheng Yi-t'ang ch'üan-shu*
ECCS	*Erh-Ch'eng ch'üan-shu*
ESWS	*Erh-shih-wu shih*
HCLC	*Han Ch'ang-li ch'üan-chi*
HJAS	*Harvard Journal of Asiatic Studies*
HSCC	*Hsiang-shan ch'üan-chi*
MJHA	*Ming-ju hsüeh-an*
MS	*Ming-shih*
PEW	*Philosophy East and West*
SBE	*Sacred Books of the East*
SK	*Ssu-k'u ch'üan-shu tsung-mu t'i-yao*
SPPY	*Ssu-pu pei-yao*
SPTK	*Ssu-pu ts'ung-k'an*
SS	*Sung-shih*
SSCC	*Ssu-shu chi-chu*
SYHA	*Sung-Yüan hsüeh-an*
TSCC	*Ts'ung-shu chi-ch'eng*
TSD	*Taishō Shinshu Daizōkyō*
TT	*Tao-tsang*
WLCC	*Wang Lung-hsi ch'üan-chi*
WWKC	*Wang Wen-ch'eng kung ch'üan-shu*

INTRODUCTION

TRUTH AND IDEOLOGY: THE CONFUCIAN WAY (TAO) AND ITS TRANSMISSION (TAO–T'UNG)

Since Han times, Confucianism has been, for over 2,000 years, the dominant Teaching . . . . And there have been disputes over orthodoxy and heterodoxy . . . [as] each [person] considers his own thinking to be Confucius' teaching, while criticizing others as not being Confucian. Thus . . . Confucius became, in turn . . . Han Ch'ang-li and Ou-yang Yung-shu, Ch'eng Yi-ch'uan and Chu Hui-an, and then Lu Hsiang-shan and Wang Yang-ming. . . . This has been the result of 2,000 years of defensive mentality. But was Confucius really [what they say he was]? . . .[1]

A HISTORICAL PATTERN

T HE EVOLUTION of Confucian teachings in China revealed a pattern that may be described as the interplay of truth and ideology. By "truth" is understood here that interpretation of reality suggested by the great philosophical minds with the help of the Classical texts. By "ideology" is meant here the institutionalization of "truth," by the state authority, which selects and manipulates the commentaries on the Classics through the education and examination system in such a manner as to present a certain interpretation of man, society, and the world, which contributes to the consolidation of that same authority. The historical process by which truth becomes institutionalized can first be discerned in the case of Confucianism around the first century B.C. during the Han dynasty (206 B.C.–A.D. 220). It was later repeated in the T'ang (618–907) and Sung (960–1279) dynasties, which witnessed another attempt by the state to reconstruct a Confucian ideology. In this case, however, the new ideology failed to take hold of men's minds, largely because of the challenges posed by Taoist and Buddhist philosophies which had not been sufficiently answered. But the movement of reinterpretation of Confucianism became important with the emergence of several independent thinkers, who sought to go beyond ideology and recover the lost truth, until, in its turn, the new synthesis that they created became established as state doctrine in the Yüan dynasty (1260–1367). Thus, the philosophy of Wang Yang-ming presented a new claim to return to the sources of Confucian inspiration in the name of truth rather than ideology. But the nature of his thought was such that it was able to resist institutionalization, thus preserving its intrinsic freshness and ambiguity, permitting a diffused influence to take place on all levels of individual and social beliefs and behavior.

It has been pointed out that the philosophy of Chu Hsi and that of Wang Yang-ming stand in relation to each other much as do the two branches of Ch'an Buddhism that differed on the issue of the nature of the inner awakening which brings about the realization of Buddhahood: the gradualist and the subtilist.[2] While affirming the general accuracy of this parallel, it is my intention also to present Yang-ming's philosophy as a reaction to the dominant system of Ch'eng Yi and Chu Hsi much in the same way as the Ch'an Buddhist movement had reacted to the more abstract and formalist elements of Buddhist thought. This analogy is to be applied with caution, on account of the penetration of T'ien-t'ai and Hua-yen metaphysics into Ch'an doctrine, and through it, into both the philosophies of Chu Hsi and Wang Yang-ming, and to avoid any misunderstanding that the description of Yang-ming's thought as "practical" indicates the absence in it of metaphysical depth. But it serves well the purpose of bringing to better light the essentially reformist or "protestant" nature of Yang-ming's philosophy with regard to the state orthodoxy of the times, and for the sake of emphasizing those more vital aspects of doctrine which have immediate relevance for the seeker of sagehood. Thus, as preparation for a rather thorough treatment of Yang-ming's philosophy in the light of its orthodoxy or heterodoxy, I propose to discuss here the historical pattern of truth and ideology, beginning with an explanation of the nature of the philosophical and religious challenges presented by Taoism and Buddhism—the so-called "heterodox" schools—and then giving an analysis of certain selected components in Chu Hsi's new Confucian synthesis, particularly of his metaphysics. I shall then proceed to a discussion of the controversy that took place between him and his contemporary, Lu Chiu-yüan (1139–92) which foreshadowed the later controversy to arise with the emergence of Wang Yang-ming in the Ming dynasty.

THE CHALLENGES: TAOISM AND BUDDHISM

Taoism and Buddhism presented serious challenges to the position in men's minds of the teachings of the Confucian school, or, more precisely, to that orthodox system which survived the end of the Han dynasty. Because of the merging process that took place between the "Two Teachings," both on the speculative and the popular levels, Taoism and Buddhism will be considered, for our purposes, as a single unit. Indeed, by the Sung and Ming times, Taoism had nearly lost its identity, having been absorbed by Ch'an Buddhism, and signifying by itself merely that esoteric movement which sought to obtain physical immortality or to prolong the human life-span. And so, for the serious student of Sung and Ming thought, in particular of the orthodoxy of Wang Yang-ming's philosophy, it is more important to concentrate on the metaphysical and psychological aspects of Chinese Buddhism, in order to understand better the nature of its challenge to Confucian thought as well as the influence it exerted on the formation of a new Confucian synthesis, firstly that of Chu Hsi, and then that of Wang Yang-ming.

The term "Chinese Buddhism" refers to that broad religious-philosophical entity against which the new Confucian philosophers of Sung and Ming times consciously voiced their opposition. It represents that which remained after the religious persecution of 845, which effectively destroyed the Buddhist domination of society and culture that had persisted for over three hundred years. It was particularly the result of a synthesis of the metaphysics of the T'ien-t'ai and Hua-yen schools with the Ch'an Buddhist concern for the practical realization of Buddhahood and the Ching-t'u or Pure Land religious devotion.[3] For our purposes, the most important component of this synthesis was that of Ch'an, which had also absorbed much of both Taoist philosophy and religion.

Chinese Buddhism and the new Confucianism that followed acquired from Taoist philosophy a basic metaphysical vocabulary of such words as *Tao* (Ultimate Reality), *Wu* (Nothingness), *Pei-t'i* (Pure Being), and *T'ai-chi* (the Ultimate). In the third and fourth centuries the tendency was to regard Confucius as the sage *par excellence,* but to consider sagehood itself as a metaphysical state of union with the Tao, and of the absence of any deliberate mind of one's own (*wu-hsin*), permitting the response in equanimity to all vicissitudes. Ensuing debates concerned the possibility of acquiring sagehood by one's own efforts, and the possession, by sages, of human emotions—usually regarded as the source of evil. While Wang Pi (226–49), the commentator of the Book of Changes and of *Lao-tzu,* spoke out in favor of the "humanity" of sages: that he has emotions, but is not ensnared by them,[4] the ideal of sagehood became more and more removed from men's minds as an attainable reality.

As an elixir cult, Taoist religion continued to have an independent existence. It was a "Way" of salvation, leading its faithful to an eternal life, not only of the soul but also of the body. Such texts as the *Ts'an-t'ung ch'i* and the *Pao-p'u Tzu* gave it a certain theoretical sophistication, while making possible also its eventual absorption by Ch'an Buddhism through the ambiguity of meaning of the so-called "inner elixir," sometimes identified with human nature itself.[5]

Ch'an Buddhism was the practical realization of the T'ien-t'ai and Hua-yen doctrines. From the latter, it took over metaphysical teachings regarding the interpenetration of the phenomenal realm of appearances, sometimes called *shih* and the noumenon or ultimate reality, variously identified as the realm of *li,* as absolute mind (*hsin,* Sanskrit, *citta mātra*) or Buddha-nature (*fo-hsing,* Sanskrit, *Buddhatā*). Ch'an Buddhism offered an intuitive method of spirituality, aimed at the recovery of the Buddha-nature present in all sentient beings, through a direct enlightenment-experience (*wu*. Sanskrit, *bodhi*) which removed the cloud of passion (*yü*, Sanskrit, *kleśa*) from men's minds, enabling them to see themselves in their true state. This was to be accomplished by the free and spontaneous operation of the human spirit, while avoiding all conscious, deliberate thought, including any anxiety involved in the conscious quest for the goal of Buddhahood itself. Thus, Ch'an considered as unnecessary the observance of rituals, the study of sutras, the recitation of formal prayers, and even conscious reflections on the ethical questions of good and evil.[6]

THE FAILURE OF IDEOLOGY: T'ANG AND SUNG CONFUCIANISM

The governments of T'ang and Sung, which ruled over a re-unified country, attempted, each in its turn, to restore a Confucian orthodoxy. A new edition of the Five Classics,[7] the Confucian deposit of wisdom, was published, together with the best available commentaries and subcommentaries, and was made into the required syllabus for examination candidates who were forbidden to deviate from the given interpretations. But these books could not command the attention of men's minds, by then habituated to Taoist and Buddhist metaphysical and religious discussions, and thirsty for wisdom rather than information. The way was thus left open for a revival of Confucianism under the leadership of individual thinkers rather than the government.

The man who raised most forcefully the banner of "orthodox" Confucianism against the continued dominance of Taoism and Buddhism was Han Yü (768–824),[8] the preacher of a return to the sources of the Confucian truth, especially the Book of Mencius, the record of the sayings of that philosopher who first gave expression to the ideas of Confucian orthodoxy and its correct transmission.[9] Han Yü's work was further enhanced by his friend and disciple, Li Ao (fl. 798), who explored, in greater depth, problems related to human nature and human emotions, bringing into greater prominence the two chapters of the Book of Rites, called the Great Learning and the Doctrine of the Mean.[10]

The notion that the Confucian Tao had not been transmitted after Mencius, and the appeal for a renewed line of "orthodox transmission," voiced by Han Yü and Li Ao, found echoes in the writings of early

Sung scholars.[11] They envisaged the true "Way" under three aspects. Its content or "substance" (*t'i*) is made up of unchanging moral ideals; its application or "function" (*yung*) is the pursuit of these ideals by right action, while its "literary expression" (*wen*) includes the whole range of Confucian classics.[12] To understand well the content and put it into practice (*yung*), however, one must first acquire insights into the mind-and-heart before expressing them in words.

This does not necessarily preclude a serious knowledge of the texts of the Classics or the help of teachers. But the work of teachers was less the transmission of exegetical skills—as was that of the great "New Text" and "Old Text" Han scholars[13]—than that of provoking thought and inspiring insight. There was no question of the passing on of a static truth, but the transmission of faith and understanding in an eternal message, unchanging, and yet to be discovered anew by every generation.

An interesting phenomenon that would accompany the development of a new, "orthodox" Confucianism was the emphasis on oral transmission. Whereas, before, scholars either spent their time annotating the Classics or writing their own treatises, based always on the appeal to the authority of the Classics, another literary genre came into vogue during the Sung dynasty. Probably following the examples of Ch'an monks who published recorded conversations (*yü-lu*) of thier great Masters, and also going back to the Confucian models in the Analects and the Book of Mencius, students of famous philosophers began to note down for later publication the conversations they had with their Masters. These *yü-lu* made up the largest repository of the new Confucian philosophy. As a genre, it expressed the attitude of the men who considered themselves to be primarily teachers of disciples, living with them in an intimate circle, and communicating to them the ineffable teaching of the Sages, which could be easily distorted when given too ornate a form.[14] Such a lack of organization in written expression stands in strong contrast to the truly organic system of philosophy that was constructed,* embracing within itself a synthetic

---

* That these *yü-lu* regard truth as the communication of insight rather than result of dialectical arguments is pointed out by D. Holzman, who has traced them to Confucius' Analects through the Ch'an Masters' dialogues and Liu Yi-ch'ing's (403–44) *Shih-shuo hsin-yü*, indicating the concrete, immediate and vital qualities*

view of the world and of man's role in it, of the deeper recesses of the human spirit and its longing for self-transcendence.

THE NEW SYNTHESIS: CHU HSI

Chu Hsi's greatness consists less in originality of thought than in his remarkable ability to adapt and fuse together in one system of thought the individual contributions of the thinkers who preceded him.† Through his numerous writings: letters, essays, poems, classical commentaries, recorded conversations, and especially the *Chin-ssu lu,* an anthology of Sung thought,[15] he greatly expanded the content of Confucian thought, giving it a metaphysical world view while keeping the emphasis on moral and spiritual issues.

Of the earlier Sung thinkers, the names of four of the so-called "Five Masters"[16] became associated with that of Chu himself in the new philosophical synthesis which he achieved. These were Chou Tun-yi (1017–73), Chang Tsai (1020–77), Ch'eng Hao (1032–85) and Ch'eng Yi.

THE NEW METAPHYSICS

The first of the Four Masters was Chou Tun-yi. According to Chu Hsi, he was the first philosopher after Mencius to discover anew the

*of this genre, and their differences from the Platonic dialogues, which present a living embodiment of the dialectic method. See "The Conversation Tradition in Chinese Philosophy," *PEW* VI (1956), 223–30.

† For this reason, Chu Hsi has been compared by Zenker, Forke, Franke, Bruce and others to Thomas Aquinas (c. 1225–74) See A. Forke's *Geschichte der neueren chinesischen Philosophie* (Hamburg, 1938), Olaf Graf, *Tao und Jen: Sein und Sollen in Sung chinesischen Monismus* (Wiesbaden, 1970), 313–14. Graf has also brought out similarities between Chu and Spinoza (1632–77). H. Bernard and others, sepecially J. Needham, have spoken of Chu's possible influence on Leibniz (1646–1716) who came to know and appreciate the *Hsing-li* philospohy through Jesuit writings and correspondence. See H. Bernard, "Chu Hsi's Philosophy and Its Interpretation by Leibniz," *T'ien-hsia* V (1937), 9–17, See also Needham's discussion of Chu's possible influence on the development of a more "organic" philosophy in 17th century Europe and after, in *Science and Civilisation in China* (London, 1956), v. 2, 496–505.

lost Confucian Tao and to transmit it to others. From Chou, Chu derived his understanding of the world both of things and of men, as the spontaneous production of the interaction between the five agents and the principles of *yin* and *yang*, which, in their turn, came from the transcendent *T'ai-chi*, a notion derived from the Book of Changes where it refers to the "Ground of Being," that which holds the universe together.[17] But Chou also described it as *Wu-chi* (literally, "limitless", or "Non-Ultimate"), thereby giving rise to later debates about his intended meanings.[18] But his effort was generally directed toward the construction of a world view that explains the countless phenomena of existence as having come from an original source, pure and undifferentiated, the totality of reality.[19] In this way, Chou affirmed the idea that reality is both "one" and "many," an idea that became basic to the Sung philosophical synthesis.[20]

Also from Chou, Chu derived his belief that man partipates in the excellence of *T'ai-chi*, possessing a "moral" nature that came to him through the cosmic transformations. Contact with external things provides the occasion for evil, as a deflection from the good rather than as a positive presence.[21] The perfect man, the sage, is completely sincere (*ch'eng*). His mind-and-heart is like a mirror, quiet when passive, upright when active or moved by emotions.[22] Chu Hsi recognized Chou's *T'ai-chi* as the source and fullness of all being and perfection, and identified it with the Ch'engs' *T'ien-li*, the embodiment of all truth, wisdom, and virtue.[23] By so doing, he also internalized this *T'ai-chi*, describing it as that which is not only immanent in the whole of the cosmos, but also in each individual person.*

For Chu Hsi—as for the later Wang Yang-ming—Chang Tsai, uncle of the two Ch'engs, had a special importance as a thinker. Chang called Chou's *T'ai-chi*, *T'ai-ho* (Great Harmony), and described it as the Tao, the undifferentiated First Principle, source of all activity as well as stillness. He also gave it the name of *T'ai-hsü* (Great Void),

---

* As the "heavenly principle" in man, *T'ien-li* is like the Divine spark which the medieval Christian mystics described as being capable of transforming the soul into what approximates divinity itself. See J. Leclerq *et al.*, *Histoire de la spiritualité chrétienne*, (Paris, 1941), v. 2, 457. For the "Mirror Image," which occurs also in Christian writings, see P. Demiéville, "Le miroir spirituel," *Sinologica* I (1948), 112–37.

describing it in another regard as the totality of formless *ch'i*, of which *yin* and *yang* are two modes.† The gathering of *ch'i* gives rise to all things, including man, who participates thereby in the *T'ai-ho*. *Ch'i* is the basic "stuff" of everything. It is characterized by constant flux, a process which man should seek to comprehend, in order that he may "harmonize" his action with it.[24] For man is, after all, part of the cosmos, and so the truer his unity with it, both morally and physically, the better becomes his own human nature. In an essay that became known as "Western Inscription" (*Hsi-ming*), Chang enunciated his doctrine of man's unity with all things, which extends to both the cosmic and the social realms.[25] He also spoke of the ability of man, by the enlargement of the human mind-and-heart until it embraces everything, to give a "heart" (*hsin*) to Heaven-and-earth.[26] This is accomplished by the knowledge that arises from sincerity (*ch'eng*) and enlightenment (*ming*)—a knowledge far superior to that gained from "sight and hearing"—and by love.[27]

The philosophy of the Ch'eng brothers, Ch'eng Hao and Ch'eng Yi, particularly of the latter, exerted a decisive influence on the synthesis of Chu Hsi. Both brothers dealt with the problems of the nature of things and of man and of a method of recapturing man's original goodness. Ch'eng Hao exalted the notion of *jen* into a vital and creative power, universally active within the operations of Heaven and Earth, through which man becomes one with all things.[28] Ch'eng Yi distin-

---

† Although Chang spoke of *T'ai-hsü* as the fullness of *ch'i*, one need not conclude thereby that he was a "materialist." Among other things, the word *ch'i* suggests the Greek *pneuma* (spirit). The entire Idealist *versus* Materialist debate is a phenomenon of European philosophy, having arisen out of the mind-matter dichotomy associated especially with R. Descartes (1596–1650). See Prof. T'ang Chün-i, "Chang Tsai's Theory of Mind and Its Metaphysical Basis," *PEW* VI (1956), 113–36.

* In translating *li* as both being and goodness, I have in mind the Latin word, *esse*, from which both *ens* and *essentia* are derived. As pointed out by R. Otto, *esse* connotes both the true and the good in the writings of medieval thinkers and 'mystics, for example Meister Eckhart (c. 1260–1327), as does also the Sanskrit word *sat* (being). See *Mysticism East and West*, Eng. tr. by B.L. Bracey and R. C. Payne. (New York, 1962), p. 34, n. 1. It may be added that for Chu Hsi, *li* as being is regarded more as essence or quiddity than existence, while, for Lu Chiu-yüan and Wang Yang-ming, it is more the reverse, or rather, that the distinction between the two tends to be overlooked.

guished between *li* (principle of being and goodness),* which belongs to the realm "above shapes" (*hsing-erh-shang*) and which gives form and identity to *ch'i* (matter-energy), the basic stuff that makes up all things, and which belongs to the realm "within shapes" (*hsing-erh-hsia*).[29] This provided a basis for a new explanation of human nature and its capacities for good and evil,[30] which confirmed Mencius' teaching regarding the goodness of human nature, while ascribing the capacity for evil to the quality of *ch'i* or physical endowment.

METHOD OF CULTIVATION

Chu Hsi sought to bring more clarity to the question of goodness and evil in human nature, incorporating the teachings of Chang Tsai and the Ch'engs, and distinguishing between *hsing* (nature) as it is endowed by Heaven, full of *li* (being, goodness), and its physical endowment, which is conditioned by *ch'i* (ether).[31] He confirmed the assertion of Mencius, repeated by Chou, Chang, and the Ch'engs, that all men are capable of attaining sagehood by their own efforts,[32] and defined this goal in terms of the possession by man in himself of perfect virtue and goodness, *T'ien-li*. Such a possession would also enable man to realize the conscious unity that exists between himself and all things. As a method of self-perfection, Chu proposed the cultivation of reverence (*ching*) through "quiet-sitting" (*ching-tso*), and the "investigation of things" through assiduous study.[33] The final goal of such a dual activity is less the acquisition of comprehensive knowledge and solid virtues than the attainment of inner enlightenment in one's mind-and-heart though the recovery of the original goodness of human nature.* The constant maintenance of this state constitutes wisdom or sagehood.[34] Seen in this light, the apparently "dualist" nature of the philosphy of Chu Hsi becomes manifestly unitary. There is only one Tao, and there is only one way of attaining it.

---

* The notion of the recovery of original goodness bears a certain resemblance to the teaching of Plotinus (3rd cent. A.D.) concerning the return of the soul to the One, the Good, a neo-Platonic teaching taken over also by the medieval German mystics, in spite of their profession of Aristotelian scholasticism. See *The Enneads*, 9th Tractate.

THE TRANSMISSION DETERMINED

Chu Hsi was the first Sung philosopher to make explicit use of the term *Tao-t'ung* (Transmission of the Way).[35] As the disciple of Li T'ung (1093–1163), the disciple of Lo Ts'ung-yen (1072–1135), the disciple, in turn, of Yang Shih (1053–1135), Chu himself could claim to be heir to a distinguished intellectual lineage that traced back to Yang's teacher, Ch'eng Yi.[36] Chu considered that the "Way" of the sages, lost to posterity with the death of Mencius, was rediscovered by the two Ch'engs. He also honored Chou Tun-yi as the teacher of the Ch'eng brothers. He spoke also of Chang Tsai's role in the "Transmission," but placed him after the Ch'engs, who were his nephews.[37]

Besides determining the "line" of orthodox transmission, Chu Hsi was also chiefly responsible for the choice of the "Four Books" as the final, authoritative storehouse of Confucian wisdom, taking precedence over the "Five Classics." He punctuated, annotated, and divided into chapters the texts of the Four Books.[38] He divided the Great Learning into eleven chapters, changing the word *ch'ing* (love) of the first part of the first chapter into the word *hsin* (renovate), and providing also material for a "missing" chapter by giving his own commentary on the meaning of the "investigation of things" (*ko-wu*) and the "extension of knowledge" (*chih-chih*).

The problem, however, arises from the contradiction inherent in a "lineal" transmission of "insights" into a dynamic truth: a problem of criteria. How can it be decided that a certain man has attained any real insight at all, and what is the nature of such insight, and of truth itself? Chu Hsi's determination of the "line" of "orthodox transmission" did not provide any external criteria. It merely set up the authority of Chu himself, as *the* criterion of judgment regarding the orthodoxy of the insights of those thinkers whose names had been included among the transmitters of the Tao.   Thus consideration is to be kept in mind in our analysis of Chu's philosophical synthesis, and of the responses he made to the challenges presented to him, in the metaphysical and ethical realms, by his chief rival, Lu Chiu-yüan and, in the realm of historical and political thinking, by his other contemporary, Ch'en Liang (1143–94). It was, indeed, a problem that has deep consequences in the later development of Confucian thought.

THE CONTROVERSIES:
CHU HSI AND LU CHIU-YÜAN (LU HSIANG-SHAN)

Chu Hsi and Lu Chiu-yüan shared similar ideals of sagehood, and believed these to be attainable by human nature. Both had a high regard for man's *hsin*, the mind-and-heart, and considered self-know-ledge, or knowledge of one's mind and heart, as very important in the quest for sagehood. However, they disagreed in their understanding of the meaning of *T'ai-chi*, of the distinction between human nature (*hsing*) and the human mind-and-heart (*hsin*), and of the best possible method for the attainment of sagehood and perfection. Chu held to Chou Tun-yi's description of *T'ai-chi* as also *Wu-chi*, explaining that the totality of *li*, the source and fullness of all being and goodness, the One behing the Many, is not subject to determinations of time and place, of shape and appearance:

> Master Chou refers to [*T'ai-chi*] as *Wu-chi* precisely because it oc-cupies no position, has no shape or appearance, and because he considers it to be prior to physical things, and yet has never ceased to be, after these things came to be. He considers that it is outside *yin* and *yang* and yet operates within them, that it permeates all form and is everywhere contained, and yet did not have in the beginning any sound, smell, shadow, or resonance that could have been ascribed to it.[39]

Lu Chiu-yüan prefers to think that the term *Wu-chi* represents either a later interpolation, or an earlier and immature stage in Chou's intellectual development, since his later work, *T'ung-shu*, contains no mention of it. The issue in question, however, was much deeper than a disagreement concerning textual problems. Lu opposed Chu Hsi's explanation of *T'ai-chi* as also *Wu-chi* on account of a "dualist" ap-proach he detected in it, of regarding the realm of the Way, to which the *T'ai-chi* belonged, as "above shape," and distinct from the realm of "usefulness," to which belonged *yin* and *yang* and the five agents, and of the dichotomy between the "principle of Heaven" (*T'ien-li*) and "selfish desire" (*jen-yü*), which Chu used to explain the *inherent* goodness in human nature and *its strange tendency* toward evil. Lu claimed that this proposition divides man's unity and bears the imprint of Taoist influence.[40]

For Chu Hsi, what is called *li* (being) in things, is called *hsing* (nature) in man. *Hsin* (mind-and-heart), however, is something different. It consists of both *li* and *ch'i* (ether; matter-energy). It is not purely good, and prevents the full manifestation of *T'ai-chi* or *T'ien-li*—in each and every person and thing.[41] He thus attempted to safeguard the transcendent as well as immanent nature of *T'ai-chi*—the totality of *li*—while explaining at the same time the origin of evil. For Lu Chiu-yüan, however, *hsin* like *hsing*, is full of *li*,[42] and so constitutes a single, undifferentiated continuum with the whole of reality. For this reason he said, "The universe is my *hsin*, and my *hsin* is the universe."[43] In other words, while Chu envisaged an *imperfect* unity of Heaven and Man with the dual presence of *T'ien-li* and *ch'i* in persons and things, resulting in a certain tension between heavenly and earthly attractions, Lu Chiu-yüan conceived of Heaven and Man as belonging to a continuum, without tension, without conflict.* Evil, he said, arises from "material desires" (*wu-yü*),[44] the origin of which he did not clearly explain.

The debate between Chu and Lu expressed itself in terms of ideology more than of truth. Lu criticized Chu for showing Taoist attachments by maintaining that *T'ai-chi* is also *Wu-chi*, while Chu attacked Lu for showing Ch'an Buddhist influence in identifying *hsin* and *hsing*. On closer examination, however, it appears that Lu was indicating to Chu the danger of dividing reality into two realms, thus making the transcendent less immanent. Chu, on the other hand, feared that Lu's identification of *hsing* and *hsin* represented a misinterpretation of "nature" in terms of its conscious activity, thus reducing that which belongs properly to the realm of *li*, to that of *ch'i*. He criticized Lu indirectly for admitting of nothing transcendent in his philoosphy.

The difficulty probably lay with the different understandings of

---

* The differences between Chu Hsi and Lu Chiu-yüan call to mind what Bertrand Russell has said about the attempt to harmonize the twofold impulse of mysticism and science in man's attempt to see the world as a whole by means of thought. Chu's teachings bear some resemblance to those of Plato, who made a distinction between the appearances of things and "forms", while Lu's doctrine aims at finding the real in the appearances without making any division. See Russell's "Mysticism and Logic," in *Mysticism and Logic and Other Essays* (London: Unwin, 1969), 9–13.

the nature and function of *hsin*. For Chu, it was the directive agent of both "nature" and the "emotions," but, on that account also, not entirely good. For Lu, however, it was much more. As he said, "Sages arise in the Eastern Seas; they have the same *hsin*, the same *li*. Sages arise in the Western Seas; they have the same *hsin*, the same *li*."[45] Thus, the human *hsin*, especially as exemplified in the sages' *hsin*, becomes universalized as a norm of truth and goodness. It remains interior, but takes on objective, even absolute qualities. He did not deny the transcendent. He merely said that it is somehow immanent in man's minds as well as in the universe.

Several years before this controversy between Chu Hsi and Lu Chiu-yüan over *Wu-chi* and *T'ai-chi*, the two men already had another confrontation over their differences on self-cultivation. This was in 1175, when they were brought together for the first time at Goose Lake Monastery (Kiangsi), by their mutual friend, Lü Tsu-ch'ien (1137–81). Lu Chiu-yüan's elder brother, Lu Chiu-ling (1132–80), was also there. The meeting was organized with the hope of reconciling certain differences between their teachings, but this turned out to be impossible, especially where the method of cultivation was concerned.* Chu insisted on the need of extensive learning, while the Lu brothers maintained that discovering and developing *hsin* was all that was necessary.[46] On that occasion, Lu Chiu-yüan wrote a famous poem to characterize the difference between his approach to sagehood and Chu Hsi's. It concluded with these lines:

> Effort easy and simple leads to lasting greatness;
> Work involved and fragmented will remain inconclusive and aimless.[47]

Needless to say, Lu's verses did not please Chu. But all three parted as friends. Six years later, Chu invited Lu to the White Deer Grotto

---

* The Ch'eng-Chu and Lu-Wang approaches to self-perfection, stressing respectively the systematic cultivation of the self through the investigation of things and the cultivation of the mind and heart respectively, call to mind clear parallels in the development of Christian spirituality, with the Dominican preference for the role of the intellect and for the systematic acquisition of particular virtues, and the opposite view, promoted by Franciscans and others, which remained closer to the teachings of St. Augustine (354–430) in giving preference to the will, and to the development of charity as the universal virtue. See J. Leclerq, v. 2, 372–77, 402–06.

Academy in Kiangsi to speak to Chu's own students. Lu gave a discourse on the text of Analects, 4:16: "The gentleman's *hsin* is conversant with righteousness (*yi*); the mean man's *hsin* is conversant with profit (*li*)." Lu spoke so earnestly that he moved the audience to tears. Chu himself was most impressed, and had the text of the discourse engraved in stone to honor the occasion.[48]

Chu's main criticism of Buddhism regards its basic nihilism. When asked once the difference between the "nothingness" (*wu*) spoken by the Taoists and the "emptiness" (*k'ung*) spoken by the Buddhists, he answered that the Taoists used the word *wu* to describe the mystery of being, and so allowed room for reality, while the Buddhists regarded Heaven-and-Earth and the elements as mere illusions. He claimed that even the Hua-yen school, which maintained an identity between the noumenal and phenomenal realms, described the phenomena as having no permanence, and so implied that the noumenal realm, even the Absolute, was itself "empty" or unreal.[49]

Lu Chiu-yüan did not refrain from criticizing Buddhism either, but his criticisms were based on practical, not speculative, reasons. He used the words "righteousness" and "profit" to distinguish between Confucianism and Buddhism, attacking the latter for its negative attitude toward human life: "[The Buddhists] consider [life] to be extremely painful, and seek to escape from it. . . . Even when they strive to ferry [all beings across the sea of suffering] to a future realm, they always base themselves on the idea of withdrawal from the world."[50]

POLITICAL PHILOSOPHY

Just as, in ethics and spiritural cultivation, man is directed to return to the source of his own being, to recover the 'original goodness of his nature," of his mind and heart, so too, in the philosophy of history, inseparably allied to that of politics, a return to the moral idealism of the Golden Age of remote antiquity is advocated by the Sung philosophers. Chu Hsi described the age of remote antiquity as the age of the dominance of the "principle of Heaven," a time when men lived according to the natural virtues of humanity, righteousness, propriety, and wisdom, bestowed on them by Heaven. He also attributed the

"success" of the Golden Past to the moral education that then flourished, which taught all to develop the goodness inherent in their
nature. This was the vision of a "moral utopia," situated in an imagi-
nary point of time rather than of place, composed of men educated in
the practice of virtue, and ruled by benevolent sage-kings and scholars
who formed a class of intellectual and moral aristocracy.[51] It implied
a dualism between the rulers and the ruled, and was therefore, in the
vocabulary of the Book of Rites (*Li-chi*), a picture of the age of "Lesser
Tranquillity" (*hsiao-k'ang*), the age of rites and righteousness, rather
than that of the "Great Unity" (*ta-t'ung*), the age when distinctions
between the self and the other had not yet arisen.[52]

Underlying Chu's philosophy of history and politics, however, was
another more important dualism, a consequence of his metaphysics
of *li* and *ch'i*, of "principle of Heaven" and of "human desire." For
Chu divided the whole past into two periods, the age of "kings" (*wang*)
—pre-Ch'in (221–06 B.C.) times—when the "principle of Heaven"
held sway, and the age of "despots" (*pa*), dominated by "human
desire." He taught that the interruption of the "transmission" of the
Confucian Way resulted also in the absence of the "Way" from the
arena of history. The best days of Han and of T'ang were thus included
in the second age, when the way of virtue, dominant during the Three
Dynasties, was forgotten.[53]

Just as Lu Chiu-yüan had opposed Chu Hsi's dualism in metaphysics and ethics, so too, another friend of Chu's, Ch'en Liang, resisted
his dualist interpretation of history with its implicit condemnation of
all government since Ch'in times. An ardent admirer of the achievements of the great Emperors Kao-tsu of Han (r. 206–195 B.C.) and
T'ai-tsung of T'ang (r. A.D. 627–49) and of the institutions they created,
Ch'en desired to see reenacted in Sung times, the success and prosperity of their governments. He declared that he saw no harm in
"mingling" the principles of "despotism" (*pa*) with those of "kingliness" (*wang*).[54]

Such arguments were powerless to move Chu, who also desired to
see a stronger Sung China, then threatened by grave external dangers.[55]
For Chu, however, the morality of "means" was just as important as
that of "ends," and the latter could never be used to justify the former.
Besides, success was no criterion in the judgment of a ruler's moral

character, which should be evaluated solely in terms of personal motivations. He pointed out the despotic actions accomplished by the two emperors whom Ch'en had singled out for praise, as well as their transgressions of moral law in private life. He also reminded Ch'en:

> You should use your enthusiasm to appreciate the work of men who lived up to the standards of the Three Dynasties and not waste your time in the defence of the Han and T'ang dynasties.[56]

Thus, in Chu's opinion, the ruler must first undergo an intense process of self-cultivation, freeing his moral nature from the impediments of its "ether," in order to follow always the "Way." Following the examples of great thinkers who preceded him, and in particular, of Ch'eng Yi, Chu wrote numerous memorials to the throne, exhorting the ruler to "rectify [his] mind and make [his] intention sincere," so that everyone of his acts may conform to the principle of virtue which should govern it.[57] In this respect, he showed himself to be the true disciple of the sage Mencius, known especially for his attitude of independence toward state authority.[58]

Chu Hsi's independent attitude is all the more significant as the Sung period witnessed the strengthening of imperial authority in theory as well as practice. The great statesmen, Ssu-ma Kuang (1019–86) and Wang An-shih, in spite of policy differences, both favored a strong central government, and preached to the people the duty of unchanging loyalty to the dynasty.[59] Indeed, a rigid interpretation of the virtue of *chung* (loyalty) became identified to the neo-Confucian movement itself, although the great philosopher had not advocated it. Certainly, Chu's attitude to the sovereign was more that of a moral judge and teacher than of a servant. In the end, he was impeached by a Censor, Shen Chi-tsu, for ten crimes, "against loyalty, filial piety, humanity, righteousness and justice"—all of these "Confucian" virtues. His teaching was prescribed as a "perverse and heretical doctrine" in 1196. Although his funeral in 1200 was well attended, all those who went were regarded as "heretics," mourning the death of the "heresiarch."[60]

THE FORMULA OF FAITH

Chu Hsi's construction of a new philosophical synthesis brought with it the definitive acceptance of a certain "formulation" of the new Confucian *credo*, a terse formula that was supposed to contain the essentials of doctrine. This was taken not from the Four Books but from the Book of Documents, considered to be one of the earliest Classics. Moreover, it was taken out of a chapter allegedly transmitted to posterity in the old, pre-Ch'in script: the "Counsels of Great Yü" (*Ta-Yü mo*). It is interesting to note that the authenticity of this chapter was subject to doubt by Chu Hsi himself.[61] Nevertheless, he did not hesitate to adopt those lines, for which the philosophers of early Sung had shown a great fondness, as containing the "original message" of the sages. All complete in sixteen Chinese characters, this cryptic formula may be translated as:

> Man's mind (*jen-hsin*) is prone to error,
> [While] the mind of the Way (*Tao-hsin*) is subtle
> Remain discerning and single-minded:
> Keep steadfastly to the Mean [or Equilibrium] (*chung*).[62]

This formula was generally accepted by all Neo-Confucian philosophers, both of the Ch'eng-Chu, *Hsing-li* school and of the school of *Hsin* begun by Lu Chiu-yüan and developed by Wang Yang-ming.[63] An examination of these lines, however, shows us very little doctrinal content. As commonly agreed, the "central message" was essentially a warning and an exhortation, presented through the statement of a certain duality between the fallibility of the human mind-and-heart, and the subtlety and evasiveness of the "Way," for the sake of encouraging a constant discernment and the maintenance of psychic equilibrium. Interpretation of the words differed slightly according to individual thinkers. While Ch'eng Yi had explained *jen-hsin* and *Tao-hsin* as opposite principles, in terms of "selfish desires" (*jen-yü*) and "heavenly virtue" (*T'ien-li*), Chu Hsi preferred to interpret the two as man's mind (*hsin*), considered first as consciousness of instinctive needs, and then as awareness of moral principles.[64] Represented as the sacred legacy of the earliest sages, these lines present the core of the Confucian transmission, visualized as the union of Heaven and

Man, with Heaven understood to be that which holds the cosmos together, the fullness of being and goodness: *T'ien-li*. Thus, the formula expresses a vision which is simple and ambiguous, which hides within itself, the depth of spiritual richness. It indicates, quite unequivocally, the goal of the entire *Tao-hsüeh* movement: the acquisition of ultimate truth and wisdom, through a "Way" of life recognized as correct and efficient. And this Tao, this "Way" of life, aims especially at the acquisition of a state of mind-and-heart—the "mind of the sage" characterized always by emotional equilibrium. Thus "orthodox transmission" (*Tao-t'ung*) emerges finally as the transmission of "the sages' *hsin*."

Admittedly, this vision comes out more clearly in the teachings of Lu Chiu-yüan than in those of Ch'eng Yi and Chu Hsi. It can be traced back to Ch'an Buddhism, with its scorn for the written word and its emphasis on direct intuition into the mind and human nature.[65] But the new Confucian line of orthodox transmission of *hsin* was established especially as an alternative to the Buddhist transmission, with a view to insisting on the Confucian interpretation of what *hsin* was: the source and principle of moral activity. For this reason too, Wang Yang-ming's teachings on the Four Maxims, which placed *hsin* beyond ethical categories, in the realm of being itself, would appear to effect a return to Ch'an Buddhist metaphysics, and so render meaningless the entire attempt to determine the Confucian transmission.

CONCLUSION

Thus, with Han Yü and Li Ao as heralds, Chou, Chang, the Ch'engs and Chu Hsi as "constructors," the "School of the Way," *Tao-hsüeh*, became systematized during Sung, to become officially approved as state doctrine by the Mongol dynasty of Yüan which succeeded it. The Commentaries of Ch'eng Yi and of Chu Hsi on the Four Bovoks and on other classical texts became incorporated into the official examination syllabus in 1313, to remain there until 1904.[66] The idea of "correctness" or "orthodoxy," inherent in the doctrine of *Tao-t'ung* or "orthodox transmission," and in the interpretation of the sacred formula of truth allegedly derived from the Book of Documents, become enshrined in the *Sung Dynastic History* which presented a novel, double classification of Sung scholars and thinkers as belonging to *Ju-lin* (literati) or *Tao-hsüeh*.[67] It is an irony of history that the system of thought, which had grown up without state support and even in spite of state opposition, should eventually come to be regarded by posterity as a great product of "Sung genius," and given official sanction by an alien dynasty.[68]

It is an additional irony that the same historical pattern that had produced the Sung *Hsing-li* philosophy should repeat itself in the Ming dynasty, to bring about a powerful philosophical challenge to the Sung synthesis. The early Ming government showed its approval of Chu Hsi's thought by ordering the compilation of three monumental collections: the *Wu-ching ta-ch'üan* [Great Compendium of the Five Classics], the *Ssu-shu ta-ch'üan* [Great Compendium of the Four Books], both of which incorporated the new commentaries of Sung and Yüan scholars, and the *Hsing-li ta-chüan* [Great Compendium of the *Hsing-li* philosophy], which presented the best of the teaching of the Sung-Yüan thinkers themselves.[69] As works of exegesis, the classical commentaries now officially approved did not on the whole equal in quality those produced in the T'ang and Sung dynasties.[70] In receiving government endorsement, however, the new Confucian synthesis, based only partly on the Confucian Classics but very much more on the syncretic backgrounds of its makers, was transformed from the charism that it had been to the ideology that it became. The inherent contradiction of Confucian orthodoxy again became manifest: as a doctrine, Confucianism had always been eclectic until officially approved and made thereby to stagnate. The price of government support, and of official promulgation in the whole country, would always be the loss of its inner vitality. Certainly, Ch'eng Yi and Chu Hsi had never desired that their opinions should become the only ones allowed circulation, to the exclusion of all others, but this was what official orthodoxy effected. It should therefore come as no surprise that the new Ch'eng-Chu synthesis of Confucianism, after receiving the ambiguous benefit of imperial patronage, should produce no more great thinkers in the wake of such support, and become merely an ideology to which lip service was paid by countless students eager to achieve an eminent position in government service. Instead of being a stimulus to thought, the officially approved commentaries only produced scholars with good memory and accurate expression. Successive generations of time-servers, of men anxious to climb the official ladder of success and to keep their political gains were thus produced. At the same time, many persons of real scholarship and tried virtue felt obliged to abstain from serving in a government which demanded the compromise of their convictions and characters.[71] Such a voluntary departure from known Confucian teachings on social commitment was made as a sign of protest rather than as a surrender of responsibility. But it could not become incorporated into the Confucian tradition as a permanent feature without distroying the tradition itself from within. The tension between the "inner" or contemplative and "outer" or active pulls of Confucian teaching became more evident than ever before, as the Chinese philosophical genius went underground again, to express itself in those students of Ch'eng-Chu orthodoxy who revolted against both these orthodox philosophers and the system of intellectual tyranny that supported them. This time, the polarization of "orthodoxy" and of "heresy" can be made more accurately, since we no longer deal with the conflict between Confucianism on the one side and Taoism and Buddhism on the other, but with that between official Confucianism and a dissident school. This was no other than that of Lu Chiu-yüan, revived and strengthened in the Ming dynasty by the appearance of several great thinkers, nourished and educated within the orthodox tradition, who reacted against its rigidity and stagnation. Of these, the greatest was Wang Yang-ming. It is to an analysis of his philosophy, of his understanding of the Confucian Tao, of the relevance of his position to the question of "orthodoxy" and of "orthodox transmission," that the bulk of this study is devoted.

PART I

THE PHILOSOPHY OF WANG YANG-MING

I

WANG YANG-MING: THE MAN AND THE PHILOSOPHER

I N ANALECTS 13.21, we find this passage:

> The Master said: "Since I cannot get men who act according to the Mean, to whom may my teaching be transmittes? I must look for the ardent (*k'uang*) and the cautious (*chüan*). The ardent will advance to lay hold of [the truth]. The cautious will desist f'm doing wrong."[1]

Three classes of men are mentioned here: those who act according to the Mean, the ardent or eccentric, and the very cautious. Elsewhere in the Analects a fourth class is mentioned: the *hsiang-yüan*— "village respectable" or "Pharisaic."[2] Confucius considers the first kind unobtainable and declares himself content to have the second and third kind among his disciples. The fourth kind, the "respectable" man of the village, who seeks to please every one, and has no firm principles of his own, he despises.

Referring to this passage, Mencius had described the *k'uang* as men who spoke eloquently and extravagantly of the ancients—whom they purported to imitate—but whose actions did not correspond to their words. He had also given, as examples of *k'uang*, Tseng Tien, Ch'in-chang, and Mu-p'i.[3] Chu Hsi followed this interpretation in his textual commentary on the passage in question. He added, according to the recorded conversations, that Confucius desired to "restrain" the *k'uang,* and help them to become "men who act according to the Mean." In so doing, he was already making reference to still another passage of the Analects, also cited by Mencius. Here, Confucius, during his sojourn in the state of Ch'en, expresses his desire to return to his disciples in his native state of Lu:

> Let me return! Let me return! The little children of my school are *k'uang* [translated by Legge here as ambitious] and *chien* [translated here as hasty]. Although quite accomplished, they do not know how to restrict themselves.[4]

Chu Hsi defines the meaning of *k'uang-chien* as "having great ambitions while being careless of one's actions."[5] He presents Confucius as having first desired to exercise his Way in the world, but had, by the time of his sojourn in Ch'en, realized that it was impossible for him to find a ruler who would make use of his talents. He decided to concentrate his attention on traininig disciples who would transmit his teaching to later generations. Not finding, however, the most desirable kind of disciples—men who acted always according to the Mean—he turned to the *k'uang*, to these highly ambitious men who were capable of promoting the true Way, but might also "fall into heresy" by their excesses. He wished, therefore, to return home to teach them restraint.[6]

The Chinese word *k'uang*, when applied to human conduct, contains unmistakable overtones of madness and eccentricity. The Analects itself distinguished between the "*k'uang* of the ancients." who paid scant attention to little things, and the "*k'uang* of the moderns, "who fell easily into licentiousness.[7] It also gave the example of the "madman of Ch'u," Chieh-yü, who sang and mocked Confucius for his "vain pursuit," presumably of looking for a ruler who would use him.[8] Throughout Chinese history, scholars who preferred a life of retirement to one of government service, and manifested a certain disdain of social conventions, were described as *k'uang*. These included the "Seven Masters of the Bamboo Grove" of the Wei-Chin period, (220–420), known for their poetry as well as their shocking eccentricity,[9] and the later "Immortal Poet" (*shih-hsien*), Li Po (c. 701–62) of the T'ang dynasty, who did not restrain himself from excessive drinking at Court, but offended the powerful eunuch, Kao Li-shih, by once obliging him to do in public the menial task of removing Li's shoes for him. In one of his poems, Li even conpared himself to the madman of Ch'u.[10]

The *Hsing-li* philosophers of Sung and Ming were not interested in literary genius, and sometimes considered it an obstacle to the pursuit of sagehood. But their disdain of conventional mediocrity, as well as their conception of the high goals of sagehood, led them back to the Confucian notion of *k'uang*, as explained especially by Mencius, and giving it an additional meaning of the experience of harmony between man and the universe. But the connotation of madness and eccentricity remained, as we have seen, in the interpretations of Chu Hsi. It is therefore significant that this word, representing both the quality of the disciple Confucius wished to choose as transmitter of his teaching, and the tendency to excess and heresy that Chu Hsi underlined, should have been used by Wang Yang-ming himself, as well as by his opponents, in describing his personality. It was also the word which the later critics of the popular T'ai-chou branch of the Yang-ming school used to condemn the movement. They called its adherents the "K'uang-Ch'an"—mad Ch'an Buddhists.[11]

A LIFE OF "ARDOR"

Wang Yang-ming is the name by which Wang Shou-jen is popularly known. Born on October 31, 1472, in Yüeh-ch'eng, near Yü-yao of the modern Chekiang province, the eldest child of a distinguished *literati* family, Yang-ming's entire life was to become an expression of mad ardor. His was the daring of a magnanimous man, driven by a restless energy, to fulfill limitless ambitions, not for worldly success, but for the attainment of absolute values. The quality appeared in him from a very early age, as when he doubted the words of his preceptor, that "the greatest thing to do in life" was to "study and pass examinations," and offered his own alternative, "to learn how to become a sage."[12] Richly endowed with a quick nature and a remarkable versatility, he was interested in everything: reading, poetry, horsemanship, archery, as well as religion and philosophy, and he was ready to pursue, and capable of developing, all these interests to a high degree of achievement. Fascinated with the profound meaning of life, he sought to probe its mystery. He believed in responding fully to the challenges of greatness, and would not stop at half measures. His multidimensional achievements in life, as a writer, statesman, soldier, philosopher, and teacher, provided material for both the conventional annalist and the historical novelist. There is a story that tells us how the young boy handled his callous stepmother after the early death of his own mother. Although difficult to confirm, the account describes for us the early manifestation of an unconstrained character, which fits in well with the brief lines of conventional biographers.[13] According to this story, the boy of twelve placed an owl in his stepmother's bed. She was frightened to discover it there, especially as the bird was, to the Chinese, an unlucky omen, and made strange noises. The boy offered to search for a sorceress, a woman who performed excorcisms and prayed for blessings on the house. He fetched home an accomplice. She pretended to have received a communication from Yangming's deceased mother, complaining of the stepmother's ill treatment of her son, and threatening dire consequences unless this was stopped. The trick proved to be quite effective.[14]

In Ming China, the ambition that all gentry families entertained for their scions was naturally the attainment of high office through success in civil examinations designed mainly to test literary skills. Yangming's father, Wang Hua (1446–1523) had distinguished himself as *optimus* at the examinations of 1481, and had taken great care to provide an orthodox Confucian education for his sons.[15] But books alone could not occupy the entire attention of the boy Yang-ming. At the age of fourteen, he learned to ride a horse, to use a bow and arrow, and to acquaint himself with military strategy. All his life, he was to show himself contemptuous of scholars who were skilled in verbal dialectic, but quite powerless in a time of military crises. At the age of fifteen, Yang-ming spent a month at the strategic Chü-yung Passes of the Great Wall in the company of his father. He observed the movements of the Tartar horsemen, as well as the physical features of these frontier regions. This experience left a deep impression on him. After his return to Peking, he was said to have offered his services to the emperor for the suppression of bandits, and was only stopped by his father who told him that he was crazy (*k'uang*).[16]

In 1488, at the age of sixteen, Yang-ming traveled from Peking to Nan-chang, Kiangsi, to fetch his bride, the daughter of the Assistant Administration Commissioner. On the day of his wedding, the absentminded bridegroom walked into a Taoist monastery, met an interesting priest, and spent the night in the monastery, in an absorbed conversation on the art of cultivating life, and in the practice of Taoist meditation. The bride's family did not find him until the next day.[17] During the rest of his sojourn with his in-laws, he also showed an absorbing interest in practicing calligraphy, using up the paper stored in his father-in-law's official residence for his exercises.[18] The next year, he took his wife back to his native place Yü-yao, stopping at Kuang-hsin, Kiangsi, to visit the philosopher Lou Liang (1422–91), and discussed with him the theory of "investigation of things."[19] His father also returned soon to Yü-yao, to mourn the death of his grandfather. Yang-ming was ordered to study the Classics in the company of four relatives. He threw himself into this work, often reading till late at night. In dealing with others, however, he remained casual and amiable.[20]

Following upon the passing visit to Lou Liang, Yang-ming's ardor for the investigation of things led him to search for all the extant writings of Chu Hsi, which he read. It was this ardor, rather than a real understanding of the intended meaning of Chu Hsi, that made Yang-ming put into application Chu's advice about a thorough "investigation of things," of every plant and every blade of grass, as a means toward attaining their inherent principle, and with the view of attaining final enlightenment concerning man's life in the universe. Yang-ming tells his own story as follows:

> People merely say that in the "investigation of things" we must follow Chu Hsi, but when have they carried it out in practice? I have attempted this earnestly. In earlier years [at the age of twenty] I discussed the question of becoming a sage with my friend Ch'ien, wondering how a person can have such tremendous energy to investigate all things under Heaven. So I pointed to the bamboos in front of the pavilion, and asked him to investigate these. Ch'ien spent three days trying to investigate thoroughly the meaning of bamboos, working hard day and night and using up his mental energy, until he fell ill. . . . So I myself proceeded to this investigation, working day and night without reaching the principle, until I also fell ill through mental exhaustion on the seventh day. So we lamented together that sagehood is unattainable.[21]

A series of minor official appointments followed his success in the *chin-shih* examinations of 1499, first in the Ministry of Public Works and then in that of Justice. Yang-ming did his work conscientiously, and also took time to visit Buddhist and Taoist monasteries in Chiu-hua Mountain, Anhwei, seeking out and speaking with Taoist recluses. Experiencing a strong desire to retire from active life, Yang-ming pleaded ill health and was granted permission to return to his home town to rest.[22]

Disagreement exists concerning where Yang-ming resided during his convalescence. The older accounts speak of his living in the so-called "Yang-ming Cave" (*Yang-ming tung*) from which he got his name. While the exact location of this hermitage is not clearly known[23] it is usually accepted that he spent his time there practicing Taoist methods of the cultivation of self. Supposedly, he acquired para-psychic powers, knowing in advance an unexpected visit from certain friends, as well as circumstances surrounding their journey. This knowledge astonished the friends but caused disillusionment to Yang-ming himself, becoming for him the occasion for an inner query that ended with a decision to return to society and active life,[24] a decision made also on the basis of his attachment to his father and grandmother, which, he thought, was something so deeply rooted in his human nature that to expunge it would involve cutting himself off from his very humanity. He returned to his official career, demonstrated his "con-version" to the school of sages by open criticisms of Buddhism and Taoism, and also began to teach students interested in Confucianism.

Just when Yang-ming was settling down intellectually and spirit-ually however, a change of fortune occurred, leading him into exile in Kweichow. This crisis was provoked by his own decision to intervene in favor of several officials imprisoned unjustly by the eunuch Liu Chin (d. 1510), the power behind the throne. The memorial which Yang-ming wrote in 1506 probably never reached Emperor Wu-tsung (1506–21) but led to his imprisonment, public flogging till loss of consciousness, and banishment to the frontier region of Lung-ch'ang Kweichow, to live among the Miao aborigines.[25] A period of great trials began, during which Heaven was to prepare him for even greater trials, as well as for the maturation of his personality and his philosophical ideas.

After an arduous journey by a devious route, during which he pre-tended to have committed suicide by drowning in the river to divert the attention of the agents of Liu Chin sent to follow and assassinate him. Yang-ming finally reached his destination in exile.[26] He found himself in the midst of the "bush."The place was infested with serpents and insects. The climate was quite different from that of Peking or Yü-yao. In the beginning he had to live in a cave. The Miaos did not speak Chinese, and he did not know their dialects. The few Chinese living there were rough men, often outlaws fleeing from justice. Some of them worked as couriers and coolies, despatching messages and official documents, and transporting supplies for the region. Yang-ming's responsibility was to care for their horses.[27]

There were other trials too, and worries and anxiety. Yang-ming knew that Liu Chin's anger had not yet abated. What would Liu do, once he found that the bold young scholar had not perished on the way, but had arrived in Kweichow? Would he not send further assassins, to pursue and put him to death? Yang-ming had been able to remain above considerations of honor or disgrace, success or failure. But he was still very much preoccupied with the question of life or death. He knew that he was not yet a sage. But then, what would a sage—a truly great man—do in such circumstances?

He knew that it was essential for him to rise above all earthly concerns. He made a coffin for himself out of stone and spent much time, day and night, in front of it, sitting in silent meditation and seeking for spiritual liberation. This brought him a certain interior peace and joy. When his servants fell sick with fever, Yang-ming personally attended to their needs, gathering fuel and water and doing their cooking. He even entertained them with songs and prosody and, when these failed to please them, told them amusing tales to help them forget their misery. It was in these circumstances that one night he suddenly received enlightenment. He was probably deep in meditation. But it seemed as though someone were talking to him. All of a sudden the meaning of "investigation of things" and "extension of knowledge" was revealed to him. Almost mad with joy, he leaped up from his place, awaking all those around him. He said to them: "I have finally understood that my human nature is quite adequate for the task of achieving sagehood. My mistake in the past was seeking principle in events and things [external to my nature]."[28] He was thirty-six years old.

In 1510 Yang-ming completed the term of his exile, and was promoted to be Magistrate of Lu-Ling in Kiangsi. After seven months of remarkable service he was summoned to Peking, where he had an audience with the Emperor, and was transferred to serve in various minor posts in Nanking and in Peking.[29] His fame as a teacher of philosophy was rapidly spreading. Through the recommendation of the Minister of War, Wang Ch'iung (1459–1532), he was promoted in 1517 to be Senior Censor and Governor of the border regions of Kiangsi, Kwangtung, and Fukien, with the task of pacifying the bandits there.[30] His military career had finally begun.

Yang-ming distinguished himself as an able administrator and a good soldier. In seven months he victoriously completed his campaigns against those rebels who had troubled the Kiangsi region for years, and put into effect many measures of rehabilitation—erecting new counties, establishing village schools, and reforming taxation.[31] And then, in 1519, while on his way to suppress a rebellion in Fukien, he received news of the revolt of the imperial prince Ch'en-hao, in Kiangsi The prince had a large army and intended to capture Nanking and declare himself emperor. Yang-ming turned his attention swiftly to Kiangsi, and was able to capture the prince. But his success also initiated the worst trial of his life.[32]

The reason for this was the jealousy of the Emperor. Wu-tsung had been delighted at the news of Ch'en-hao's rebellion, which, he thought, provided him with an occasion for going south at the head of an expedition that would bring him military glory. Yang-ming was urged to release Prince Ch'en-hao and his men in P'o-yang Lake, so that the Emperor might himself "defeat" his forces.[33] Yang-ming found himself in a terrible predicament. Either he had to violate his conscience for the sake of pleasing the Emperor, in which case there would also be needless bloodshed, or he must resist pressure and run the risk of becoming the object of intrigue. He chose the latter course of action. His enemies, the Emperor's favorites, did their best to injure his reputation, accusing him even of having been the rebel prince's accomplice. To this end, they imprisoned one of his students who had earlier visited the prince. Although no evidence was ever produced of the involvement of either Yang-ming or the student, the latter was to die in prison.[34]

The following poem, written about that time, expresses well the sentiment of frustration and of disgust with political life that Yang-ming surely experienced:

> Not the least merit have I gained in the service of his sage and
>   august majesty,
> Helplessly I watch the graying of hair on my temples.
> Han Hsin was surely never a true credit to his country,
> While Shao Yung certainly was a hero among men.
>
> The times are hard, and allow no ease:
> No longer able to improve the state of affairs, I wish to keep
>   my knife intact.
> I go to seek my old place of retirement east of the Yüeh waters,
> In a thatched hut, high above the mountains, in the company
>   of clouds.[35]

The death of Emperor Wu-tsung, and the accession of his cousin, Emperor Shih-tsung, brought Yang-ming a certain change of fortune. His military merits were finally recognized, and he was awarded the title of Earl of Hsin-chien.[36] The death of his father in 1522 however obliged him to spend the next three years in mourning in his native place. He was there during the so-called "Rites" controversy, concerning the awarding of posthumous titles to Emperor Shih-tsung's deceased father. He expressed no opinion in public on this issue, although the general trend of his teaching, as well as conversations he had with disciples, seem to indicate his approval in principle of the Emperor's filial desires.[37] In 1524, when the period of his mourning was over, Yang-ming's talents were recommended to the Emperor by the Minister of Rites, Hsi Shu (1461–1527). But the jealousy of high officials at Court, including that of Yang Yi-ch'ing (1454–1530), who was made Grand Secretary, prevented him from being summoned to serve at the highest level of government.[38] He continued to live in virtual retirement until 1527. Most of his important letters were written during this time when he finally developed the doctrine of "extending liang-chih." Ironically, his philosophy was officially regarded as a "heterodox teaching," and as the reason why he should be banned from high office.[39]

In 1527, after nearly six years in retirement, Yang-ming was called upon to undertake another military campaign against rebels, this time in Kwangsi.[40] On his way, he passed by Nan-chang, in Kiangsi, where he was formerly stationed.

> The village elders, soldiers and common people all came to welcome him, holding incense in their hands, and lining the streets. They filled the roads and the streets, so that it became impossible for him to move. The elders, therefore, held up [Yang-ming's] sedan, passed it along over the heads of the crowds until they reached his quarters in the city, Yang-ming invited the elders, soldiers, and the common people to come in to see him. They came in through the east gate and came out through the west gate. Some could not bear to leave him, and went in again. This went on from seven in the morning until four in the afternoon.[41]

Surely this was a sign of sincere gratitude on the part of those people for whom he had toiled and suffered in the past. It was also a very timely expression. For this was to be Yang-ming's last visit in life to Nan-chang. He was, indeed, on his last military expedition. For he was already sick when he began the journey. He managed to pacify Ssu-en and T'ien-chou by early 1528, after which he ordered the erection of village schools and put into effect other measures of rehabilitating the people.[42] As his health steadily deteriorated he begged for leave, and started, eventually, on his journey home without having received official permission. He died on the way, on January 9, 1529, near Nan-an in Kiangsi. He was fifty-seven years old. His last words were: "My heart is full of brightness; what more can I say."[43]

The trials and opposition that had constantly beset Yang-ming's life did not leave him even at death. His better enemy, Kuei O, then Minister of Rites, accused him of having left his post without permission, and of teaching heretical doctrines.[44] In spite of the protests of his friends, Yang-ming's infant son was prevented from inheriting his father's title. The bereaved family, indeed, was reduced to dire straits, and had to seek the protection of Yang-ming's friend Huang Wan (1477–1551). It was not until 1567, thirty-eight years after his death, and after the accession of a new emperor, Mu-tsung (r. 1567–72), that Yang-ming's case was finally vindicated. His son was given the title of Marquis of Hsin-chien. Yang-ming himself received another posthumous dedication, that of Wen-ch'eng (Accomplished Culture).[45] Seventeen years later, in 1584, Yang-ming was given sacrifice in the

Temple of Confucius.[46] It was the highest honor any scholar could expect. It was also a sign that his teaching was regarded officially as a part of Confucian "orthodoxy." His name was finally associated with the names of all the other distinguished philosophers of both the Sung and the Ming dynasties.

The best eulogy of Wang Yang-ming that was ever delivered was probably that of his friend and disciple Huang Wan who describes him in these words:

> By nature, he was endowed with an extraordinary intelligence, and could retain by memory whatever he had once read. In youth, he was fond of knightly ventures; in adulthood, of prose and prosody, and of Taoism and Buddhism. After taking upon himself the mission of [restoring] the true way [of Confucius], and with the belief that sagehood is attainable, he changed his ways and corrected his faults. He responded courageously to the difficulties and challenges of the times, assisting, with his learning, the sovereign above, and serving the people below. Earnest and untiring, he counselled others to the practice of good, desiring by *jen* to save all living beings under Heaven. He showed no ill will toward those who hated him Even when he was in a position of wealth and honor he frequently manifested a desire to leave all things and retire into the mountains. Money was to him as mud and grass. He regarded with the same equanimity the amenities and comforts accompanying high rank, such as rare food, silk robes, and a spacious dwelling, and the inconveniences of poverty and lowliness, such as coarse soup, hemp garments, and a thatched roof. He was truly a born hero, and stands high above all others of the world. There has not been anyone like him in recent ages.[47]

THE "FIVE FALLS" AND THE "THREE CHANGES"

Wang Yang-ming's intellectual and spiritual evolution has been described in terms of "Five Falls" and "Three Changes." The "Falls" refer to his unorthodox interest in knightly ventures, sporting, and warlike skills, letters, pursuit of physical immortality and Buddhist religion, which preceded his final conversion to the Confucian Way of sagehood. Strictly speaking, they did not represent consecutive events, but rather, simultaneous and frequently recurring interests. The "Changes" refer, not to ruptures with the past, or even evolution in the direction of his life, but to the different shifts of emphases which occurred in his teaching, or, more precisely, in his practical direction of his disciples. All these occurred after his definitive return to Confucianism, and marked the stages of the development of his own philosophy,

Yang-ming's friend, Chan Jo-shui (1466–1560), has described for us the "Five Falls":

> His first fall was an absorbing interest in knightly ventures; his second was in the skills of horsemanship and archery. His third fall was an absorbing interest in letters; his fourth was in the art of pursuing immortality, and his fifth was Buddhism. Only in the year 1506 did he return to the orthodox teaching of the sages.[48]

Yang-ming has compared the "ardent" man to a phoenix, flying above, at a height of ten thousand feet.[49] His own inner evolution is an illustration of this truth. His dynamic vitality did not allow him to stop anywhere, but led him from one interest to another, from one spiritual adventure to another.

He was a precocious child, and as such, tended to be difficult. His biographer relates how, at the age of eleven, he was given a preceptor to supervise his studies, but manifested a greater fondness for roaming in the streets of Peking. Once he tried to obtain a bird from a seller without paying for it. The ensuing dispute attracted the attention of a physiognomist in the crowd, who paid for the bird, encouraged the boy to study, and left him with some cryptic words about his future greatness. Such adventures could hardly have been pleasing to his father, a compiler in the Hanlin Academy, who "frequently worried about him." The "knightly ventures" probably started to fascinate him in the streets of Peking, where he led other boys in battle games. The four Chinese words used to describe his character, as it first unfolded in these days of his carefree youth, are *hao-man pu-chi*.[50] They mean: "he was bold, fearless, and totally uncontrollable."

A hero of Yang-ming's youth was Ma Yüan (14 B.C.–A.D.49), the conqueror of Cochin. At the age of fourteen, Yang-ming visited in a dream the temple dedicated to Ma's memory, and composed a poem for that occasion. Over forty years later, shortly before his death, Yang-ming had occasion to visit the real temple, during a military campaign which he conducted in Kwangtung and Kwangsi.[51]

As we have already said, Yang-ming was early introduced to the art of horsemanship and archery. After his return from the sojourn at the Chü-yung Passes, he kept up this interest in military affairs, and had to be desisted by his father from submitting a memorial to advise the Emperor on this subject and to offer his services. At twenty-five, he studied military science more seriously, even playing war games at table while entertaining guests, using fruit kernels as soldiers. He regretted that the military examinations held by the state required only knowledge of horsemanship and archery, and not military strategy. He continued to study military science even during his period of repose in 1502, while living in his hermitage, with the help of Hsü Chang, a scholar conversant with astronomy, geography, and the art of war, who preferred a life of retirement to official service.[52]

That Yang-ming was an excellent archer was demonstrated at a public contest held between him and the two favorites of Emperor Wu-tsung, the eunuch Chang Chung and the general Hsü T'ai. This was in 1519, soon after his capture of Ch'en-hao. The two men had imagined it an easy task to win such a contest with a scholar. They were astonished and frightened to watch Yang-ming hit the target everytime.[53]

The art of letters also began to fascinate Yang-ming at an early age. At ten, he had surprised his father's friends with his impromptu verses. He did so again at twenty, when he associated himself with several others in a poetry club (shih-she) that included the elder scholar, Wei Han. His other friends included the "Four Talents" (ssu-chieh) of his times: Li Meng-yang (1472–1529), Ho Ching-ming (1483–1521), Hsü Cheng-ch'ing (1479–1511) and Pien Kung (1476–1532). Advocates of the movement calling for a return to a classical style in Ming prose and poetry, these men were to consider Yang-ming's development of other interests stronger than that of literary writing a real loss to their cause.[54] For a time, however, Yang-ming devoted himself to modeling poems and essays on pre-Sung and earlier pieces. He has left us examples of fu-sao and of imitations of T'ang poetry. His prose has been much acclaimed, especially for the independent style which he developed later. His "Yi-lü wen" (Burying the Dead Travelers), written at Lung-ch'ang, concludes with a song of lament, and is a moving essay.

His letter to Yang Sui-an (Yang Yi-ch'ing), dated 1523, is another expression of a simple and dignified style.

Until the age of thirty, literary writing was one of Yang-ming's principal occupations. He read avidly the pre-Ch'in and Han writings, staying up till late at night until his health was seriously damaged. He also kept up his exercises in callingraphy. He was finally obliged to practice more moderation when he started vomiting blood. Said he in the end: "How can I waste my finite energy in the writing of useless and empty compositions?"[55]

According to Yang-ming himself, he had been in contact with Taoism and Taoists since the age of seven.[56] At the age of eleven, he met a physiognomist in the streets of Peking. The words of the physiognomist, describing his future greatness, are full of Taoist allusions:

> When the beard brushes the collar, you will enter sagehood,
> When the beard reaches the upper cinnabar field, you will form a sage-embryo.
> When the beard reaches the lower cinnabar field, your sagehood will be perfect.[57]

In Taoist terminology, "cinnabar field" refers generally to the part of the body below the navel. *Pao-p'u tzu* refers to the "three cinnabar fields": the lower one below the navel the middle one below the heart, and the upper one between the eyebrows.[58] In the lines quoted above, only two, upper and lower, are mentioned. Since they are mentioned especially in relation to the length of the beard, it is safe to suppose that they indicate the parts below the heart and the navel. Those special terms are usually associated with the Taoist practice of breath control and breath regulation, considered as one of the means conductive to the prolongation of life, or even to the attainment of physical immortality. The "formation of a sage-embryo," is also a Taoist expression referring to a certain degree of progress made, for example, through practice of breath control, leading to the growth within oneself of the "inner pill."[59]

Yang-ming's feeble health might have been one reason for his interest in popular Taoism. Mention has already been made of his excursion to a Taoist temple on the night of his wedding. He persisted in seeking out unusual Taoist priests, asking them questions about the art of cultivating life. It is, besides, perfectly consonant with his restless, insatiable nature to desire to "steal the secret springs [of the creative operations] of Heaven and Earth."[60] After all, did not Chu Hsi himself make textual studies for those Taoist classics which describe such "theft": the *Yin-fu Canon* and the *Ts'an-t'ung Ch'i*?[61]

At the age of thirty, Yang-ming retired to a little hermitage near his native-place. We have already spoken of his practice of assiduous cultivation, and of his acquisition of a kind of "prescience." If he finally decided against a life in retirement, it certainly goes to show that he had frequently entertained the desire to be a "mountain man," and indeed, he delighted in calling himself *Yang-ming Shan-jen* (the Mountain Man of Yang-ming).[62] Whether his hermitage of 1504 was situated in a cave is not so important. But he definitely manifested, all through his life, a fondness for caves. He named his cave-dwelling in Lung-ch'ang the "Little Yang-ming Cave,"[63] and wrote several poems on it. In 1518, during one of his campaigns, he visited a double cave south of Lung-ch'uan in Kwangtung, and fell in love with it. He gave it the name "Another Yang-ming Cave," and again wrote a series of poems to commemorate the occasion. Connected with his love of caves, of course, is his passion for nature itself. Habitually, he instructed his disciples while roaming about in the mountains or near the lakes.

Yang-ming's frequent travels and visits to famous mountains brought him to many Buddhist as well as Taoist monasteries. The Japanese author, Kusumoto Fumio, has made a careful study of Yang-ming's peregrinations, noting a total of forty Buddhist monasteries with given names, which Yang-ming had visited. They were spread out in eight different provinces. Kusumoto claims that there were another forty or more monasteries which Yang-ming also visited, the names of which are unknown to us. These visits occurred not only in his early life, but also after his conversion to the Confucian quest for sagehood. At the age of thirty-one, Yang-ming spent eight months in a Buddhist monastery—the longest sojourn recorded. At the age of forty-nine, he made thirteen visits to Buddhist monasteries, spending one or two weeks there every time.[64] Certainly, Yang-ming regularly met and taught his disciples in such monasteries. While these contacts do not necessarily indicate heavy influence, and Yang-ming's biographers have said much less of his Buddhist than of his Taoist practices, we should recall firstly that the two religions, Taoism and Buddhism, experienced a "merging" process during the Yüan and Ming dynasties, and secondly, that Yang-ming himself admitted to "thirty years of interest" in Taoism.[65]

True, starting from 1504, when he set questions for the Shantung provincial examinations, Yang-ming expressed his repudiation both of Taoism and Buddhism.[66] Nevertheless, his conversion to Confucianism did not seem definite until his meeting with Chan Jo-shui in 1505, or according to Chan, in 1506.[67] And then, as we shall see, he was to develop his own "Confucian" doctrine, a response to the Taoist-Buddhist challenges, which shows that he has not been able to throw away the formative influences on his early life and thought. Indeed, as we must have discerned, the "Five Falls" were not consecutive but represented sometimes simultaneous and frequently recurrent interests. Among them, certainly, Taoism and Buddhism lasted longer, and left deeper imprints.

Not only do the "Five Falls" refer to recurrent temptations, but they had also competed all along for Yang-ming's attention with a sixth attraction: Confucian learning. His father was known as a scholar who refused to have anything to do with Taoism and Buddhism, and had given him an "orthodox" education in the Confucian Classics. Yang-ming never seemed to have questioned the value of the Confucian goal of sagehood. He had only objected to making compromises, to regarding success at examinations and in an official career as the ultimate goal. Even when practicing calligraphy, he recalled to mind the words of Ch'eng Hao: "I write with great reverence, not for the sake of writing beautiful words, but in order to learn [virtue]."[68]

He also explained: "When I started to learn calligraphy, I used to copy from model writings, and could only imitate the shapes of the characters. Later on, I no longer used the writing brush so flippantly. I first concentrated my attention and meditated upon the characters in my heart [or mind] . . . . Once the heart knows, the characters will naturally be well written."[69] This contains already the whole of his philosophy in embryo form. It explains why Yang-ming's philosophy became an inspiration for the Ming *literati* painters.[70]

The philosophy of Yang-ming cannot strictly be traced through a direct line of teachers, as can that of Chu Hsi, or even that of Chan Jo-shui. Much, however, has been said of Yang-ming's meeting with Lou Liang, the disciple of Wu Yü-pi. Certainly, Lou's remark that "Sagehood is possible of attainment through learning,"[71] is extremely significant. Yang-ming was undoubtedly aware of the intellectual controversy that raged in the Chin dynasty concerning whether sages have feelings and whether "sagehood" is attainable by one's own means."[72] It must certainly have been his own problem too. He is described as having searched everywhere for the extant writings of Chu Hsi in order to read them. His zeal for putting into practice the words of Ch'eng Yi and Chu Hsi led to his "investigating" the bamboos. He did so until overtaken by sickness. He also sought to follow Chu's counsel to "study systematically, in order to become excellent in learning," and once again he fell sick. It was therefore his supposition that only a "select" few can become sages and so was tempted to abandon the Confucian quest, and leave the world in order to practice the cultivation of life.[73] In other words, he was ready to give up Confucian ideals of sagehood only because he did not regard himself as being capable, physically and otherwise, of attaining them.

The Taoists must have disconcerted him since they treated him as a Confucian scholar, destined to an official career, rather than as one of themselves. Determined to search for a more profound meaning in life, he then retired to his hermitage for nearly a year. However, he was to find the result of Taoist cultivation also disappointing in itself. Without having discovered a solution to the problem of "whether sagehood is possible of attainment," he decided to return to worldly society and an official career, armed now with a crusading zeal to persuade others also to "remain true to their human nature," by adherence to Confucian social morality.[74]

Friendship with Chan Jo-shui was an important factor in Yang-ming's inner evolution. He had longed and looked, but without much success, for teachers and friends, for men who were his own intellectual equals, who had the same kind of boundless desires as he. In 1505 or 1506 the two men met for the first time in Peking. Yang-ming was then thirty-three and Jo-shui thirty-nine. Of this meeting, Yang-ming was to say: "I have lived in official circles for thirty years, without having met such a man." Chan, in his turn also said, "I have

traveled widely and seen much, but without having met such a man."[75]
Together, they discussed the learning of sages, in particular the teaching
of Ch'eng Hao, that "the man of *jen* forms one body with Heaven and
Earth and all things."[76] On Yang-ming's exile to Kweichow, Chan
presented him with nine poems, including the following:

> We form one body with Heaven and Earth,
> One family with the Universe,
> Since our minds are already at one,
> Why should we complain of separation?
> The floating cloud cannot stay fixed;
> The traveler on the route must make his turn.
> Let us honor brilliant virtue,
> And explore the boundless vastness.[77]

In reply, Yang-ming also presented Chan with several poems,
including these lines, which express succinctly his desires for greatness as well as the assistance and encouragement he had received from
Chan's friendship:

> The currents of Chu and Ssu have weakened,
> The waters of Yi and Lo appear to be only a thread.
> As to the three or four later gentlemen—
> Their merits cannot adequately make up for their defects.
> Alas, that I should refrain from measuring my own weakness:
> Limping in my walk, yet I desire to go so far.
> So many times, I fall down and I rise up again,
> Breathing heavily, often near the point of breaking.
>
> On the way I met a man with the same mind.
> Together, we dare to proclaim the greatness of virtue,
> We fight for the important differences which exist between
>   nuances,
> And encourage each other to go forward ten thousand *li*.
> The winds and waves are rising; I suddenly lose sight of you—
> As I utter these words, my tears are vainly falling.[78]

At that time, there was no doubt that, of the two men, Chan was the
"senior" philosopher, older and more mature. He had already spent

the past nine years of his life in the study of Sung philosophy. Yang-ming, on the other hand, was only *beginning* to settle down intellectually. Friendship with Chan certainly contributed to the firmness of his determination to seek for Confucian ideals, until, during his exile, he was once more faced with the same question: how could one, in those circumstances, become a sage? He would discover the answer for himself, and it was to change, not only his own life, but the lives of many others.

In his Preface to Yang-ming's Collected Writings (*wen-lu*), Ch'ien Te-hung (1497-1574) proposed two "triple changes" in Yang-ming's life, first as a student, and then as a teacher. As a student, Yang-ming first went through a phase of fondness for letters, then passed on to an absorbing interest in Buddhism and Taoism, and finally, during the hardships of his exile, understood the meaning of the Confucian Way.[79] All this we have already treated in our description of the "Five Falls," while noting that, given the shifts in emphasis in the general direction of his life, these "changes" or "falls" represent, to a large extent, recurrent rather than consecutive interests. The three changes in his life as a teacher, however, refer to something different. Although closely related to his own inner development, and to the refinement of his teaching, they have particular reference to the spiritual direction which he gave to his disciples, and so arose as much from his experience of their needs and responses as from those of his own. On the basis of Ch'ien's theories of the double "triple changes," and also on that of his own observations, Huang Tsung-hsi has presented his own version of a double set of "triple changes," which occurred before and after Yang-ming's development of his own teaching.[80] Since the two versions do not differ very much from each other, and for the sake of convenience, we shall adopt the earlier, or Ch'ien's version. According to him, Yang-ming first taught at Kweiyang the doctrine of unity between knowledge and action, then in 1513, after his arrival in Ch'u-yang, Anhwei, he gave special emphasis to quiet meditation. Lastly, after 1521, having experienced all 'the trials that accompanied his victory over Ch'en-hao, he began to teach the doctrine of the extension of *liang-chih*, going right to the heart of the matter, in order to bring insight to his hearers.

Yang-ming was primarily seeking an answer to the burning question of how to become a sage. Chu Hsi's suggestion was to cultivate an attitude of reverence in one's life and by the "investigation of things" which is achieved through extensive knowledge. His belief, and that of Ch'eng Yi, was that such a diligent pursuit of learning—primarily moral learning—would bring with it eventually a kind of sudden enlightenment, powerful enough to give meaning to the whole of life: "There is *li* (principle) in everything, and one must investigate it to the utmost. . . . One must investigate one item today and another item tomorrow. When one has accumulated much knowledge, he will naturally achieve a thorough understanding all of a sudden."[81]

Earlier in his life, Yang-ming had attempted to follow this advice to the letter, and hae found it wanting. Instead of bringing him closer to the goal of sagehood, the exhaustive investigation of *li* discouraged him and even affected his health. Moral principles, after all, are inexhaustible, just as life itself is unfathomable. If their knowledge was necessary for virtue, then very few men would be competent to the task of pursuing virtue. This, however, would not be in accordance with the writings of the sages, especially of Mencius. It is characteristic of Yang-ming's mentality, and of the nature of the Chinese language, that he should have sought to solve this problem, not by denying the value of knowledge, but by giving it a new meaning. By proposing the doctrine of the unity or identity between knowledge and action, he placed emphasis on a very special kind of experience: that of practicing virtue. One can become a sage only by acting in a sagely way, and this action itself is knowledge.[82]

That this insight should have come to Yang-ming during his exile was no coincidence. Mencius had said that every man can be a Yao or a Shun,[83] but Chu Hsi had specified that the road to becoming Yao and Shun lies in moral cultivation and the intellectual pursuit of moral knowledge. Yang-ming, however, found himself in the midst of people who had never heard of Yao and Shun. Had they, and their ancestors, been banned from reaching sagehood? Should they be instructed in the intricacies of investigation of principles? The Confucian had always been aware of his civilizing mission toward the barbarians. Yang-ming could not help asking himself how a sage would act in these circumstances.

The unity of knowledge and action was, in a sense, the only rationalization one could make in order to justify Mencius' teachings. He began to teach it, first to the few humble Chinese living there and then to the even humbler and less civilized Miaos. The response was gratifying:

> When I spoke to [the Chinese] of the theory of knowledge and action, they were all very much pleased to hear it. After a while even the barbarians became interested and reacted in the same way. But when I came out of my exile and spoke of it to scholars and officials, they raised diverse opinions, often refusing to accept what I said. And why is it so? Because they [have been biased] by having heard other opinions.[84]

The unity of knowledge and action provides a necessary foundation for the proposition that sagehood is attainable by all, but gives no instruction regarding what is virtuous action. If this need not be learned from books, then there must be another way of learning. Life, of course, is the best teacher, but is it also an ambiguous one. The human subject cannot always remain intent, waiting to hear the instructions that life might unfold to him. A certain "formal" learning is necessary, which is not the perusal of Classics. Yang-ming suggested the method which he himself had found fruitful: that of quiet meditation. During this exercise, one seeks not thought nor understanding, but the recovery of one's original nature—the nature that is perfectly good. In the light of its discovery, the principles of sagehood and virtue would naturally reveal themselves.

The great Sung philosophers—Chou Tun-yi, the two Ch'engs, Chu Hsi and Lu Chiu-yüan—as well as Ch'en Hsien-chang and Yang-ming himself, all had a general knowledge of the principles of "meditation," common to Taoism and Buddhism. These include the "remote" preparation for this exercise, which is a morally upright life, and a more "immediate" preparation, the control and regulation of one's emotions. An erect, sitting posture, whether on a chair, or, for the Buddhist, on a rush mat and in a lotus position, is always recommended. Attention is also given, both by the Taoists and Buddhists, to the control and regulation of breathing during the exercise of meditation. Chu Hsi himself had written a famous instruction on breath control, for which he recommends "watching the white on the nose," a Taoist practice. Control should also be exercised over one's sensations, with a view to keeping external stimuli away from the senses. The mind should be concentrated upon itself, to the exclusion of all distracting thought, and for the sake of attaining unity and harmony between consciousness and the object of consciousness, which is one's innermost self.[85]

Yang-ming practiced such meditation himself, and also recommended its exercise to his disciples. Soon after his exile in 1509 while on his way to Lu-lin in Kiangsi, he had met several of his disciples in Ch'en-chou and had sat with them in meditation in a temple. Afterward, he wrote to explain to them the purpose of such an exercise:

> What I have said earlier in the temple about sitting in meditation was not meant for the sake of attaining Ch'an impassivity.[86] Rather, since people like us are usually distracted by our many occupations, and do not know how to recollect ourselves, I wish to recommend such a remedy to our lack of study by the recollection of the mind.[87]

But Yang-ming found that meditation can also be a temptation, that one may be inclined to meditate for the sake of resting in the tranquility which it gives, rather than for the purpose of recovering one's innate principle of moral activity. If knowledge is action, meditation surely should not be an end in itself. Besides, for the "initiated" meditation becomes much less necessary. If one is habitually conscious of the demands of *liang-chih,* one need do nothing more than live up to them in depth and fullness.

This extension of *liang-chih* represents the culmination of Yang-ming's teaching. According to Ch'ien Te-hung, he began developing this theory around 1521, after his experience of the great trials that followed the victory he had won over the rebel, Prince Ch'en-hao.[88] Yang-ming spoke of *liang-chih* as a discovery he had made through a hundred deaths and a thousand sufferings. It was to be his guiding principle for the rest of his life. It was also the guiding principle he gave to his disciples.

> "Extension of knowldge" is not what later scholars understand as enriching and widening knowledge. It means simply extending my *liang-chih* to the utmost. This knowledge of the good is what Mencius meant when he said: "The [moral] sense of right and wrong is common to all men." This sense of right and wrong requires no deliberation to know, and does not depend on learning to function. This is why it is called *liang-chih*.[89]

The development of this doctrine, however, did not entail a repudiation of Yang-ming's earlier teaching regarding the unity of knowledge and action, or of the important role of quiet sitting, in one's understanding of self and perception of this knowledge of the good. It was rather the result of a fusion of these two, and of their simplification in practice. Since extension implies action, the extension of *liang-chih* necessarily presupposes the recognition that true moral knowledge lies only in action. Moreover, it includes also the meaning of acting always as one would in meditation without losing sight of one's virtuous nature, or rather, of permeating one's life and action with the spirit of quiet contemplation. For this reason, Yang-ming admitted that, in principle, ever since his exile of Lung-ch'ang he had not taught anything but this "knowledge of the good."[90]

Since the time of Confucius, and even more since the time of Chu Hsi, the "school of sages" had become identified with Confucian "scholasticism." Yang-ming desired to lead his students back to the sources—beyond Chu Hsi, beyond Confucius and the Classics, beyond even the first sages—who had attained sagehood without first studying the Classics. He desired to lead them back to the deepest faculty within themselves, to the principle of their originally good human nature, to *liang-chih*. And, after having done so, he knew that they would be able to live—as did Confucius, as did Yao and Shun—by practicing the simplest human virtues, those which make a man human, those which make him also a son, a brother, and a member of the human society in association with other men.

But the meaning of *liang-chih* extends beyond the realm of cultivation into that of the luminous, the term and goal of the entire method and process. For Yang-ming, its discovery signifies the fulfillment of a quest for the absolute. He had received certain insights into its nature during his exile, in 1508, in an experience which also summed up for him a methodology of self-cultivation. With the passage of time, he penetrated further into this mystery, discovering in it the beginning and end of the quest itself. To him, the extension of *liang-chih* eventually came to represent the continual discovery, within one's entire being, of that which is greater than oneself—the absolute.

Beyond "Ardor"

The "Five Falls" describe Yang-ming's mad ardor, which led him, during his early life, from one interest to another, without resolving the problem of his fundamental restless search for absolute values. The "Three Changes," on the other hand, present to us the gradual evolution of the substance and method of his teaching, after his definite return to the Confucian Way. He remained, even then, madly ardent, but his ardor was tempered with peace and serenity. He had become totally independent of the vicissitudes of life and the judgment of others.

His development of a new philosophy, interpreting the investigation of things as the rectification of the mind or heart, brought him criticisms, including the charge of preaching heresy. In 1523, students sitting for civil examinations in Peking were questioned about the "philosophy of the mind"—in an attempt by the authorities to discredit Yang-ming's teachings. Among the candidates, one disciple of Yang-ming, angered by the move, walked out of the examination hall. Others, too, were very much provoked. Yang-ming's reaction, however, was very different. "The learning of the sages will, from now on, be well known," he said, "because. . . . if my teachings are held [everywhere] to be false, there must be people in the world who will do their best to find out the truth."[91]

He went on to explain that, before, during his sojourn in Nanking (1515–16) he had yet something of the "Pharisaic" in him. But by this time he only believed in *liang-chih*:

> Where truths and falsehood are concerned, I no longer need to hide or be on the defensive. This is how I can be "ardent." Even if the whole world says that my actions do not measure up to my words, I would still act according to *liang-chih*.[92]

When questioned further concerning the distinction between the "Pharisaic" and the "ardent," Yang-ming explained:

> The "Pharisaic" seeks approval of the gentleman (*chün-tsu*) by being faithful and incorrupt. He also seeks not to offend the mediocre men (*hsiao-jen*) by doing what they do. . . . His mind is therefore corrupt,

and he cannot enter the way of Yao and Shun. The "ardent" aims at emulating the ancients. No turmoil or worldliness is sufficient to disturb his mind. He is like a phoenix flying above at height of ten thousand feet. With one more motion, he can become a sage.[93]

We should not be surprised, therefore, to find Yang-ming praising that man of strange ambitions, Tseng Tien, without reservation. Using the words of the Doctrine of the Mean, he remarked that Tseng was a man who "can find no situation in which he is not at ease with himself."

> If he is in the midst of barbarous tribes, he does what is appropriate to being in the midst of barbarous tribes. If he is in danger and difficulty, he does what is appropriate to this situation of danger and difficulty.[94]

Besides, he added: "The other three disciples may be described as *ch'i* (utensils), Tseng Tien showed that he was no *ch'i*."[95] Neither, of course, was Yang-ming.

A man who admired Yang-ming's accomplishments as a writer, statesman, soldier, and man of virtue, but disapproved of his philosophy, once remarked: "Men of old become famous, sometimes for their literary writings, sometimes for their political achievements, sometimes for their high virtue, and sometimes for their military victories. But you possess all these titles to fame. If you would only abandon your work of teaching, you would be a perfect man." With a smile, Yang-ming replied: "I would prefer to give up the other four titles to fame, and only teach [philosophy]. I believe that this would not make me less perfect."[96]

In the autumn of 1524, during Yang-ming's period of retirement from public office, he prepared a banquet for his students on the night of the Mid-Autumn Festival. The tables were set outdoors, at the Pi-hsia Pond near the T'ien-ch'üan Bridge. Over a hundred persons were present. Wine was served, after which the guests enjoyed themselves by singing, pitching darts, beating drums, or boating. Pleased and a little gay himself, Yang-ming composed a poem to honor the occasion. Its first verse concludes with these lines:

> Old as I am, I sing wild (*k'uang*) songs tonight,
> To be transformed into heavenly music, filling up the Great Purity.[97]

The second verse goes on to say:

> Everywhere brightly shines the midautumn moon,
> Where else can you find another assembly of such talents?
> Alas, that learning should already have been interrupted for a thousand years!
> Waste not your one life, men born to greatness!
> Whether our influence will outreach Chu Hsi's is a matter of doubt,
> Yet in no wise shall we imitate Cheng Hsüan's quest for details and fragments.
> Setting aside the lute while the notes are still vibrating in the spring breeze,
> Tseng Tien, the ardent and eccentric (k'uang), understands my mind best.[98]

However, the next day, when his disciples came to thank him for the feast, he said some very remarkable words, which show that while he approved of "mad ardor" he aimed at something even higher. Referring to the passage from the Book of Mencius where the philosopher explained to one of his disciples why Confucius, during his sojourn in the state of Ch'en, expressed his desire to return to his "ardent" (k'uang) students of Lu,[99] Yang-ming offered his own reflections. He said that while scholars of the world, shackled by considerations of wealth, honor, and profit, might be able to liberate themselves from these vanities when they heard the teaching of Confucius, yet they still ran the risk of giving only notional assent to the sage's words without really putting them into practice:

> And so they might gradually suffer from the defect of despising worldly affairs, and of paying scant attention to questions of social morality. Although they might be different from the commonplace and mediocre people of the world, they also have not attained the Way. That was why Confucius wanted to return [to Lu] from Ch'en in order to instruct them, and lead them onto the Way. When you, my friends, discuss learning, you should also fear not having understood this message. Now that you have seen it you, make assiduous efforts to reach the Way. Do not be satisfied with some small insight, and stop at being "ardent" (kiuang).[100]

If Yang-ming valued the quality of "ardor," it was for the sake of a higher goal. He was to reach beyond ardor, on to sagehood.

And this was also the verdict of his favorite disciple, Hsü Ai, who was to die eleven years before the Master. In his introduction to the first part of *Ch'uan-hsi lu,* Hsü had this to say about the person of Yang-ming:

> The master is naturally intelligent and perceptive. But he is also serene, joyful, straightforward, and easygoing. He pays no attention to his appearance. People who knew how impatient of restraints and conventions he had been as a young man, and how he was once absorbed with the writing of artful prose and poetry, and with the teachings of Buddhism and Taoism, regarded his new theories as novel doctrines, unworthy of careful study. They did not realize that his three years of exile among barbarians, and his efforts to keep [his mind] at peace while in the midst of difficulties, had brought him a degree of discernment and of single-mindedness that indicates his *penetration into* the state of *sagehood,* and his attainment of supreme harmony and truth.[101]

II

THE STARTING POINT: HSIN

When a person devotes himself to study (*hsüeh*), he must have a "starting point" [*t'ou-nao*, literally, "head"]. Only then can his effort become fruitful. . . .He will [have a definite direction] as a boat can have when [provided with] a rudder.[1]

AN EXAMINATION of Yang-ming's life prior to 1508, the year of his enlightenment, has yielded a recurrent pattern of two apparently contrary tendencies—attraction to silence and contemplation, and interest in scholarship and political action. At first sight, the enlightenment of 1508 might appear to be the maturation of his fondness for contemplation, a fondness which he had carefully and systematically cultivated. He admitted to having erred in his practice of the investigation of things external to himself. And since in Chinese, the word "things" (*wu*) contains the meaning of affairs (*shih*), it may be argued that he finally realized the folly he committed in having engaged himself in the active life of a scholar-official, a life which brought him to the loneliness of exile, where he discovered the value of solitude and the self-sufficiency of his own nature.

However plausible this explanation may appear, a glance at his subsequent life and activities is sufficient to dispose of it, Yang-ming was to show himself far more active after 1508 than ever before. He would never lose his fondness for silence and contemplation, but he was to give less and less importance to the practice of meditation. Eventually he would seem to have succeeded in uniting the two contrary attractions of stillness and activity, by his elaboration of the

famous doctrine of the "extension of *liang-chih*," according to which
every interior and exterior act of the human person can contribute
to the development of his *hsin* or character.

To understand the real meaning of Yang-ming's discovery—the
meaning he himself held—we must constantly keep in mind the vital
character of the need that it answered. The two contrary tendencies
of involvement in the world and withdrawal from it not only reveal
the tensions inherent in his exuberant temperament. They also express his restless search for the "right method" that would direct
him to the ultimate goal of human life: sagehood. It would have been
meaningless for Yang-ming to recognize the theoretical possibility
of every man attaining sagehood, unless he could also find the correct
method for this attainment. The agreement of Mencius and Hsün-
tzu on the universal possibility of sagehood did not solve the problem
for the later generations who purported to see passages in the Classics
susceptible of a different interpretation, and who were disconcerted
by the scarcity of sages since the time of the end of Chou. It was in
fact almost contradictory that philosophers such as Ch'eng Yi and
Chu Hsi should accept so earnestly Mencius' notion of this universal
possibility while considering him as the last sage. Probably they regarded the loss of orthodox Confucian teaching since the death of
Mencius as the cause of this very scarcity. Certainly, the long prevalent
belief that sages were born, not made, offered little encouragement to
the pursuit of sagehood. Even if the dominance of the philosophy of
Ch'eng Yi and Chu Hsi spelled the triumph of the *idea* of the universal
possibility of sagehood, sages did not thereby become more abundant.
Somehow, the ideal of sagehood still remained the reserved goal of a
few selected scholars, who always risked the danger of being considered
mad (*k'uang*) for daring to have such an ambition. It was against this
situation that Yang-ming revolted, and, in revolting, would present
his own discoveries—that every man not only *can* be a sage, but possesses within himself all the *means* necessary to become one, and that
sagehood is not a remote, impersonal ideal, but a concrete goal, well
within reach, *a state of mind*, self-transcending and yet to be made
immanent, to become internalized.

The enlightenment of 1508, with its assertion of the entire adequacy
of human nature itself as the agent and cause of sagehood, appeared

at first to be the parting of ways for Wang Yang-ming and Chu Hsi. In reality, it represented the fruit of Yang-ming's labor in attempting to give consistency to Chu's teaching of the universal capacity for sagehood. Yang-ming had tried Chu's *method* for acquiring wisdom— that of investigating things and extending knowledge—and had found it inadequate. He finally discovered a new basis that would provide the foundation for a different method. His goal remained the same as Chu's. The shift, however, is evident. Where knowledge of the Classics, and of all the moral principles expressed therein, as well as those present in external events and things, was for Chu Hsi the basis of his thought and the critieria for his action, for Yang-ming it was of much less importance. His emphasis would be rather on personal insight, the result of evidences drawn from life as well as from books, but completely internalized. Words are important to him no longer because they come from Classical texts, but because they are meaningful to the mind—to *hsin*.

Nevertheless, Yang-ming refrained for the time being from criticizing Chu Hsi. His first preoccupation after his enlightenment experience was to seek for confirmation in the canonical texts which he knew by heart, as proof of his convictions. He committed to writing the findings, entitling the collection "My Personal Explanations of the Five Classics." It was, at the same time, an appeal to authority, an attempt to remain within the orthodox tradition, as well as a subtle declaration of independence. He selected what he remembered of the words of the Classics, interpreting these according to his needs, and presenting them as *internal evidence* for his own thought. Besides, said he, the Classics were only *instruments* to be used in one's quest of the "Way." Once the "Way" had been found, the instruments should be put aside, just as the fishing trap should be put away once the fish has been caught, and the dregs of rice should be discarded once the good wine has been extracted from them.[2] The mistake of the worldly scholar, however, was to look for fish in the rod itself and consider the dregs to be wine. Yang-ming then went on to describe the writing of his "Personal Explanations":

> As I have not been able to bring books with me [to Lung-ch'ang] I have been sitting daily in the mountain cave, noting down what I remember by heart of the books which I studied in the past. I have

given explanations on those points which have impressed me. After seven months I have virtually covered the ideas of the Five Classics. I call [this work] "Personal Explanations" because [the ideas I offer] are not necessarily in accordance with those of the worthy [scholars] of the past.[3]

And so, quite early in his philosophical career, Yang-ming adopted the attitude characteristic of that great rival of Chu Hsi's, Lu Chiu-yüan: "The six Classics are all my footnotes."[4] He made a strong assertion of the validity of his personal insights, assigning to the texts of the Classics a secondary, supporting role. He also set aside quite completely those authoritative commentaries on the Classics, written by Ch'eng Yi and Chu Hsi. The "enlightenment" was to mark a "beginning." Yang-ming had decided to make the "journey" to sagehood all alone, relying completely on his own internal spiritual resources.[*]

THE MEANING OF "HSIN"

Yang-ming asserted the importance of having a correct "starting point" before any effort to attain sagehood can become fruitful.[5] According to him, this starting point is, without doubt, *hsin* (mind-and-heart). He described it as a life-giving power, and as the source and principle of goodness in man. Yang-ming brought this out in his "Personal Explanations of the Five Classics," where he gave a rather arbitrary and symbolical interpretation of the beginning line of the Spring-Autumn Annals: "[It was his] *first* year . . . the King's *first* month."[6] Yang-ming believed that, just as Heaven possesses the power of *jen*, by which it brings forth living beings, so too, man is endowed with *hsin*, the power and capacity that comes to him with life, and gives meaning to life. And so, what is called "origin," or "beginning"

---

* Regarded in this light, Yang-ming's enlightenment may be compared to René Descartes' (1596–1650) experience of 1619, when Descartes decided to make a clean sweep of the confusing ideas of other philosophers, and to bring new clarity and system into the sciences by relying upon the pristine powers of his native intelligence. This is given in his "Private Thoughts" and in the *Discourse on the Method*, Parts 1 and 2.

(*yüan*), is, for Heaven, the power of *jen* that brings forth living beings and, for man, *hsin*. "*Hsin* is that which comes [to us] with life."[7]

He brings out that which, after long reflections upon the experience of his recent enlightenment, he considers to be the central idea of his philosophy: the living, human *hsin* as that "beginning" from which philosophical thinking should start and to which it should frequently return. It is no wonder that his school of thought, as s development of those ideas already present in the philosophy of Lu Chiu-yüan, should be known to posterity as *Hsin-hsüeh*.

Already in these earliest extant writings that have come down to us from the time of his exile, Yang-ming has spoken of "making clear virtue manifest" (*ming ming-te*)[8] in terms of making *hsin*, the mind-and-heart, manifest. For him, *hsin*, which is one with nature, is the source of all goodness as well as the principle of all conscious and moral activity, possessing within itself the power of conducting the human person to the highest goals of sagehood. This does not necessarily mean that it is completely free of any or all imperfections, but rather that it possesses within itself the power of controlling these imperfections, and so, of perfecting itself. Comparing therefore *hsin*, the mind-and-heart, to the sun, which is naturally bright, and becomes obscure only when hidden from view by some obstacle, Yang-ming described the earth as that which, at the sun's setting, blocks from view what is of itself total brightness.* This can happen for the individual too, when his mind is obscured by "selfishness."

> There is nothing of the virtue of *hsin* that is not originally bright. That is why we speak of "clear virtue." If, at times [*hsin*] is not bright, it is merely obscured by selfishness. When selfishness is removed, there will be nothing that is not bright. Just as the sun rises of its own accord [up the horizon] from under the earth, without relying on the help of heaven [or the sky] (*t'ien*), so too the gentleman of his own accord makes clear virtue manifest, without requiring the help of another.[9]

---

* This calls to mind Plato's parable of the cark cave of ignorance with an opening to daylight, through which men ascend till they reach the Form of the Good, represented by the source of light. In Yang-ming's case, the implication would be that light is only hidden by darkness, and the action required is less to "ascend" to light, than to "dispel" the darkness. See *Republic*, Book VII.

And so, according to Yang-ming, *hsin*, the mind-and-heart, is that which refers to three things: the perfect *hsin* of pristine purity, the actual *hsin* obscured by selfishness, and the restored, acquired *hsin* of the gentleman who attains wisdom and sagehood. Yet the whole process is a self-determining one: *hsin* is capable of improving and restoring itself without requiring any outside help.

HSIN CHI LI

Yang-ming's determination that *hsin* should be the great "starting-point" of his philosophy proceeded naturally from the discovery he made in 1508—that his *hsin* was itself adequate as an instrument in the pursuit of sagehood, and that he had made a mistake in the past by seeking for this instrument outside the self. It also led him to formulate the propostion: *hsin chi li*.

The Chinese word *hsin* refers, in the Book of Mencius, to that center in man's being that is the source of all his conscious and moral activity.[10] In the Mahāyāna Buddhist, especially Ch'an texts, it signifies "reality" or "being," even "ultimate reality."[11] Thus, it extends well beyond the meaning of the English word "mind." Even in its moral connotation alone it is probably better translated by the Latin world *"mens,"* taken to mean the innermost point or apex of the soul, or the French word *"coeur,"* in the sense assigned to it by Blaise Pascal. It is, in this sense, the meeting point of the intellect and the will. For that reason, its activity, *yi*, translated sometimes as "thought," refers also to all conscious activity, including prereflective as well as volitional acts, that is, "intention." The word *li*,[12] on the other hand, refers, in the system of thought constructed by Ch'eng Yi and Chu Hsi, to the "essence" or "nature" of things as well as of man, that which constitutes their organizing principle, but that which also, in the Chinese interpretation, has a moral dimension, since human nature, and the world with which it is existentially one, is fundamentally moral. And since the Chinese language lacks a definite verb *to be*, the proposition, *hsin chi li*—literally, *hsin* and *li* are one and the same—can be translated as "the source of all being and virtue lies in *hsin*, in man's mind-and-heart." Initially, this proposition represents Yang-ming's attempt to internalize the moral quest, by claiming for the mind-and-heart, the possession of all moral principles, and even by identifying *hsin* with virtue or the sum total of moral principles. But it contains also the more hidden, metaphysical depths of Yang-ming's discovery, which is the understanding of the dynamic, existing self, *hsin*, as that which is somehow identical to *li*, previously understood as the more static principle, but now given a new dynamism in Yang-ming's teaching.

Our exploration of the meanings discovered in *hsin* will begin with Yang-ming in the moral sphere. In the year 1512, during a discussion with his favorite disciple and brother-in-law, Hsü Ai, Yang-ming had to answer the objection put forth by Hsü, who thought, like Chu Hsi, that the "highest good" should be sought in external things and affairs, because all these possess in themselves a definite *li*. Yang-ming's reply was to identify the "highest good" with *hsin chih pen-t'i*, that is, the "original substance" of *hsin*, or "*hsin* in itself," an expression already rich with metaphysical significance derived in part from Buddhist philosophy. Yang-ming commended Chu Hsi for having explained 'the words "making clear virtue manifest," in terms of "realizing fully *T'ien-li* (heavenly principle or virtue)."[13] He added:

> *Hsin chi li*: Is there any affair (*shih*) in the world which is outside [the realm of] *hsin*? Is there any virtue (*li*) which is outside [the realm of] *hsin*?[14]

Hsü gave as examples of moral principles that reside in affairs outside of the mind, those relating to the virtues of filial piety in serving one's parents, and benevolence in governing the people. In other words, he was thinking of the whole world of moral relationships, which form the recognized core of Confucian ethics. He gave to *hsin* an epistemological function as well as a moral one. But he did not understand how it could be the sole agent of its own perfection.

Wang Yang-ming replied that the principles of filial piety or loyalty and the rest can hardly be looked for in the parents or the ruler. These principles are all in *hsin*. Repeating here that *hsin chi li*, he continued:

> When *hsin* is free from hindrance of selfish desires, it is the embodiment of heavenly virtue (*T'ien-li*). . . . When this *hsin*, which is the pure and perfect virtue, is applied to serving parents, there is filial piety, to serving the sovereign, there is loyalty, [and so on]. . . .[15]

On that occasion he sought thus to answer Hsü's question by

limiting the meaning of the word *li* purely to its ethical dimension, as that which constitutes virtuous behavior. "Heavenly virtue" [*T'ien-li*] is, of course, that totality of goodness, present in the universe as well as in man; present, however, in its fullness and purity only in the sage, the perfect man, whose *hsin* is free from all traces of selfishness.

Yang-ming also agreed with Hsü that practical matters relating to caring for the parents' comfort in winter and summer and the like deserve investigation. But he did not think that the pursuit of virtue should begin with such details. He suggested that the filial son develop within himself a deep love for his parents, a love which as the "root" of virtue will make possible the growth of filial piety, blossoming into all the minute points of observance that constitute the "branches."[16] And so, instead of seeking to acquire moral knowledge of virtuous behavior through the study of details and techniques discovered by chance occasions, he envisaged the pursuit of virtue as being best carried out by the development of the inherent goodness of *hsin*, the seat of man's personality and the source of all moral activity.

> . . .The Book of Rites says: "A filial son who loves his parents deeply is sure to have a peaceful disposition. Having a peaceful disposition, he will surely have happy expression. And having a happy expression, he will surely have a pleasant countenance."[17] There must be deep love as the root and then the rest will naturally follow.[18]

About the same time that the discussion with Hsü Ai took place, or perhaps a year after, Yang-ming wrote a letter to another friend, in which he also spoke of the teachings of the Great Learning, in particular those regarding sincerity and the understanding of the good. He said:

> What one calls *li* (moral principle) in an object or event, righteousness in the manner we relate ourselves to it, and good in nature, is differently designated on account of the things to which they refer, but in reality are all manifestations of my *hsin*. There is no object, no event, no moral principle, no righteousness and no good that lies outside *hsin*. . . . To insist on seeking the supreme good in every event and object is to separate what is one into two things.[19]

And so Yang-ming directs the seeker of the highest good to an inner quest of the fullest moral development of himself. This would not isolate him from reality, nor remove him from the world of active involvement. Rather, it represents the fusion of inner and outer concerns. The development of an ever-deepening mind-and-heart in the aspirant for sagehood brings about a union between the agent and the object of his intentions and actions, thus transcending the dualism between the self and nonself, between *hsin* and *li*.

Yang-ming sought to justify his identification of *hsin* with *li* by pointing out that what makes the act virtuous is the intention of the mind rather than the act itself, or the object to which the act is directed. He used as example the Five Despots of the Spring-Autumn times, who gave the appearance of practicing virtue by resisting barbarian invasions and honoring the house of Chou, but who really acted out of selfish motivations.[20] The people who make a distinction between *hsin* and *li* may express admiration for such historical figures, on account of their external achievements, and neglect to consider their unworthy motives. They may even imitate such conduct, doing deeds that appear virtuous without ascertaining that these are in conformity with their intentions. "[These people] make two things of *hsin* and *li*, and drift unwittingly into the kind of hypocrisy that is characteristic of the way of Despots. I speak of *hsin* and *li* as identical so that people may know . . . and devote their efforts to [cultivating] *hsin* instead of accumulating isolated and external acts of righteousness."[21]

It is the inherent goodness of *hsin*, rather than external relationships, that prompts us to the practice of virtue. It is the *moral* or virtuous nature of *hsin*, which manifests the presence of a natural knowledge of the moral nature of human relationships and of a natural ability to act in accordance with such knowledge. And so, "on seeing the father, one naturally knows how to be filial; on seeing the elder brother, one naturally knows how to be fraternally respectful; on seeing a child fall into the well, one naturally knows how to be compassionate."[22] The moving power of such virtues as filial piety, fraternal respect, and compassion for the helpless are not present in the father or brother or child but in one's own *hsin*.

> If the principle of filial piety was present in the parent, would it. . . not cease to affect my heart after my parent's death?. . .The substance of the heart is nature (*hsing*). Nature and virtue (*li*) are one. And therefore, where there is a mind (*hsin*) of filial piety toward the parent,

there is the principle of filial piety. Where there is no mind of filial piety, there is also no principle of filial piety.[23]

Yang-ming appealed to the authority of Mencius as support for his proposition, *hsin chi li*. The sage seldom mentioned *li*, a word largely unknown to the early philosophers.[24] But the sage frequently discussed both *hsin* (nature) and *hsin* (mind-and-heart), often using the two words interchangeably. He had particularly stressed the innate human capacity for goodness and of the presence in it of the bour beginningsof virtue.[25] Yang-ming declared that the dichotomy of *hsin* and *li* and the quest for moral principles outside *hsin* implied the acceptance of Kao-tzu's proposition that righteousness was an exterior virtue,[26] and so indicate a lack of the proper knowledge of righteousness itself. "[Neither] humanity . . . nor righteousness can be sought outside *hsin*. How then could *li* alone be sought outside? To seek *li* outside *hsin* would divide knowledge and action into two things. To seek *li* in *hsin* is the teaching of the Unity of Knowledge and Action given by the school of the sages."[27]

Obviously, the practical and moral implications of such a proposition represents a radical departure from the practical, moral teachings of Chu Hsi, who had always insisted on the investigation of things outside of self as a help to the practice of virtue. Yang-ming never denied that human affairs and the events of life as well as person and things with which we come into contact are a good *test* of the reality of our knowledge of moral principles.[28] He only preferred to regard all affairs, events, persons, and things in terms of their relationship with *hsin*. To him, the moral dimension of the whole lived world of human relationships and affairs connotes somehow the *inseparability* of these relationships and affairs with *hsin*, the source of morality.[29]

UNIVERSAL CAPACITY FOR SAGEHOOD

Yang-ming made the goal of sagehood accessible to all, bringing a higher sense of consciousness and understanding of man's innate dignity and potential greatness, the foundation itself of man's basic equality with man. He also discovered the real meaning of sagehood, and of the word *sage*. This is not a being with superhuman powers as described by the Han apocryphal classics; or a person born great, with extraordinary intellectual and moral capacities, identified with the Way or original nonbeing, as presented by the neo-Taoists, or a *bodhisattva* prepared by innumerable previous lives of high virtue and merit for the bliss of Nirvana, but who prefers to remain within the cycle of life and death, of change and transmigration, in order to help and save others, to bring them also over to the other shore of eternal rest. Yang-ming described the sage very simply as a man whose *hsin* is filled with the pure heavenly virtue (*T'ien-li*) without any admixture of selfish desires. The sage is born like everyone else. He has no special knowledge other than the capacity for knowing the good in every man and woman. He does not necessarily know, by innate endowment and without the need of study, all the information pertaining to the rites, music, systems, and institutions.[30] Indeed, it is not even necessary that the sage should study all things and be prepared in advance for every kind of situation. Even Confucius had to ask questions on rites and ceremonials when he went inside the grand temple.[31] The sage is, in a sense, an *improvisor*. He responds to the needs of the times, learning to do so as these needs arise. Neither is he necessarily impeccable. Yang-ming cited the famous formula of the doctrine of the sages supposedly transmitted by Yao to Shun, remarking:

> If Yao and Shun really considered themselves as faultless, they would not be sages. The advice they gave each other was: "Man's *hsin* (mind) is prone to error; but the *Tao-hsin* is subtle. Keep always to the Mean; practice discernment and singlemindedness." Since they themselves regarded man's mind as being prone to error, it shows that their own minds are also prone to faults. Only because they were always wary, were they able to hold fast to the Mean and avoid transgressions.[32]

To learn to be a sage is therefore simply to keep and cultivate *T'ien-li*, that inborn power of goodness, or *liang-chih*, our inborn capacity to know the good and, in so doing, to eliminate selfish desires. Sagehood is a quality with which every man is born. To become a sage is simply to recover one's original innocence, to take over one's self completely by recapturing one's pristine state of mind and of heart.

Yang-ming likes to compare the mind of the sage to a bright mirror,[33] endowed with the power of reflecting all things as they come. By itself, it does not engage in either activity or stillness. It merely responds to all events, without allowing anything to tarnish it, without retaining any of the images. Thus the emotions of the sage are in accord with all things and yet of himself he has no emotions.[34]

The work of striving for sagehood resembles that of polishing the mirror, or of the mirror polishing itself. Fro while "the mind and heart of the sage cannot tolerate the least particle of dust and has naturally no need of polishing, the mind and heart of the average man . . . resembles a spotted and dirty mirror, which needs thorough polishing, to have all its dust and dirt removed. Then will the tiniest speak of dust become visible, and only a light stroke will wipe it away, without [anyone] having to spend much energy."[35]

Yang-ming placed much emphasis on the need of polishing the mirror. This image expressed for him the effort of removing selfish desires and of developing *T'ien-li* in the mind. He explained to his disciples the simplicity of such an effort:

> Listening first with mixed doubt and belief.
> My students find their heart finally revealed.
> [Their hearts] are like mirrors in the mud,
> Enclosing the light within the darkness.
> Dust and dirt once removed,
> The mirror will reflect the beautiful and the ugly.[36]

But how must one go about this work of polishing the mirror? The answer to this question has been given to us by Hsü Ai. He said that this should be done according to Yang-ming's instruction on *ko-wu*, or so-called investigation of things.[37] By this, Yang-ming refers to the work of making the intention sincere. He had earlier told Hsü Ai: "The teaching in the Doctrine of the Mean (Ch. 25) that 'Without sincerity, there is nothing,' and the work of 'making manifest clear virtue' of the Great Learning (Ch. 1) means simply that [one should seek] sincerity of intention. And the work of seeking sincerity of intention is [the same as] that of investigation of things."[38]

Such sincerity is not easily acquired. In the work of self-mastery, Yang-ming admits of no compromise. Speaking of selfish desires, he declares that "these must be thoroughly and completely wiped out, without the least bit being left behind."[39]

That such an assiduous watchfulness over self, over the least movements of *hsin*, was directed to the acquisition of perfect sincerity and perfect rectitude of thought and intention, is confirmed by his teachings elsewhere. When criticized by others, Yang-ming had sought not to justify his own actions or teachings but to benefit from the criticisms. Writing in 1523 to a friend, he quoted Mencius' sayings that "if anyone loves others but is not loved in return, let him examine himself to see whether his *jen* is perfect"[41] and "if anyone does not attain the goal sought after in his actions, let him examine himself."[41] Then, with characteristic directness, and employing the shock technique so well developed by Ch'an Buddhist Masters, he explained the task of establishing sincerity:

> Recently, whenever I discussed learning with friends, I spoke only of two words: establishing sincerity (*li-ch'eng*). As in killing a man, the knife ought to be placed on the throat, so in learning [to be a sage], efforts should be made to enter the fine points of the mind (*hsin*). Then would our learning become earnest and solid, and radiate brightness. And even if selfish desires sprout up, they will disappear in the same way as a few flakes of snow melt upon a fiercely burning stove.[42]

Sincerity lies at the heart of sagehood, and perfect sincerity makes of the would-be sage the real sage. Even more than a virtue to be acquired it is a state of being, into which one gains entrance, almost as though by violence. It is the *locus* in which one establishes oneself, and in so doing, establishes one's own sincerity, one's total integrity and authenticity.

Yang-ming developed his doctrine of sagehood especially in his conversations with Ts'ai Tsung-tai [Ts'ai Hsi-yüan] and others. Ts'ai agreed that one can *learn* to be a sage. But he could not understand why such different people, as Confucius, Po-yi and Yi-yin, should all be considered sages.[43] In other words, he had such a high ideal of sagehood and of Confucius, the sage *par excellence*, that he could not understand how other men, in his view inferior in character to Confucius, should also be venerated as sages. Yang-ming replied by another parable. He compared the work of achieving sagehood to that of refining gold. When a man has completely identified his mind and heart with "heavenly virtue" or "heavenly principle," the state of perfection he had attained may be likened to that of pure gold, which is no longer mixed with copper or lead. Men, however, differ in capacity (*ts'ai*), just as gold pieces may differ in weight. But the purity of gold is decided on the ground of its perfection in quality, not quanitity.[44]

> Therefore, even an ordinary person who is willing to learn to have his mind become completely one with heavenly virtue can also become a sage, just as a piece of gold weighing one tael is inferior in quantity, but not necessarily in quality, to another piece weighing 10,000 *yi*.[45] This is why we say, "Every man can become Yao and Shun."[46]

Yang-ming went on to explain that some men are born with a greater capacity for sagehood, and can practice virtue naturally and with great ease, whereas others are obliged to make greater effort to learn how to do so. Those who are less "talented" must make one hundred efforts where others need make only one, and one thousand efforts where others need only make ten. But they can all achieve the same kind of success. He then criticized the scholars who regarded sagehood as something determined by "knowledge and ability." Thinking that a sage must know all and be able to do all, they aim at encompassing all the knowledge and ability that they attribute to sages, and so devote themselves to acquiring "extensive knowledge" instead of to the only thing necessary—developing and realizing in themselves the Heavenly principle (*T'ien-li*). In the end, as they become more and more learned, they also become more and more selfish, more and more estranged from this *T'ien-li* itself. Their condition resembles that of a person who puts lead, brass, and iron into gold so as to increase its weight in quantity, thus lowering its purity of quality, until it is no longer fit to be called gold.[47]

To a disciple, who was not so happy with the "allotment" of 10,000 *yi* of gold to Yao and Shun, and only 9,000 to Confucius, Yang-ming also explained that the comparison with gold should not be taken too seriously. Sagehood, after all, is a transcendent state, and cannot be weighed quantitatively. Natural endowments differ from person to person, but all can achieve a certain capacity of self-realization, developing their given talents according by as they are big or small.[48]

Yang-ming made the ideal of sagehood possible of achievement, accessible to all men. This made a strong impression on his disciples. On two separate occasions two of his disciples told him that they had discovered that all the people walking in the streets were sages. Yang-ming took it calmly, remarking that this was just a natural fact.[49] However, while he believed in the universal capacity for sagehood, he was careful to see to it that none of his disciples assume the artificial "bearings" of a sage. To those who complained to him that many did not listen to their teachings, he said: "You assumed the bearing of a sage, and so scared people away. How could you succeed in lecturing to others? You must become like one of the people of ordinary intelligence. Then you can discuss learning (*hsüeh*) with them."[50]

UNITY OF KNOWLEDGE AND ACTION

The proposition that "the source of all being and virtue lies in in *hsin*," laid the foundation for Yang-ming's affirmation of the universal capacity for acquiring wisdom. It provides also the basis for his practical doctrine, his method, since *hsin* is capable of determining itself through a process of knowledge that involves experience and action. This will be clarified later on by Yang-ming's adoption of the term *liang-chih*—literally, good knowledge, or rather, knowledge of the good—as the basis of both his thought and method. To act, therefore, was to become for Yang-ming to "extend and realize our knowledge of the good."

Since for Yang-ming being and virtue are mutually identical, "knowledge" (*chih*) refers primarily to moral knowledge, and ultimately to wisdom, by which one's life is ordered in a meaningful manner. On the other hand, the word "action," *hsing*, does not simply designate any movement whatsoever, but only that by which one acts in conformity to his "knowledge of the good." In other words, just as true knowledge is always knowledge of virtue, true action should always be virtuous action. "The unity of knowledge and action" is primarily a moral ideal rather than a principle of epistemology.

Yang-ming began teaching "the unity of knowledge and action" in 1509, the year following his enlightenment. He was still living then in Kweichow, the place of his exile, and had been befriended by Hsi Shu, Assistant Superintendent of Education, who asked him about the similarities and differences between the teachings of Chu Hsi and

Lu Chiu-yüan. Refraining from answering directly, Yang-ming explained instead to Hsi his own recent discoveries. He spoke of the relationship between knowledge and action, proving his points by quoting the Five Classics and the ancient philosophers. Hsi finally understood and said, "The teaching of the sages has become clear again [for me] today. The similarities and differences between Chu [Hsi] and Lu [Chiu-yüan] show that each had his insights as well as his weaknesses. Instead of resorting to argumentation, it is better to seek for answers in my own [human] nature. Then I shall naturally understand." He ordered the repair of the Kwei-yang Academy, and personally led the students of Kwei-yang in paying respects to Yang-ming as their teacher.[51]

In another conversation with his disciple Hsü Ai, Yang-ming outlines his ideas on the unity of knowledge and action. When Hsü points out that there are people who *know* they ought to serve their parents with filial piety but do not put this knowledge to practice, which shows a clear distinction between knowledge and action,[52] Yang-ming answers that, in such a case, knowledge and action are being separated from each other by selfish desires, and thus are no longer knowledge and action "as they ought to be."[53] In his own opinion, however, there have never been people who "know" but do not "act." Those who seem to know but do not act simply do not know.

> Seeking beauty pertains to knowledge, while loving it pertains to action.[54] However, beauty is no sooner seen than loved. One does not first see it and then make up one's mind to love it. . . . It is like saying that so-and-so knows filial piety . . . . [or] fraternal respect. This must be due to his already having practiced filial piety and fraternal respect. . . . . It is also like the knowledge of pain. One can only know pain after having experienced it.[55]

Interestingly, Yang-ming illustrates the unity of *moral* knowledge and *moral* action by giving examples taken from the experience of sense perception which provokes an immediate and instinctive desire—or sometimes, aversion—for the objects perceived. He makes no distinction between knowledge and the broader human consciousness. For him, the cycle of reflection begins with a more passive activity, that is, with sensation, and proceeds to a reflective, moral knowledge, involving choice or action. Thus, where prereflective or sense knowledge is by nature "knowledge in action," so too moral knowledge reflective or prereflective—should be one with action.[56] Yang-ming knows, or course, that the perfect unity of moral knowledge and moral action is only a reality in the ideal man, the sage, who acts spontaneously according to his deep moral convictions, which have become to him like second nature. Such a man acts always according to his originally good nature, practicing all virtues instinctively. But the ideal exists for all. As Yang-ming puts it, "Knowledge is the direction for action, and action is the effort of knowledge,"[57] and "knowledge is the beginning of action and action is the completion of knowledge."[58] He also says:

> People today distinguish between knowledge and action and pursue them separately, believing that one must know before he can act. . . . They say that [they will wait] till they truly know before putting their knowledge into practice. Consequently, to the end of their lives, they will never act and also will never know. This doctrine of knowledge first and action later is not a small sickness. . . . . My present advocacy of the unity of knowledge and action is [made] precisely as medicine for that sickness. . . .[59]

This is the language of a prophet, seeking to arouse the moral conscience of his fellow countrymen to the recognition of certain ethical ideals. For Yang-ming the "return to *hsin*" can only mean going back to the original source of both knowledge and action, to that power which is productive of all goodness. As he put it: "If one understands my meaning [and purpose], there is no harm in saying that [knowledge and action] are two things, since they will still be only one *in reality*. If one does not understand my meaning, even if he says [knowledge and action] only make up one thing, it will still be as useless as idle gossip."[60]

The teaching of the unity of knowledge and action also seeks to reform and rectify men's characters by going right to the heart of their troubles: to their thoughts and intentions. To his disciple Huang Chih, Yang-ming explains that those people who divide knowledge and action into two things do not make any effort to remove their evil thoughts and intentions so long as these remain as such, and have not been translated into "action." On his part, however, he advocates the unity of knowledge and action precisely so people may understand that "when a thought is aroused, there is already action. If there is anything evil there. . . . one must overcome it at once. One must go to the root and the bottom of [things] and not allow the evil thought [or intention] to lie latent in one's chest. This is the basic purpose of my doctrine."[61]

All his life Yang-ming never got tired of speaking of this "unity of knowledge and action." He discussed it in his letter to Ku Lin, saying that "where knowledge is genuine and earnest, it is also action, and where action is intelligent and discerning, it is knowledge."[62] He kept repeating that a true understanding of this unity between knowledge and action would lead a disciple of the Confucian Way to seek for the source and principle of all perfection and goodness in *hsin*— the mind-and-heart.[63] In a long letter, written in 1526, he took up the subject again in response to questions posed by a friend,:

> Knowledge and action are really two words describing the same, one effort. This one effort requires these two words in order to be explained completely. If one sees clearly the essential point of departure, he would know this is only one, and that though [knowledge] and [action] may be described as two activities, they really remain one effort.[64]

SITTING IN MEDITATION

The teaching on the "Unity of Knowledge and Action" sets forth an ideal for both knowledge and action, foreshadowing a method to be developed for its attainment. By personal practice, Yang-ming discovered the merit of the "technique" of quiet sitting. The stillness it inculcates in the heart enhances the deepening of a genuine self-knowledge, opening to the person who practices it a new world of life and conscious activity within himself.[65] However, as it is only a technique, which can be practiced from time to time but remains subject to abuse, its importance is yet secondary. It was not the method for which he was searching. All the same, Yang-ming frequently practiced sitting in meditation, and advised others to do the same. Many of the poems he wrote before 1520 and even after manifest his deep love of silent contemplation. In one of them, probably written in 1514, he had this to say:

> If our Master Confucius desired to remain silent and wordless,
> We ought to believe that wordlessness expresses great joy.
> When one wakes to the hidden meaning of hawk flying and fish
>   leaping
> One knows that moral striving does not lie in expounding texts.
> Self-cultivation and mind-culture are not Ch'an practices.
> In attempting to correct errors, one may go to the opposite.
>
> Under the influence of hearsay and rumor,
> True learning has long been interrupted.
> I need to sit in silence in the woods,
> Green mountains understand well my unspoken words.[66]

In the Buddhist and Taoist schools, meditation was made for the sake of gaining inner calm, of reaching pure consciousness, of reducing the body to "dry wood" and the mind to "dead ashes."[67] Yang-ming, however, promoted this exercise for a different goal. It was to be a "remedy" for the lack of study, to help toward the recollection of the mind. "If, during the day, our work and effort begin to annoy us, we can practice sitting in meditation. [and] If, we feel lazy and uninclined to read, we should [go against this inclination] and read. This is like applying a remedy according to the disease."[68] It is not an end in itself, but a means to an end.

Yang-ming regards sitting in meditation as an especially good method by which the beginner may acquire enough peace and strength to discern and eliminate his selfish desires. This, he says, resembles the work of getting rid of bandits. One must be determined to wipe them out completely.[69] The root of the trouble—that is, the unruly desires—whether for sex, money, or fame, must be discovered, pulled up, and thrown away so that it will never grow again. "Act at all times like a cat trying to catch a mouse, with eyes intent on watching and ears intent on listening. As soon as a [bad] thought takes rise, overcome it at once, as decisively as [a blacksmith] removes a nail or saws iron."[70] It is not, he says, the concern of the beginner to abandon all thought and reflection. He must first examine himself. He must think of sincerity and "heavenly virtue." When he has acquired, in his *hsin*, the pure "heavenly virtue," he will also have attained a state of emptiness or void regarding thoughts and reflections.[71]

In answer to a disciple who expressed disappointment in the effort of "putting a stop" to thoughts and deliberations through meditation, Yang-ming explains that thought is never, and never can be, absent. There is, after all, no stillness without activity as there is no activity without stillness. What is aimed at, rather, should be the elimination of selfish desires (*yü*). And then nature can be calm whether in a state of activity or stillness. When reminded of Ch'eng Yi's praise of a man who was able to sit absorbed in meditation, becoming completely unaware of the doings of his son who was near him, Yang-ming merely remarks that Ch'eng was probably speaking in jest and mocking the man. Distractions after all will always be felt. What is important is not be misled by them.[72]

When one of his disciples, Liu Chün-liang, expresses a desire to retire into the mountains for the sake of sitting in meditation, Yang-ming replies that such a course of action can be recommended only if his motive is to cultivate himself in a quiet place. But the same practice would not be helpful if Liu was seeking stillness for its own sake, and through disgust with the affairs of the world and of society.[73] Thus, sincerity of intention is not only to be cultivated in meditation, but used also as a criterion to judge the practice of meditation itself and the appropriateness of such a move.

All his life Yang-ming himself yearned for silence and quiet. As far as he could, he also gave himself and his disciples every opportunity of retiring to a quiet place, or at least of spending some days or weeks, from time to time, in such places. But just as he had repented of his repented of his retirement to Yang-ming Cave in 1504, when he had achieved a certain measure of success in acquiring "parapsychic" powers, which he recognized to be merely the result of "playing with [his] mental powers,"[74] so he would always be wary of practicing sitting in meditation for its own sake. He wanted, through both meditation and the activities of daily life, to attain a fusion of the "inner" and "outer" realms of his mind and spirit, or rather, he could not see these realms divided into two. For him, life was thoroughly one, with the "inner" permeating the "outer." His goal was not self-perfection for its own sake. It was to be a Confucian sage, a man who united "kingliness witout" with "sageliness within," a man who "manifested" his "clear virtue"'not only by cultivating himself, but also by allowing self-cultivation to overflow into the fulfillment of responsibilities toward the family, the state, and the world.[75]

Nevertheless, sitting in meditation, while geared to action, remains in itself a technique. It cannot take the place of an all-embracing, universal method. It contains, besides, the risk of making its practitioners prefer silence and contemplation to action. From the beginning, Yang-ming was well aware of these risks and dangers. Writing in 1511 to Wang Chün [Wang Shih-t'an] on the subject of Chu Hsi's commentary on the Doctrine of the Mean, Yang-ming had objected to the work of self-cultivation being divided into two sections, with a special time set aside for quiet and passivity:

> I would recommend that you pay more attention to activity, without allowing such effort to suffer any interruption. When activity is not without harmony, passivity [or stillness] will not lack equilibrium.[76]

Already in 1515, soon after his departure from Ch'u-yang, Yang-ming issued a warning regarding the danger of being turned away from a life of action by the practice of contemplation.[77] In later life, he described clearly his own shift from an emphasis on sitting in meditation to that of "extending [and realizing] *liang-chih*", achieved either through quiet reflection, in or out of meditation, or through action itself:

> When I was in Ch'u-yang, I saw that my students were mostly concerned with intellectual knowledge, and spent time debating on similarities and differences of meanings of words, which did them no good. For a while, they realized the situation better, and achieved some immediate results. But in time they gradually developed a fondness for silence and a disgust for action, thus falling into the pitfall of becoming lifeless like dry wood. There are people who advocate abstruse and subtle theories to startle others. But I expound now only the doctrine of extending *liang-chih*. If *liang-chih* is clear, one can either try to attain truth through quiet reflection, or through efforts made in the midst of activity.[78]

Yang-ming broadened the quest for wisdom and sagehood, freeing it from a narrow, academic focus on intellectual knowledge and textual studies—though these be of hallowed Classics extolling eternal virtues—to include a particular emphasis on meditation and silence and then, even more, to embrace the confronting of life on all its levels, especially in the midst of activities. By doing so, he is already offering a glimpse of his own understanding of wisdom itself and of the way to acquire it. Wisdom does not mean intellectual knowledge. The latter does not necessarily preclude it, but may sometimes hinder its achievement. Wisdom is rather the harmony and purity of the mind-and-heart, perfect in its spontaneity, true to its pristine nature. Wisdom is also the proven ability of dealing with a variety of human situations according to an inborn moral intuition, developed and realized to its fullest by earnest self-cultivation, unchanging in its constant attachment to goodness and virtue, and yet flexible in its judgments of variables and in its freedom of decisions. Wisdom is a constant becoming. For its starting point, *hsin*, the mind-and-heart, is the self, which is both given and to be created, possessing the seed of perfection and yet in need of continual purification, finding and fulfilling itself through testing itself in the ebb and flow of stillness and activity which makes up the whole of life.

For this reason, Yang-ming cannot limit his understanding of "extending *liang-chih*" to merely "increasing" or "developing" a basic, given, moral sense. There is, indeed, nothing to increase, if the word is understood in terms of quantity. As Yang-ming would frequently repeat, *liang-chih* can neither be increased or diminished.[79] It is the fully given. It requires rather discovery, deepening, realization. If Yang-ming retains the word "extend" (*chih*) on account of its classical origin, *chih-chih* (extension of knowledge), coming, as this does, from the text of the Great Learning (Ch. 1), he only does so to give it an enriched meaning. If knowledge, whether of intellectual truths or moral relationships, can be extended through a gradual accumulation of information and a development of sensitivity and discernment, wisdom, which allied with virtue is all-comprehensive, transcends information, understanding of particular truths, moral judgment, and sensitivity. Wisdom can only be acquired paradoxically. It is the realization of what we already possess in potency. It can only be extended through a process of unfolding and of becoming. And this will be the burden of the following chapters, as we attempt to follow Yang-ming in his paradoxical, even dialectical, expositions of his views on investigation of things and extension of knowledge, all of which led to his ultimate perception of wisdom itself and of his way of acquiring it.

III

THE CONTROVERSIES: KO-WU

Whenever [philosophical] teaching is given, there must be similarities and differences. It is not necessary for all to have the same opinions; that is the way to seek the same [truth][1].

Y ANG-MING realized that his own teachings—"the source and principle of all being and virtue lies in *hsin*" and "knowledge and action are one"—clashed with the accepted teachings of Chu Hsi regarding *ko-wu*—investigation of things—and *chih-chih*—extension of knowledge. Chu had spoken of such "investigation" and "extension" as "developing the mind to the utmost, knowing one's nature, and knowing Heaven." But he tended to see a certain sequential order in which this self-cultivation is organized. He spoke of investigating things and extending knowledge in nearly quantitative terms. He regarded that as the first step to take in the pursuit of sagehood. He said that "sincerity of intention, rectification of mind, and cultivation of person" should follow the first step. He also said that perfect wisdom and virtue (*jen*) lies in "remaining single-minded regardless of whether one's life will be long or short."[9] In other words, he envisaged such perfection as the crowning achievement of a long life of investigating things and extending knowledge—personal perfection coming to fruition after a life of diligent scholarship and careful, moral cultivation—a sum total of various individual decisions and actions. For Chu Hsi, only the perfect man, who has passed through every one of the steps outlined for the quest of sagehood, will have the detachment necessary regarding his own life—after his desires have been carefully purified.

Yang-ming disagreed with such teaching. He preferred to see the end in the beginning. For him, sagehood is more than a goal to be attained. It is a state in which one places oneself, engages oneself. It is a state of consciousness in which one grows continually. It is a state into which one must gain entrance by a firm, resolute act of giving oneself over to the quest for sagehood. The beginner must already have a certain single-mindedness and dedication and be detached from all consequences that may befall him, as, for example, regarding the length or shortness of his life. Yang-ming always equated Chu Hsi's first steps—investigation of things and extension of knowledge—with the cultivation and realization of the Heavenly principle, T'ien-li, and with the concluding state suggested by the Great Learning, that of "abiding in the highest good."

PRELIMINARY DISCUSSIONS

In the famous conversation with Hsü Ai, Yang-ming explained that Chu Hsi made the mistake of reversing the proper order that should be observed in the work of study, requiring of the beginner what could be done only by the moral genius or expert. He considered rather becoming "single-minded,"* regardless of whether one's life is long or short, as the first step, equivalent to establishing one's hsin (li-hsin)[3]. For hsin, the mind-and-heart, is at the same time the starting point as well as the goal to be achieved and realized. It is the given; it is also to be created, discovered, realized. It is potentiality and freedom, gradually shaping itself, establishing itself, through an act by which one's entire being engages itself in the quest for wisdom, an act which must be constantly renewed, until it is coextensive with

---

* This is very suggestive of the contemporary existentialist emphasis of authenticity as the process of becoming, especially of M. Heidegger's interpretation of Dasein as the call of conscience to authenticity, which requires a certain existential "resoluteness." It is an aspect of existentialist thought which has evoked Christian theological thinking, as for example by Paul Tillich. See Heidegger, Being and Time, Eng. tr. by J. Macquarrie and E. Robinson (London, 1962), 312–14, and P. Tillich, The Courage to Be (New Haven, 1952), 148–56.

one's whole life and existence. This is the same as what Yang-ming has said about "establishing sincerity."

Yang-ming admitted that this first step involved, as do most beginning, painful and arduous labor. But this was basic and essential. Only he who desires wisdom with his whole being, and gives himself in exchange for it, will find wisdom and become himself a sage. But the man who gives himself merely to the accumulation of knowledge, through the process of investigation and extension, will never find it. And so, Yang-ming added: "Chu Hsi reversed the proper order [of things], so that the beginner has no place to start."[4]

Yang-ming declared that he preferred to use the word *ko* as "rectifying" rather than "investigating" or "reaching," and the word *wu* as "affairs" (*shih*) rather than "things." For whereas "investigating or reaching things" implies a linear movement of the person who reaches out of himself to attain to the so-called principles (*li*) of things, "rectifying [oneself in the handling of] affairs" connotes a circular movement involving the dynamic activity of *hsin*, the mind-and-heart, engaged in perfecting and determining itself. Let us listen to his own words:

> The master of the body (*sheng*) is the mind (*hsin*). That which proceeds from the mind is intention (*yi*). Intention-in-itself [literally, the "original substance" (*pen-t'i*) of intention] is knowledge. That to which intention is directed is affair (*wu*). For example, when the intention is directed to the service of one's parents, then such service is an "affair" or action. . . . There is no *li* (virtue, moral principles), no *wu* (affair, action) outside of *hsin* (mind, mind-and-heart).[5]

Following this line of reasoning, Yang-ming concludes that the central moral teaching of both the Doctrine of the Mean and of the Great Learning lies in "seeking the sincerity of the intention," and this, in turn, is the meaning of *ko-wu*, called "investigation of things."[6]

Yang-ming objected to Chu Hsi's new arrangement of the text of the Great Learning, which put the section of the "investigation of things" before that on "making the intention sincere." For him, "making the intention sincere" is the principal message of this book, and the starting point of the entire task of study or personal cultivation. Chu's rearrangement confused the order of importance as well as of precedence. He referred to it as the "infinitesimal mistake in the beginning which led to an infinite mistake in the end."[7] He remarked that Chu's effort to interpret the whole text in terms of reverence (*ching*) and of sincerity (*ch'eng*) was superfluous, like "drawing a snake and giving it feet."[8] It would have been much better if he had left the entire text intact without additions and without changes.

In a letter written in 1513 Yang-ming gave a thorough discourse on this question of the "investigation of things." He says that "sincerity of intention" is the essential principle and basis of learning, while the "investigation of things and the extension of knowledge are the results achieved by sincerity of intention." He also stated that Chu Hsi's teaching of "intention becoming sincere after exhausting the principles (*li*) of things," while not contradictory in itself, does not completely conform to the original meaning of the text of the Great Learning or of the Doctrine of the Mean. Unfortunately, this teaching became accepted by "later scholars," who "adhere to the added commentaries, and do not investigate deeply the meaning of the Classics."[9]

Yang-ming attempted for a long time to accommodate Chu Hsi's teaching by a process of reinterpretation, presenting what he considered to have been the "real meaning" of Chu's words, and appealing from a "misunderstood" Chu Hsi to the "real" one. Later on, he would take a further step, and move from an "immature" Chu Hsi to a "mature" Master who allegedly, in his old age, reached virtually the same position as did Yang-ming himself.

In his "*Tzu-yang shu-yüan-chi hsü*" [Preface to the Collected Works on the Tzu-yang Academy], dated 1515, Yang-ming tries to reconcile his teaching that "the source and principle of all virtue and perfection lies in the *hsin*" with Chu Hsi's famous "Rules for Instruction of Po-lu-tung Academy."[10] He claimed that his desire is to present a systematic methodology for the acquisition of virtue through learning. For him, this means going from the roots to the branches, cultivating the mind-and-heart (*hsin*) and expressing this cultivation through the practice of such virtues as humanity and righteousness. He says that this was also the inner meaning of Chu's "Rules," which first set forth knowledge of the five moral relationships as the "essentials" of learning, and then prescribes for the student a graded program of "study, inquiry, reflection, and discernment," which, in turn, is followed by certain "main points" on practical moral behavior in the management of affairs. He admits the danger that arises when Chu's words are taken in a detailed and fragmentary manner, adding that his own teaching is designed to clarify what Chu Hsi had not been able to explain completely. Thus, according to Yang-ming, *hsin* remains always as the object of "study, inquiry, reflections and discernment."[11] In other words, all efforts of learning or self-cultivation should be concentrated on the cultivation of one's *hsin*.

So long as Yang-ming kept his teaching on the "investigation of things" private, in letters and discussions with disciples and friends, he was able to avoid public controversy. The situation changed, however, in 1518, with the publication of his two works: *Ta-hsüeh ku-pen p'ang-chu* [Old Version of the Great Learning, with Side Commentaries] together with the Preface he wrote for it three years before, and the *Chu-tzu wan-nien ting-lun* [Definitive Ideas of Chu Hsi as Developed in His Later Life], also with his Preface.[12] These works indicated Yang-ming's state of mind at that time. The first was an open assertion of views on the Great Learning which differed from Chu's, while the second work represented an effort to defend himself against possible accusations of "heterodoxy," by a strange appeal to Chu Hsi himself. The text of the Great Learning had been divided into small chapters, punctuated and explained by Chu Hsi, who had also altered the expression *ch'in-min* (love the people) to that of *hsin-min* (renovate the people). This edited text, together with Chu's commentary, had gained wide acceptance and official approval during Yüan and Ming to such a point that many forgot the original text was an integral part of the Book of Rites.[13] Yang-ming, however, preferred the pre-Sung text as found in the T'ang edition of the Nine Classics, and had it published, together with his own Preface, prepared three years earlier, as well as certain brief side commentaries.

Yang-ming's second publication consisted of a collection of excerpts from thirty-four letters written by Chu to twenty-four disciples and friends, and a selected passage from the writings of Wu Ch'eng (Wu Yü-ch'ing, 1249–1333), who expressed regret at the degeneration of Chu's school of thought into a school of exegesis, and declared his own "conversion" from a fondness for fragmentary knowledge to the cultivation of real virtue.[14] To these, Yang-ming added his own Preface, written three years earlier. He claimed here that he had found proof that Chu had reached in later life the same conclusions as himself on what was the correct Way of the Confucian school.[15]

These publications established Yang-ming's reputation as a thinker, and also stirred up a great deal of controversy, which was to last throughout the Ming and well into the Ch'ing dynasty.[16] This controversy can best be seen through the letters and remarks exchanged between Yang-ming and two of his friends: Chan Jo-shui and Lo Ch'in-shun (Lo Cheng-an)—the latter being a renowned scholar and follower of the Ch'eng-Chu school, Yang-ming's senior in age and official rank. It revolves around the question called "the investigation of things," so much a part of the teaching of the Great Learning, and generally associated with the interpretations given it by Ch'eng Yi and Chu Hsi. And it also calls to question the authority of Chu Hsi, till then unchallenged.

I propose to study the controversies aroused by these two publications by discussing the debates between Yang-ming and his friends, concerning both the "investigation of things" and the authority of Chu Hsi, and then move on to a more thorough treatment of Yang-ming's entire attitude toward the Classics and the role of intellectual inquiry in the quest for wisdom and sagehood.

THE CONTROVERSIES

In the preface to the *Ta-hsüeh ku-pen p'ang-chu,* Yang-ming presented his reasons for the publication of the old version of the text. He began by saying that the essential teaching of the Great Learning, including that of the "investigation of things," lies in "making the intention sincere." This is also the meaning of "extending knowledge," which is achieved through the "rectification of *hsin*" as expressed in the "cultivation of self," which is nothing else than "manifesting clear virtue"—with reference to self—and "loving the people"—with reference to others. He thus internalizes the whole quest for wisdom and sagehood. Self, mind-and-heart, intention, knowledge, and even things [in his case, referring to action] are all one and the same, are all different manifestations of the same reality, or better still, of the same process.* Let us listen to his own words:

> The work of making the intention sincere lies in the investigation of things. To seek such sincerity means, at its utmost, to rest in the highest good. To rest in the highest good requires the extension of knowledge. The rectification of the mind (*hsin*) is aimed at the recovery of the pristine goodness (*pen-t'i*) [of the mind]. The cultivation of self expresses the effort (*yung*) [of such rectification]. This is called manifesting virtue with reference to self, and loving the people with reference to others.[17]

After this explanation, Yang-ming goes on to say that when the entire text of the Great Learning is taken as a whole, and meditated upon in an attitude of reverence, everything falls into perspective and the meaning of the sages is clear. When, however, the text is divided into sections and given a commentary, the doctrine transmitted by Confucius to Tseng-tzu and contained therein is lost. "Fragmentation [of knowledge], emptiness [of mind] and falsehood" are the results. The highest good disappears from sight.[18]

KO-WU: "WHOLE" or "PARTS"?†

Lo Ch'in-shun was Yang-ming's elder by nine years and a known scholar of the time. He had studied Ch'an Buddhist writings and

---

* Yang-ming's confidence in the capacity of *hsin* to improve and perfect itself, and to attain the "highest good," recalls to mind, even more than does the philosophy of Chu Hsi, the concern of Baruch Spinoza (1632–77) for the acquisition of wisdom through a method of "improving the understanding" by which one rises to the intellectual love of God, the highest good. Both by his life and teachings— he believed in the identity of intellect and will, of thought and action, and in an immanent God, the highest good—Spinoza resembles Yang-ming to an unusual degree. Even Spinoza's effort to complete and correct Descartes' view of clear and distinct ideas, which require the support of a God outside of the self, by accepting the human understanding to be its own guarantee, reminds one of Yang-ming's faith in the self-determining nature of *hsin*. The Chinese thinker differs from the Dutch Jew, however, because he grew up in a tradition that did not know the "geometrical method" of reasoning and concentrated much more on intuitive perceptions.

† This "whole *versus* parts" discussion is more concerned with knowledge or truth than with action. It shows how Yang-ming's integrated approach to the "investigation of things" flows from his basic understanding of reality and of the nature of wisdom.

followed Buddhist practices, but had later discarded them in favor of the "orthodox" teachings of Ch'eng Yi and Chu Hsi. But he was not lacking in originality, and his own understanding of the inter-relationship between *li* and *ch'i* differed from that of Ch'eng and Chu, and was to exert a special influence in the development of the so-called Ch'eng-Chu school in both Korea and Japan.[19]

After reading Yang-ming's two publications of 1518, which had been sent to him in 1520, Lo wrote to tell Yang-ming of his reactions.

Like Ch'an Jo-shui, Lo pointed out that Yang-ming advanced his own teaching on the "investigation of things" by taking the two words *ko-wu* out of context. He added that Yang-mings' interpretations appeared to exclude the "investigation of things" outside of the mind-and-heart for the sake of cultivating the mind-and-heart alone. This, Lo said, would result in a direct contradiction of the words of the text of the Great Learning, and would come dangerously close to the teachings of Ch'an Buddhism.[20] He also remarked that Yang-ming's interpretation of the sentence, "the extension of knowledge is in the investigation of things" (Great Learning, Ch. 1), made of it, "the investigation of things is in the extension of knowledge," that is, by emphasizing "extension of knowledge."[21]

Lo also insisted upon Chu Hsi's distinctions between *hsin*, the mind-and-heart, and *hsing* (nature), which makes up its "content," and causes it to become the *locus* of *li* (reality, moral principles). Lo did not share Yang-ming's optimistic estimate of the power of the mind-and-heart to acquire wisdom and sagehood. He pointed out that if Wu Ch'eng finally attained insights into the nature of sagehood, it might have occurred as the fruit of his long years of devoted study on the meaning of words in the Classics and the Commentaries, to which he therefore owed his enlightenment.[22]

In his reply, Yang-ming concentrated on explaining to Lo his own *basic* position regarding the "unity" or "wholeness" of the quest for sagehood. It is, he said, the whole personality that should be developed, not by investigating one thing after another in the manner of an as-siduous scholar and exegete, but by cultivating and realizing *hsin*, the mind-and-heart. He admitted to Lo that the text of the Great Learning makes mention not only of sincerity of intention and recti-fication of mind, but also of investigation of things and extension of knowledge—as "methods" of personal cultivation. However, this does not justfy the separation of learning into two realms, inner and outer. The four "methods" or procedural steps—investigation of things, extension of knowledge, sincerity of intention and rectification of mind—are in reality four aspects of the same effort, an effort directed at the integral development of the *character* of the *whole* man by the cultivation of his personality at its deepest recesses, its *hsin*.[23] And then, propounding a thoroughly unitary philosophy to support his single, universal method of self-cultivation, Yang-ming presents his own understanding of *li*. This time, it is in terms of this word that he seeks to explain the other words—of *hsing* (nature), *hsin* (mind-and-heart), *yi* (intention), *chih* (knowledge), and *wu* (thing).

> There is only one *li* (principle of being). When concentrated in an individual, it is known as *hsing* (nature). As master [or moving principle] of this nature, it is known as *hsin* (mind-and-heart). In terms of the operation of this [*hsin*], it is known as *yi* (intention or thought). In terms of the clear consciousness [one had] of this intention, it is known as *chih* (knowledge). And, from the point of view of [the object of] experience of this [knowledge] it is known as *wu* (act or "thing").[24]

Yang-ming speaks here of *li* as the one hidden reality made manifest through human nature and its activities. According to his view, the investigation of *li* would therefore become the investigation of human nature itself, and this is to be done by the control that the mind-and-heart exercises over its acts and operations, which means over its "intentions." By this control, the mind-and heart assures the sincerity of its intentions, which, in turn, assures the sincerity and rectitude of the mind-and-heart itself and of the whole person. Yang-ming therefore gives a renewed statement of his views on the method of self-cultivation, flowing from the above explanation of *li*:

> To rectify is to rectify this [*hsin*], to make sincere is to make this [*hsin*] sincere, to investigate is to investigate this [*hsin*]. This is what is meant by investigating *li* to the utmost for the sake of completely developing human nature. There is no *li* outside human nature; there is no *wu* ("thing," for him, really "act") either outside human nature.[25]

In later life, Yang-ming frequently had to answer his disciples' questions concerning his teaching on the investigation of things—on *hsin* and on *li*. Once a disciple asked how Yang-ming would reconcile his own teaching with that of Ch'eng Yi on these questions, and quoted this sentence from Ch'eng Yi: "In things (*wu*), [it] is called *li* (principle)."[26] Yang-ming must have known very well the context of this sentence, taken from a passage in which Ch'eng had discussed the goodness of *hsin*. Therefore he promptly replied that the word *hsin* should be inserted: "In things, *hsin* is called *li*." He went on to explain how this meant that when the mind applies itself to the practice of serving one's parents, then this virtuous action is *li*, and when the mind applies itself to the practice of serving the ruler, this virtuous action also becomes *li*. In this way, he asserts over and over again that *li* is not an abstract principle of being or virtue. For him, being and virtue cannot be separated from life and action. *Hsin* (mind) and *li* (virtue) are inseparable, because it is the mind that *makes* virtue.[27]

On that same occasion, Yang-ming continued his discourse by explaining his underlying reason for teaching such a doctrine. He said that to regard *li* as abstract principles, albeit principles of virtue, but separate from and outside of *hsin*, the center of moral activity, had led to the abstraction of the concept of virtue itself and the divorce between virtue and life.

> There are people who only strive to make their actions look good on the outside, while separating them completely from *hsin*. They make *hsin* and *li* into two things, drifting unconsciously into hypocrisy as did the [Five] Despots. I speak of *li* as being present in *hsin*, so that . . . people may make efforts on *hsin* and not accumulate individual acts of righteousness externally. . . . This is the basic reason for my teaching in this respect.[28]

When the disciple posed a further question as to why Yang-ming always tried to synthesize the teachings of the many sages and worthy men of the past by his own holistic view of sagehood, Yang-ming replied: "There is only one Way. . . . Heaven and Earth and the sages are all one. How can they be divided?"[29]

KO-WU: KNOWLEDGE OR ACTION?

Wang Yang-ming was a self-taught philosopher. Chan Jo-shui, on the other hand, was the recognized disciple of Ch'en Hsien-chang, the disciple, in turn, of Wu Yü-pi. At the time of their first meeting, Chan was without doubt the senior philosopher, older and more mature. Chan's friendship certainly contributed to Yang-ming's resolution to engage himself in the quest for wisdom, and to do so by relying on personal insight acquired through the practice of virtue.

Unlike Lo Ch'in-shun, with whom Yang-ming appears to have had no real discussion until 1520, Chan had discussed with Yang-mnig the problems related to the Great Learning over a long period of time. These revolved around the question of knowledge and action. Where Chan insisted upon the role of classical knowledge in the quest of sagehood, Yang-ming replied that there was no genuine knowledge outside of action. But the basic positions of the two men were not very far apart. Both believed in the mind-and-heart, as the self-deter- mining principle capable of bringing a man to his highest goals, al- though Chan would have added, *provided* he made certain efforts to study the Classics.

Late in 1511, Yang-ming wrote an essay in Chan's honor, in which he openly expressed his gratitude:

> For twenty years I had meddled with perverse doctrines and heresies .... Later, I made friends with Master Chan Kan-ch'üan [Jo-shui], and my determination to seek after the Confucian ideals of sagehood became firmer and stronger, and quite irrevocable. This shows how much I have received from Kan-ch'üan.[30]

Yang-ming continued to praise Chan's insistence on the role of per- sonal insights in the quest for sagehood, defending Chan from the accusation of being tainted with Ch'an Buddhist influence by ap- pealing to Chan's high ideals:

> The teachings of Kan-ch'üan insist upon acquiring for oneself personal insights. The world has not been able to understand them. ... Many suspect it to be Ch'an Buddhisn. If that be so, then I do not yet know Ch'an Buddhism. For, with such sublime ambitions as his, how can someone like Chan Kan-ch'üan not be a disciple of the sages?[31]

The seeds of disagreement, however, were already present. Having received, through Chan, the legacy of Ch'en Hsien-chang concerning the importance of acquiring for oneself personal insights, as well as the teaching of the unity of man with all things, Yang-ming had also gone beyond these horizons. The period between 1512 and 1518 had already witnessed his gradual development of an independent philosophy. From then on he was to influence Chan more than Chan could influence him. The two engaged in philosophical disputes in letters and conversations, which ended with Yang-ming's death in 1529. As Chan was himself accused of having Ch'an Buddhist sympathies, his disagreements with Yang-ming were less on ideological grounds than on nuances of meaning concerning *hsin*.

Chan's teaching centers on the notion of *T'ien-li* or "Heavenly principle," a notion that calls to mind again the teaching of Ch'eng Hao and his emphasis on acquiring insight for oneself.[32] But it also gives some importance to Chu Hsi's notion of *li*. This later brought Chan into conflict with Yang-ming, who objected to Chu's doctrine of an "exhaustive search for *li*" by the "investigation of things." The dispute was to focus on the differences of methodology of self-cultivation. It brought out Yang-ming's entire dependence on personal insight, as opposed to Chan's admission of the role of the Classics as the ultimate corrective criteria to such insights, which, no doubt, he valued too. It also brought out certain subtle nuances in the understanding of the word *hsin*. For Yang-ming, *hsin*, the mind-and-heart, which is one with all things, is in itself independent and sufficient, without necessarily requiring the help of the Classics in its quest for wisdom. For Chan, *hsin*—understood also as one with all things—must on that account accommodate also the Classics as the deposit of truth and wisdom.

Already in 1515, Yang-ming had discussed with Chan the relative merits of the Old and the New Versions of the Great Learning, as well as the interpretation of the words *ko-wu*, "investigation of things." They were at that time unable to reach an agreement. According to one of Yang-ming's disciples:

> Kan-ch'üan held the old theory [of Chu Hsi]. The Master said: "This would be seeking wisdom in external things." Kan-ch'üan replied, "If you regard the investigation of the principles (*li*) of things as external, you are belittling your mind (*hsin*)." . . . Then the Master proceeded to give a discourse on Mencius' chapter regarding the complete development and realization of *hsin*. [Book of Mencius, Ch. 7].[33]

The next day, Chan explained his own ideas further in a letter addressed to Yang-ming, objecting to the latter's interpretation of the word *wu* (thing) as "that to which the intention of the mind (*hsin*) is directed." For Chan, this implied that things were outside of the mind. He suggested an alternative understanding: that the mind comprehended all things, and so, the investigation of things would be no longer an external quest. "For the mind [which] investigates 'things and extends [knowledge] is not external [to oneself]."[34]

In his own work, *Explanation of the Diagram of Mind and Nature* (*Hsin-hsing-t'u shuo*), Chan Jo-shui gave a fuller development of his ideas regarding the interaction that takes place between mind-and-heart, human nature, and all things. The diagram presents a big circle, enclosing within itself three small circles. According to Chan, the big circle represents the mind and human nature as "embracing" all things, while the small circles signify the "penetration" of all things. This is effected through the practice of reverence (*ching*)— through vigilance over the self when one is alone, and achievement of harmony or equilibrium of emotions, which in turn permits the cultivation of virtues leading to unity with all things, again in an attitude of reverence. In this sense, the diagram represents the whole of reality, and the participation of mind and nature in that reality. "To embrace and to penetrate are not really two separate functions. The mind-and-heart is that which embraces Heaven and Earth and all things without, and yet penetrates Heaven and Earth and all things within. The "within" and "without" are also not two different [realms]. There is no such division with regard to Heaven and Earth nor, for that matter, with regard to the mind. This is only a question of words."[35] Chan was to accuse Wang of regarding merely the physical heart, located in the breast, as *hsin*—mind-and-heart. He claims that, for himself, it is something much greater: "To say that mind-and-heart is inside self, while Heaven and Earth and all things are outside, is to belittle the mind-and-heart."[36]

But did Chan correctly understand Yang-ming's position, in particular his understanding of "things" (*wu*)? Could he, perhaps, have misunderstood Yang-ming, by placing "things" in the context of investigation and of knowledge, where Yang-ming himself had referred rather to action, that, namely, of "polishing" the mind and heart by removing from it all selfishness? In other words, was not Chan's idea of self-cultivation that of the mind-and-heart expanding itself through a deepened understanding of all things, while Yang-ming preferred that mind-and-heart empty itself of all unruly desires through a process of purification? To one of his own disciples, Ch'en Wei-chün, who shared Chan's misgivings regarding Yang-ming's position, Yang-ming explained how he himself did not consider "things" (*wu*) to be outside of "mind." He regarded "things" as somehow one and the same with *sheng* (self, or body), *hsin* (mind-and-heart), *yi* (intention), and *chih* (knowledge). He said: "The sense organs of eyes, ears, mouth, and nose, together with the four limbs, make up the body [or the self]. Yet, without mind-and-heart, how can they see, hear, speak, or move? And also, if the mind-and-heart wishes to see, hear, speak, or move, it too would be powerless without the eyes, ears, mouth, nose, and the four limbs. Hence the mind-and-heart is nothing without the body, and the body is nothing without the mind-and-heart."[37]

Thus, the mind-and-heart is that which is the master of the body, or of the whole self, and the two cannot be understood in isolation from each other. And the dynamic activity of this mind-and-heart is called intention, whereas the intelligence which permeates this activity is called knowledge. And since it is intention that directs itself to "things" (*wu*), these—which, for Chan, make up the object of knowledge—must involve action.

And so, Yang-mind internalizes the whole quest for truth and wisdom. His method of self-cultivation lies in the rectification of intention, a process in which knowledge and action are one, in which truth or wisdom is discovered by action. For Yang-ming, action contains knowledge.

Between 1517 and 1520, when Wang was busy suppressing rebellions, Chan was back in his native place, mourning the death of his mother. He gradually lost his former misgivings concerning the old version of the Great Learning, coming around to Wang's point of view especially in expressing preference for the words *ch'in-min*—loving the people—which Chu Hsi had altered. He also regarded the investigation of things as "realizing personally the Heavenly principle everywhere." This seemed to move his position closer to Wang's although they still remained one step apart:

> [Chan's] present view on the investigation of things is much nearer [the truth]. However, there is no need for him to substitute the word

li (virtue) for the word *wu* (thing). Let the word *wu* be restored, and his teaching will be correct.[38]

For Yang-ming, Chan's use of the word *li* implies his continued adherence to the importance of the role of knowledge—of knowing the principles of things and attaining the supreme reality in *T'ien-li*.

For Chan Jo-shui, on the other hand, to reduce the teaching of the Great Learning to "making the intention sincere" is tantamount to saying that the universe is empty and unreal. While he admits to a *mystical unity* between self and the universe, he also maintains that the two are distinct in existence. The investigation of things would refer to the attainment of "principles" residing in the universe. For Chang, to "investigate" is to "reach" or "arrive," while "things" refer to *T'ien-li*, the principle of Heaven, which can be attained through study, inquiry, thought, discernment, and action.[39] He therefore visualizes a certain *ascent* to perfect virtue or "Heavenly principle," which forms the supreme reality, the fullness of all goodness and perfection, that involves a man in becoming wise so that he may be good. Action, therefore, depends on knowledge, as does the attainment of sagehood itself.

In a letter written to another friend, Ku Lin, some time before 1524, Yang-ming has left us with his reply to Chan's interpretation of the investigation of things. After saying that to develop one's nature and know Heaven, all that is needed is to extend one's *liang-chih* to the utmost, an effort that in turn includes that of "carefully examining *T'ien-li*," he declares that he has never discouraged others from investigating things to the utmost, nor has he urged them to live in seclusion and do nothing. Rather, he holds that "if an unenlightened student can really carefully examine *T'ien-li* . . . in connection with things and events as they come, and extend his knowledge of the good, then though stupid, he will surely become intelligent, and though weak, he will surely become strong."[40] However, he continues:

> Who knows that the investigation of things of the Great Learning should not be interpreted in the sense of "rectifying" rather than in the sense of "reaching"? If it must be interpreted in the sense of "reaching," it would be necessary to say, "investigating things to the utmost until you reach the principles of all things," in order to make sense. . . . To mention only the investigation of things and

dogmatically to say that it means the investigation of the principles of things to the utmost is to regard the latter as belonging entirely to the sphere of knowledge and the investigation of things as involving no action. . . That is why later scholars have separated knowledge and action into two sections and have been constantly caught up in fragmentary knowledge and dissociated details, and why the doctrine of the sages has been declining and fading away.[41]

Hence, with regard to the doctrine of investigating things, the chief *difference* between Wang's and Chan's teachings is that of spiritual practice. For Wang, the quest for sagehood is mainly moral and mystical. In his view, the Unity of Knowledge and Action implies that moral knowledge and moral action are almost indistinguishable; that the former lies in the latter. His overwhelming emphasis is therefore upon moral and spiritual ascesis, through the individuals' continual responses to the movements of his own mind and to the events of life that act upon the mind. Chan, however, insists upon the necessity of intellectual effort, of the study of Classics. He considers it difficult to ascertain the correctness or orthodoxy of one's thoughts and concepts without making intellectual efforts. To break out of the narrow boundaries of a purely internal quest for sagehood, as consisting in the purification and rectification of one's inner thoughts and motives alone, he expresses preference for the realization of *T'ien-li* as the meaning of investigating things. True, Yang-ming also speaks of developing *T'ien-li*. But he envisages it being done when selfish desires are removed, and the mind or heart is rectified. He does not consider classical learning as absolutely essential. Chan, however, regards classical learning as an integral part of this realization. The mind-and-heart—according to Chan—can only become perfect if it avails itself of the instructions of the ancients. In other words, where Yang-ming considers *T'ien-li* to be perfect virtue, acquired by the mind-and-heart in purifying itself, Chan takes the same word to refer to the *knowledge* of such perfect virtue, and as such, it must accommodate the knowledge of the Classics. Chan was to publish, several years after Yang-ming's death, a one-hundred-*chüan* work under the title, *Sheng-hsüeh ko-wu-t'ung* (A Penetration of the [Doctrine of] Investigation of Things of the School of Sages). It was addressed to Emperor Shih-tsung. There, Chan developed his own understanding of *ko-*

wu, making it an all-reaching formula, extending from the practice of "making the intention sincere" to that of "governing the country" and "giving peace to the world."[42]

WANG AND CHU: FROM APPEAL TO OPPOSITION

Yang-ming did not purposely disagree with Chu Hsi. He admitted that he and Chu shared the same ultimate goal—that of directing men to sagehood. He did not wish to alter any of Chu's sayings, wherever these appeared clear and proper.[43] He differed with Chu only on certain specific points, such as regarding the doctrine of investigating things. To one of his disciples, Yang-ming said that he considered Chu Hsi to have been a very intelligent man, dedicated from early youth to the pursuit of intellectual inquiry, for the sake of transmitting the heritage of the past and of enlightening future generations. While he did not give priority to personal cultivation, he did reach a state of eminent virtue. Unfortunately, he did not follow the example of Confucius, who "eliminated superfluous writings" and only noted down the simple and essential. In old age, however, Chu regretted having written so much, and directed his attention to the cultivation of genuine virtue. But he did not have enough time before death to correct the many mistakes he had made during his life.[44]

Yang-ming presented these attitudes in a short treatise, *Chu-tzu wan-nien ting-lun*, which he published in 1518. In the preface to this work he gave a short account of his own spiritual odyssey, describing how he had prepared for the civil examinations and had become interested in writing prose and poetry; how he had devoted his mind to Confucian learning but was confused by the great variety of theories and interpretations regarding the texts, how he had turned to Taiosm and Buddhism for an answer to the meaning of life. Then he went on to describe his exile, the enlightenment received and the confirmation of it by his meditation on the Classics. He explained how he was troubled by the fact that his insights were not in agreement with the teachings of Chu Hsi, whom he so respected. Finally, after searching through Chu's writings, he found that Chu's ideas had changed remarkably in later life, when he "expressed regret" at the mistakes he had made in earlier years. And so, with great joy, Yang-ming decided to make open Chu's spiritual evolution and the insights of his later life, which were largely unknown to the scholars of the world, attached only to the *tentative* doctrines developed by Chu during an earlier period.[45]

In the same letter in which he discussed Yang-ming's publication of the old version of the Great Learning, Lo Ch'in-shun also gave his criticisms of Yang-ming's second publication of excerpts from letters that Chu was supposed to have written in later life. Lo indicated how Yang-ming had selected these passages arbitrarily, taking them out of context to underscore Chu's teaching on inner cultivation. Besides, Yang-ming had presented, as written late in life, four letters composed in Chu's middle age or even earlier, certainly before the publication of his *Collected Commentaries* and *Questions and Answers on the Four Books* which, Yang-ming asserted, incorporated Chu's tentative doctrine.[46] Lo also pointed out that if Wu Ch'eng had finally acquired insights into the teachings of the sages, these probably came as a sudden culmination to his long years of devoted study of the Classics and the Commentaries, thus proving that assiduous study of the Classics should be promoted rather than discouraged. After all, Lo said, one might forget the fish trap on catching the fish, and the rabbit's traces on catching the rabbit, but there was no reason why one should also regret having used the fish trap and followed upon the rabbit's traces.[47]

In his answer, Yang-ming insisted that *most* of the letters in his selection were written by Chu Hsi toward the end of that philosopher's life, although he admitted that he had not taken care to establish the correct chronology of *all* the letters. He acknowledged that he had published the selection for the sake of "reconciling," as much as possible, Chu's teachings on the "investigation of things" and his own insights. But he denied that he had made this work public with the motive of deceiving his readers.[48]

> All my life, Chu Hsi's teachings have been like a revelation from the gods or from divination and oracles. I could hardly bear to depart from his teachings so abruptly. In my heart, I cannot bear to contradict Master Chu, and yet I cannot but contradict him, because the Way is what it is and the Way will not be made clear unless I am forthright.[49]

This was in 1520. Yang-ming had made an attempt to reconcile his own teaching with Chu Hsi's, or rather, to reconcile Chu Hsi's teaching with his own, and his attempt had been largely unsuccessful. One can hardly blame him for any intellectual dishonesty. He had merely acted in accordance with Lu Chiu-yüan's remarks, of the Six Classics being only footnotes to one's insights, and had applied it to the writings of Chu Hsi. In doing so, he had been grossly careless of chronology, and quite unfair to Chu Hsi's intended meanings. And he had admitted his errors. Yang-ming's differences with Chu Hsi were only made clearer by this publication, aimed originally as an appeal for support for Yang-ming's own teachings. There would be no reconciliation possible. If the ideas of Chu Hsi were the criterion for Confucian orthodoxy, then Yang-ming was without doubt a dissenter and even a heretic.[50] But there can be other ways of looking at this picture.*

To Acquire Wisdom

Classics Versus Commentaries

How much value Yang-ming attaches to intellectual inquiry as well as to the authority of the ancients can be seen in his attitude toward the Classics. He has spoken at length on this subject, especially in a conversation with Hsü Ai.[51] He gives his reasons for favoring a return to the sources, the classical texts themselves, without paying attention to the commentaries. He says that Confucius' merit was in abridging and transmitting the Classics, reducing their contents, purifying them of accumulated dross. This was done in order to help people more easily find the real message of the Classics. And this message lies, not in the words or narratives given by the texts, but in the spirit in which these were recorded. The Classics represent a portait of the principle of Heaven. They can be compared to the por-

---

* The experience of the medieval European scholastics can also shed light on this point. The philosophical method they followed was to resolve every question in some precise sequence of authority and refutation and resolution. A good scholastic was one who could find authority for either side of the question and who was convinced further that truth could be discovered best by examining all the contradictory statements. See Richard McKeon, ed., *Selections from Medieval Philosophers* (New York, 1929), v. 1, Introduction, xiv–xv.

trait of a human being, portrayed by a painter who offers the outlines
of a man's appearance in such a way as to communicate something of
his genuine, spiritual personality. Those who view the portrait should
use it in order to seek out this true personality. The commentaries,
however, were written by later men, who came after the sages. They
are like *copies* of the masterpieces. The copies have changed and added
to the originals until the true likeness has been lost.[52] One should
therefore return to the sources, to the texts of the Classics, in order
to recover the primary purpose for which Confucius and other sages
transmitted the sacred books, and this was: "to rectify men's *hsin*,
keep intact the principle of Heaven, and eliminate selfish desires."[53]

In an essay he wrote on the Tsun-ching Pavilion [literally, Respect-
the-Classic Pavilion] of the Chi-shan College, Yang-ming describes
the Classics as the "constant Way," which "penetrates persons and
things, reaches the four seas, fills up Heaven and Earth, goes through
past and present, comprehends all that exists, is identical to all that
exists without changing anything."[54] And also:

> When responding to events, it becomes compassion, sense of shame,
> modesty in yielding to others, and discernment of right and wrong.
> When expressed in affairs, it becomes the affection between father
> and son, righteousness between sovereign and subject, differentiation
> between husband and wife, order between elders and juniors, fidelity
> between friends. . . .The Six Classics are nothing other than this
> constant Way in my mind.[55]

Yang-ming explains that sages of old had committed these Classics
to writing for the sake of giving support to the ultimate human criteria
of morality. Such action can be compared to that of the ancestors of a
rich clan, who committed to writing the record of their property,
which they bequeathed to their descendants.[56] "Thus the reality of the
Six Classics resides in my mind, just as all kinds of amassed wealth
and each little item of these are preserved in the rich family, while
the inventory book merely gives an account of their names, kinds, and
numbers." And so, worldly scholars who do not seek the reality of the
Classics in the mind, and search for it in words and sounds, resemble
the descendants of the rich family, who squander their heritage, while
pointing vainly to the inventory books, saying, "Here is our amassed
wealth!"[57]

The primary purpose for which the Classics have been handed down determines also the manner in which they should be studied. Yang-ming is against merely understanding the words themselves. He recommends that the texts be read over and over again, until they have yielded their spiritual meaning. This spiritual meaning cannot be separated from virtuous action:

> One should make efforts [to develop] *hsin*-in-itself.[58] Whenever something is not understood and cannot be put into practice, one should enter into oneself and seek to realize [what is said] in one's *hsin*. Understanding will surely come. For the Four Books and Five Classics talk about nothing but *hsin*-in-itself. And this is nothing other than the Way. When *hsin*-in-itself is understood, the Way is also understood.[59]

For the philosopher of the unity of knowledge and action, there can be no other answer than that the Classics should be the object of an intellectual inquiry that is permeated by virtuous intention and activity. Yang-ming says elsewhere of the different books of the Classics, their various *genres* and the different truths which they seek to communicate:

> In using the Six Classics, the gentleman seeks the movements of *yin* and *yang* of the mind (*hsin*), in order to act according to them, by his respect for the Book of Changes. He seeks the laws and regulations and government of the mind, in order to practice them, by his respect for the Book of Documents. He seeks the musical and lyrical expressions of nature and emotions of the mind, in order to develop them, by his respect for the Book of Odes. He seeks the rules of deportment and propriety of the mind, in order to pay attention to them, by his respect for the Book of Rites. He seeks the joy and peace of the mind, in order to give expression to them, by his respect for the Classic of Music. He seeks the distinctions between sincerity and hypocrisy, perversity and orthodoxy of the mind, in order to discern their differences by his respect for the Spring-Autumn Annals.[60]

It is by reverent contemplation of the Classics, the portrait of *T'ien-li* or of *hsin*-in-itself, that the student is able to benefit from the spiritual richness hidden in each book, for the development of his own *hsin*—his own personality.

Yang-ming recognizes that many of the Classical texts are obscure and in need of clarification. He does not discount the role of simple commentaries. He wrote a preface to a new edition of Wu Ch'eng's *Li-chi ts'uan-yen* (Annotated edition of the Book of Rites), in which he warmly praised this attempt to elucidate the confusing and complicated body of ritual texts, which had already accumulated many commentaries. But whereas other commentaries often consist of detailed explanations of articles and numbers of sacrificial vessels as well as minor items of criminal law, the *Li-chi ts'uan-yen* seeks to bring the student back to the foundation of the rites, putting various issues in a proper order of moral values.[61]

Speaking of the fundamental unity underlying the many ordinances of the ritual texts, Yang-ming has this to say:

> There are three hundred rules of canonical rites (*ching-li*) and three hundred additional rules of demeanor (*ch'ü-li*).[62] Not one of them is not based on humanity; not one of them is not based on human nature. Such are the directives and arrangements of Heaven.[63]

It would be a mistake to pay so much attention to the details of rites and propriety as to forget this very reason for which the ritual texts exist: to expound the mind of the sages. Yang-ming quotes the Analects, saying: "Do rites refer merely to jade and silk?"[64] and also, "If a man is lacking in the virtue of humanity, what can the rites do for him?"[65]

Voicing sympathy for the followers of Lao-tzu[66] and Chuang-tzu,[67] who claimed that the rise of ritual law and the practice of particular virtues followed the decline of real virtue (*tao* and *te*), and who preferred to overlook propriety and talk only of human nature, Yang-ming went on to give his own views of ritual observance and propriety:

> Rites are to the ceremonies what compass and quadrant are to the shapes of circles and squares. Without circles and squares there can be no use for compass and quandrant; without ceremonies there can be nothing visible called rites. Yet circles and squares are made by compasses and quadrants, and without being themselves compass or quadrant. . . . . For compass and quadrant are not limited to making certain definite circles and squares, while circles and squares are [in their turn] rules by definite compasses and quadrants.[68]

These words help us to understand what Yang-ming said on an earlier occasion: that the two words, homophones, *li* (rites, propriety) and *li* (organizing principle, being, virtue) have the same meaning. For—he claims—to restrain oneself with the rules of propriety implies that one's *hsin* is already full of the Heavenly principle, *T'ien-li*.

Yang-ming has left us two long letters on the subject of propriety. From these we discover the rich knowledge he possessed of the Classics, including detailed questions of rites and of historical precedents, as well as of Chu Hsi's work, *Chia-li* (Family Rites).[69] From these we also discover his constant preoccupation, which is to direct his friend or disciple away from an excessive fondness for ritual hair-splitting, and on to a new awareness of and respect for genuine human feeling. Without such, the rites would be dead. And so, while Yang-ming has made no explicit pronouncement on the matter of Emperor Shin-tsung's desire to transgress precedents by giving posthumous imperial honors to his deceased father,[70] it might safely be presumed that he was sympathetic to such expressions of genuine filial feeling. Some of his poems, written in 1524, have been interpreted by his disciples as expressive of Yang-ming's attitude toward the controversy aroused by the emperor's gestures.[71] In one of them he attempts to lift men's minds from petty preoccupations with ritual observances to a higher plane:

> An autumn rain brings in the newness of a cool night:
> Sitting on the pond's edge, I find my spirit brightened by the
> solitary moon.
> Swimming in the depths, the fish are passing on words of power;
> Perched on the branches, birds are uttering the true *Tao*.
> Do not say that instinctive desires are not mysteries of Heaven:
> I know that my body is one with the ten thousand things.
> People talk endlessly about rites and music;
> But who will sweep away the heaps of dust from the blue sky?[72]

PERSONAL INSIGHT VERSUS AUTHORITY

In 1522, Chan Jo-shui wrote a long letter to Yang-ming, explaining clearly the differences between his own understanding of the investigation of things and that of Yang-ming's. He presents four objections to Yang-ming's interpretations. Of these, the first two concern textual problems. He claims that Yang-ming did violence to the meaning of the whole text of the Great Learning by taking the word *ko-wu* out of context. His fourth objection is a corollary of his third or main objection, which regards the criteria of correctness or rectitude of one's intentions. He said that by explaining *ko-wu* as rectifying intentions (*cheng nien-t'ou*) Yang-ming has overlooked the fact that the intention as such does not supply by itself any proof for its correctness. Without Confucian criteria of orthodoxy, Buddhists and Taoists who consider the world as empty and unreal, and who follow the teaching of the Diamond Sutra by striving to "produce a [pure] *hsin* (mind or thought) that is unsupported [by *rupa*, *i.e.*, sights, sounds, smells, tastes, touchables or mind-objects]" might well regard themselves as "orthodox."[73]

> During the time of Yang Chu and Mo Ti, people all thought of the two men as sages. Did they consider themselves as being unorthodox? In fact, they did not know what it meant to be upright, since they did not make any serious effort to study. They were heretics without being conscious of it themselves.[74]

Chan Jo-shui then goes on to explain the importance of intellectual inquiry, of basing one's insights on the knowledge of ancient Classics. After all, why should Tzu-ssu proclaim the need of "study through inquiry," if only "respecting virtuous nature" is adequate?

> A person interrogating [me] may say: "What had Confucius to learn? All is in *hsin*. He does not know that while Confucius was the greatest sage, the man who developed *T'ien-li* to the utmost, and was mature in the practice of righteousness, yet even he had to reach the age of seventy before he could follow the wishes of his mind and heart, without transgressing what is right.[75] If one does not study, he will grow old and die as fool. Of course, your intelligence is far superior to that of anyone else. I would not dare say this of you. But as I observe how Confucius exhorted himself to study, and was worried about not studying, and as I realize how you occupy a high position in the world, and are esteemed by the scholars of the world, I wish to remind you that one must be cautious in his learning, and balanced in his teaching. . . .[76]

It is not known to us whether Yang-ming ever answered this letter from Chan Jo-shui. But in a letter he wrote to Lo Ch'in-shun, he has expressed his thoughts on the role of intellectual inquiry in the quest for sagehood, as well as on the role of the authority of Confucius himself as the teacher of wisdom. He maintains here that he includes the "Nine items" of self-cultivation set out by Chu Hsi in his own interpretation of the investigation of things.[77] But he acknowledges also that he differs from Chu Hsi in the relative emphasis made on these items. After this, he attacks the so-called disciples of Chu Hsi of his own times, whom he compares unfavorably with Yang Chu and Mo Ti,[78] the two "heretics" whose fallacies had been exposed by Mencius himself. He also likens himself to Han Yü, who had been audacious enough to combat the harmful teachings of Buddhism and Taoism, without being equal to Mencius in virtue.[79]

That Yang-ming accepts in all sincerity the role of intellectual inquiry in personal cultivation can also be seen in the explanation he gave for "honoring virtuous nature" and "following the path of study and inquiry." Commenting on Chu Hsi's admission that Lu Chiu-yüan taught more of "honoring virtuous nature" while Chu himself gave greater emphasis to "study and inquiry," Yang-ming told his disciple, Huang Chih, that the two could not be separated from each other. He said: "Is there such a thing as "honoring virtuous nature" in a vacuum without also pursuing "study and inquiry," or pursuing "study and inquiry" in a vacuum without relating it to "honoring viruous nature"? If there is, I do not know what we are seeking to learn in our present studies and discussions."[80] It would seem that his main preoccupation was to permeate intellectual inquiry with the desire for virtue, while at the same time subordinating it to the cultivation of this desire itself, and of one's capacity for virtue. But he did not give a direct and satisfactory reply to Lo's criticism, that he was influenced by Ch'an Buddhism.

Yang-ming's attitude to intellectual inquiry can be discerned in his teaching concerning the role of the arts (yi) in the quest for wisdom. With his eyes fixed always on the ultimate goal of life, he declares that the word yi (arts) is related to its homophone, yi (righteousness). The arts ought to lead man to the practice of virtue. Such activities as poetry recital, reading, playing of lutes and practice of archery are all intended to give greater harmony to hsin, and to help it proceed with the quest of the great Way. "The man who does not first set his will firm on the Way, and only seeks amusement in the arts, is like a fool who does not first plan the building of a house, but attends only to the purchase of paintings which he can hang up as show, without knowing where he is going to hang them."[81]

Yang-ming also affirmed the positive contribution of music to the work of self-cultivation. He expressed the desire of purifying theatrical music of its licentious words and tunes, and of keeping only stories with moral lessons in theatrical performances, to help the people extend and realize their *liang-chih*. But he did not recommend a return to the lost, ancient, musical tunes. He said merely that one should attempt to keep to the *intention* of the sages who first devised those tunes, by having such music as would be helpful to the achievement of peace and harmony in the mind and heart.[82]

To the difficulty that reading or intellectual effort sometimes brings with it ideas of vanity connected with the desire to succeed in civil service examinations, Yang-ming replies that such desires should not be any hindrance to the man whose *liang-chih* is genuine and earnest. This man knows that he should not force himself to commit things to rote learning, or to yield to impatience or vain ambitions. As long as he overcomes such temptations immediately, he will remain in perfect accord with the Heavenly principle. "Let him read. He will be merely refreshing an giving harmony to his mind-and-heart. What difficulty is there?"[83]

But there is no doubt that for Yang-ming, reading (*tu-shu*) is a means toward an end: the quest for wisdom. He excuses those persons who read or study with the ambition of passing examinations, so long as they have need of official emolument for the support of their parents or family.[84] But he is anxious to point out that intellectual inquiry should be carried out only as a help to the acquisition of wisdom. Care should be taken that such inquiry does not absorb the mind and lead it astray.[85] For this reason, he is against the laborious work of writing long commentaries on the Classics. He warned his disciple Chi Pen (Chi Ming-te) in these words:

> If you wish to divide up every section of the Classical texts, giving commentaries and citing proofs, taking these to be systematic steps of the path by which a sage advances in the Way. . . .then you will not be free from the defects of making [useless] comparisons and of being fettered by words. To show in this way the fact that sagehood is attainable by learning may give some insight, but would tend to make of the status of sagehood something very high and far away. . . .[86]

Reading, after all, is only one exercise of the task of study. As already mentioned, the word *hsüeh*, usually translated as "study," means to learn or to acquire by learning—whether through moral effort or intellectual inquiry. For the philosopher who teaches the unity of knowledge and action, there can be no distinction between the two. Yang-ming generally means by *hsüeh* a method by which selfish desires may be removed. It is no different from the effort of extending *liang-chih*. As he put it:

> A scholar who has already determined to become a sage, need merely extend his *liang-chih*, in its intelligent and conscious aspects, to the uttermost, proceeding gradually day by day. He does not need to worry about externals and details. Criticisms, praise and blame, can also be used profitably. . . but without having these affect his *hsin* in the least. . . .[87]

Given this view of intellectual inquiry, it is easy to see why Yang-ming regards as suitable objects of study, not only the recognized books of the Confucian canon, but also the so-called Taoist and Buddhist scriptures, so long as these contribute to the realization in oneself of *T'ien-li*.[88] These unorthodox texts are not required for the passing of official examinations, but they contain insights that are nonetheless valuable. This concession, which Yang-ming has made, is important to the student who wishes to understand the universal character of his "Way" of acquiring wisdom. But it cannot be denied that Yang-ming values the Confucian classics far above those of the other two schools.

THE APPEAL TO CONFUCIUS

Lo Ch'in-shun had criticized Yang-ming for putting forward views that differed from those of Ch'eng Yi and Chu Hsi, and in direct contradiction of the words of the Classical texts. To this charge of heresy, Yang-ming replied in self-defence that he had merely attempted to return to the sources of Confucian teaching by restoring an old text with which Chu Hsi had tampered. Appealing directly to the authority of Confucius, he said:

> The old version of the Great Learning is the original version transmitted from generation to generation in the Confucian school. Master Chu, suspecting that errors and gaps have crept in, corrected and amended it. But I believe that there has not been any errors and gaps. That is why I followed the old version completely. Perhaps, my

mistake has been in believing too much in Confucius. I did not omit Master Chu's chapter divisions or delete his commentary on purpose.[89]

The appeal to Confucius was no sooner made then Yang-ming went beyond it. He went on to say that true learning is only that which is personally acquired in one's *hsin*, without regard to the authority of other scholars, even of Confucius:

> If [words] are examined in the *hsin* and found to be wrong, then even if they have come from [the mouth] of Confucius, I dare not accept them as correct. How much more so for what has come from people inferior to Confucius! If [words] are examined in the *hsin* and found found to be right, then even if they have come from [the mouths] of mediocre people, I dare not regard them as incorrect. How much more so for what has come from Confucius![90]

He then criticized Chu Hsi for having tampered with the old version, which had been handed down for several thousand years. "By what authority did Chu Hsi decide that this paragraph should be here and that one should be there, that this part had been lost and should be provided for . . . ? Are you not taking too seriously my divergences from Chu Hsi and not seriously enough Chu's rebellion against Confucius?"[91]

Wisdom, after all, is no static deposit of unchanging truths that have been discovered by any one man who can therefore claim for it a certain monopoly. Wisdom means the ability to deal with different circumtances. It presupposes an open mind, without set judgments and ready answers, but looking for the answers in the circumstances themselves. For this reason, every sage understands wisdom and virtue in his own unique way. For this reason, too, even Confucius himself would never present any simple, rustic questioner with a standard answer. He would merely try to direct the man himself to see the right and wrong of a situation in his own heart and with his own judgment.[92] The words of the ancients are all results of deep personal experience, acquired frequently through trials and tribulations. In order to attain the wisdom contained in them, the student himself must not stop at the words; he must also rediscover wisdom at its source, through the complete engagement of his *hsin* in its quest, permitting the whole of life to strengthen his nature and so improve his understanding.[93]

Yang-ming's answer to the question concerning the role of authority in the quest for sagehood is one that points beyond the authorities, beyond Chu Hsi, beyond Confucius and the Classics, beyond even the first sages, to the source and fountainhead of all wisdom and sagehood: the self-determining, self-perfecting *hsin*, the deepest and most dynamic principle within man. As Yang-ming says in one of his poems, every man possesses a Confucius in his own heart, a need of greatness quite sufficient in itself and capable of developing into a powerful tree with many branches. In another poem, written in 1524, he speaks again of sages and of the Classics, of their function of helping to purify man's mind and heart of its accumulated dross, and of the ultimate authority of the "polished mirror," of *hsin* alone, as that which reflects both truth and error.[94] His words are:

> Under the new autumn moon, I sit alone in the courtyard.
> Where else between Heaven (*Ch'ien*) and Earth (*K'un*) has man
> more freedom and ease?
> My loud songs move away with the fresh breeze,
> My quiet feelings follow the stream and turn to spring.
> The thousand sages have no word of power outside of the mind;
> The Six Classics should wipe away the mirror's dust.
> Alas, for those disturbed by dreams of Duke Chou,
> They have not tasted the joys of a quiet life in a poor alley.[95]

Yand-ming's attitude toward one specific Classic, the Book of Rites, as well as the application of the moral principles set forth in it to real life, can enlighten us with regard to his general attitude toward all the Classics and the use one should make of them. The Classics are made for man, not man for the Classics.

IV

THE "WAY" DISCOVERED:
CHIH LIANG-CHIH

> The greater simplicity and perfection (*ching*) one attains in his effort (*kung-fu*) of [self-cultivation], the more difficult verbal expression and discussion of it becomes.[1]

HE PERIOD from mid-1519 to early 1521 witnessed the climax of Yang-ming's career as soldier, statesman, and philospher, and marked the final crystallization of his thought. But this climax and crystallization did not come without a price. Just as Yang-ming's first great philosophical discovery—the recognition of *hsin* as the basic principle in man's quest for wisdom, and the formulation of the proposition, *hsin chi li*—came to him during the time of exile, so too his greatest discovery, the elaboration of his basic principle into an all-embracing method, occurred at a time of great stress. The spectacular victory he won over the rebel, Prince Ch'en-hao, became for him the occasion of great trial. Yang-ming was faced with the dilemma of abandoning his captives for the sake of giving pleasure to an irresponsible emperor, and thus provoking another battle at which unnecessary losses of lives would surely occur, or of withstanding the caprice of his enemies, the Court eunuchs, at the risk of encountering serious danger to himself, his family, and his faithful subordinates. He was, at the same time, pained by his own powerlessness to relieve the sufferings of the population under his government,[2] and by the news of his grandmother's death and his father's illness.[3] He was also under attack for his teaching of "novel doctrines." In such circumstances and under such pressures, it is easy to understand why many people, including some of Yang-ming's own disciples, decided to avoid his company. Only in early 1521, when Emperor Wu-tsung left his temporary capital of Nanking to return to Peking, did the tension begin to relax.[4]

Nevertheless, these severe trials, accompanied by the continued controversy aroused by Yang-ming's publication of the Old Version of the Great Learning and of what he considered to have been the proofs of Chu Hsi's "change of mind" in late life, contributed eventually to the development of his famous doctrine, *chih liang-chih*, literally, "the extension of *liang-chih* or of one's knowledge of the good," and of his own mature views on the Confucian Way and its transmission through history.

That Yang-ming had been fumbling over a verbal formula with which to express his inner discovery is clear from his own words. He had been teaching for a long time on the importance of developing "heavenly principles," (*T'ien-li*) and of eliminating "selfish desires" (*jen-yü*). But he had never explicitly described "heavenly principle." He had merely told his questioners to find out for themselves. Once he told his friends: "I desire to elaborate upon this [discovery], but feel that I cannot utter the word. It is as though I have something in my mouth [but cannot pronounce it]."[5] He also said: "More and more I feel that there is nothing in this learning [of the sages] outside of this little thing.'"[6] Ch'ien Te-hung also relates:

> The Master once said: "Since my experience at Lung-ch'ang, my thoughts have not been outside of the two words, *liang-chih*. However, I have not been able to articulate these two words [until now]. So I have had to use many words and expressions [to explain myself]. Fortunately, I have now made this discovery. I now see the whole [of truth] in one expression."[7]

Yang-ming learned to articulate his thoughts in terms of the word *liang-chih* during the trials and tribulations that visited him after his battle with Prince Ch'en-hao. These experiences proved to him the reliability of his own "way," the way to sagehood which follows the promptings of the human heart and its desire for the good. In a letter to a friend, written in 1526 toward the end of his life, Yang-ming described the experience of being guided by the inner light, his own *liang-chih*, during his difficulties of 1520, and of the peace and equanimity this had generated within:

> Formerly, when His Majesty, Emperor Wu-tsung, was in Nanking
> [1520], his entourage vied with one another to slander me in his
> august presence. At that time, I faced unknown calamity, and my
> equals and subordinates all feared for me, saying that. . . .I ought to
> attempt to explain myself. I answered that the gentleman does not
> expect the world to believe him, but is rather satisfied with his belief
> in himself.[8]

Yang-ming made up the formula, *chih liang-chih*, to "extend [and
realize] the knowledge of the good," by inserting the word *liang*—good
or innately so—between the words *chih-chih*, extending knowledge
of the Great Learning.[9] The expression *liang-chih* also came from the
Book of Mencius,[10] where it refers to the "inborn capacity to know
the good," which, together with "the inborn ability to do good," or
liang-neng, enables man to act according to his originally good nature
by the practice of virtue leading to complete self-transcendence. In
an age when many philosophers searched for a universal method of
attaining sagehood, the formula *chih liang-chih* became identified with
the Yang-ming school. It is to day the best known of many others,
including, for example, Chan Jo-shui's *sui-ch'u t'i-jen T'ien-li* (recognizing everywhere the principle of Heaven),[11] Huang Wan's *ken-chih* (acting and reposing harmoniously),[12] and Liu Tsung-chou's
shen-tu (vigilance in solitude).[13]

Yang-ming had met with much criticism for his explanation of the
investigation of things in terms of making the intention sincere. He
had attempted to defend himself by explaining that this manner of
interpretation allowed for the "path of study and inquiry," but subordinated it to, or incorporated it into, the practice of "honoring virtuous
nature." As this did not adequately satisfy his critics, and after having
been tested by trials and tribulations himself, he presented the final,
synthesizing concept of extending *liang-chih* as an all-inclusive way of
self-cultivation transcending all divisions between the inner and outer
realms of life, between activity and tranquility. He sought to interpret
in this way the Great Learning by means of the Book of Mencius. He
affirmed that the extension of knowledge refers to extending the
knowledge of the good, or better still, of all that goes to make the person

good, by developing the capacity for virtue which he possesses in his mind, heart, and nature. And since genuine knowledge must involve action, then knowledge that makes a person virtuous or good necessarily flows into action.

THE GREAT PRINCIPLE: LIANG-CHIH

In the method of cultivation developed by Chu Hsi, the attitude of reverence (*ching*) and the exhaustive, assiduous investigation of principles (*li*) occupy positions of primary importance. The mind (*hsin*) is limited in meaning to that source of human activity and consciousness that is composed of both *li* and *ch'i*. While *hsin* controls both nature and emotions, it does so only in the human being. It is inferior in importance to nature, which is identified with principles, and is therefore present in all things.[14] For Yang-ming, however, mind and nature are one and the same and, so to speak, coextensive. The ability of the mind-and-heart "to know the good" is somehow identical with the mind-and-heart itself, with nature, with "being" or "virtue," and even with *T'ien-li*, "heavenly principle."[15] It is upon this principle—*liang-chih*—that Yang-ming built his own thought and method. It is from this principle that Yang-ming elaborated the entire interpretation of his thought and method.

> If an unenlightened scholar is able to discern *T'ien-li* carefully in his heart, as things happen and as events occur, in order to develop his *liang-chih*, then. . . . .he will surely become intelligent and strong. The great Foundation will be established and the universal Way will prevail.[16]

Yang-ming describes *liang-chih* as an inborn moral sense, common to all, whether sages or men in the street, which gives everyone their fundamental dignity and equality. It enables a man to discriminate between right and wrong, not by providing him with ready-made concepts that can be applied *a priori* to individual, particular situations, but because it directs him to search for the good through a moral experience acquired in this orderly manner.

> Our knowledge of the good (*liang-chih*) does not come from seeing and hearing, and yet seeing and hearing are all functions of *liang-chih*.[17]

He goes on:[18]

Our capacity to know the good (*liang-chih*) is in the human heart, the same through all time and in the whole universe. It is the "capacity for knowledge which does not depend on reflective thinking"[19] which "works with ease and knows where danger is."[20] It is "the ability for action which does not depend on learning,"[21] which works with simplicity and knows where obstruction is."[22]

To be genuine, *liang-chih* must be spontaneous, prereflective. It is the feeling of alarm and commiseration any man would have when he sees a child fall into a well.[23] "It is no other than *T'ien-li* in its [power] of natural consciousness."[24] Its "original substance" (*pen-t'i*) is "genuine sincerity and compassion."[25] It is the foundation of all knowledge, embracing within itself all true learning. "There is no knowledge outside of his knowledge of the good (*liang-chih*), and no work outside that of extending this knowledge (*chih liang-chih*). He who seeks knowledge outside of this knowledge, finds only vain knowledge. He who seeks to perfect himself without extending this knowledge, falls into error."[26] It is the inner forum, where each man passes judgments on the moral rectitude of his own thoughts and intentions.

Your *liang-chih* is your own criterion. As your thoughts and intentions arise, it knows what is right and what is wrong.* You cannot deceive it at all. . . . Follow it faithfully in everything you do. Then good will be preserved and evil will be removed. How secure and joyful [one can be] with it! This is the true secret of the investigation of things, and the real effort of extending knowledge.[27]

It is compared to the Buddhists' "spiritual seal," which gives certitude to the truth they know, to the "stone" by which gold is tested, to the "mariner's compass" which gives direction to the traveler, to a secret medical formula, a miraculous pill, a magic wand by which iron can be changed into gold.[28] "If you see clearly into this 'little thing' [*liang-chih*] . . . all right and wrong, sincerity and hypocrisy, will become manifest in front of it. What is in accord with it is right, what is not, is wrong."[29]

* Yang-ming's *liang-chih* is sometimes compared to Kant's "categorical imperative," the moral law which obliges human beings *a priori* to strive for the highest good through the correct use of freedom. But where Kant made his discovery through analytical examination of common knowledge, and considered it the basis of his ethics, Yang-ming discovered *liang-chih* through an experience of inner enlightenment, and made of it the core of his entire philosophy: both ethics and metaphysics.

However, although *liang-chih* begins as an inborn moral sense, it does not always offer a clear program of detailed action. There is often need of reflection, of careful deliberation, for the sake of clarifying the basic response given by this "inborn moral sense." When made sincerely, such effort becomes at once part of the moral sense itself, continually increasing the original capacity for goodness. "In our countless thoughts and deliberations, we must only extend *liang-chih*. The more we think, the more *liang-chih* becomes clear and discerning. Unless one thinks carefully, without responding haphazardly to the affairs that arise, *liang-chih* would become rusty."[30] Emperor Shun, for instance, was also known as a man who was fond of discernment and inquiry, but only for the sake of putting his *liang-chih* to use. He did not give himself to "seeing and hearing" for its own sake. He always united knowledge and action.[31]

In order to explain how *liang-chih*, an *inborn* moral sense, is at the same time a disposition that can be *acquired*, Yang-ming gave two allegedly historical examples. These concern the legendary Shun, and the sage King Wu, founder of the Chou dynasty (c 1122–249 B.C.).[32] Emperor Shun was described as having married the two daughters of Emperor Yao without having first requested permission of his own parents, an omission which, according to known Confucian norms, should have constituted a breach of filial piety. King Wu of Chou was reported to have launched a miliatry expedition against the house of Shang before burying his own father, an act which, according to Confucian norms, should also have constituted a transgression of filial piety. But Mencius voiced approval of both men and their actions, because, in each case, the son was moved by a greater motive of filial piety than that required by social convention. Emperor Shun realized that his parents might refuse him permission to marry, and so prevent him from assuring them proper descendants. King Wu urgently desired to save the people suffering under the tyrannical rule of King Chou of Shang. In each case, the person was faced with certain moral options, without the benefit of recourse to any historical precedent recorded by the Classics. Each chose to act as he did, after having "queried his *liang-chih* in an instant of thought, and weighed all the factors involved."[33]

The capacity to know the good, while being inborn, relies not on abstract principles which can be applied universally, but on the guidance of experiential wisdom. This may be acquired through reading the Classics, especially when such reading is united to the activity of the virtuous intention, but also and more particularly through options made in perfect sincerity and often after much agony and reflection. It is in the depths of the human heart, the *hsin*, and through the activity of *liang-chih*, that virtue and vice are discerned by the judgment and sealed by action. "If Emperor Shun's heart was not sincere about having no posterity, and if King Wu's heart was not sincere about saving the people, then the former's marriage . . . and the latter's expedition . . . would be acts of great filial impiety and disloyalty."[34]

For *liang-chih* is to "detailed actions and changing circumstances as compasses and measuring rods are to areas and lengths."[35] Detailed actions and changing circumstances cannot always be known in advance. But if *liang-chih* is genuine, and its basic and pivotal role well understood, detailed actions can always be decided upon as the changing circumstances arise. When seen in this perspective, a place can even be found for the study of ancient instructions.[36] Yang-ming, however, is loath to admit as proper object of study for a Confucian scholar, those matters not directly pertinent to the cultivation of virtue. He does not consider the details of ritual matters and of music to be worthy of the attention of disciples of the sages.[37] For him, the whole of education should be moral, in spirit and in content, being directed entirely to man's real goal in life: sagehood.

Since *liang-chih* is present in all men, and can be developed by them all, and since this development or extension is the sine qua non of sagehood, it follows that the difference between the sage and the ordinary man is one of degree rather than of kind, a degree of the intensity of the presence of *liang-chih* in each. Yang-ming explains that the belief that a sage is "born with knowledge" refers to a capacity to know the good, and not to "innate knowledge" concerning all matters of life and culture. He also says that ordinary people are also "born with knowledge"—with the same moral sense.[38] All must make efforts to deepen and develop this capacity, acquiring more and more of the knowledge of the good. The sage, indeed, may be more gifted at birth. He may not need to make such strenuous efforts. Nevertheless, if he becomes a sage, it is less through his natural endowment and propensity for good than through his efforts of cultivating *hsin*. And even the least-endowed person can attain sagehood, provided he is willing to make a hundred or thousand times the effort required of a moral genius. For example, with the practice of filial piety, the better endowed may have more facility than the less gifted. But both must sincerely follow the light of *liang-chih*, and so unite knowledge with action and increase their original capacity for both.[39]

Yang-ming was fond of comparing *liang-chih* to the sun. He uses this comparison to describe the differences between the moral knowledge of the sage, the worthy man, and the fool. In each case, knowledge concerned is not only the inborn capacity, but also what has been acquired, what has passed from potentiality to act:

> The knowledge [or wisdom] of the sage can be compared to the sun in a clear sky, that of the worthy man to the sun in a sky that is partly clouded, and that of the fool to the sun on a dark and dismal day. These three kinds of knowledge seem to differ in clarity, but have all the power of discerning between black and white, although with unequal efficacy. . . . The work of learning through assiduous study or effort begins with the light [one has] as a starting point, in examining things (*wu*) carefully.[40]

All men have *liang-chih*. Its presence in individual persons differs, however, according to the natural endowment of each, and, even more important, according to the degree of realization to which each has brought his natural endowment.

HSIN-CHIH PEN-T'I

The Doctrine of the Mean, ch. 1, speaks of the state of equilibrium (*chung*) that characterizes the mind-and-heart before the rise of emotions, and the state of harmony (*ho*) that characterizes it afterward—provided that the emotioas arisen are in due proportion to the events which aroused them. Chu Hsi has said that equilibrium is characteristic of *hsing-chih pen-t'i*, that is, pure "nature" as such, full of goodness or good potential.[41] Yang-ming identifies *hsin* to *hsing*. He spoke, therefore, of *hsin-chih-pen-t'i*, that is, of the pure mind-and-heart, which he also identifies to *liang-chih*. "*Liang-chih* is [*hsin* in] equilibrium before [emotions] are aroused. . . . It is what every man has."[42]

The meaning of *hsin-chih-pen-t'i* is better clarified when it is discussed in terms of *t'i* (substance) and *yung* (application), the inner (*nei*) and the outer (*wai*). It is as though *hsin* has many layers, one deeper than the other.* Its *pen-t'i* is *hsin* at its deepest level, where it is totally itself, unchanging and unchangeable. There, it is "active without activity and tranquil (still) without tranquillity. [It] is neither that which precedes or follows any state; it is neither internal nor external. It is totally undifferentiated, a unity in itself."[43]

Contemplating *hsin* at its deepest level, Yang-ming also redefines "activity" and "stillness". His criterion is not the movement of emotions, but the moral intention. When the intention is correct, no distinction need be made between states of mind as stillness and activity.* *Hsin* would remain in peace, even when it is responding to events and affairs, just as it would not lack anything that activity may give, even when it is engaged in quiet meditation.

> The state before the emotions arise exists in the state in which emotions have already arisen. . . . The state after the emotions have arisen [also] exists in the state before the emotions arise. Neither is without activity or stillness and neither can be separately described active or still.[44]

Where Chu Hsi had sought to unite activity and stillness through the practice of reverence, Yang-ming attempts to find it at the source of one's being itself, in this *pen-t'i* of *hsin*, which possesses the ability of perfecting itself. For him, this union of activity and stillness is accomplished not merely by the continual exertion (*kung-fu*) through self-cultivation, and watchfulness over one's least movements, but also by the awareness that *hsin-chih-pen-t'i*, the source and origin of

---

* Karl Jaspers' teaching of the two modes of the Encompassing, and Martin Heidegger's doctrine of being as *Dasein*, and its participation in Being-itself, open insights into Yang-ming's vision of the various levels of depth in *hsin*, both as the individual principle of life, consciousness, and activity and as the *pen-t'i* in which all things are one.

† Yang-ming's emphatic assertion of the unity of knowledge and action, as well as the importance he gives to moral intention, underlines the central role given to the fundamental moral choice in his philosophy. On this point, see David S. Nivison, "Moral Decision in Wang Yang-ming: The Problem of Chinese 'Existentialism,' " *PEW* XXIII (1973), 121–38.

activity and stillness, is itself one and indivisible. For this reason, Yang-ming declares that *pen-t'i* (ultimate reality, wisdom) is present in *kung-fu*, and *kung-fu* in *pen-t'i*.[45] For this reason too, he says that it is very difficult to describe *kung-fu*, which represents that which is continually simplifying ,tself.[46]

Anxious to do away with unnecessary, subtle distinctions between stillness and activity, and to maintain that "equilibrium" and "harmony" penetrate each other, Yang-ming emphasizes the dynamic function of *liang-chih*, ever still and ever active. "*Liang-chih* makes no distinction between doing something and doing nothing."[47] It is foolish to seek after stillness for its own sake, because *liang-chih* itself is always still, as it is also always active. Rather, one should simply stay alert, remaining always attentive to the task of keeping the heart as such pure and free from selfishness. This is what the Book of Mencius [2A, 2] means by "Always be doing something."[48]

Yang-ming describes *liang-chih* as the "shining *hsin*,"[49] and also compares it to a mirror. "*Liang-chih* always knows and always shines. It is like a bright mirror, hung [on the wall]. The things which appear before it cannot conceal their beauty or ugliness."[50] It is also identified to the "heavenly principle" (*T'ien-li*) which fills the pure mind-and-heart. "There is only one *liang-chih*. It is where *T'ien-li* is bright and spiritual. Therefore *liang-chih* and *T'ien-li* are one and the same thing."[51]

THE GREAT METHOD: CHIH-LIANG-CHIH

The "extension [and realization] of *liang-chih*" is a possible task because *liang-chih* is at once inborn and acquired and because *liang-chih* "originally knows everything and yet knows nothing."[52] It is also an all-important task, because it alone can bring one to the desired goal of sagehood. Yang-ming is fond of saying that while sages and ordinary men all have *liang-chih*, sages differ from ordinary men by the fact that they know how to "extend" *liang-chih* and really do it.[53]

> The knowledge of the good (*liang-chih*) which is [present] in the mind and heart may be called sagehood (*sheng*). The learning of sages lies precisely in extending [and realizing] this knowledge of the good.

The sage is he who extends it with ease. The worthy man is he who extends it with some effort. The fool or the good-for-nothing is he who hides himself from the truth and refuses to extend it. However, no matter how great is his ignorance and foolishness, the good-for-nothing still possesses this capacity to know the good. If only he would extend and realize it, he would be no different from the sage. . . . There is no [other] knowledge beyond this knowledge of the good.[54]

A moral doctrine is always ordained to practice. Yang-ming's teachings concerning *liang-chih* are given for the sake of moral action. It is important, therefore, to find out how to "extend" or "realize" this capacity for goodness, which is at once inborn and acquired. Yang-ming himself is most emphatic about this. He considers "the extension of *liang-chih*" to be an "easy and simple" method, which is sure to bring man to sagehood. Nevertheless, one must understand it correctly. One must not, especially, take for granted the word *chih* (extend).

Among our companions now, there is not one who does not know this theory of the extension of *liang-chih*. Yet, there are very few who really apply their efforts in this direction. This is so because they do not yet see their *liang-chih* clearly, and especially take the word *chih* (extension) too light-heartedly, so that from many points of view they do not gain much in strength.[55]

In his teachings on the subject, Yang-ming is careful in pointing out that the "extension of *liang-chih*" is not the acquisition of abstract principles of morality—for example, of filial piety—or of simple techniques for performing moral duties—for example, of how to care for one's parents in hot or cold weather. It is simply the great principle, to do always in one's life what one's mind-and-heart says is right and good. And this involves both knowledge and action, or rather, of knowledge that is also action. As he told his disciple Lu Ch'eng:

All men have this moral ability to judge between right and wrong.[56] This is what we call *liang-chih*. . . . There are [however] people who do not know how to extend it. The Book of Changes speaks of "knowing the utmost point to reach, and reaching it."[57] To know the utmost point is real knowledge. To reach it is to extend knowledge. This is how knowledge and action become united. In recent ages, the teaching concerning *ko-wu* (investigation of things) and *chih-chih* (extension of knowledge) covers only one word: $chih_2$ (knowledge), and [even] that it has done quite inconclusively. As to the effort of $chih_1$ (extension), this has been completely omitted. This is why knowledge and action have been made two separate things.[58]

The meaning of the semantic shift from Chu Hsi's formula, the extension of knowledge (*chih-chih*), to Yang-ming's extension of the knowledge of the good (*chih liang-chih*), is thus explained in terms of an increasing emphasis on the first word, $chih_1$ (extend), understood as self-exertion, and receiving a clearer ethical reference with the substitution of *liang-chih* for $chih_2$ (knowledge). It is in order to preserve and strengthen this meaning of "self-exertion," of continual striving, that Yang-ming keeps to the usage of $chih_1$ (extend). Knowledge of the good cannot be realized without self-exertion, discipline, attentiveness.

And again, in this discussion of the "extension of *liang-chih*," Yang-ming returns to his earlier teaching of the Unity of Knowledge and Action. Whether *liang-chih* pertains more to knowledge or action has been a subject of academic dispute. But, where Yang-ming himself is concerned, there can be no doubt that knowledge and action necessarily penetrate each other, and that there is no true moral knowledge outside of action.[59]

PURITY OF MIND-AND-HEART

As said before, Yang-ming is much concerned about the proper understanding of *liang-chih*. He calls it the basic idea, the great principle, or the great starting point. Yet he says remarkably little about *how* it is to be extended or realized. He prefers rather to approach it from different angles, to see the work itself always as a whole rather than a s parts or steps. Man is a unity, and the work of acquiring wisdom is a unique endeavor. It is a work which takes up the whole of man, the whole of his time. It can neither be broken into fragments, nor organized into a system.

One angle from which Yang-ming contemplates the work of extending *liang-chih* is that of purifying *hsin*. For although the extension of *liang-chih* is a simple task, its practice can be quite difficult, on account of the resistance of *hsin*. This arises from man's "selfish desires" (*wu-yü*), which prevent the proper functioning of our movement toward the good.[60] Without explaining the origin of these desires, Yang-ming urges their removal in view of making possible the spontaneous operation of *liang-chih*:

> The determination to have the mind-and-heart completely identified with *T'ien-li* and devoid even of the least bit of selfish desire is the work of becoming a sage. But this is not possible unless such desires are prevented from arising. . . . To do this is the task of caution and apprehension, as taught in the Doctrine of the Mean, and of the extension of knowledge and the investigation of things, as taught in the Great Learning.[61]

This does not mean that a two-fold labor is required, first negative and then positive. On the contrary, the removal of selfish and material desires is accomplished, quite simply, by "making intention sincere." When our intentions are correct, *liang-chih* is thereby being extended.

> To remove a bad intention is at once to have a good intention and to recover *hsin-chih pen-t'i*. This is like the sun which had been hidden by clouds, and which becomes bright again when the clouds disappear. If, once the bad intention is gone [one attempts] to have some good intention, it would be like lighting a lamp under the bright sun.[62]

Yang-ming especially singles out pride as the great danger to virtue. The proud son, he says, cannot be filial, the proud minister cannot be loyal, the proud father cannot be affectionate, and the proud friend cannot be faithful. His exhortation is that one should always keep the "heavenly principle" pure and integral in the heart, for purity of heart means selflessness. The virtue of the ancient sages lies in their selflessness. Only the selfless can be humble. Humility is the fountain of all virtue, just as pride is the source of all vice.[63]

To have no selfish desires one must be able to get rid not only of one's desires for renown and profit, and for other particular interests, but also of the attachment to life itself. It is only when one is totally detached and unconcerned with life or death, that a man is single-minded. Only then will his heart be completely free, able to operate in every direction without encountering any obstacle.[64]

Yang-ming asserts that selfish desires can be discerned and eliminated by meditation. He even rebuked a disciple who questioned the effectiveness of such a practice, saying that he had found it useful after having done so for more than ten years. But he would never limit the task only to a time of formal "quiet sitting." He believes that *hsin* should be always active, even in meditation, just as it should remain always still, even in the midst of activity.[65]

PERFECT HARMONY

By harmony, Yang-ming refers to a natural state of the mind-and-heart, free from any affectation or insincerity. "The excess of emotion is not harmony. The movement of temper is not harmony. To be attached to selfish desires and stubbornness is not harmony. The infant cries all day without hurting his throat.[66] This is the extreme of harmony."[67]

Yang-ming criticizes Chu Hsi for making the work of maintaining harmony of the emotions too complicated, and for overemphasizing the role of stillness. He prefers to give more attention to activity, that is, to an attitude of constant vigilance and caution over one's least movement. "When activity is not without harmony, passivity or stillness will not lack equilibrium."[68]

When asked about the control of anger, Yang-ming replies that it is natural to men to get angry sometimes. The important thing is not to let our anger go to excess.[69] To another question, as to how joy can be maintained when a person is experiencing a great sorrow, such as the death of his parents, Yang-ming's answer is quite different from the conventional one. There can be no joy, he said, unless the son has cried bitterly. "For joy means that *hsin* is at peace. [It means that] *hsin*-in-itself has not been perturbed."[70]

To follow the course of nature in the control of emotions, one must see to it that the emotions are in proportion to the events which arouse them. One must control anger, even in face of provocation, in order to avoid being carried away by anger. On the other hand, one need not fear giving in to sorrow, when there is just reason for it. The essential thing to do is to keep peace. Where there is peace, there is equilibrium and harmony.

For Yang-ming, *hsin* is a dynamic principle of moral activity. It is "always doing something."[71] To be more precise, it should always be "accumulating righteousness" (*chi-yi*).[72] *Hsin* should be always intent upon the practice of virtue, without ever forgetting this great objective, and without allowing itself to become impatient, and to seek for quick results. "If one accumulates righteousness in and through his own heart every hour and every minute, *liang-chih pen-t'i* will be absolutely clear and will spontaneously see right as right and wrong as wrong."[73]

The extension of *liang-chih* refers to the whole task of pursuing wisdom, but the "accumulation of righteousness" speaks of the performance of individual acts of virtue. However, if every individual act one performs is just and right, *hsin* itself will certainly be in peace and harmony and the capacity to know the good will be developed. For this reason, Yang-ming states that the "accumulation of righteousness" is nothing but the extension of *liang-chih*. And, to use the vocabulary of the Great Learning [ch.1], the extension of *liang-chih* in daily affairs means "investigating things" and "making the intention sincere." It effects also the "rectification of the *hsin*." To use the vocabulary of the Doctrine of the Mean [ch.1], it is the same as being constantly alert when alone, practicing vigilance without being seen, and apprehension without being heard.[74]

To the question whether the constant practice of vigilance over self, of respect for one's virtuous nature, entails the loss of spontaneity and freedom, thus bringing about a state of tension, Yang-ming's answer is negative. For him, it is less a question of "practice," than one of "attitude." He does not require *hsin* to be always making conscious efforts. He merely insists that it be kept always free from unruly desires.[75] "Always be doing something" is therefore merely a positive manner of stating the negative imperative, "Do away with your selfish desires."

> To practice caution when one is not seen, and vigilance when one is not heard, refers to a *state* of mind-and-heart which one ought to have. [It is not the same as] being fearful and anxious. . . .Respect and reverence arise out of the natural operation of the mind-and-heart. To arise out of the natural operation of the mind-and-heart, to do something without conscious action, refers to natural spontaneity.[76]

Chu Hsi had spoken of vigilance in solitude, but largely in terms of self-exertion.[77] Yang-ming opposes the forcible exertion of effort in the practice of virtue. To him, this would be indicative of impatience and selfishness. After all, too much anxiety to attain perfection is in itself an imperfection and a hindrance.[78] A beginner, he said, cannot suddenly jump into the position of a sage. Rise and fall, advance and retreat make up the natural rhythm of the task of extending *liang-chih*.

> Whether the task advances or recedes, remain always [your own master] and extend *liang-chih*. Do this without cease, and in time [your] effort will bear fruit and no external events can disturb you.[79]

INSEPARABLE FROM SOCIAL RESPONSIBILITY

Yang-ming teaches very clearly that the extension of *liang-chih* is inseparable from the fulfillment of one's social responsibilities. For the gentleman who extends *liang-chih* naturally comes to regard others as he does himself, to look upon the country as his family, and Heaven and Earth and all things as one. "[When this is the case], even if we want the world to be without good government, it would not be possible. The ancient sages developed their knowledge of the good to such an extent that they felt the good flowing from themselves when they saw others doing it, and evil flowing from themselves too when they saw others doing it. They regarded others' hunger . . . as their own, and felt that when a needy man had not been properly assisted, it was as if they themselves had pushed him into a ditch."[80]

> The sage-emperors Yao and Shun and the Three Kings[81] spoke and all the people believed them, because in speaking they extended their knowledge of the good. They acted and all the people were pleased with them, because in acting they merely extended their knowledge of the good.[82]

"The Way of Yao and Shun was simply that of filial piety and fraternal respect."[83] Not everyone is a ruler. But everyone can practice the simple virtues of filial piety and fraternal respect, and so contribute to good government of the world.

This does not mean that conventional standards of behavior associated with filial piety, loyalty, or other virtues governing human relationships must always be adhered to. Mention has been made of the exceptions—Emperor Shun's marriage and the military expedition of King Wu of Chou. Events and circumstances of life cannot always be foreseen. One should reamin always sincere, free from self-deception. "Given sincerity, there will be enlightenment."[84]

> Throughout the countless changes which occur in his relationships
> with others, the gentleman acts if it is proper to act, stops if it is proper
> to stop, lives if it is proper to live, and dies if it is proper to die.
> In all his reflections and responses, he is always extending his *liang-
> chih* to the utmost.[85]

Moral endeavor aims at the highest goals of virtue which makes a
man completely sincere, free from all hypocrisy and duplicity, through
a process of inward transformation rather than outward imitation. To
a friend who agrees that from the beginning the student should recognize the goal of sagehood as the final end of his studies (*hsüeh*), but
who prescribes that such a student must first know "what the emotions
and dispositions of a sage" are like, in order to be able to model his
own inner responses upon them, Yang-ming explains that the sage's
emotions and dispositions cannot be "experienced" by someone else.
Unless a person seeks to learn from his *own liang-chih*, he is behaving
like a man using an unmarked scale to weigh things or looking for his
own reflection in a covered mirror.

> My *liang-chih* is originally the same as that of the sage. If I can ex-
> perience my own *liang-chih* properly, then I shall find that the sage's
> emotions and dispositions are present within myself as they are within
> him. Master Yi-ch'uan [Ch'eng Yi] once said,[86] "If one merely con-
> templates [Emperor] Yao and imitates his actions [externally], without
> having also his quickness of apprehension, his intelligence, insight
> and wisdom, how can one act and appear [as did he], always in accord
> with propriety?"[87]

And so, throughout his life, a man's effort to cultivate virtue is to
consist only of one task. From youth to old age, from dawn to dusk,
he has only to extend his *liang-chih* in response to affairs and circumstances as they arise, and so render his *hsin* ever more sincere and transparent, open to life and its challenges, to the calls of responsibility
which bind him to others in a society which is fundamentally a moral
order.[88]

THE TRANSMISSION REDEFINED

Yang-ming placed great importance on his discovery of a universal
method. The formula *chih liang-chih* represented the acquisition of an

infallible starting point for the quest of sagehood. It was the prize he
had acquired in the midst of "a hundred deaths and a thousand difficulties." He hoped that later scholars would not take it for granted.
He considered it the precious legacy of the sages.[89] In a letter dated
1521, he spoke of his discovery in the following words:

> What I say about the extension of knowledge is the "treasure of the
> orthodox dharma-eye"[90] of the Confucian school. He who sees the
> truth "sets it up before Haven and Earth, and finds nothing in it
> which he transgresses. He presents himself with it before spiritual
> beings, and finds no doubt regarding it, He examines it by comparing
> [it] with the doctrines of the three [sage] kings, and finds it free from
> error. He is ready to wait for a hundred years for a sage, without
> harboring any misgiving.[91]

Yang-ming considers this discovery not as a *new way*, but rather as
the only and universal Way, the Way of the sages: of Yao, Shun,
Confucius, and Mencius. He identifies his teaching of *chih-liang-chih*
to the "orthodox" Confucian doctrine, that which was first discovered
by the earliest sages, but which became lost with Mencius' death, and
was expounded anew centuries later by Lu Chiu-yüan. This new
presentation of *orthodox transmission*, the establishment of a *new line*
as well as the new interpretation of the *sacred legacy* of the sages, was
given by him first in 1520,[92] probably a little before his public teaching on *liang-chih*. It was reaffirmed in 1521 and after, reiterated time
and again till the end of his life.

Yang-ming declares that the teaching of the sages is of *hsin*, the
profound and unitary source of man's moral judgments, actions, as
well as of his vital consciousness, the "substance" of which he calls
jen.[93] He recalls Confucius' instruction to Tzu-kung, who had imagined
virtue as the fruit of abundant learning and who regarded as *jen* the
effort of "securing extensive benefits for the people." The Master
taught him instead to seek for *jen*, humanity, in an all-pervading
unity, in the quest for perfect virtue, and to learn to judge others by
what was near oneself,[94] by seeking the Way in one's own *hsin*. Yang-
ming also relates how Mencius had combatted the teachings of both
Mo Ti and Kao-tzu. The former had practiced the virtue of humanity
to the point of "rubbing his head and wearing out his heels,"[95] while
the latter had taught that if the virtue of humanity resided in the person,

that of righteousness was exterior to man. But Mencius resisted such tendencies of externalizing virtue, insisting that both humanity and righteousness were present in *hsin*.[96] He said, "There is naught else in learning except the recovery of the lost *hsin*."[97]

According to Yang-ming, the Way of the sage-kings was lost when *hsin* and *li* were divorced from each other, giving scholars an excuse to seek external and fragmentary knowledge regarding "laws, useful things, and numbers," for the sake of understanding the "principles of things" (*wu-li*). By doing so, they deserted *hsin*, which was in reality identical with true *li*. But the Buddhists and Taoists erred in another direction. While they sought the understanding of *hsin*, they did not realize that it was the principle of all *moral* perfection and responsibility. They abandoned their social responsibilities in order to indulge in idle talks of emptiness and the void.[98]

Fortunately, the transmission was resumed in Sung times. Yang-ming spoke explicitly of Chou Tun-yi and his teachings of *Wu-chi* and *T'ai-chi*, and of the practice of stillness, of Ch'eng Hao and his teaching of *hsin* as that which is always the same in both activity and stillness. But he did not consider either Chou or Ch'eng as the direct transmitter of the Confucian teaching.[99] This honor was reserved especially to Lu Chiu-yüan.

> Although his teaching might not appear to have as much purity and harmony as Chou's and Ch'eng's, it was nevertheless simple and direct, genuinely going back to the teaching transmitted by Mencius. If certain features of his doctrines also opened new vistas, and differed somewhat from Mencius, these were due to particular differences of temperament and opinion. He remained one with Mencius in teaching others to seek the Way in the mind. For this reason, I decided that Lu's teaching was the very teaching of Mencius.[100]

THE SACRED LEGACY

Like Ch'eng Yi and Chu Hsi, Yang-ming regarded the "formula" taken from a forged chapter of the Book of Documents to contain the sacred message handed down by the early sages. But whereas Chu had interpreted *jen-hsin* as man's mind, regarded as the seat of consciousness and composed of blood and ether (*ch'i*), and *Tao-hsin* as the same mind, considered as the source of moral discernment, or the embodiment of principle of Heaven in the sage,[101] Yang-ming offers a much simpler explanation. He understands *Tao-hsin* to refer to the pure mind-and-heart, without the least trace of selfishness, and described as "subtle" on account of its spiritual character, and *jen-hsin* to refer to the mind-and-heart contaminated by selfish desires and so become prone to error. As to the remainder of the formula, he explains "discernment" and "single-mindedness" as practices that reinforce each other and together make up the task of achieving sagehood.[102]

Yang-ming identifies *Tao-hsin* to *liang-chih*, our capacity to know and do good.[103] He says that the extension of this capacity enables us to "keep steadfastly to the Mean." And since the Mean refers to the state of equilibrium preceding the rise of emotions as well as to principle of Heaven (*T'ien-li*) and *hsin-chih-pen-t'i*, it too is no different from *liang-chih*.[104]

Yang-ming also identifies the task of "being discerning and single-minded" to the extension of *liang-chih*. He believes that this should be done gradually and attentively. He compares this work to that of watering a growing plant or tree. One must go on watering the tree. One must not give it more water than it can take.[105]

Yang-ming reportedly said that, just as a man could prove his genuine ethnic descent from his ancestors by a certain test that involves mixing his own blood with the ancestor's dry bones to see if these would absorb it, so too, the word, *liang-chih*, "is the drop of blood transmitted from antiquity by the sages."[106] In a poem written a few years later, he expressed this same idea in different words:

> The sages' instruction lasted a thousand years;
> *Liang-chih* is its oral transmission.
> Compasses give circles and quadrants squares,
> To discover pristine unity, do not wield an axe.
> Without leaving the ordinary realm of actions and movements,
> Go straight to the primeval moment, before any diagram was
>   made.[107]

For the rest of his life, Yang-ming continued to meditate upon this word. He spoke of it day and night to his friends and disciples. His teaching became increasingly simplified, as the expression *liang-chih* came to represent all he had ever discovered and taught. He described with some humor how a certain retired official once invited him to give a lecture, saying, "Besides *liang-chih*, is there anything else [you can] talk about?" His answer was straight and direct: "Besides *liang-chih*, is there anything else [to] talk about?"[108]

V

THE CULMINATION: LIANG-CHIH PEN-T'I

Hsin (the mind-and-heart) is *Tao* (the Way), and *Tao* is *T'ien* (Heaven). If one knows [his own] heart, he would also know the Way and Heaven.

THE YEARS 1522–27 were spent by Yang-ming in virtual retirement in his native place. During these years he taught his disciples and all who came to listen to him.[2] From 1523 on, so many people came to Yü-yao to hear him that the local Buddhist temples could hardly provide enough room for the lodgers.[3] The Chronological Biography says, "Disciples came to him from all parts. [Frequently], over three hundred people would sit around and listen to him. The Master came and discoursed on the meaning of the unity of all things according to the Great Learning. [He spoke of] how every man should seek in his own nature and extend to the utmost his *liang-chih*, in order to reach the state of supreme goodness."[4] Whenever any of these disciples took their leave, Yang-ming would sigh and say, "Although you gentlemen are going away, you will not go ouside Heaven-and-Earth. So long as you share my basic outlook of life, I can be so happy as to forget my own self."[5] As a disciple, Huang Mien-chih explained:

> . . .While the Master had many friends and followers even before the Nanking days [1514–16], there were never as many as in Yüeh [Yü-yao] This is partly because the more lectures he gave, the more people believed him. Essentially, however, it was because the Master's daily progress in learning gave him a mysterious power of attraction and influence. . .[6]

It is the aim of this chapter to examine the results of this period of the culmination of Yang-ming's teachings. It is my assertion that this culmination lies in a form of "mysticism," taking this word to refer to the total vision of life and reality, which he developed, as well as to the transcendent ideals of sagehood, which he outlined. In this connection, it may be claimed that Yang-ming himself attained an enduring state of mind, both sublime and human, which made him regard himself as being related to all reality in a dynamic unity of heart and spirit. However, since it is his thought more than his personal life that interests us—although the two can hardly be separated— I shall present Yang-ming's enunciation of his total vision, and then proceed to an examination of his teaching of *hsin*, this time not only as a principle of moral activity but also as the dynamic principle of vital consciousness which united man to the universe and makes of him its psychic center, its heart, its *hsin*.

ALL IN ONE

"All in One" refers to Yang-ming's basic teaching of *Wan-wu yi-t'i*, the "Unity of All Things," which permeates his entire teaching. He likes to cite Analects 15:2, where Confucius declares: "There is one [unifying thread] which runs through all my teachings."[7] He also alludes to the T'ien-t'ai and Hua-ven insight, which had been absorbed into Ch'an Buddhism, of "*yi chi yi-ch'ieh, yi-ch'ieh chi yi*.[8] But it is in his famous essay of 1527, the "Ta-hsüeh wen" (Inquiry into the Great Learning), that he gives full expression to these ideas of the harmony and mutual interpenetration of reality.

In this respect, in the letter addressed to Ku Lin, the long passage on "Pulling the Roots and Stopping the Source" (*po-pen sai-yüan*),[9] probably written in 1524 or earlier, is noteworthy. Out of these texts emerges a unified picture, rich with meaning, of Yang-ming's understanding of sagehood as culminating in an experience of oneness with Heaven and Earth and all things, an experience which permeates the sage's thinking and being and acting, which becomes identified with his *hsin* or *liang-chih* and its *pen-t'i*, overflowing into a concrete awareness of his social and political responsibliities.

"An Inquiry into the Great Learning" begins with an explanation of its title. Whereas Chu Hsi had interpreted the "Great Learning" as "education for an adult,"[10] Yang-ming gives it greater importance, explaining the words as "the learning of a great man," of a person who regards Heaven-and-Earth and the myriad things as one body, the world as one family, and the country as one person. But this state of mind is less the result of deliberate efforts of his will, than the natural and spontaneous outcome of his "humane" heart, full of *jen*, and unobscured by selfishness.[11] To prove this, Yang-ming gives as example the spontaneous, prereflective reactions of the "small man," the one mediocre in virtue and learning:

> When he sees a child about to fall into a well, he cannot help having a feeling of alarm and commiseration. This shows that his humanity (*jen*) forms one body with the child. It may be objected that the child belongs to the same species [as he]. Yet when he observes the pitiful cries and frightened appearance of birds and beasts [about to be slaughtered], he cannot help feeling an "inability to bear" their suffering. This shows that his humanity forms one body with birds and beasts. It may be objected that birds and beasts are sentient beings too. But when he sees plants broken and destroyed, he cannot help having a feeling of pity. This shows that his humanity forms one body with plants. It may be said that plants are living things too. Yet even when he sees tiles and stones shattered and crushed he cannot help having a feeling of regret. This shows that his humanity forms one body with tiles and stones. This means that even the heart of the small man must have [in potentiality, this humanity which unites him to all things].[12]

The great man "cultivates his moral qualities to such a point as to enable a happy order to prevail throughout Heaven-and-Earth and all things to flourish."[13] He has been compared, time and again, to a bright mirror. He has been compared to Heaven itself. He is one whose nature has been completely transformed, who is completely identified with goodness. He practices virtue by instinct. He is always joyous and peaceful. In the words of the Book of Changes, his character, one with that of Heaven and Earth, possesses a brilliance equal to that of the sun and the moon, in harmony with the universe, and participating in its creative processes.[14]

According to Yang-ming, this "humane" heart which unites man to all things is rooted in our Heaven-endowed nature, and is in itself clear and intelligent. For this reason it is called *ming-te*, clear virtue. It is present in all men, great and small alike, so long as their minds and hearts are unmoved by selfish desires. When aroused by such, and when compelled by greed for gain, fear of harm, or impulse of anger, man becomes capable of destroying, of killing members of his own species, slaughtering his own brothers—evil actions which cause his "humanity" to disappear. The universal task of self-cultivation, for both the small and great man, lies therefore in removing selfish desires and in making manifest clear virtue, so that the "original condition (*pen-t'i*) of the unity of Heaven and Earth and the myriad things may be restored."[15]

And then, with some caution, Yang-ming added: "This does not mean *adding* anything from the outside to this original condition (*pen-t'i*)." For, just as in speaking of "extending *liang-chih*," he was careful to point out that its *pen-t'i*—one with the *pen-t'i* of all things, that is, with ultimate reality—can neither be augmented nor diminished, that its "capacity" for knowing the good is at once inborn and possible of development.[16] In this way he safeguards the independent and transcendent character of *pen-t'i*, while allowing for the possibility of that which is latent to become manifest by a process, so to speak, of development, or better still, realization.

JEN (HUMANITY) VERSUS AI (LOVE)

A difficulty arises however in this view of *jen*, the Confucian moral virtue that becomes the means by which unity between the self and all things is established. Would not such an interpretation obliterate the basic difference between Confucian and Mohist ethics, between the virtue of "humanity" or *jen* as a "graded love" and the Mohist virtue of equal and universal love (*chien-ai*)? Early in Yang-ming's career as a teacher of philosophy, a disciple had raised this question in relation to Ch'eng Hao's statement that the man of *jen* was one with Heaven and Earth and the myriad things.[17] In giving his answer, Yang-ming admitted the difficulty of distinguishing between such *jen* and the Mohist "love." Emphasizing the life-giving quality of the virtue of *jen*, he gave the example of a tree or plant, beginning as a sprout, growing strong and developing a trunk with branches and leaves. He recommended that distinctions be observed in our practice of love, the love of parents and kin resembling giving water to the "roots," while the love of others being compared to the extension of life from the roots to the branches:

> The love between father and son and between elder and younger brothers is the starting point of the life-giving power of man's *hsin*. . . . From there it is [extended] to [the practice of] humanity toward all people and to love of all things. . . . Mo-tzu's universal love makes no distinction in human relations, [causing the person] to regard his own father, son, elder or younger brother as he would any man in the street. And so, this [love] has no starting-point. . . . How can it be called humanity? Filial piety and brotherly respect are the roots of humanity. This means that the principle of humanity grows from within.[18]

The Confucian virtue, humanity, is the natural development of spontaneous feelings of commiseration, coming from within man's mind-and-heart, and overflowing to embrace all others from his nearest kin on. The Mohist notion of love, on the other hand, disregards the spontaneous quality of this love itself as well as the natural distinctions inherent in social relations and in the order of things. The danger is that, by promoting an "equal love of all," the very nature of love be denied. For if love springs spontaneously from man's nature, it must also recognize the order of nature itself, with its inherent distinctions, based on natural kinship and obligations.

And so Yang-ming seeks to preserve a certain distinction in the practice of *jen*, which is based on human nature itself, rather than by allotting it arbitrary "grades." Understanding universal love as an ideal to be achieved, he does not see it as an excuse for "leveling" human affection and responsibility.

In this regard, a letter Yang-ming wrote to Huang Hsing-tseng in 1524 is also significant.[19] Huang had spoken approvingly of Han Yü's definition, that "universal love is called *jen* (humanity),"[20] calling to mind also Chou Tun-yi's statement, the "love is *jen*."[21] To him, it seemed that both these sayings gareed well with the meaning given to the word by Mencius. He was however puzzled by the fact that other Sung thinkers had criticized Han Yü, preferring rather to relegate love to the realm of emotions (*ch'ing*), while using *jen* to signify a virtue pertaining to nature (*hsing*).[22] Yang-ming was in agreement with Huang, and recalled how Confucius himself had said that the meaning of *jen* lay in "loving others."[23] He then gave an exposition of a "correct" kind of love and an "incorrect" kind of love:

> But while the *pen-t'i* of love can be called *jen*, there is a kind of love that is correct, and a kind that is not correct. Only the correct kind of love is the *pen-t'i* of love, and can be called *jen*. If one knows only universal love, without distinguishing between the correct and incorrect kinds of love, there will be a difference.[24]

However, what does Yang-ming mean by the "correct" and the "incorrect" kinds of love? For the answer to this question, we must once again go back to the "Inquiry into the Great Learning," and examine his teaching concerning the order of "relative importance" among things, that is, whether all things are equally important, or whether some are more important than others, and should be recognized as such. The specific question posed to him is, if the great man forms one body with all things, then why should the text of the Great Learning refer to things as possessing a "relative importance"?[25] Again, Yang-ming answers by giving the example of a living organism, this time of the human body. The body is of course a unity. However, the nature of things being what they are, we use our hands and feet to protect the head, without intending to show less regard for the hands and feet, but rather for the sake of the whole body. So too, we love both plants and animals and yet feed animals with plants. We love both animals and men, and yet allow the animals to be slaughtered in order to feed our parents, to provide for religious sacrifices, and to entertain our guests at table. The same can be said of our love for our parents and for the man in the street. If we have only a little bit of food with which to save from hunger either our parents or the man in the street, we will prefer to save our parents instead of the man in the street. And so, to love all things, to be one with all things through the practice of the life-giving virtue of humanity, does not necessarily preclude distinctions in the concrete application of our love and humanity. In fact, the humane feeling we may have for all people is itself somehow derived from the affection we bear for our parents. It is again the question of roots and branches, because it is a question of the communication of life within the living organism. We must accept both our own limitations and the natural order of things. What the Great Learning describes as [an order of] natural importance refors to the natural order derived from our knowledge of the good (*liang-chih*). Not to transgress this [natural order] is called righteousness (*yi*). To act according to this order is called propriety (*li*). To know this order is called wisdom (*chih*). To follow this order from beginning to end is called fidelity (*hsin*).[26] Fidelity, therefore, sums up righteousness, propriety and wisdom.*

CH'IN-MIN: LOVING THE PEOPLE

Proceeding with the text of the Great Learning, Yang-ming explains the expression of "loving the people" (*ch'in-min*). Making the distinction between *t'i* (substance, reality) and *yung* (activity), he says that "making manifest clear virtue"—the perfection of self—refers to the work of "establishing the reality (*t'i*) of the unity of Heaven and Earth and the myriad things," whereas "loving the people" is the "activity" that flows from this same unity. In other words, making manifest our clear virtue lies in loving the people, and loving the people is the way to manifest clear virtue; these being two aspects of the same work. And then, in the concrete, practical language so characteristic of him, Yang-ming gives examples of how the practice of filial piety and of other social virtues, when extended to embrace not merely one's own parents and kin but the parents and kin of all men, brings about this unity of man with all things:

> Only when I love my father, the fathers of others, and the fathers of all men, can my humanity really form one body with my father, the fathers of others, and the fathers of all men. . . . Then the clear virtue of filial piety will be made manifest. . . .[27]

Even the world of spirits, of beasts and of plants and of inanimate beings are to be included in this all embracing *jen*:

> Everything from ruler, minister, husband, wife, and friends to mountains, rivers, heavenly and earthly spirits, birds, bests, and plants,

---

* Together, these five virtues are usually known as the five "constant virtues" that are based on human nature. The notion of *hsin* (fidelity) recalls the Hebrew, '*emet* while *jen* suggests *hesed*. But the Hebrew virtues describe the Divine-human relationship more than that between human beings themselves.

> all should be truly loved in order that the unity may be reached
> [through] my humanity (*jen*). Then will my clear virtue be completely
> made manifest; then will I really form one body with Heaven and
> Earth and the myriad things.[28]

Just as in personal life the quest of sagehood lies in the "recovery"
of one's original nature, so too, in social and political life the same
quest lies in recapturing a Goldern Past, a moral "Utopia." Yang-
ming's sage is not a contemplative lost in the wonder and admiration
of his own unity with the world, but a man with social and political
responsibilities striving to make this reality a social and political
fact. For him, the world of nature and of human society are fundamentally one, and unity with other men extends itself to unity with
birds and beasts and the whole cosmos.

Thus the love which Yang-ming recommends operates in the manner
of a ripple in a pond, expanding itself continually, until it effects a
unity between man and his family, society at large, his physical environ-
ment, all his fellow creatures, and even with invisible spiritual beings.

In a letter he wrote to Ku Lin some time before 1524, Yang-ming
explained the chief ideas of his "utopian theory." Beginning with the
doctrine of the unity between the self and all things, he says:

> The mind-and-heart of the sage considers Heaven-and-Earth and the
> myriad things as one body and regards all men under Heaven, whether
> inside or outside [his family], near or far, all with blood and breath,
> as his brothers and children and kin. He wants to give peace and se-
> curity, education and nourishment to all, in order to fulfill his desire
> of [really] forming one body with all things.[29]

In this ideal society, everything contributes to helping the people
live a moral life and attain the highest goals of sagehood. There is no
fear of envy or discontent. Division of labor is done to assure better
service of the common good, but no social distinctions are made between the various ways of serving all. Rather, each man shares in the
effort and merit of all. Those with special abilities contribute their
specialized knowledge, whether it be in agriculture, education, music,
or the rites. In a passage strikingly reminiscent of St. Paul's Epistle to
the Corinthians [1 Cor. 12: 14–21] Yang-ming described the coherent
and harmonious functioning of the ideal society in terms of a living
organism:

The eyes see, the ears hear, the hands hold, the feet walk—all fulfilling the functions of the body. The eyes are not ashamed of their not being able to hear. When the ears hear something, the eyes will direct their attention toward it. The feet are not ashamed that they are not able to grasp. When the hands feel something, the feet will move forward. . . .[30]

But, the moral greatness of the Golden Age is the only aspect of the past that Yang-ming desires to recapture. Unlike Chang Tsai, the Ch'eng brothers, and Hu Hung (1100–55), he never speaks about the restoration of Chou feudalism of or the well-field system. Yang-ming desires to strike at the root and the source: to heal the moral sickness of society. If he seems to be too idealistic in his hopes of moral restoration, he is at least realistic in his belief that ancient institutions could no longer be restored.

Yang-ming regards the governing of a family, of a country, and even of the world as nothing else than the extension of love and affection between the self and others. For him, the final goal is the recovery of the unity that should rightfully exist between the two, so that there is essentially no difference between "loving" one's self and "loving" the people:

When I extend affection for my father to other people's fathers, there will be affection between all the fathers and sons of the world. When I extend love for my elder brother to other people's elder brothers, there will be affection between all elder and younger brothers of the world. The same can be said about sovereign and subject, husband and wife, friend and friend, and even about birds and beasts and trees and grass. One can have affection for all. And this affection will always develop more completely one's mind-and-heart, and make manifest its clear virtue. This is the meaning of making manifest clear virtue in the world, giving order to the family, good government to the country, and peace to the world.[31]

Certainly, this is a vision which goes beyond that of a political and social "utopia." It bears within itself a tremendous moral and mystical idealism and dynamism, an enormous confidence in the basic goodness of human beings and of their capacity for self-transcendence, and a consciousness of the inner unity of man and the whole of nature. But is this vision possible of realization in political life? If it not, perhaps, the expression of a naive idealist unacquainted with the realities of human existence and of human nature?

As a philosopher or wise man, Yang-ming's proposed remedy for society's ills, the method he suggests as a means of restoring the purity of heart necessary for the recovery of the Golden Past, is moral education. For him, loving the people necessarily means educating the people in the right way, in the philosophy of *hsin*, in the ways of extending *liang-chih*. As an experienced administrator, however, he does not forget the more concrete needs of life. He gives his reason for preferring the phrase, "loving the people" (*ch'in-min*) to that of "renovating the people" (*hsing-min*), saying that the former reading allows room both for "educating the people" and for "feeding the people." This does not mean merely giving food to the people in times of famine. It means, essentially, making the people wealthy and self-sufficient. In a certain memorial to the throne, he says:

> Wealth is what the people want. When wealth is given to the people, they will live together [in peace]. The people make up the foundation of the state. When the foundation is secure, the state will be in peace. That the ruler and the people *make up one body* is a perennial truth.[32]

However, it was not easy for Yang-ming to convince his disciples that his substitution of "loving the people" for "renovating the people," and his identification of the former work with the great task of "manifesting virtue," was correct. They remembered Chu Hsi's explanation of "manifesting clear virtue" as the "root"—the fundamental task—and of "renovating the people" as the "branch"—a work of less importance.[33] Yang-ming's teaching seemed rather to obscure the difference between the "roots" and the "branches," thus confusing the methodical pursuit of self-cultivation.[34]

In his answer, Yang-ming voices approval of making a distinction between "roots" and "branches," but warns against understanding them as two different things. After all, both "roots" and "branches" belong to the trees. In the same way, "manifesting clear virtue" and "loving the people" are basically two aspects of one same task. So too are the efforts of "investigating things," "extending knowledge," "making the intention sincere," "rectifying *hsin*," cultivating self," "ordering the family," "governing the state," and even "giving peace to the world." All are aspects of the same task, for all are aspects of the basic work of "extending *liang-chih*." And this work of "extension" lies in "investigating things." "To investigate," however, means "to rectify," while "things" means "affairs" or "acts." Thus, "when we come into contact with the 'thing' to which our intention is directed, if we really do good and avoid evil to the utmost, as our innate faculty knows and [directs us to do], then everything will be investigated . . . and our knowledge of the good . . . will be extended [and realized] to the utmost."[35]

JEN (HUMANITY) AND LO (JOY)

The "Inquiry into the Great Learning" concludes on a note of joy (lo). Yang-ming has described the task of the great man—the extension of liang-chih. He has said that this task involves many dimensions, many steps to be taken one after the other. Both as a whole and also in each of the steps, what is involved is "doing good and avoiding evil," developing to the utmost the capcity of our liang-chih. "And then the heart will be naturally joyous, happy, and without regret. And then there will be no deception in the functioning of our intentions, and sincerity may be said to have been attained."[36]

Joy is an important tenet of the philosophy developed by the Hsing-li thinkers of Sung and Ming times. Chou Tun-yi used to ask his disciples, the Ch'eng brothers, to describe the joy of Confucius and Yen Hui.[37] In answering a question as to whether this joy of the sages is the same as that joy which is given as one of the seven emotions, Yang-ming answers that the joy of the sage is characteristic of hsin-in-itself. Without being one of the seven emotions, it is not totally outside the realm of these emotions. True joy can be possessed by ordinary people as well as by sages, except that ordinary people are not aware of this. They allow themselves to become overwhelmed by sorrow and grief and confusion. And yet, even in the midst of all this, as soon as the light shines through, and the person examines himself and becomes sincere, joy is immediately within his reach. To look for joy outside of oneself is thus like "looking for a donkey while riding on it."[38]

Joy comes from the practice of jen, The man of jen is capable of deepening his emotions, and of incorporating them on a higher level, while purging them of a mere emotion. In Yang-ming's terms, he is thus one with Heaven-and-Earth and all things, being united to all in harmony. Joy is the natural and spontaneous consequence of this harmony. The only effort required for the maintenance of this true joy is an attitude of constant vigilance over self when one is alone, a vigilance which is itself spontaneous and without tension. Yang-ming describes this "vigilance in solitude" (*shen-tu*) as 'the "extension of *liang-chih*," and *liang-chih* as nothing other than "joy-in-itself."[39]

Joy is the expression of the peace of mind-and-heart of a man at ease with himself and with others, united by virtuous action to Heaven-and-Earth and all things in a marvelous harmony that allows him to be always natural and spontaneous, always his True Self.

LIANG-CHIH PEN-T'I

Yang-ming's teaching on the unity of man with all things represents the culmination of his practical doctrine on the extension of *liang-chih*. It also contains certain metaphysical implications and presuppositions, relating especially to the nature of *hsin*-in-itself [*hsin chih pen-t'i*] or of *liang-chih*-in-itself [*liang-chih pen-t'i* literally, the "original substance" of *liang-chih*].

The word *hsin* refers to the principle of our conscious and moral activities, as well as to the metaphysical self or "being." The word *liang-chih* refers primarily to the capacity of *hsin* to know and do good. Yang-ming's introduction of this term in his philosophy has already served to point out the richness of the notion of *hsin*. He speaks interchangeably of *hsin* and *liang-chih*, of *hsin*-in-itself and of *liang-chih*-in-itself. It is also obvious from the context that he sometimes refers to *liang-chih*-in-itself when he is using the word *hsin* or simply *liang-chih*, with the result that his meaning is not always clear. Nevertheless, from many unequivocal references to *hsin*-in-itself and to *liang-chih*-in-itself, he obviously wishes to use these terms to speak of *hsin* and *liang-chih* at a deeper level.

Yang-ming speaks of *liang-chih pen-t'i* as both the agent that achieves a certain end and as the end itself. Just as in his practical doctrine, the same word represents both the starting point and the end achieved. No doubt to Yang-ming's mind, the end is always present in the begin-

ning. One can become a sage because he already carries within himself
the seeds of sagehood, and self-realization is what brings the seeds to
their full development. The end, the goal, is never something out of
oneself. It is a presence that is already possessed, that can be developed
to the utmost, to the point at which one can truly say: "All things
are present in me. I have no greater joy than to find, when I look deep
into myself, that I am true to myself."[40]

PRINCIPLE OF LIFE AND CONSCIOUSNESS

Yang-ming speaks of *hsin*, the mind-and-heart, not merely as the
source and center of man's thoughts and intentions, emotions, and
decisions, but also as the source and center of his vital functions and
movements, and of all his conscious activities, sensory, and supra-
sensory. It is that which gives unity to multiplicity, which organizes
all our multiple experiences into one meaningful experience to which
we ourselves are identified.*

For this reason, Yang-ming explains that *hsin* or *liang-chih* is
present in every part of man, being that which unites the whole man.
It is present wherever consciousness functions. For "*hsin* (the heart)
is not just a piece of flesh with blood. It is wherever [we experience]
consciousness. For example, the ears and eyes can hear and see, and
the hands and feet can experience pain and irritation. All this consciousness [comes from] *hsin*."[41]

> Seeing, hearing, speaking, and moving are all [activities of] *hsin*
> (principle of consciousness). *Hsin*'s ability to see has the eyes as its
> channels. Its ability to hear has the ears as its channels. Its ability
> to move has the four limbs as its instruments. Without your *hsin*,
> there would be no eyes, ears, mouth, or nose.[42]

Yang-ming identifies the principle of moral activities to that of
vital consciousness. He also recommends that the gentleman's practice
of watchfulness over *hsin*, over the least movements of his mind-and-
heart, include as a matter of fact a certain control of the senses and

---

* Yang-ming is using a language akin to that of Aristotle, who defines the soul as
the determining principle of the living body—that which gives it life and unity,
motion, and essential nature. See his *Psychology*, Book II.

of the physical activities of the body. Recalling Lao-tzu's teaching that becautiful colors cause the eyes to be blind; beautiful sounds cause the ears to be deaf; beautiful tastes spoil the palate; and hunting and racing make a man mad,[43] he draws from it the moral exhortation that one should only see, hear, speak, and move when the occasions to do so are in accordance with propriety.[44]

Hsin, of course, is nothing other than *liang-chih*. Just as *hsin* is present in the senses, so it also is in the thinking mind, in our intentions and decisions; the same can be said of *liang-chih*.

Through conscious activity and experience of reality, man's mind-and-heart and senses penetrate all things, uniting, and even identifying, *hsin*-in-itself to Heaven-and-Earth and all things:

> The eye has no "substance" (*t'i*) of its own. It regards as [its] "substance," the color of all things. The ear has no "substance" of its own. It regards as [its] "substance," the sounds of all things. The nose has no "substance" of its own. It regards as [its] "substance," the odors of all things. The mind-and-heart has no "substance" of its own. It regards as [its] "substance," the right or wrong of the operations and responses of Heaven-and-Earth and all things.[45]

Color, for example—or sound in the case of the ear—is a quality of the object of perception as well as of the sense organ, the eye that sees it. Yang-ming resolves a problematic relationship between this "quality," and the "sensation" through which it is perceived, in terms of potentiality and actuality. Instead of denying the separate existence of the senses apart from the reality which they experience, or of *hsin* from the whole of the cosmos, he is asserting that, in the case of sensation, the "source" (*t'i*) of the activity (*yung*) meets the activity itself, which flows from and fulfills the very nature of the sense organ in the actualization of sight or hearing. Thus, according to him, neither the eye nor the ear can be properly understood outside of the experience of reality that it has. And also, eye, ear, or any or all of the other sense organs, together with *hsin*, the central unifier of all our experiences, sensory or otherwise, work together to bring the human person into dynamic contact with the whole of reality, and in so doing, unite him to the whole of the cosmos.

A SELF-TRANSCENDING STATE

Yang-ming has referred to *hsin* or to *liang-chih*-in-itself in negative terms, as the Taoist "Void" (*hsü*) and the Buddhist "Nothingness" (*wu*), and as the Great Void (*T'ai-hsü*). He is giving the cosmic connotations already associated with these terms to his *hsin*-in-equilibrium. This is hardly astonishing, especially since the Doctrine of the Mean Ch.1 has described "the *hsin*-in-equilibrium" as the "great root of all under Heaven," and "the *hsin*-in-harmony" as the "universal path of all under Heaven," and has added: "when equilibrium and harmony are realized, a happy order will prevail throughout Heaven-and-Earth, and the myriad things will flourish."[46]

Hence, "*hsin*-in-itself" represents, for Yang-ming, a psychological as well as metaphysical view of reality. It is a state of consciousness, a disposition of the spirit, which is to be achieved. Yang-ming is saying that so long as one follows spontaneously the naturally good promptings of the mind-and-heart, he will keep his *liang-chih*-in-itself free from unruly desires. When this is done, nothing in life can hinder the continual operation of *liang-chih* as it responds to events and affairs, entering into reality, absorbing reality by its activity, until it becomes one with all reality, and even the heart of all reality.

Yang-ming identifies *liang-chih*-in-itself to the Great Void, which "embraces all things without letting anything become a hindrance to itself":[47]

> The vacuity of *liang-chih* is [one with] the vacuity of the Great Void (*T'ai-hsü*). The nothingness (*wu*) of *liang-chih* is the formlessness of the Great Void. Sun, moon, wind, thunder, mountains, rivers, people, and things—all that have figure, shape, from, and color—all operate within this formlessness of the Great Void. None of them ever becomes a hindrance to Heaven. The sage merely follows the functioning of his *liang-chih*. Heaven, Earth, and the myriad things are all contained in its functioning and operating. How can there be anything else transcending *liang-chih* which can become a hindrance [to it]?[48]

For the man who strives after sagehood, wealth, proverty, gain and loss, love and hatred—desires for the one and fear of the other—all are worth as much as the passing storm and the floating smoke, which move and change in the Great Void, while the substance of the Great Void remains always vast and unlimited.[49]

A HIGHER REALITY

The Taoist notion of Void, the Buddhist notion of Nothingness, and the Sung philosophers' Great Void, do more than provide an insight into *liang-chih*-in-itself as a self-transcending state. They indicate that this state is symbolic of a higher order of ontological reality, which is contained in *liang-chih*-in-itself.

Yang-ming's writings and recorded dialogues present metaphysical discussions in contexts that are rather different from those in which the metaphysical vocabulary used by him first appeared in the writings of the Sung thinkers. Except for one known instance, he usually discusses *li* and *ch'i* less in relation to each other than in the relation of each to *hsin*, the mind-and-heart, his principal moral, psychological, and metaphysical interest.[50] He speaks little of *T'ai-chi*, the absolute, "ground of being," so prominent in the thought of Chou Tun-yi, Chu Hsi, and even of several early Ming thinkers who showed a much greater interest in the practice of self-perfection than in its metaphysical implications. When discussing Chou's teaching, he seems more concerned with explaining how *yin* and *yang* refer to the same *ch'i* that contracts and expands, while *tung* (activity) and *ching* (stillness) refer to the same *li*, which is sometimes hidden and sometimes manifest.[51] Thus, his emphasis is that *tung-ching* and *yin-yang* refer not to two different stages in the cosmic process, but to one and the same transformation. Given his understanding of *li* and *ch'i*, as also of his apparent approval of Chang Tsai's teaching of *T'ai-hsü* as the fullness of *ch'i*,[52] one may assume that he understands *T'ai-chi* to be that which gives a pattern of organization (*li*) to *T'ai-hsü*, and *T'ai-hsü* as that through which *T'ai-chi* functions and is made manifest. Together, they may be said to describe the absolute, the ground of being. And since *liang-chih*-in-itself has been identified to the Void (*hsü*), to Nothingness (*wu*), and to the Great Void (*T'ai-hsü*), there can be no doubt that it signifies the absolute—the one behind the many.

The absolute is by necessity that which transcends all other concepts, that which need not be only understood by one particular school of thought. As already mentioned, the discovery of the absolute by the Sung thinkers had been greatly aided by centuries of Buddhist-Taoist metaphysics and religious thinking. Yang-ming himself alludes to this when making use of the negative language of Buddhist-Taoist philosophical vocabulary:

> When the Taoists conclude that [*hsin*] is vacuous, can the sage himself add a bit of reality to that vacuity? When the Buddhists conclude that [*hsin*] is nothingness, can the sage himself add a bit of being to that nothing?[53]

Yang-ming's understanding of the absolute character of *hsin* or *liang-chih* is especially borne out on one occasion, when he was questioned by his disciple, Wang Chi, on the reality or illusoriness of all that makes up life and existence, as expressed by the Buddhist word, *hsiang* (*lakṣana*). His answer was:

> If *hsin* is present, there is reality,
> If *hsin* is absent, there is illusion.
> If *hsin* is absent, there is reality,
> If *hsin* is present, there is illusion.[54]

This seeming riddle can be interpreted in various ways. Taking the words as they are given, especialy *hsin* (mind), *wu-hsin* (no-mind or absence of the mind), *shih* (reality) and *huang* (illusion), and the method of negative logic that is used here to prove certain metaphysical affirmations,[55] one cannot deny the emphatically Buddhistic implications. This is further confirmed by the response it elicited from Wang Chi, who gave his own spontaneous interpretation:

> [When you say], "If *hsin* is present, there is reality, if *hsin* is absent, there is illusion," you are speaking of effort (*kung-fu*) from the point of view of [its] source and principle (*pen-t'i*).
> [But when you say], "If *hsin* is absent, there is reality, if *hsin* is present, there is illusion, you are speaking of the source and principle [of effort] from the point of view of effort [itself]."[56]

Yang-ming expressed approval of these words, which Ch'ien Te-hung, the editor of this part of the *Ch'uan-hsi lu* acknowledged not to have understood on that occasion.[57] If *pen-t'i* is the ultimate reality, as Wang Chi would have it,[58] and as Yang-ming's teachings on the *pen-t'i* of *hsin* would tend to support, then he seems to be saying that *hsin* and *wu-hsin*, just as reality and illusion, interpenetrate each other, and that the ultimate transcends metaphysical categories of "reality" and "illusion." On the basis of given language, Yang-ming was using the discrimination of opposing terms to obtain a meaning that answered Wang Chi's question.

Writing years later, Ch'ien Te-hung would remark that the answer indicated the fundamental unity, in Yang-ming's thinking, of *pen-t'i* (ultimate reality) and *kung-fu* (effort);[59] in other words, of Yang-ming's metaphysics and his ethics, of the discovery of the absolute in one as well as in the other.

ROLE OF CH'I

When asked whether inanimate beings also have *liang-chih*, Yang-ming replied:

> Man's *liang-chih* [acts also as] the *liang-chih* of plants and trees, tiles and stones. Without man's *liang-chih*, there can be no plants and trees, tiles and stones . . . . This is true not just of plants and trees, tiles and stones. Heaven-and-Earth will not be Heaven-and-Earth without man's *liang-chih*. For Heaven-and-Earth and the myriad things form basically one body with man. And this unity is best manifest in the spiritual understanding of man's *hsin*.[60]

It is the dynamic power of man's *liang-chih* which differentiates all things, knowing plants to be plants, and stones to be stones. It is also the dynamic power of man's *liang-chih* that overcomes the differentiations between various orders of beings, and even between the duality between the self and the nonself, by merging all into a higher form of unity. This is possible, Yang-ming asserts, because wind, rain, dew, thunder, sun and moon, stars, animals and plants, mountains and rivers, earth and stones, are all "one body with man." The same *ch'i* permeates all. For this reason—and Yang-ming offers this fact almost as a scientific proof for his "mystic" view of reality—grains and animals can nourish man's life, while herbs and minerals can heal human diseases. "Because they share the same *ch'i*, they can enter into [the bodies of] one another."[61]

In other words, if *liang-chih*-in-itself is capable of achieving unity out of the multiplicity of things, it is on account of a certain component that permeates all things. And this component is called *ch'i*.

And so, *liang-chih*-in-itself, the principle of life and consciousness, is not just a spiritual power or capacity. It too is spirit-in-matter.

For it too is permeated with *ch'i*, the same *ch'i* that permeates all other things, and which makes possible the passage from duality into non-duality.

Nevertheless, it would be a mistake to think that Yang-ming merely reduces *liang-chih*-in itself to *ch'i* or material force. The universal presence of *ch'i* is only given as a proto-scientific explanation of the unity of all things. But the only way man achieves this unity in himself is through *liang-chih*. And certainly, Yang-ming himself is more interested in the self-transcending state, which can be realized by *liang-chih*, than he is in the ubiquitous *ch'i*.

A puzzled disciple once questioned Yang-ming concerning his teaching about Heaven-and-Earth and all things having no meaning apart from man's *liang-chih*. He reasoned that since Heaven-and-Earth, the spiritual beings, and the myriad things had all existed since time immemorial, how could one presume that they would disappear, when the end came for the man whose *liang-chih* had attained this unity with all things? Yang-ming's answer shows that his teaching on unity and multiplicity, and the role of *ch'i* in this unity, concerns less the objective existence of the universe than the state of consciousness by which man's heart attains a certain oneness with all things:

> Consider the dead man. His spirit has drifted away and dispersed. Where are *his* Heaven-and-Earth and myriad things?[62]

Another example is given of the person when he is asleep. Yang-ming claims that *liang-chih* is always conscious, or rather, is always capable of consciousness, even when the person is asleep.

> As night falls, Heaven-and-Earth becomes an undifferentiated continuum. All forms and colors disappear. With man too, the ears hear nothing, the eyes see nothing .... It is the time when *liang-chih* is collected and concentrated. As Heaven-and-Earth open up again, all the myriad things reveal themselves .... With man also, the ears and eyes now hear and see .... It is the time when *liang-chih* begins its wonderful functioning.[63]

For Yang-ming, it is incomplete to speak of the nature of man and of things without also speaking of *ch'i*; just as it is incomplete to speak of *ch'i* without also speaking of nature (*hsing*) and even mind-and-heart (*hsin*). He has said: "*Ch'i* is [indistinguishable from] *hsing*, and *hsing* is [indistinguishable from] *ch'i*"[64] And he has also spoken of *hsin chih pen-t'i* as the True Self, master of the physical body:

> The *pen-t'i* of *hsin* is nothing other than *T'ien-li* (principle of Heaven). It is originally never out of accord with *li* (propriety). This is your True Self. This True Self is the master of [your] physical body. Without the True Self, there is no physical body. With it, one lives, without it, one dies.[65]

Thus, for the good of the physical body itself, one should take good care of the True Self,* keeping always intact its *pen-t'i*, and practicing caution and apprehension even when one is not seen or heard.[66] And then, as a man shreds off the superstructures that his "false self"— his ego—has erected as barricades behind which he has formerly attempted to hide himself and to limit his activity, as he clears away the selfish desires which hinder his inner vision, he will naturally discover this innermost core of his own being, this *liang-chih*, always shining even when it is temporarily obscured from view. He will then become transformed, completely true to himself, completely true to the universe in which he lives and acts, and following its natural courses of operation that will lead him to the realization of perfect goodness, which is the ultimate revelation of the absolute in himself.

HEART OF THE UNIVERSE

Once, when Yang-ming was taking a walk in the mountainous region of Nan-chen, one of his friends pointed to the blossoming trees, and asked: "If there is nothing in the world that is not outside of *hsin*, how is it that these trees hidden in the mountains can produce flowers that bloom and die without my *hsin* being in anyway involved?"

Yang-ming replied: "Before you see this flower, the flower and your *hsin* are both dormant. When you see this flower, its color suddenly becomes clear. This shows that the flower is not outside of your *hsin*.[67]

---

* The notion of the True Self suggests strong Buddhist influence, with truth understood as opposite of illustion. It also reminds us of a theme underlined by Hegel and repeated in his own way by F. H. Bradley (1846–1924), who speaks of the ultimate transformation of the true self in the Absolute. See especially *Appearance and Reality*, ch. 26.

For him, reality is always dynamic, related to man's *hsin*. By themselves, flowers in the wilderness can hardly be called "things" (*wu*). It is only when they have become known to man's *hsin* and, by being known, have become somehow activated by man, that they take on this status. Thus, Yang-ming presents man's *hsin* and *liang-chih* as the cause of the fundamental unity of all things: that which *knows* all things and has the power to direct all things to their proper ends.

In this context, one can also understand better Yang-ming's words concerning the "creative" power of *hsin* and *liang-chih*. In extravagant language, he has described *liang-chih* as the spirit which creates all things, Heaven, Earth, ghosts, and gods. "It is that to which there is no opposite [or equal]."[68]

Yang-ming speaks of man as "the heart (*hsin*) of Heaven-and-Earth."[69] For him, it is man, with his spiritual understanding and dynamic power for self-transcendence, who alone is capable of knowing and of reflecting all things, of giving ultimate meaning to all things as well as to his own existence. Man occupies the position of "heart," as the psychic center of the universe. For while men may be separated from one another and from all things on account of their physical forms or bodies, which limit them to specific positions in time and place, the heart of man transcends such limitation. It fills up Heaven-and-Earth and all things by means of its dynamic spirituality. In it, the unity of Heaven-and-Earth and all things is most clearly seen.

> My luminous spirit is the master of Heaven-and-Earth and all things. If Heaven is deprived of my luminous spirit, who is going to look into its height? If Earth is deprived of my luminous spirit, who is going to look into its depth? If spiritual beings are deprived of my luminous spirit, who is going to distinguish between their good and evil fortune, or the calamities and blessings they will bring? Separated from my luminous spirit, there will be no Heaven, Earth, spiritual beings, or myriad things, and separated from these, there will not be my luminous spirit.[70]

VI

THE CULMINATION: WU-SHAN WU-Ô

"Universal virtue" *(t'ung-te)* is that which one shares with ordinary men and women. "Heresy" *(yi-tuan)* is that which differs from what is present in ordinary men and women.[1]

So far we have spoken of the evolution of the "Confucian Way," and in particular, of the opening of new vistas on this Way by Wang Yang-ming. We have discussed the emergence of certain of his key ideas, the controversy resulting from them, and the gradual formulation of his all-embracing method of cultivation: *chih-liang-chih.* We have attempted to draw out certain spiritual and metaphysical implications of this doctrine, giving special attention to the notion of *hsin*-in-itself or *liang-chih*-in-itself, and discussing the problems ensuing from this teaching. It is the aim of this chapter to discuss the controversial aspect of Yang-ming's philosophy—that regarding the problem of evil, and the transcendance of both good and evil. From there, we shall see too how Yang-ming's insights took him beyond the traditional boundaries dividing orthodoxy and heresy, to the belief in the oneness and universality of the true Way, and in the validity of the insights of all—Taoist, Buddhist, and Confucian—as well as the subtle differences which divided the Taoist and Buddhist from the true Confucian. It will be pointed out that Yang-ming considered as real heretics, not the Taoists or the Buddhists, but the renegade Confucians, men who voiced admiration of and desire for wisdom but acted in contradiction to their words. We shall then discuss the "Way of Wang Yang-ming," making a few comments on the new criterion which he set for the judgment of truth and error: *liang-chih*. Regarded as that in us which is greater than ourselves—the absolute—it becomes therefore the authority for its own truth in the person whose mind-and-heart has become pure and transparent.

BEYOND GOOD AND EVIL

Yang-ming's treatment of the problem of evil is related to his discussions of *hsin*-in-itself. Where ontological imperfections are concerned, he says of flowers and weeds that the distinction made between them is purely arbitrary, since the same principle of life flows through both.[2] In the human realm, when *hsin* is full of the pure "principle of Heaven" (*T'ien-li*) and empty of all selfishness, it is then resting in the state of highest good, and may be described as being "neither good nor evil," should the word "good" be used merely in opposition to that of "evil." While Chu Hsi had never asserted clearly that emotions were not in themselves evil, Yang-ming pointed out this fact, affirming that evil only arises with deviation of the mind-and-heart from a state of equilibrium or harmony, before (*wei-fa*) or after (*yi-fa*) the rise of emotions:[3]

> The highest good [refers to] *hsin*-in-itself. When one deviates a little from this, there is evil. It is not as though there are two given opposites: good and evil. Good and evil are [two possible states] of one and the same thing [*viz.*, *hsin*].[4]

Without really explaining the rise of evil, Yang-ming's understanding of it stems from his holistic view of reality.[5] He recognizes that human nature-in-itself (the *pen-t'i* of *hsing*) is neither good nor evil, while capable of either. For both good and evil flow from the deepest recesses of man's mind-and-heart, being dependent on the activity of his intention. Neither can be defined in terms of social conventions, exterior to the person and his convictions. Offering as an example the human eye, which takes on different expressions of joy or anger, which may glance fully or directly at its object or merely glimpse it from its corners, he says that the eye itself should not be identified with any of its expressions but should be understood in terms of the distinctions between *t'i* (substance) and *yung* (activity). In describing human nature as good, Mencius was looking at it from its "substance" or source, as principle of its activity. In describing it as evil, Hsün-tzu was speaking mostly of abuses occurring in its activity. Mencius was anxious that efforts be made to keep nature-in-itself clear and manifest. Hsün-tzu desired that measures be taken to correct the abuses of its activity, an approach however that made the task of self-cultivation more difficult.[6]

For Yang-ming, the question of good and evil lies simply in following the "principle of Heaven" or in deviating from it. When asked whether the desire to remove weeds has at all a moral character, he refers the questioner back to his *hsin*-in-itself. All depends on the intentions, and that which moves the intentions. If *hsin* is moved inordinately by wrath or attachment, its desires are tainted by selfishness. If *hsin* is correct, the desires and the acts which flow from them will also be.[7] The act of removing weeds is in itself indifferent, but takes on a moral character when the mind-and-heart, with its intentions, intervenes.

While Yang-ming holds that *hsin* in a state of tranquility is in possession of the highest good, which, in turn, is beyond conventional distinctions of good and evil,* he does not require that a person make a special effort to "acquire" such a state. He expressed this opinion in a letter written in reply to questions from his disciple Lu Ch'eng.[8] Lu had questioned him on the Buddhist method of striving to "recognize one's original countenance (*pen-lai mien-mu*) at the time when one's mind-and-heart is clear of either good or evil thoughts."[9] He knew it to be different from the Confucian way, recommended by Yang-ming, of "investigating things as they come," that is, of attending to affairs with a sincere heart. He said that the only time he knows

---

* As Bertrand Russell asserts, mystical thought tends to regard a lower kind of good and evil as that which belongs only to the world of appearances, while the higher good is said to belong to Reality in its own nature, and is not opposed by any correlative kind of evil. See his essay, "Mysticism and Logic," 26. Russell supports his assertion by references to Hegel and Spinoza. In *Mysticism East and West*, R. Otto points out this characteristic as being common to both the medieval Christian, Meister Eckhart and the Indian, Shankara (9th cent. A.D.). See the Eng. trans., 23.

of, when one's *hsin* is without good or evil thoughts, is when he is passing from sleep to waking. But this condition does not last long. In an instant, thought and deliberation will quickly arise. Lu himself had frequently sought to recapture and maintain the point of stillness when the mind-and-heart is without good or evil thoughts, but found it extremely difficult to do so.

Yang-ming characterizes the Buddhist method mentioned 'by Lu as an "expedient" technique which may be practiced by those who do not yet understand or recognize their "*hsin*-in-itself." 'For those, however, who already understand *hsin*-in-itself, or *liang-chih*-in-itself, there is no longer any need to make use of this technique. Besides, he explains that to *desire* to think of neither good nor evil involves already some selfishness, for this implies the wish to recapture some past experience of [partial] enlightenment, which has served one well but is no longer necessary for self-cultivation.[10] A person who does so resembles a man who constantly keeps vigil at the site of a tree where he had once captured a hare. He ought rather to look for hares elsewhere.[11]

THE FOUR MAXIMS

In late 1527, Yang-ming was called back to active service from his life of retirement and was given the task of suppressing rebellions in Kwangsi. As he was about to start, two of his disciples, Wang Chi and Ch'ien Te-hung, were discussing the Master's teachings. Wang Chi recalled four sentences which, according to him, Yang-ming was fond of repeating in his instructions on *liang-chih*. They are:

1. The absence of good and evil (*wu-shan wu-ô*) characterizes the mind-in-itself (*hsin-chih-t'i*)
2. The presence of good and evil (*yu-shan-yu-ô*) characterizes the movement of its intentions (*yi-chih-tung*)
3. The knowledge of good and evil (*chih-shan chih-ô*) characterizes its innate capacity for wisdom (*liang-chih*)
4. The doing of good and ridding of evil (*wei-shan ch'ü-ô*) characterizes its investigation of things (*ko-wu*)[12]

These sentences comprise Yang-ming's well-known "Four Maxims," which, together with his publication of the Old Version of the Great

Learning, and of Chu Hsi's "mature views," left behind a legacy of controversy that continued long after his death. Certainly, the expression is ambiguous enough to allow a wide diversity of interpretations. If the explanation of *hsin*-in-itself as "a state of equilibrium" is kept in mind, we may seek to understand the first of his "Four Maxims" as referring to *hsin*-in-equilibrium, before it has been aroused (*wei-fa*) by the movement of emotions or desires, which, in turn, explains the second Maxim. According to this interpretation, the third and fourth Maxims treat of *liang-chih*, first as a capacity for the knowledge of the good, and then as a dynamic tendency that follows its own knowledge and judgment through the investigation of things that, for Yang-ming, means the rectification of the mind-and-heart. Thus it is a method that makes action of knowledge.[13]

At that time already, in 1527, Wang Chi and Ch'ien Te-hung could not agree on a definite interpretation of these Maxims. Ch'ien's great admiration for his Master caused him to consider the words to be part of Yang-ming's sacred teaching in its final form, while Wang Chi regarded them as a "tentative" explanation of *liang-chih*, saying that Yang-ming's insistence on personal insight precluded any desire to impose on others the definitive formulation of his thought. Following from the First Maxim, Wang Chi drew the inference that with the realization of *hsin*-in-itself being "neither good nor evil," would also come the understanding that its intentions, its knowledge, and all its acts could and should be "neither good nor evil."

> If we say that *hsin*-in-itself is characterized by the absence of good and evil, then [we should be able] to say the same of the intentions, of knowledge, and of things [or acts]. And if we say that the [movements of] the intentions are characterized by the presence of good and evil, then [we should also] say the same of *hsin*-in-itself.[14]

Wang Chi is speaking here of a complete "transcendence" of the ethical categories of good and evil which occurs with the recognition in oneself that *hsin* is, fundamentally speaking, independent of moral judgments while being at the same time the source of such judgments. The best example is of the sage, whose mind-and-heart is so well in tune with ultimate reality—the "highest good," which is beyond good and evil—that he can follow all its dictates without fear of making any moral transgression. But since every man is potentially a sage, the same truth can apply to every one provided he gains this realization that constitutes the experience of total, inner enlightenment.

On the other hand, Ch'ien has in mind, not enlightenment, but self-cultivation. He sees the First Maxim as expressive of our given *hsin*-in-itself, as it is in the state of "equilibrium," the recovery of which is the objective of all self-cultivation. The following three Maxims would therefore be the embodiment of a practically oriented teaching, aimed at the instruction of all whose hearts are no longer in possession of pristine innocence and purity. The distinction between good and evil should be maintained for the activities of the intentions, for the moral judgment exercised by *liang-chih*, as well as for the practice of "investigation of things" understood as "extension of *liang-chih*"—following always the judgment of our *liang-chih* in our acts. For "if there were no such distinctions between good and evil, where would there be any need for such effort [of self-cultivation]"?[15]

As the two disciples could not reach an agreement concerning the correct interpretation of the Master's teaching, they raised the issue again in the presence of Yang-ming. The Master declared that both were right. For him it was a question less of doctrine than of pedagogy. He said that the man of superior intelligence was capable of penetrating at once into the nature of *hsin*-in-itself and able to unite the internal and external in his efforts of self-cultivation. But for those men whose minds-and-hearts were less open to truth—being hindered by passions—it was more important to learn how to do good and avoid evil in their thoughts and intentions. Gradually, their minds-and-hearts would be freed of impurities, and *hsin*-in-itself would become clear and manifest. Yang-ming then added that Wang Chi's interpretations were suited for students of superior intelligence, whereas Ch'ien Te-hung's views could be useful to those less endowed. But he warned that there were few men in the world so intelligent that they would not need to make the effort to do good and avoid evil, but had merely to meditate upon *hsin*-in-itself. Rather, this could lead to the danger of emptiness and the void.[16]

If Yang-ming's teachings on the problem of evil and on the nature of *hsin*-in-itself are understood, there is no difficulty in accepting his conciliatory reply to both Wang Chi and Ch'ien Te-hung. It would seem that Wang Chi interpreted all Four Maxims as indicative of a superior stage of development and that, granted the truth of the First Maxim, as well as the attainment of a total, inner enlightenment, one could also say that all the spontaneous functionings of *hsin* should be as perfect as *hsin*-in-itself, and so need no longer be qualified either as good or evil. Action, after all, follows being.

Nevertheless, the fact that such a superior state of enlightenment, which brings about a transformation of all a man's interior and exterior activitism may be attained, and even instantaneously, does not necessarily mean that it will be attained by everyone. Just because a sage can always "follow the dictates of his own heart without transgressing the Mean" [*Analects* 2: 4] it does not follow that the ordinary man or woman can abandon all effort of self-cultivation and merely follow his or her instinctive desires.[17] The risk is quite obvious. Yang-ming's awareness of this made him utter the Four Maxims in their given form, and moved him to counsel the two disciples to give instruction on these according to the capacity of the student concerned.

> [For] it is not easy to find [many] persons of superior spiritual intelligence. Even Yen Hui and Ming-tao [Ch'eng Hao] dared not assume that they could [attain a] full realization of *hsin*-in-itself as soon as they applied themselves to the task.... Men's hearts are [usually] governed by [deep-seated] habits. If we do not teach them to devote themselves concretely and sincerely to the task of doing good and avoiding evil in their *liang-chih* rather than merely visualising in a vacuum their [*hsin*-in-itself], what they do cannot all be genuine, and what they cultivate will only be an empty and tranquil heart. This is no small mistake and should be exposed as early as possible.[18]

Yang-ming recognizes the possibility of a shortcut to wisdom and sagehood in a sudden, penetrating understanding of one's *hsin*-in-itself, which constitutes the experience of enlightenment, and which may suffice to keep the person in an enduring state of perfection. But he also knows that such an experience, while theoretically within reach of everyone, is not at the beck and call of anyone. It comes as a pure gift, to men of usually superior spiritual intelligence, who have kept their minds-and-hearts ready and alert. Nevertheless, for all who wish to perfect themselves, the great Way and the correct path remains that of extending and developing their *liang-chih*, through the acquisition of great sincerity of will and intention, and the conformity of every one of their acts with the inner light given to them all.

Enlightenment may act as a shortcut to wisdom. But there is no method for inducing this experience. It cannot and should not be sought after for its own sake. But enlightenment, and wisdom itself, is present seminally in *liang-chih*. A person need merely to follow its promptings, attentively but without fear or anxiety, to predispose himself for this gift, should it come. And then, failing its arrival, he can remain confident that wisdom is yet within reach, since wisdom is virtue, and virtue is practiced by the extension of *liang-chih*, which slowly makes of one, his *hsin* and ultimate reality, Tao. And then, once united with ultimate reality, this *hsin* becomes also its own authority, the reason for its having faith in itself, because it is the cause of its own attainment of sagehood and wisdom.

It may be said that Yang-ming advocates a kind of cultivation that akin to noncultivation, reminiscent of the ideas of both Chuang-tzu and the Ch'an Buddhists. This method is basically rooted in faith in the presence and possession within the self of the object of one's desires, hence excluding all anxiety concerning its acquisition. But a certain delicate balance must be maintained between the quest for *pen-t'i* (ultimate truth) and the need for *kung-fu* (self-exertion), to avoid such a proposed method of cultivation becoming mere hypocrisy. For while Yang-ming himself offers the example of a life of action permeated by contemplation, many of the restless and eccentric among his latter-day disciples would prefer to pass their time in empty speculation on the *pen-t'i* of their *hsin*, without embracing any discipline which a life of cultivation must require. As a result, even the understanding of the absolute character of *liang-chih* would be lost.

BEYOND ORTHODOXY

The doctrine of "Beyond Good and Evil" has important consequences for the problem of orthodoxy. The notion that the absolute is neither good nor evil is liberating to the human spirit, who realizes that value judgments are man-made whereas the real Good is suprahuman. It thus forces the mind to reconsider the question of the openness of truth and disregard the ideologist's tendency to regard truth as the possession of a few, usually of those steeped in classical learning. In Yang-ming's case, this insight has led him to another insight: that of the basic unity underlying all schools of thought dedicated to the quest of truth.

THE UNITY OF THE THREE WAYS

The movement of amalgamation of the Three Teachings began very early. The gradual fusion of Buddhist and Taoist teachings and practices with Confucian doctrine during the Sung dynasty has been described in Chapter 1. Chu Hsi's philosophical system and Lu Chiu-yüan's rival synthesis each represents a certain aspect of this fusion. Yang-ming took another, firmer step in this direction by his open discussion of the basic unity underlying the Three Teachings.[19]

Yang-ming was fond of saying, "Tao is everywhere." This can be understood in two ways. First, truth is seen as that which is within the access of all, rather than the private property of any one man or any one school of thought. It is both interior to man and universally present in all things through man. Second, the Way of acquiring this truth is also broad and open. Whichever "way" brings one there is the true Way.

One consequence of this attitude is his openness of mind regarding Buddhism and Taoism. The Two Teachings had long been regarded as standing in opposition to the Confucian Way. Yang-ming's attitude served to clarify the difference between truth and ideology, the latter implying the belief that truth is the possession of a select few, that falsehood reigns everwhere else.

This does not mean that Yang-ming does not recognize important differences existing between the Confucian teachings and the known doctrines of the Taoist and Buddhist schools. Where the differences were acute, he was unhesitating in pointing them out. But his continued tolerance of mind drew to him many disciples sympathetic to Taoism and Buddhism. Quite early in his career as a Confucian teacher, Yang-ming discussed with a disciple, Wang Chia-hsiu, the relative merits of the Three Teachings, agreeing with him that Buddhists and Taoists shared with Confucians the same ultimate quest but differed in their methods of going about it. "Students today need not attack Taoism and Buddhism. They should rather fix their determination earnestly on the doctrine of the sages, As this. . .is made clear to the world, Taoism and Buddhism will disappear of themselves. Otherwise, I fear that what we wish to learn will not be considered worthwhile by Buddhists and Taoists."[20]

The way of the sages, he said, was nothing other than that which was written in the human heart, notwithstanding the different names it might be given. "The man of humanity sees it and calls it humanity. The man of wisdom sees it and calls it wisdom. The common people act daily according to it without knowing it. . ."[21]

Yang-ming's teaching of *liang-chih* began around 1521. In 1523, he told his disciples that he was content to follow this inner light without regard of human respect. In speaking with Chang Yüanch'ung, he revealed that he no longer even wished to distinguish between the Three Teachings:

> The practices of the Two Teachings [Buddhism and Taoism] can all be my practices. When I complete and cultivate myself while developing my nature and fulfilling my destiny, [what I do] may be called Taoist. When I refrain from worldly contaminations while developing my nature and fulfilling my destiny, [what I do] may be called Buddhist. But certain scholars of these later ages have not understood the completeness of the Teaching of the Sages. For this reason, they have distinguished themselves from the Two Teachings as though there exist two views [of truth]. This is like having a large hall which can be separated into three rooms. The Confucians did not know that the whole place could be used by themselves. When they saw the Buddhists, they separated the room on the left to give it to them. When they saw the Taoists, they also separated the room on the right to give to them. And so the Confucians themselves remain in the middle.[22]

The Three Teachings, he said, were all at the disposal of the sage. He was free to follow the "Great Way", to accept the good and the true from everywhere. He added, however, thet a certain selfishness manifested by Buddhism and Taoism caused them to be known a "Small Way."[23]

Given the understanding of Yang-ming's openness regarding the universality of truth and the transcendence of orthodoxy, we can proceed to an examination of his conscious attitudes toward Taoism and Buddhism, as these are known to us through his writings and recorded dialogues.

YANG-MING AND TAOISM

Yang-ming had early contacts and long associations with Taoism and Taoist practices. He was even regarded by some people as being in possession of preternatural knowledge and powers. When Tung Chen, Prefect of Shao-hsing, wrote to ask for information regarding the "art of making rain," Yang-ming had to reply that he did not have any to impart, and that the virtuous behavior of the responsible official would be in itself much more important than any such knowledge, and also more efficacious in its power of moving Heaven. He dismissed the claim of those persons who specialized in the preternatural skills:

> All such reports [of their success] came to us from miscellaneous accounts of minor importance and not from the Classics. The gentleman tends to consider these happenings as coincidences. As to our present-day priests and sorcerers, many of them are little different from the loafers and ruffians of the marketplace. How can we expect them to rebuke the thunder, to call forth wind and rain?[24]

A later letter, dated 1508, to an unnamed friend, gives us Yang-ming's attitude toward "spirits and immortals." Admitting his own long-standing interest in the practice of Taoist methods of cultivation, he said with some irony:

> More than thirty years have passed. . . . My teeth are becoming unsteady, several of my hairs have turned white, my eyes cannot see beyond a foot's distance, and my ears cannot hear beyond the distance of ten feet. Moreover, I am often bedridden with sickness for entire months. My need of medicine as well as my capacity for it is growing. These are all the results of my interest in spirits and immortals.[25]

Yang-ming praised the Taoist sages and immortals, Kuang-ch'eng tzu[26] and Li Po-yang (Lao-tzu), as "perfect men, of genuine virtue and mature Tao, who lived in harmony with *yin-yang* and the four seasons, away from the world and its vanities." But they had unusual gifts, which come from "the work of Heaven, and are not what human force can bring about."[27]

To Lu Ch'eng, who was interested in Taoist methods of cultivating life, he cited the line from the epilogue of the treatise, *Wu-chen p'ien* (On Awakening to Truth): "The Yellow Emperor and Lao-tzu took pity on [the people's] covetous desires, and used the art of immortals to give them gradual and systematic direction."[28] He also argued that had an art of immortality really existed, the sages of antiquity, from Yao and Shun to Confucius, would have known it and would have revealed it to others too.[29] Disassociating himself explicitly from the Taoist concern for physical immortality, he spoke rather of the "immortality of virtue," reminding his friend that Yen Hui, the disciple of Confucius, died at the age of thirty-two, and yet continued to live.[30] "The cultivation of virtue and of life are the same thing. If what you call True Self (*Chen-wo*) could remain vigilant when not seen, and apprehensive when not heard. . .then your *ch'i* (ether) and your *ching* (sperm) would be collected, and what the Taoists call physical immortality would also be present."[31]

> There is only one *liang-chih*. In terms of its marvelous functioning, it is called "spirit"; in terms of its universal operation, it is called "ether," and in terms of its concentration and coagulation, it is called "sperm." How can it be understood as [objects with] shapes and forms and locations?[32]

The Taoist language of cultivation is thus applied to a higher plane —of ultimate truth. In identifying *liang-chih* to spirit, ether, and sperm, Yang-ming indicates the deeper longing of Taoism—to discover one's True Self, to unify the profound energies of body and spirit, and to extend this unity to all things.

Toward the end of his life, he expressed in a poem the fulfillment of all his desires in the discovery of *liang-chih*. It presents a summary of his personal evolution:

> Immortality—I covet in vain
> Lacking pills and money
> Famous mountains I have combed,
> Till my temples yield silken hairs.
> My light body fettered by *smṛti* (*nien*)
> Daily move I farther from *Tao*.
> Awakened suddenly, in middle age, I find

The Pill of Nine Returns,
No need for oven, nor for tripod:
Why seek I *k'an* and why *li*
No end is there, nor beginning.
So too, for birth and death—
The magicians' wise words
Only increase my doubts;
Confusedly these old men
Transmit arts difficult and complex,
In me is *Ch'ien* (Heaven), in me *K'un* (Earth)
I need not seek elsewhere—
The thousand sages pass as shadows,
Liang-chih alone is my guide.[33]

Yang-ming and Buddhism

In the Intruduction, mention has already been made of the gradual fusion between philosophical Taoism and Buddhism, which led to a gradual loss of identity on both sides.[34] This is to be kept in mind while discussing Yang-ming's overt attitudes to Buddhism. Indeed, in spite of his stronger recorded contacts with Taoism, Yang-ming has been more often accused of being a Ch'an Buddhist in Confucian disguise than for his Taoist connections. This can be understood from the greater antagonism in which orthodox Confucianism held the Buddhist teachings, for their alleged alien origins, as well as for the stronger appeal which Ch'an Buddhism had for the more speculative minds. Yang-ming himself displayed both a fondness for Buddhist vocabulary, parables and riddles, and even fundamental insights, as well as a disapproval of the Buddhist tendency of withdrawal from society. His language abounds with Buddhist allusions, to a greater extent than that of the Ch'eng brothers, Chu Hsi, and even Lu Chiu-yüan. Yang-ming manifests his acquaintance with many important texts of Mahayana Buddhism, including the *Saddharma pundarīka* (Lotus Sutra), the *Sūrangama* (*Leng-yen ching*), the *Vajracchedikā Prajñā-Pāramitā* (Diamond Sutra), the *Lankāvatāra* (*Leng-chia ching*), the *Parinirvāna* (*Nieh-p'an ching*), the *Yüan-chüeh ching* ("Perfect Enlightenment" Sutra), and the *Ch'uan-hsin fa-yao* of Hsi-yün. He cites most frequently from the *Platform Scripture* of the Sixth Patriarch, and the *Transmission of the Lamp*.[35] He shows a certain familiarity with the biographies of many eminent Ch'an monks and their sayings.[36] He uses quasi-Buddhist techniques in the instruction of disciples. When asked by Hsiao Hui how selfish desires were to be overcome, his reply was reminiscent of the words of the Ch'an patriarch Hui-k'o (486–593) to his disciple and successor, Seng-ts'an (fl. 592): "Give me your selfish desires, and I shall overcome them for you."[37]

Yang-ming's metaphysical discovery of *hsin-chih pen-t'i* or *liang-chih pen-t'i* as ultimate reality, together with his assertion that *pen-t'i* is identical to *kung-fu* (self-exertion) and *vice versa*,[38] is especially reminiscent of the Buddhist teaching of the interpenetration of the real and the phenomenal, of the presence of wisdom or enlightenment (*bodhi*) in the concrete human existence with its limitations and afflictions (*kleśa*),[39] and of the identification of the "ordinary mind" (*p'ing-ch'ang hsin*) with the Way (Tao)[40]—that which is beyond knowledge and action, good and evil. On the practical level, this insight explains Yang-ming's preference for a method of cultivation which emphasizes joy and spontaneity, and his attitude regarding any anxiety for the acquisition of wisdom as being harmful to its very acquisition. This recalls to mind the Ch'an Buddhist expression of having "no-mind" (*wu-hsin*),[41] that is, of emptying one's mind of attachment to particular desires.

An examination of Yang-ming's writings shows a stronger Buddhist influence in Parts II and III of *Ch'uan-hsi lu* than in Part I, which was first published in 1518. Although one must take into account the persons to which Yang-ming was addressing himself, whether in writing or in speech, and the type of questions he was endeavoring to answer, it appears rather certain that his spiritual and intellectual evolution led to an increasing acceptance of Ch'an Buddhist philosophical ideas, although he had earlier repudiated the Buddhist-Taoist practice of withdrawal from secular affairs. This is also borne out by the study of his poems. Although these are difficult to date, it seems that those poems generally considered to have been written before 1515, while containing Ch'an Buddhist allusions, frequently offer also an explanation that the teaching itself is not Buddhist,[42] whereas those poems written much later, especially around or after 1524, no longer express such reservations.[43] For this reason also, Ch'en Chien cited many of Yang-ming's poems to demonstrate the extent of Buddhist influence on his thought.[44] In one such poem, Yang-ming visualizes his own role of prophet to a world of inert men:

> The whole world is drowned in sleep.
> But the lonely man—who is he?—by chance still sober
> Cries aloud but cannot stir the others,
> Who stare at him in great astonishment.
> Calling him mad, they rise up
> Only to surround him and belabor him.
> The waters of Chu and Ssu covered the sounds of the Golden Bell
> The rivers Lien and Lo carried faint echoes.
> Who is sounding the poison-painted drum,
> While the hearers remain dull and unresponsive?
> Alas, what are you all intent on doing,
> Going about, toiling so restlessly?
> How can you be made to hear this drum,
> Which can open your Heaven-endowed intelligence?[45]

The language of this poem is certainly Buddhist. The concern of awaking the sluggish world is also in accord with Mahayana teachings. But the persevering endeavor expresses a deep sense of social responsibility that is more Confucian, unless it be said that Yang-ming has carried the insights of Ch'an Buddhism to their logical conclusions, by deriving from the teaching of the interpenetration of the real and the phenomenal, of the sacred and the profane, the understanding that the Confucian ideal of social involvement is quite compatible with the highest goals of sagehood, as these are understood by Ch'an Buddhism itself.[46] As he has said:

> The Buddhists are afraid of the burden involved in the father-son relationship and so run away from it. They are afraid of the burden involved in the ruler-minister relationship and so run away from it. They are afraid of the burden involved in the husband-wife relationship and so run away from it. They do all this because [these] . . . relationships involve attachment to the phenomenal order (*hsiang*, Sanskrit, *lakṣana*) . . . . We Confucians accept the father-son relationship and fulfill this [responsibility] with humanity. We accept the

ruler-minister relationship and fulfill it with righteousness. We accept the husband-wife relationship and fulfill it with attention to the separate functions it involves. When have we been *attached* to these relationships?[47]

THE REAL HERETICS

In the final analysis, Yang-ming considered as the worst enemies of the school of sages, not the Buddhists and Taoists, but the "mediocre scholars" of his own days. He compared these scholars to Yang Chu and Mo Ti, and himself to Mencius, who condemned them as "heretics" and exposed the fallacies of their teachings. While Mo Ti supposedly erred in preaching a universal love that went too far in the practice of humanity, and Yang Chu erred in advocating an individualism that went too far in the practice of righteousness toward one's self, Yang-ming considered the scholars of his days who treated the study of Confucian doctrines as a means of personal advancement on the official ladder to be teachers neither of humanity nor of righteousness.[48] Their misinterpretations of true doctrine misled others, turning them to the study of Taoism and Buddhism, the teachings of which, he claimed, were in fact superior to those of the mediocre Confucians.[49] All his life, Yang-ming showed his great abhorrence for such hypocrites, who paid lip service to the words of the sages, while contradicting them by their manner of life. If, on the one hand, even Buddhists and Taoists possessed valid insights into the true Way, on the other, the false doctrine of the worldly scholars was to the true teaching of the sages what *mock jade* was to jade.

> There is only one Tao . . . . The mediocre Confucian scholars all start from a partial view of it, and embellish their image with comparisons and imitations giving expression to it through divisions of chapters and sentences and borrowed explanations. They are used to such practices, which can instill enough self-confidence producing sections and items which give them a sense of make-belief security, with which they can deceive themselves and others, remaining in this pitfall for a whole lifetime without realizing it.[50]

The root of their evil was less the fragmentary nature of their insights than the moral bankruptcy of their intentions. For selfishness

corrupted their knowledge, enlisting their learning in service of hypocrisy.

> The width of their knowledge of memorized texts merely serves to
> increase their pride. The wealth of learning they possess merely con-
> tributes to their evil actions. The breadth of information they have
> accumulated by hearing and seeing merely helps them to indulge in
> arguments. Their skill in prosewriting merely covers up their hypoc-
> risy.[51]

Yang-ming's attitude toward the mediocre Confucians was not
lost on those who were the object of his criticisms. These scholars
never ceased to launch counterattacks of heresy and of false learning
against Yang-ming himself. They pestered and persecuted him all
during his life and even after his death. Yang-ming's student, Ch'ien
Te-hung, has testified to this fact:

> Our Teacher was, during his whole life, the object of criticisms,
> slander, intrigues, and other attempts to destroy him. He survived the
> dangers of ten thousand deaths. Yet he always kept himself busy
> and never relaxed his effort of teaching, lest we might fail to hear the
> real Way, and fall into the pitfalls of worldly honor and profit and
> unprincipled opportunities, and degenerate unconsciously to the
> manners of barbarians and beasts. . . .[52]

And so, Yang-ming has always advocated an authentic humanism,
based on the self-perfecting *hsin*, while opposing a false humanism,
which pays lip service to moral ideals, but risks the loss of its own
hsin, through a pattern of behavior which is not in accord with it.

THE NEW CRITERION

For Yang-ming "virtue" is that which is universally present in
ordinary men and women. "Heresy" (*yi-tuan*), on the other hand,
is that by which one diverges from this universal "virtue."[53] He was
anxious that no exterior criterion be set up for truth and orthodoxy
and the quest for sagehood, which should discourage people from
its pursuit. He said to his disciple Lu Ch'eng, "If one has faith in
liang-chih and makes effort only [to extend] *liang-chih*, one will find
that the thousand classics and canons will all conform to it and all

heretical doctrines. . . .will be destroyed when measured against it."[54]

For Yang-ming, *liang-chih* is the only criterion of truth, just as its extension to the utmost is the only requisite for the attainment of sagehood. He recalled to Nieh Pao the experiences of Confucius himself—how he was criticized, ridiculed, slandered, denounced, and insulted. "People like the gatekeeper [of Shih-men] and the basket-carrier, [considered] at the time to be virtuous men, said of [Confucius] that 'he knows a thing cannot be done and still wants to do it,' and that 'he is contemptible and obstinate, and should stop seeking [official service] when no one really knows him.' Even his disciple Tzu-lu rebuked him for going to see a woman of ill repute."[55] And yet— Yang-ming reasoned—the Master could not but act as he did because he was so keenly aware of his responsibilities toward the world.

Yang-ming declared that he had the same *hsin* as Confucius—he felt the same urgent responsibility to save a world that was proceeding headlong to destruction. It did not matter to him that others might consider him insane. For his was the insanity of a man willing to risk drowning himself to save those who were sinking. "The minds (*hsin*) of all the people in the world are my mind (*hsin*) also. If there are people in the world who are insane, how can I not be insane also? If there are people who have lost their minds, how can I not lose my mind?[56] And then, expressing belief in his own charismatic mission, he says:

> How dare such an unworthy person as I regard the Way of the Master to be my own responsibility? However, to some extent, I realize in my mind that there is [the same] sickness and pain in my own body, and so I look everywhere for someone who may be able to help me, with whom I may discuss ways and means of removing this sickness and pain. If I can really find heroic men who have the same ambitions, in order to help one another to promote the spreading of the learning of *liang-chih* in the world . . . and bring about a state of Great Unity [*Ta-t'ung*], then my insanity should certainly be cured all of a sudden, and I can finally avoid losing my *hsin* . . . .[57]

Is it, after all the Classics, together with the officially approved commentaries, that define the meaning of wisdom and point out the way toward its acquisition, or is it rather the sage, the man who has succeeded in finding and becoming his True Self, whose mind-and-heart has become completely identified with the true and the good and the beautiful, who fixes the criteria for true wisdom and authentic learning? And, if the sage, the man qualified to write new Classics, is the best arbiter of matters orthodox and heretical, the judge of true and false wisdom, may one not say, with Yang-ming, that he is so by right of, and through the use of, that which makes him a sage: his *liang-chih*? And again, is not this *liang-chih* present in every man, the seed of his possible greatness and sageliness, the criterion of its own movements, the authority for its own beliefs, and its own wisdom?

In a series of four poems written for the instruction of his disciples, Yang-ming has expressed his ideas of *liang-chih* as the criterion of true doctrine, which can be compared to the authority of Confucius himself, to that of the Taoist text, the *Ts'an-t'ung ch'i*, which "tallies the ideas of the Confucian Book of Changes with those of the Taoist classic, *Lao-tzu*,"[58] and to the mariner's compass:

> Confucius resides in every man's *hsin*,
> Hidden by distractions of ears and eyes.
> The real image being now discovered,
> Doubt longer [your] *liang-chih*.

> Why, sir, are you always agitated:
> Wasting efforts in the world of sorrows—
> Know you not the sages' occult word,
> *Liang-chih* is your *Ts'an-t'ung ch'i*,

> In every man there is a [mariner's] compass,
> His mind-and-heart is the seat of a thousand changes.
> Foolishly, I once saw things in reverse:
> Leaves and branches sought I outside.

> The soundless, odorless moment of solitary self-knowledge
> Contains the ground of Heaven, Earth, and all beings.
> Foolish is he who leaves his inexhaustible treasure,
> With a bowl (*t'o-po*), moving from door to door, imitating the
>   beggar.[59]

Indeed, the line that divides the authentic disciple of the sages from the Ch'an Buddhist is a very narrow one. Yang-ming knows that scholars who are interested in the inner cultivation of mind-and-heart are frequently accused of being Ch'an Buddhists in Confucian disguise. He has now given his own criterion, *liang-chih*, and radically changed the notion of orthodoxy, declaring as real heretics, not the adherents of alien creeds or practices, but the hypocrites of the Confucian school itself, who mouth traditional ideals but deny them in life and action. By rendering obsolete the old criteria of correctness and orthodoxy, which were applied to a man's thoughts rather than to his life and action, and by substituting a new one, that of personal insight into the good, he has performed a signal service to the cause of sagehood itself. He has declared himself in favor of truth rather than of ideology and of virtue rather than of worldly success. He has also pointed out that sagehood confers an assurance of its own correctness or "orthodoxy," because it reveals to man that in him which, united to all things is greater than himself: his *hsin*, which is also called Tao.

VII

CONCLUSION

How perfect are the secret springs of Heaven and Earth! A divine abyss separates madness (*k'uang*) and sagehood—Truth and error diverge on an infinitesimal point.[1]

A_S A STUDY of the philosophy of Wang Yang-ming, with special reference to its "correctness" or "orthodoxy," the underlying polarity in the foregoing chapters of analysis has been that of "orthodoxy *versus* heterodoxy." I have pointed out the inherent ambiguity of the problem, with reference to the development of the Confucian tradition as a whole, and particularly with regard to the "Confucian *versus* Ch'an Buddhist" debate generally associated with the criticisms of Yang-ming's philosophy. I have also indicated how Yang-ming's fundamental insight into the absolute nature of *hsin*-in-itself as being neither good nor evil brought his thinking beyond the ordinary notions of orthodoxy and heresy. But I have not settled certain problems that arise from these insights. Granted that Yang-ming was influenced by Ch'an Buddhist thinking, one might yet ask how much of his thought was Buddhist, and how much Confucian, at least as these were understood to be in his own days? Besides, a deeper question could emerge concerning the nature of Yang-ming's thinking, whether that it be more philosophical or religious. Was the experience that underlay his metaphysics and ethics of a religious and mystical kind, or was it rather the result of speculative, even dialectical reasoning?

In this final chapter of critique and inquiry, it is my intention to review the results of the analysis of the preceding chapters, in terms of certain polarities that are present within the framework of the broad "Orthodoxy *versus* Heresy" controversy. I have in mind the tensions between the Inner (*nei*) and the Outer (*wai*), between Enlightenment (*wu*) and Cultivation (*hsiu*), and that which has greater relevance to the problem of orthodoxy: between Self and Authority. There is also a very basic dichotomy, which Yang-ming had sought to reconcile, and which I have termed, between the Metaphysical (*t'i*) and the Moral (*yung*).[2] I propose to do this by examining at closer range the similarities and differences between the philosophy of Chu Hsi on the one side, and that of Wang Yang-ming on the other, referring back to Lu Chiu-yüan, Chu's contemporary and Wang's "mentor"— although separated from him by three hundred years of history— whenever this seems helpful. And then, I shall discuss in greater detail the questions as to whether Yang-ming could be considered Confucian at all, whether his teaching is "simple and easy," or profound and subtle, and whether it is more religious than philosophical. In other words, was he a sage, a mystic or a thinker, or was he all three? And was his discovery an immanent reality, or was it also transcendent?

THE POLARITIES IN YANG-MING'S THOUGHT

I admit readily that, of the polarities just mentioned, the *nei-wai* and *t'i-yung* may be understood in a similar way, both to refer to the "latent" and the "manifest," and even the *wu-hsiu* tension may be explained in terms of the emphasis on one or the other of this same metaphysical dichotomy, For the sake of inquiry, when I refer to the *nei-wai* or Inner-Outer tension in this chapter, I have in mind the attractions of the contemplative and the active ways of life; when I refer to the *t'i-yung* pattern, I am speaking in terms of the Metaphysical-Moral concerns; when I speak of the *Wu-hsiu* debate, it will be with regard to the roles of Enlightenment and Cultivation in the quest for sagehood. Thus, within the context of this chapter, the Inner-Outer and Enlightenment-Cultivation tensions both pertain more to the realm of *yung* (ethics) than to that of *t'i* (metaphysics). But it should be kept in mind that Yang-ming himself saw a fundamental unity between *t'i* and *yung*, finding the former in the latter, just as he regarded contemplation as that which should permeate action, and enlightenment as that which could be attained through cultivation.

At first sight, it may seem that Lu's attempt to internalize the whole pursuit of wisdom to his philosophy of a self-determining, self-perfecting *hsin*, tends to the "inner" pull of self-cultivation in silence and contemplation at the expense of social involvement. Chu's balanced method of both "reverence" and "extending knowledge," on the other hand, appears to be more "outer"-oriented, since it takes the person out of himself, to the investigation of truth in classical texts. In reality, however, Chu's attention was focused on *hsing* (nature), which he regarded as containing all "goodness" (*li*) in potency but which awaits the effort of being cleared from the obscuration cast upon it by passions or evil desires. It is therefore a more passive principle, which must be acted upon, through the work of *hsin*, the mind-and-heart, which controls both *hsing* (nature) and *ch'ing* (emotions). Chu placed much emphasis on quiet-sitting, as a technique that helps to restore to man his originally good nature. Lu's vantage-point was quite different. His basic principle, *hsin* (mind-and-heart), is a source of dynamic action.[3] While its development is promoted by the practice of quiet-sitting, it is not necessarily dependent upon this "inner"-oriented technique. It is, by nature, independent. Thus it need not appear so remarkable that, with all his desires for social involvement, Chu had led the life of a near-recluse, while Lu, who never attained a very high position, was content to exercise the duties of the minor official posts entrusted to him.[4] But the culmination of Lu's philosophy would come only with Wang Yang-ming, whose life revealed the same contrary pulls between concerns for the "inner" and "outer" realms of existence, but whose method of self-perfection, based on a dynamic *hsin*, which confronted all events as they occur, would direct him to undertake social and political activities as the opportunities arose.

Yang-ming moved from Confucian studies to the investigation of Taoist and Buddhist beliefs and practices, even abandoning the world for some time. This gave him a certain peace. He came near to believing that he had found in this "unorthodox" way of life the secret of attaining sagehood. But he was troubled by their divergences from Confucian teaching, and by their lack of attention for action and social involvement. "I was torn between following them and rejecting them, between believing them and doubting them."[5] Not satisfied with whatever gains he made in insight and virtue, he was several times near the verge of declaring that sagehood was not universally accessible, since he himself could not get within sight of the goal.

The quest for a method brought Yang-ming first to the doctrine of the "Unity of Knowledge and Action," which evolved, through personal effort of realization accompanied by refinement of thought, to the "extension and realization of the Knowledge of the Good," and to "Unity of Man with All Things." For Yang-ming's understanding of "knowledge" was not the knowledge of particular truths, but that of universal truth, of wisdom, of the Tao, the possession of which must necessarily be accompanied by the development of a perfect, moral character. The same, however, cannot be said of his understanding of "action," which, by its very nature, refers to innumerable, particular acts. But for the man determined to find wisdom through the development of his *hsin*, every act merges with the whole effort (*kung-fu*) of self-realization, eventually bringing him into the consciousness of the very oneness of his being with all things. He will then find Heaven (*T'ien*) and Earth (*Ti*) and the myriad creatures in himself. Seen 'in this perspective, one may explain the assertion, *yü wan-wu yi-t'i* (being one body with all things), as "making all things (*wu*) one." Through moral action allied to knowledge, man comes into vital contact with things—whether persons or events—and transforms all into his own life, making of all, a unity identified with himself. For Yang-ming, the reconciliation of the "inner-outer" tension was clearly in the realization of "sageliness within and kingliness without."[6]

ENLIGHTENMENT (WU) VERSUS CULTIVATION (HSIU)[7]

Ch'eng Yi and Chu Hsi both recognized the universal capacity for sagehood and wisdom. For them, however, its acquisition was a task that required tremendous effort, usually the fruit of a sudden inner enlightenment, which follows the accumulation of encyclopaedic knowledge, and the permeation of the spirit of "reverence" and "stillness" into daily living. Lu Chiu-yüan disagreed with the assumption underlying this approach. For him, human nature is, in itself, an entirely adequate instrument of its own perfection. It is not merely the tranquil locale where enlightenment occurs. It is identical with the dynamic *hsin* (mind-and-heart). Lu regarded this *hsin* to be somehow one with ultimate reality (Tao). Whoever sought enlightenment should therefore grapple with this *hsin*, this Tao, without allowing himself to be distracted by other affairs and persuits. Lu once said of Chu that he could be compared to the sublime Mount T'ai, "but, unfortunately, in spite of his [great] learning, he has not seen Tao. He merely wastes his own energy."[8] It was the comment of an "en-lightened" man, on an "unenlightened" man.

Lu pointed out the correct direction to sagehood. But he merely spoke of it in random fashion, as a support for his exclusive concern for "honoring one's virtuous nature." Yang-ming pushed it to its final conclusions. Much more than Lu, he always referred to his personal experience as the proof for the truth of his words. Yang-ming's inner life developed through a series of enlightenments.[9] But the insights he attained in these experiences helped him to develop a method, not of "enlightenment"—for there is no such method—but of "cultivation." The "extension of *liang-chih*" refers not to the application of innate, unchanging, ready-made concepts of right and wrong to life and action,[10] but rather to the gradual and steady development of one's character, through an experience acquired in an orderly manner, with emphasis on searching in one's personal behavior, although without discounting the role of classical learning. It was his way of coming to grips with life at its deepest level, of pre-disposing the self for entrance into a state of vital sympathy and cosmic consciousness with all things.

The formulation of the "Four Maxims" has often been interpreted as Yang-ming's preference for enlightenment and rejection of culti-vation in the quest for wisdom. A careful study of his answer to Wang Chi and Ch'ien Te-hung shows that this was not the case. Yang-ming saw clearly that enlightenment could not be induced at will. But there is no reason why wisdom itself would not be within the access of all. Yang-ming was a teacher of virtue, a man who believed in "polishing the mirror," in developing the mind-and-heart. He in-dicated a "Way" of acquiring wisdom; he did not presume to have the power to "give" it to others.

A sudden, traumatic experience of "enlightenment" is useful but not absolutely essential to the quest for sagehood, which can also be attained through constant development by cultivation of the dynamic *hsin*, The effort of cultivation is not to be strained or painful, but spontaneous and confident. After all, the quest is for that which one already possesses, if only in potentiality.[11] The discovery will come as a revelation of that which is hidden within oneself. And it will be a revelation of all things, as reflected in a clear mirror. Instead of deepening a dichotomy between "enlightenment" and "cultivation," Yangming opted for their reconciliation. Enlightenment need not be sudden; it may come gradually, through the process of cultivation.

A question that naturally arises is the foundation of the reality of one's "enlightenment," and finally, of one's "sageliness." How can a man decide that his experience of enlightenment is genuine, or that his many insights derived from earnest inquiry in reflective thought as well as from virtuous behavior, are authentic? How indeed can a human being, so limited in his capacity for that which is unlimited—wisdom— know for sure that he has acquired enough of this ultimate truth to consider himself "wise"? It is a question of authority. But whose authority?

This question must have pursued Yang-ming throughout his own quest for wisdom, for virtue, for the absolute. It colors the entire evolution of his thought. It underlines the whole foundation of his method.

"SELF" VERSUS "AUTHORITY"

At first sight, the philosophy of Ch'eng Yi and Chu Hsi seems to support the role of authority in the acquisition of wisdom and in the ordering of society. The harmonious universe of *li* and *ch'i*, which revolves around the notion of *T'ai-chi*—the Ultimate in being and goodness—may argue well for a hierarchic structure of a strongly centralized government.[12] The appeal to the Classics and to the sages, considered as "lineal forebears" of the exponents of this philosophy, provides another cornerstone for a regimented system of education. The truth however is far more complex. The philosophy that Ch'eng Yi and Chu Hsi developed was founded on an independent interpretation of the Classics. Until such time when they were officially recognized as transmitters of the Confucian heritage,[13] the authority to which they gave adherence was indeed higher than the state—that regarded itself as guardian of classical exegesis—higher, indeed, than the Classics. In fact, they relied primarily on their own authority, as self-appointed interpreters of the sacred message. For this reason, they acted as moral judges of their sovereigns rather than as dutiful ministers.

Lu Chiu-yüan, on the other hand, appears to be a rebel against the entire classical tradition, and a prophet of pure insight. He proposed the recognition of *hsin* (mind-and-heart) as Tao (ultimate truth). He sought to internalize wisdom and virtue completely, and to make the pursuit of sagehood entirely independent of classical studies. Naturally, such a rejection of external authority did not bring to his philosophy, the favor of state power, which always relies on external sanctions.

In fact, Lu was only inferring certain logical conclusions from Ch'eng Yi's and Chu Hsi's attitudes toward the Classics. He clearly pointed out the significance of that "higher authority," to which appeals had been made: it was the sages' *hsin*, as Ch'eng and Chu also acknowledged, but it was seminally present in man's *hsin*, a fact that neither Ch'eng nor Chu clearly demonstrated. In Yang-ming's case also, instead of being accepted as an important contribution to the "Confucian quest," his teachings were criticized as "heresy" on doctrinal grounds—because based on "private interpretations" of the Classics, through his accommodation of Ch'an Buddhist ideas. The controversies he sustained led Yang-ming eventually to question not only the exact role of personal insight or of intellectual inquiry, of inner enlightenment, which relies solely on insight, and of cultivation, which includes studies, in the quest for wisdom, but even of the very role of "authority" itself—whether of the sages, of the Classics, or of government—in the determination of truth. For if authority can be detrimental "to that which it claims to defend, by what right does it continue to demand respect and adherence?

Yang-ming's debate with Chan Jo-shui put the focus on the problem of the "criteria" of truth. Chan admitted the value of insight, but regarded the Classics as a source of rich inspiration and insight that should not be set aside. Yang-ming, on the other hand, tended to give other pursuits in life equal value with the study of the Classics. But then, to what authority can the man of insight appeal as a support for the correctness of his views? If truth is only regarded as the product of action—of trial and experience—and therefore quite independent of intellectual knowledge, he can only appeal to his own moral character as final arbiter. His only authority is himself.

This would be the case if man's moral character, his *hsin*, contains nothing greater than itself. Yang-ming, however, discovered in it a certain self-transcending quality. It is the agent as well as the goal of sagehood. It is also the meeting place of Heaven-and-Earth and all things. Yang-ming spoke of *hsin* and *liang-chih* as the ultimate authority of wisdom and perfection. He formulated the first of the Four Maxims in this light, explaining how *hsin*-in-itself, the final and most profound center in man, that which is beyond ordinary consciousness and yet capable of being "awakened" to itself through enlightenment, defies ethical differentiation and judgment. Basically, it is responsible to itself alone. Its authority, with regard to itself, is absolute. It is a more fitting object of "faith" than the Classics.

Thus the authority to which Yang-ming appealed, as support for the truth of his teaching, and as guarantee for the success of his "Way," is identical with the core of his teaching: *hsin*, or *liang-chih*. This self-determining agent of wisdom and perfection, is transformed into an absolute norm, an authority for itself. Yang-ming advocated having faith in *liang-chih*.[14] He identified the object of faith with this authority itself. He was speaking of ultimate truth, the possession of which is wisdom.

Paradoxically, this philosopher who acknowledged no earthly authority, who desired to subject the words of Confucius himself to the examination of his own *hsin*, recognized one sole authority: that of *hsin*, the vehicle itself of wisdom. For him, this refers not merely to his own mind-and-heart, which is one and the same with the minds-and-hearts of all the sages, past and present, but also to what constitutes the sacred legacy of all orthodox transmission. It is what he called *hsin*-in-itself or *liang-chih*-in-itself. It is also, according to him, the Tao (ultimate truth) and even Heaven.

In this light, Wang Yang-ming merely gave the finishing strokes to the work which Lu Chiu-yüan had begun. He developed a philosophy of *hsin* which sees everything only in relation to *hsin*. He also formulated a new "line" of "orthodox transmission"—and why should he not do so, if Chu Hsi could do it?

THE METAPHYSICAL (T'I) VERSUS THE MORAL (YUNG)

Lu Chiu-yüan and Wang Yang-ming both speak of *hsin* as that which explains the meaning both of the universe and of man. Yang-ming also took a further step, going deeper into *hsin*, and discovering therein the meaning of *liang-chih*—that in man which enables him to transcend himself, which is identical with *Ti'en-li*. with Tao, with the Absolute. In order to discern between the unstable, changing "mind-and-heart" of man, and that in him which is constant and unchanging, he speaks of *hsin-chih pen-t'i* and *liang-chih pen-t'i*. And since he discovers *pen-t'i* (ultimate reality) in *hsin*, he is obliged to describe *hsin chih pen-t'i* as the undifferentiated First Principle, that which is above ethical categories of good and evil. The search for a method has thus brought him to the metaphysical heights of the transcendent and unknowable.

The dichotomy between the Metaphysical and the Moral concerns in Yang-ming's philosophy can be best seen—as also that between Enlightenment and Cultivation—in the debates over the Four Maxims. Wang Chi and Ch'ien Te-hung represents respectively the emphasis on one and the other. For Wang Chi, the issue at stake is the ontological nature of *hsin* in-itself, in which he sees all other questions, including those regarding the movement of the intention, and those two processes under its control: knowledge, that is, *liang-chih*, and action or *ko-wu*. He therefore reformulates in a negative formula the last three Maxims, bringing them into consistency with the first one.[15] He is in a realm that transcends ethics, which deals with the metaphysical basis of ethics: with the source and fountain of man's being.

Ch'ien Te-hung, on the other hand, prefers to see the First Maxim in a class by itself, as expressive of a state of mind to be achieved, and to concentrate on the other three Maxims, which he interprets in a practical manner, as the guideline of a method of cultivation. For him, the important categories are good and evil, even more than *hsin*-in-itself. He has no interest in metaphysical speculation, no desire to bring Yang-ming's teachings to further heights of insight and discovery.

He desires a way of life, and believes to have found its simplest, methodological expression.

Yang-ming's attempt to reconcile the differences between the two men on a pedagogical level reveals his own understanding of both the methaphysical and the ethical aspects of his philosophy. For him, the two are almost inseparable; his ethics contain metaphysical insights while his metaphysics has ethical connotations and makes ethical demands. His interest in the attainment of sagehood has led him to inquire into the nature of sagehood, and of wisdom itself. But he realizes that discoveries in such ultimate concerns can only accompany the search for self-perfection in one's existential situation.

Far from being merely a practical doctrine, Yang-ming's philosophy has truly metaphysical dimensions. But when metaphysics seeks to penetrate the secret of being, the ultimate and unknowable, it can become gradually divorced from the concerns of real life, while expressing its insights in a language that must remain, per force, symbolic. The efforts of Yang-ming's disciples, especially of Wang Chi, Wang Ken, and their followers, to emphasize the metaphysical dimensions of sagehood, led eventually to a distaste with metaphysics, and a gradual return to classical exegesis, to the meaning of words and texts. The scholar Li Chih, who claims to be disciple of the school of Wang Chi, through the teachings of such men as Ho Hsin-yin and Yen Chün, no longer sees any metaphysical oneness behind the manifold phenomena. While keeping broad Confucian interests in history, government, and philosophy even as a tonsured Buddhist monk, Li's anti-metaphysical biases underline the eventual breakdown of Ming thought,[16] and foreshadow the rise to prominence, in the Ch'ing dynasty, of exegetical, classical scholarship. A full cycle is thus effected, beginning with the early Ming preoccupation with practical, moral cultivation and the quest for a universal method of sagehood, and concluding, after the practical as well as speculative discoveries of Wang Yang-ming and his school, in the abandonment of metaphysics and, with it, of the quest for a universal method itself, and a return to the preoccupations of the Han and T'ang dynasties.* The method of

---

* The reaction against the abstract metaphysics of nineteenth-century Europe that culminated in the Hegelian system, and the tendency in twentieth-century*

cultivation became once again identified with the pursuit of scholarship.

A QUESTION OF ORTHODOXY: CONFUCIAN OR HERETIC?

The examination of the various tensions in the development of a "new" Way of acquiring wisdom helps to clarify the issue concerning the "orthodoxy" of Yang-ming's thought. Was he, after all, a Confucian or a heretic? The answer to this question will be given after a review of the basic content of his all-embracing vision, and especially of the culmination of this vision as expressed in the Four Maxims. Consideration will also be made of the many implications of the method of cultivation which he formulated, and toward which his entire thought was oriented.

Yang-ming's exposition of the Unity of All Things (*wan-wu yi-t'i*) manifests similarities as well as dissimilarities with the early idea of the Unity of Heaven and Man (*T'ien-jen ho-yi*) and the later vision developed by Ch'eng Yi and Chu Hsi, Yang-ming accepted the thought-content of the Confucian Tao, as already modified by his Sung predecessors. But his focus on the self-determining *hsin*, made the "unity" between Heaven and Man more dynamically conscious of itself. He did not return to the old idea of a personal deity, which became, quite early, one of the many components inherent in the meaning of the word "Heaven" (*T'ien*). But his descriptions of Man in terms of the dynamic *hsin*, and his insistence on the oneness between man and all things, suggest the discovery in the conscious and dynamic spiritual nature of man, the presence of a greater, more dynamic principle, present in the depths of the self and yet master of the entire universe. But this was never articulated in unequivocal terms. According to Yang-ming's usage, the word Heaven (*T'ien*) remains ambiguous, with the emphasis on the continuum comprising man and all things predominating over the presence of a transcendent Other. Nevertheless, the notion of the

---

*Analytical philosophy to insist on the proper understanding of the meaning of words to the point of excluding metaphysical discussion from philosophy itself, is a good parallel. See Preface.

absolute cannot be denied. Whereas other Confucian thinkers have frequently spoken of this in terms of *wu-sheng wu-ch'ou* (without sound or odor),[17] Yang-ming adopts, in the First of his Four Maxims, the expression *wu-shan wu-ô* (neither good nor evil).

A closer examination of the vocabulary of the Four Maxims can further clarify the continuities and discontinuities between Yang-ming's thought, and that of early and Sung Confucianism. The words, of good and evil, of the mind (*hsin*), of the movement of the intention, of knowledge of the good (*liang-chih*), and of the investigation of things are all derived from Confucian texts, especially from the Book of Mencius, the Great Learning and the Doctrine of the Mean. The innovation appears with the term, *hsin-chih-t'i*, mind-in-itself, and its description in the negative expression, "neither good nor evil" (*wu-shan wu-ô*). This is confined to the First Maxim. But given the innovation, and the interpretation of it by Wang Chi, which Yang-ming personally approves, there is no doubt that a shift has been effected. With the words *wu-shan wu-ô*, Yang-ming has openly adopted a Buddhist expression. He is taking a step further from the position that the absolute cannot be attained by sense perceptions. He is also describing it as that which transcends all ethical categories. Thus, while his concerns remain Confucian and ethical, his interpretation of the ultimate truth appears clearly Buddhistic. He has given a new meaning to an old vocabulary. And if, on the one hand, he is liberating man from the bondage to established patterns of morality, on the other, he must seem to the orthodox Confucians of his time, to be destroying the cornerstone of Confucian society and the *raison-d'etre* of Confucianism itself.

In terms of content, therefore, while Yang-ming's basic vision appears to have effected a lesser shift than that made by his predecessors of the Sung dynasty who had already expanded the Confucian context to embrace Buddhist and Taoist vocabulary and insights, his interpretation of the absolute or ultimate as that which is beyond good and evil represents a radical, albeit logical, departure from the orthodox system of Ch'eng Yi and Chu Hsi.

Certainly, Yang-ming reveals a deep concern for the continuity of the Confucian transmission. He proposes *liang-chih* as the sacred legacy in question, using it as a key in his explanation of the "formula of faith" which had been crystallized earlier, and establishing in retrospect a new line of transmission. But such daring is sufficient to indicate his entire independence of the officially approved Ch'eng-Chu philosophy, while declaring fully his faith in the correctness of personal insight, so long as the mind-and-heart (*hsin*) remains open and sincere. free from unruly passions. If the Confucian classics preserve a place of honor in his heart, the gates of sagehood have been clearly flung open to all, whether Confucian or barbarian.

And it is this teaching which resolves the inherent contradiction contained in the doctrine of "orthodox tramsmission." For insights, unlike techniques of exegesis, cannot be transmitted.[17] They must be acquired anew, by and for oneself. But faith in *liang-chih*, which deepens itself into faith in ultimate truth, in what is called, "the sages' *hsin*," can be passed on, by inspiration. Just as Confucius had inspired it in Mencius, without having known or taught him personally, so too Mencius inspired it in Lu Chiu-yüan, after an intervention of over 1,500 years. And Lu Chiu-yüan, in turn, had inspired it in Yang-ming, after another interval of over 200 years. In other words, the transmission of *hsin*, an entirely interior process, requires the person to look into his own *hsin* to discover the orthodox legacy itself, which, in turn, is sometimes described in a negative vocabulary, for the sake of emphasizing its undifferentiated character and the consequent ineffability.[18]

In this way, Yang-ming completed and perfected certain teachings of Chu Hsi, while rejecting others. He taught the doctrine of "orthodox transmission," and of a truth that was transmitted. But he did so only in order to show that truth or wisdom cannot be delineated by human ideas of "correctness." There is ultimately only one truth and it is everywhere, our *hsin* being fundamentally one with all things. Ch'eng Yi and Chu Hsi had both incorporated Taoist and Buddhist ideas into their system. Yang-ming declared that this was perfectly natural and legitimate. There are no Confucian, Taoist, or Buddhist *taos*. There is only one Tao.

In terms of the method for attaining sagehood that Yang-ming developed, the picture is somewhat different. The formula, *chih liang-chih*, represents, at the same time, a call to awaken to the seed of enlightenment already present in the hearts of all, as well as a method of spiritual cultivation which reduces to the essentials, the task at hand. Yang-ming is a teacher of wisdom, but not of enlightenment, for which there is no method. But if one is to judge the orthodoxy of his "method," of extending *liang-chih*, one faces the fact that "orthodoxy", strictly speaking, pertains to thought. Where methods are concerned, correctness can only be decided by the test of their effectiveness.

Effectiveness requires testing through experimentation. Yang-ming had personally experimented with Taoist-Buddhist methods of cultivation and meditation. He had approved of many insights which these brought him, but had rejected some of their techniques and presuppositions.[20] He had based his judgments and selection on his *liang-chih*, thus admitting the inevitability of a certain circular process: *liang-chih* enables the discovery of the correct method, which is no other than the "extension of *liang-chih*." For this circular process to have validity, one must acknowledge, with Yang-ming, the presence of a greater-than-*liang-chih* in *liang-chih*, as well as be able to judge, in Yang-ming's life itself, the effectiveness of his method.

And so, how effective was the method of Wang Yang-ming? The answer lies partly in what it produced. The best example is the life and character of Yang-ming himself. From all evidences, his was the exemplification of a life which fused together the "inner" and "outer" pulls of contemplation and of intense activity, of wisdom sought for and discovered through enlightenment and virtuous action, of the harmonious integration of such diverse pursuits as philosophy, statesmanship, and even war. The tensions were not always completely resolved. Yang-ming continued to show throughout his life of activity, a desire for stillness. He made intermittent attempts of withdrawal from active life. But his strong sense of social responsibility, inherent both in his vision of the "unity of all things" and in his practical ideal of sagehood, always brought him back into the arena of active affairs and their resultant conflicts. It was the best demonstration of his inner adherence to his own method: the extension and realization of *liang-chih*, the knowledge of the good, gained through life and action, making of one, stillness and activity, permeating all decisions and acts with its own inner light.

And what repercussions does this have on the question of orthodoxy? Here too, a certain circularity of reasoning appears inevitable.

The effectiveness of Yang-ming's method in his own quest for sagehood serves as recommendation, both for the method itself and for the discovery of the absolute in *liang-chih*, of the sages' *hsin*. According to Yang-ming, so long as *hsin* or *liang-chih* is kept free of selfishness, which alone obstructs the discovery of the absolute, interrogation regarding the orthodoxy of one's vision is unnecessary. Seen in this light, the whole question of orthodoxy *versus* heterodoxy becomes irrelevant.

EASY AND SIMPLE, OR SUBTLE AND PROFOUND?

A few words of evaluation concerning Yang-ming's thought—whether it is "easy and simple" (*yi-chien*)[21] or profound and subtle—may also be relevant in this final, concluding chapter. For Yang-ming has been described as both,[22] and has also described his own thought as possessing at the same time these opposing qualities. He said: "This Way is most simple and most easy. It is also most perfect and most subtle."[23] Also: "These two words *liang-chih* can be understood at once on hearing. Who does not know them? But where perception (literally, "seeing") is concerned. . .who is there that really perceives [their meaning]? . . .The man who does this throughly is already a sage."[24]

The answer to this problem will appear to resemble strangely attempted answers to other problems dealt with in the course of this work. I should like to describe Yang-ming's philosophy as both simple and subtle. But I should like first of all to define my terms carefully.

If "simplicity" is to be understood as easily comprehensible, and lacking in speculative profundity, then Yang-ming's thought can hardly be called simple. On the contrary, it is possible to read his writings, admire the lucidity of his style, and yet fail to comprehend his real meaning. He appears deceptively simple and yet unreasonably paradoxical. He uses certain words common to the Confucian and neo-Confucian vocabulary to weave arguments against the followers of the Ch'eng-Chu school, and he does so by giving these same words deeper levels of meaning, frequently with Buddhistic allusions. But the word "simplicity," as opposed to that of "complexity," also connotes single-ness and unity, the integration of parts in the whole, or rather, the absence of discernible parts. A movememt to simplicity is, in this sense, a movement away from multiplicity, toward the oneness of all things. It is in this way that I understand Yang-ming's philosophy which treats of this very Oneness, by contemplating it from various angles. It is for this reason that I have proceeded, as explained in the book's Preface, in a "spiral" fashion, dealing with Yang-ming's teachings as with a series of concentric circles, moving ever more to the central focus of his own intuitions.

The word "simplicity" (*chien*), when used together with the word "ease" (*yi*)—which, also carries the connotation of unity and singleness, as well as other meanings—makes up the expression "easy and simple." This has especially been used in descriptions of a certain "way" or method of acquiring wisdom, traced out by Lu Chiu-yüan and completed by Wang Yang-ming. In this sense, it stands in contrast to the "method" of Ch'eng Yi and Chu Hsi, which requires a more scholastically laborious preparation. This does not mean, that Yang-ming actually made the quest of sagehood "easy"—more accessible and less exacting. The truth is rather the opposite. He has clearly presented this quest with all its exigences. It is a case of losing all to gain all, of losing oneself to discover a new self, the True Self. It is a quest in which the goal will always remain elusive, in which success can hardly be measured in quantitative terms. It can hardly ever become a "popular" quest—although momentary fervor and a short-lived enthusiasm may cause it to appear so, and may also contribute to the understanding of certain features of this quest, as also of its object and goal. And it is probably on account of such contradictions inherent in the way of Wang-Yang-ming that, for all its simplicity and profundity, sages—real sages—will not thereby become more abundant. Wisdom is by nature such that every seeker must find his own way to it, although the insights of those who have gone before can be helpful. The acquisition of wisdom will remain, for all, a *personal* experience. And it is to Yang-ming's credit that he has so emphasized the personal and experiential nature of this Way.

For wisdom is more than a highly developed moral sense, an ability to discern, to make choices, which has been confirmed and consolidated by wide practical experience of life and its activities and problems.

Wisdom is more than an integrated body of knowledge, of both speculative and practical matters, which gives unity to one's learning and
insights. Wisdom is even more than virtue, emotional equilibrium
and serenity. Wisdom is all of these and more. It is the final goal that
is already present in the starting point, the end that is already present
in the means. It is the desirable and elusive object of striving for the
disciple of the sages, the philosopher. But the wise man is he whose
life and struggles, whose activities and stillnesses, have shown him
that search and discovery, quest and goal, are one. Wisdom *is* the un-
failing experience of its own quest.

SAGE? THINKER? MYSTIC?

I have spoken of Yang-ming's philosophy as that which precludes
the use of such time-honored categories as "orthodox" and "heretic,"
of Confucian or Buddhist-Taoist, since it represents an attempt to
attain ultimate truth, beyond the considerations of ideologies. I have
also explained how it can be described at the same time as being
"simple and easy," and yet "subtle and profound," how it represents
a movement from multiplicity to unity, through reconciliation of
certain qualities considered sometimes as opposites. A final question
now arises near the end of this study. It concerns the nature of his
discoveries. Are these of the order of philosophical thought, or religious
vision? Was his wisdom born of a religious experience of reality, which
consists primarily in certain special moments of "enlightenment" or
suprarational consciousness, and only secondarily in continual reflection upon the meaning of the insights received, especially as confirmed and enriched by new experiences in the realm of ordinary life?
In other words, is Yang-ming to be described more as a thinker, a
mystic, or a sage?

The examination of his life and inner evolution has shown that he
had definitely enlightenment-experiences, acknowledged by himself
as such, and confirmed by his disciples, especially by him who was the
preacher of enlightenment, Wang Chi. Besides, if the latter's interpretation of the Four Maxims, in terms of the Four Negatives, is
accepted, then it appears obvious that what is being referred to is
ultimate reality, which is known and grasped in an experience that

transcends thought.* Indeed, Yang-ming has objected to making an artificial effort of "not *thinking* of either good and evil" because it implies in itself a deliberate thought. But he has not hesitated to identify *liang-chih* with the Ch'an Buddhist *pen-lai mien-mu*, that is, the absolute self, described also as the nonself, the ultimate, that which lies beyond the reach of dialectical reasoning.

Another reason for favoring the argument that points to the religious, or suprarational nature of Yang-ming's experience, is his exhortation to secrecy regarding the real meaning of the Four Maxims. Mystical knowledge means, by definition, secret knowledge. The mystic, who has grasped reality in a suprarational experience, feels personally responsible about the effects on others, which such insights he possesses may have, for whom the experience itself is lacking. For while the notion of the absolute being neither good or evil is liberating to the human spirit, who realizes that ethical distinctions are man-made whereas the real good is suprahuman, it can also cause confusion to those who cannot see any deeper level of meaning in the words.

This does not mean that Yang-ming is more of a religious genius than a thinker. It just implies that he is both: after having reached the peak of thought that reason could bring him, he has also been favored with certain experiences and insights that effected a certain "leap" beyond the realm of reason and dialectic, beyond even that of spiritual cultivation and the study of Classics. Yang-ming is above all a sage, a wise man. As such, he is also a thinker and a mystic. And he attained the goal that any man, Confucian, Taoist, or Buddhist can reach, with the help of the self-determining principle of wisdom present to all.

---

* Yang-ming's thought displays those characteristics of mysticism pointed out by R. Otto, regarding the concern for the ontological relationship of the One with the many, and the description of the One, pure Being, in negative language, in a doctrine that is primarily directed to personal salvation, through a knowledge of the ultimate or absolute as true knowledge, in contrast with the "false" knowledge that reaches only the appearances of things. In Yang-ming's case, this true knowledge is especially that which is united with action. See *Mysticism East and West*, 23–24, 33–25.

IMMANENCE OR TRANSCENDENCE?

And what of Yang-ming's fundamental insight, granted that the religious and mystical dimensions of his thought are acknowledged? In speaking of the discovery, in *hsin*, of the unity of all things, is Yang-ming expressing a totally nondual vision, with no difference at all between the self and the other, or is he speaking more of the interpenetration of one in the other, which does not necessarily imply the absorption of one by the other?

First of all, the "Unity of All Things," although presented as an existential "truth," remains a goal that must be personally realized on the moral, psychological, and metaphysical-mystical planes, by the aspirant of sagehood. It is a reality that must be restored, revivified, recreated. It is not the existential condition in which all things find themselves. For if there is no distinction at all between one and many, self and other, there would be no need either to seek to realize any such unity, or to speak of it at all.

Secondly, although the conscious realization of a state of mind that sees unity and harmony in all things is characteristic of the possession of the absolute *liang-chih*, or the sages' *hsin* (*Tao-hsin*), this does not necessarily imply that a sage is one who has lost his own identity, which has become merged with a higher reality, or that all sages lose their individualities through union with the Tao. On the contrary, sages have always remained highly individual, as Yang-ming is fond of repeating.[26]

But, if the Unity of all Things does not refer to loss of identity either on the part of self or of other, it must refer rather to a relationship of harmony, which does not destroy the distinction between one and the other. And since this relationship of unity and harmony is most realized in the sage's *hsin*, this means that a certain difference remains between his own *hsin*, and the *pen-t'i* of this *hsin*, which is discovered therein, but which is greater than himself, because transcending himself. In other words, Yang-ming's teaching of *hsin chih pen-t'i* and *liang-chih pen-t'i* not only suggests the presence of the absolute within the contingent self, but provides also a description of the process of transformation by which the contingent self becomes more and more related in harmony with the absolute within, without ever destroying the tenuous balance between immanence and transcendence,[27]

For the process that is being described by Yang-ming's life and teachings is one which stretches human language beyond its possibilities for precision of expression. It can only be expressed symbolically by words that hide as much as they reveal the truth. One will, therefore never attain the truth if one only stops at the words. Such neologisms introduced by Yang-ming, like *liang-chih pen-t'i*, are intended to express the inexpressible, of that which lies at the heart of nonduality as well as duality, that is, of the mystery that is present in human existence, and which can also be called wisdom.*

And this wisdom, according to Yang-ming's teaching, is both immanent and transcendent, because it is at the same time present in the self and the others, while transcending both self and the others.

THE AMBIGUOUS LEGACY

It is a truism to say that ambiguity belongs to the essence of wisdom. We have so far attempted to explore into the meanings of the many ambiguities of Yang-ming's philosophy. We have not yet exhausted their whole richness. Indeed, his philosophical legacy was so ambiguous that diverse interpretations soon set it, putting once more into motion the various tensions in thought and action of the "inner-outer" pulls. of the "enlightenment-cultivation" debate, of the "self-authority" dichotomy, and of the "metaphysical-moral" polarisation. The group that followed the leadership of Wang Chi and Wang Ken sought particularly to draw certain logical conclusions from the enlightenment *versus* cultivation debate, arguing in favor of an instantaneous enlightenment of the mind-and-heart, *hsin*, which is sufficient to assure

---

* The discovery of the "absolute" in the self implies also the discovery of that which is somehow "other" than the self. This is characteristic of the mystics who find the absolute in an inward vision. R. Otto describes the tendency in mysticism to follow the *via negationis*, by which every predicate that can be stated in words becomes excluded from the absolute Numen until the absolute is designated as "nothingness," to be expressive of this feeling of "otherness" or the "suprapersonal." See *The Idea of the Holy*, Eng. tr. by J. W. Harvey (London: Oxford University Press, 1950), 197.

the acquisition of wisdom.[28] But it offered no way of determining the authenticity of such enlightenment and such wisdom. In the end every "aspiring" sage considered himself an already "made" sage, and acknowledged only the rules of behavior that he himself had made. This development contributed to the growth of the Yang-ming school into a popular movement, penetrating into all segments of the stratified society of late Ming times, and effecting a marked tendency toward individual and eccentric behavior, and of an attitude of independence and resistance with regard to all authority, especially that of the political state.

Other followers of the Yang-ming school sought to prevent or remedy the above tendency, which contributed to the promotion of social egalitarianism based on men's equal dignity, but brought havoc to the orderly pursuit of philosophy and of wisdom. They either emphasized the importance of silence and of stillness, acquired in quiet-sitting, for the sake of confronting events and circumstances, or insisted upon the development of moral virtues in the "extension of *liang-chih*". In both instances a certain return to some of the ideas of the Ch'eng-Chu school was achieved.[29]

It is interesting to note here that the development of a popular, protest movement in the Yang-ming school also prevented it from being ever clearly accepted as official doctrine. But the rich ambiguity of Yang-ming's legacy, which allowed such diversity of interpretation and of application in practice, permitted the eventual development in Japan of a movement of thought and action that drew from the fusion of moral ideals, social commitment, and the cultivation of an "inner" personality, a certain strength and freedom of action that served well the later, midnineteenth century Meiji reforms.[30] Yang-ming's method functioned well in producing many inspiring individuals of high character in Japan and Korea as well as in China. In Japan especially, it helped to effect a certain social transformation, based on ancient moral ideals, but looking forward to an independent confrontation with new political, social, and intellectual realities that entered Japanese life and awareness with the incursion of European and American interests.

And so, as we look back five hundred years and more to the life and thought of Wang Yang-ming, and wonder at its fruitful ambiguity, we may be led, as was Yang-ming himself, to the Ch'an Buddhist belief that the best transmission of the Way of Wisdom is that which takes place in silence. This is the logical conclusion of him who wished to go beyond the words of the Classical texts, to the spiritual meaning that inspired the earliest sages, including those who had left behind nothing in writing. At the end of this analytical and exegetical study of Yang-ming's philosophy, it may serve well to recall to mind his frequent allusions to Analects 17: 19, as, for example, in the following lines of a poem:

> Confucius desired to become silent and wordless;
> The perfect man attained a glimpse of reality's foundations.
> Is this past Way different from today's
> Though this man has gone so far away?[31]

And so too can one say of the Way of Wang Yang-ming himself.

EPILOGUE

NOTES ON THE "YANG-MING CONTROVERSY"

LOOKING BACK upon the many things that have been said by Yang-ming's admirers and critics during a period of nearly five hundred years one can see the gradual shifts of focus in the "Yang-ming controversy." During and after his lifetime, lasting until the early nineteenth century, the issue was over his "orthodoxy": whether his philosophy should be called "Confucian" or "Ch'an" [Japanese: Zen]. Debates regarded particularly his interpretations of the "investigation of things" (*ko-wu*) and of the so-called "absence of good-and-evil" (*wu-shan wu-ô*). In the nineteenth and twentieth centuries, with the introduction of Western philosophical ideas, Chinese thinkers are being reexamined in the light of Western philosophical categories. The entire *Hsing-li* movement of the Sung and Ming dynasties, with its two branches—the school of Ch'eng Yi and Chu Hsi, and the school of Lu Chiu-yüan and Wang Yang-ming, usually known to the Chinese as *Hsin-hsüeh*, is being represented as a "neo-Confucian" philosophy, divided into the so-called "rationalist" Ch'eng-Chu and "idealist" Lu-Wang branches. And so, although the "Confucian *versus* Ch'an" issue has not yet disappeared, the tendency today is to praise or dismiss Yang-ming's thought as a system of "idealist" metaphysics.

"Confucian" or Ch'an "Buddhist"?

Yang-ming's contemporaries, including Lo Ch'in-shun, reproached him for departing from the accepted lines of the Ch'eng-Chu school of thought, and for yielding to Ch'an influence. Ch'en Chien, Feng K'o, Lu Lung-ch'i, and Chang Lieh continued these criticisms in a much stronger language.[1] The change of dynasties that took place in the middle decades of the seventeenth century was a traumatic experience, and many scholars—Wang Fu-chih (1619–92),[2] Chu Chih-yü (1600–82),[3] Ku Yen-wu[4] and others—criticized Yang-ming's philosophy for having contributed to the Ming downfall. In his History of Ch'ing Philosophy, T'ang Chien (1778–1861) accused the Yang-ming school of having caused men to "lose heart" by empty, irresponsible talk, "destroying the morality of the times, and leading to the final annihilation of the Ming dynasty."[5]

Among the most famous critics of Yang-ming's philosophy were the leading scholars of the Tung-lin Academy: Ku Hsien-ch'eng and Kao P'an-lung. Both regarded Ch'eng Yi and Chu Hsi as the orthodox heirs of the Confucian tradition and attacked Yang-ming for rebelling against the authority of the Classics and their "correct" commentaries, and for strong Buddhist-Taoist sympathies.[6] Kao said:

> "Not satisfied with remaining as an adherent of Buddhism and Taoism, Yang-ming was determined to usurp a position in the orthodox Confucian line. That was why he took great trouble to match his own discoveries with the teachings of 'extension of knowledge' and 'investigation of things,' moving left and right, back and front in his arguments. One need merely give his thought a calm look, to find all his inconsistencies."[7]

The Opinions of Huang Wan (1477–1551)

Whether during or after his lifetime, Yang-ming's critics usually took for granted the Confucian orthodoxy of the Ch'eng-Chu school, to which the "unorthodox" Ch'an Buddhist teachings were polarized. The criticisms of Huang Wan were an exception.

Huang had been an ardent disciple of the Ch'eng-Chu school before his meeting with Wang Yang-ming (1501), whose close friend and disciple he became. After Yang-ming's death, he assumed the role of guardian to Yang-ming's infant son, who was also engaged to his own daughter. Still later in life, however, Huang underwent another intellectual evolution, as his published notes, the *Ming-tao p'ien,* still testify.[8]

Huang's main target of attack were those disciples of the Yang-ming school who tended to neglect completely the discipline of intellectual inquiry and the established standards of moral behavior. He referred to them as "the gentlemen of today" or "[our] friends today." But he also criticized Yang-ming himself, although he did so without mentioning his name. He took issue especially with Yang-ming's teaching of *ko-wu,* which he regarded as more Ch'an-Buddhist than Confucian, and also with the doctrine that "the man of *jen* (humanity) is one with Heaven-and-Earth and all things,"[9] which he said was contrary to the Confucian idea of "graded love," and could easily degenerate into a complete disregard of basic moral relationships.[10]

Huang's criticisms are all the more significant because he openly pointed out the deep Taoist-Buddhist influences that had penetrated into the entire *Hsing-li* movement ever since the Sung dynasty, mentioning by name Chou Tun-yi, Chang Tsai, Ch'eng Hao, whom he called "inferior Ch'an Buddhists," according to the extent of Buddhist influence they manifested.[11] He said:

> Although it is [usually] said that the School of Sages became dominant in the Sung dynasty, [this was not really so] . . . . That is why Ch'an teachings have become even more widespread today. True doctrine has been lost, but people are still unrepentent.[12]

Nevertheless, Huang's indictment remained an exception in an age when the basic assumptions of the state-approved Ch'eng-Chu school were little questioned. Other Yang-ming critics of his time and after continued to adhere to the simplist "Confucian *versus* Ch'an" argument, writing polemics that tended to become diatribes.[13] It was only in the Ch'ing dynasty, with the gradual revival of classical exegesis according to rediscovered Han techniques, that criticisms of both the Ch'eng-Chu and Lu-Wang schools were again heard.[14]

Strangely enough, this restoration of "Han learning" led later on
to a renewal of the ancient "New Text" "Old Text" controversy which
was occasioned by the intrusion of Western influence in nineteenth-
century China. But the extraordinary K'ang Yu-wei (1858–1927)[15]
and his disciples T'an Ssu-t'ung (1865–98)[16] and Liang Ch'i-ch'ao
(1873–1929)[17] expressed a certain predilection for Yang-ming and
considered his philosophy as capable of inspiring new hope in the
minds of a people then facing the serious political, technological, and
intellectual challenges of the West. Anxious to promote a synthesis
of Confucian, Buddhist, and Taoist ideas with the religious and political thinking of Western Europe, K'ang and his disciples praised
Yang-ming's openness of mind. For them, there is no question of
"Confucian versus Ch'an" controversy.

K'ang's political misfortunes prevented him from carrying out pro-
jected institutional reforms. But feelings for or against Yang-ming's
philosophy continue today to be colored "politically," and Chiang
Kai-shek's effort to promote Yang-ming's philosophy had been followed
by attacks made against Yang-ming in the People's Republic.

"METAPHYSICAL IDEALISM"?

The expression, "Metaphysical idealism" (wei-hsin) carries an
ambiguous connotation. For some, it refers to a philosophical attitude
that regards all reality in terms of the subjective self. For others, there
is a question of a certain ultimate and transcendent reality, of which
the objective world is the manifestation. Yang-ming's metaphysics
has been described as "idealist" by both European and Chinese
scholars. A. Forke said so in 1939,[18] J. Needham in 1956,[19] Carsun
Chang in 1962.[20] It represents the tendency to reevaluate Chinese
thinkers in terms of European philosophical categories. In Yang-
ming's case, he has been compared especially with such European
thinkers as Berkeley (1685–1753) and Hegel.[21]

There are two problems associated with the use of this expression,
which has arisen out of a European philosophical context following the
Cartesian mind-body dualism. The first is that the Chinese word hsin
refers not merely to the mind as intellect but also as vital principle,

source, and center of all human activities. The second concerns the special meaning which the expression *wei-hsin* (mind-only) has assumed in the writings of Chinese intellectuals in the mainland, where the criterion of orthodoxy has become Marx-Lenin-Maoism. The whole range of the history of Chinese thought has been reexamined in terms of the materialist *versus* idealist struggle, with idealism represented as the villain of philosophy. The Ch'eng-Chu and Lu-Wang schools are both classified as "idealist," with the former described as "objective idealism," and the latter, "subjective idealism." Yang-ming's role as a commanding officer against peasant rebels has also contributed to the criticisms against his philosophy. Hou Wai-lu summarized Yang-ming's thoughts in a sentence taken from one of his letters: "It is easier to defeat the bandits in the mountains than to defeat those in one's mind and heart (*hsin*)," and judged him accordingly.[22]

Hou and others of his persuasion have also chosen to praise the so-called "leftist" branch of the Yang-ming school, in particular Wang Ken and his T'ai-chou followers, including Yen Chün, Ho Hsin-yin (1517–79) and Li Chih, for such reasons as humble origins, egalitarian ideas, protest, or rebellion against the Confucian establishment. But Yang-ming's influence over the development of such a popular movement is not acknowledged. How even states that the T'ai-chou branch only "pretended" to belong to the Yang-ming school![23] These men who had been criticized by Ming and Ch'ing writers as "mad Ch'an Buddhists," escaped even the charge of being "subjective idealists" in Hou's book.

It should be pointed out here that the scholar, Fung Yu-lan, has sought to be more impartial in his judgments of both the Ch'eng-Chu and Lu-Wang schools. While making use of the orthodox Marxist framework of the conflict of thought between Materialism and Idealism, he has enumerated the merits of the Lu-Wang school in propagating a philosophy of protest and opposition against the established authority of the time, through their liberating teaching on mind-and-heart.[24] He claims that Yang-ming helped to "bring the Ch'eng-Chu abstract world back into the concrete world."[25] He also praises Yang ming's doctrine of *liang-chih* as the discovery of a moral criterion that is independent of the traditional teachings and of state authority.[26]

And so, with both earlier and later critics of Yang-ming's philosophy, the underlying assumptions were more frequently questions of ideology rather than of truth. Yang-ming was judged wrong, either because he differed consciously from Chu Hsi, or because, in today's China, he differed—quite unconsciously, of course—from the present ideology. Even in labeling him an "idealist," the issue remains that of orthodoxy, although the doctrine to which this word refers has changed drastically.

PART II

SELECTED ESSAYS AND POEMS IN TRANSLATION

The following pages present certain selected essays and poems written by Wang Yang-ming that provide supporting evidence for the interpretation of his thought as it has been given in this work. The texts have been classified roughly in chronological order. The poems are difficult to date accurately, and most of them have never been translated into English before. On account of their content, some of the translations of the poems will more resemble prose than poetry.

SECTION A

THE ESSAYS

1. A Farewell Essay in Honor of Chan Jo-shui (1511)

The teaching of [Confucius] the Sage virtually died with [his disciple] Yen-tzu. Although Tseng-tzu passed on its one-pervading meaning[1] to Mencius, [the transmission ceased] with the latter's death. Only two thousand-odd years afterward did Chou Tun-yi and Ch'eng [Hao] resume this teaching.[2] But from that time on, the more words that were used the less clear was the Way, and the better *li* (principle, being) was analyzed, the more fragmented and without foundation the tradition of learning became, as it preoccupied itself increasingly with externals, getting more complicated and difficult.

Mencius had feared the growing influence [during his time] of [the heretics] Yang-tzu and Mo-tzu,[3] The heterodox teachings of Buddhism and Taoism were still widespread at the time of Chou [Tun-yi] and Ch'eng [Hao]. But today, all our scholars honor Confucius and Mencius, despise Yang-tzu and Mo-tzu, and keep away from Buddhism and Taoism. Our world seems to understand well the Way of the Sages. And yet, when I look around, I can find no sage. In fact, is there even anyone today who can practice Mo-tzu's doctrine of universal love, or Yang-tzu's teaching of [enlightened] self-

---

[1] Analects 4:15; Legge, *Classics*, v. 1, 169.
[2] Reference to the interruption and resumption of the transmission of orthodox teaching. See Introduction and chapter 4.
[3] Book of Mencius, 7A: 26; Legge, *Classics*, v. 464–65.

interest, or keep himself pure and undefiled as the Taoists, or investigate the mind and destiny as the Buddhists? Why do I think of Yang-tzu, Mo-tzu, Taoists, and Buddhists? Because they had at least their own insights, although their ways differed from the Way of the Sages. But our scholars today spend their time underlining texts and decorating sentences in order to attract attention flattering others with their cunning and protecting one another by hypocrisy. They say that the Way of the Sages is wearisome and unrewarding, no longer possible to human efforts. They engage solely in verbal arguments, saying: "In the past, there were scholars who were unable to understand what they studied after having spent their entire lives in such investigation. Now, we all can talk about their general ideas." And they think that if they do this, it is enough. In this way, the teaching of the sages has gradually been abandoned.

Is not therefore the greatest threat confronting us today this habit of chanting and rote learning [of the Classics] and scrutiny of words and sentences [in textual studies]? And do not these bad habits come from giving explanations which are too detailed and making analyses that are too minute? After all, Yang-tzu, Mo-tzu, Taoists, and Buddhists all studied about humanity and righteousness, nature and destiny, but did not find the Way on account of their partiality. They are not like our scholars of today, who consider humanity and righteousness to be impossible, nature and destiny to be useless. And so I should regard as worthies those men today who still study humanity and righteousness, nature and destiny, and avoid rote learning and textual studies, even if they may make the same mistake of partiality as did Yang-tzu, Mo-tzu, Taoists, and Buddhists. These men still seek personal insights (*tzu-te*)[4] in their minds, and personal insights are indispensable for those who wish to discuss the Way of the Sages.

I was not a serious student in my youth. For twenty years I had meddled with perverse doctrines [and heresies], before even beginning to study the mind (*hsin*) in Taoism and Buddhism. Thanks to Heaven,

---

[4] Both Chan Jo-shui and his teacher, Ch'en Hsien-chang, emphasised the role of personal insights in the quest for wisdom and sageliness. See Chien Yu-wen, "Ch'en Hsien-chang's Philosophy of the Natural," in de Bary, ed., *Self and Society in Ming Thought*, 81–82.

I had some enlightenment (*chüeh*), and started the [real] quest according to the teachings of Chou [Tun-yi] and Ch'eng [Hao], and acquired certain insights. I had then only one or two friends to help me in this endeavor. Time and again, I fell down only to rise up once more. Later, I made friends with Master Chan Kan-ch'üan, and my determination to seek after the Confucian ideals of sagehood became firmer and stronger, and quite irrevocable. This shows how much I have received from Kan-ch'üan. Kan-ch'üan's teachings insists on acquiring for oneself insights. The world has not been able to understand it. Those who know of it suspect it to be Ch'an Buddhism. If that be so, then I still have not known Ch'an Buddhism. For with such sublime ambitions as his, how can someone like Chan Kan-ch'üan not be a disciple of the Sages?[5] As to people's talk, why should that be a problem? After all, I believe that people's talk cannot discredit Kan-chüan, just as Kan-ch'üan does not allow himself to become troubled because of such. As friends, Kan-ch'üan and I understand each other without words, and reach the same [philosophical] conclusions without too much prior discussion. We are committed to this Way, and shall strive for it until death.

Today, at this parting, should I remain silent? After all, the teaching of the Sages is hard to comprehend and easy to misunderstand; the standards of moral life are always lowering and can hardly be restored. You have a great responsibility and a far way to go, and already expect nothing of words. But when I look into my heart, I cannot help saying what I have to say. And I know that you, Kan-ch'üan, will not consider my words to be only artificial and decorative.

WWKC 7: 232a–233a.

[5] Part of this paragraph is quoted in chapter 3.

2. PREFACE TO THE OLD VERSION OF THE GREAT LEARNING (1518)

The essential teaching of the Great Learning concerns the sincerity of the intention. The work of making the intention sincere lies in the investigation of things. To seek such sincerity means, at its utmost, to rest in the highest good. To rest in the highest good requires the extension [and realization] of knowledge. The rectification of the mind (*hsin*) is aimed at the recovery of its substance (*t'i*). The cultivation of self expresses the effort (*yung*). This is called manifesting virtue with reference to self, and loving the people with reference to others. It is complete with reference to all between Heaven and Earth. And so the highest good refers to the *pen-t'i* of the mind. Only after this *pen-t'i* is activated can anything which is not good happen. But the *pen-t'i* itself is never without such knowledge [of good and evil]. The word intention (*yi*) refers to activity; the word things (*wu*) refers to affairs. When one extends the knowledge of *pen-t'i*, such activity is always good. But unless one investigates such affairs as they arise, knowledge cannot be extended. That is why extension of knowledge is the root of sincerity of intention, and investigation of things is the core of extension of knowledge. When things are investigated, knowledge is extended, intention becomes sincere, and the *pen-t'i* of the mind can be recovered. This is the meaning of resting in the highest good.[1]

Fearing that people would seek all this outside of themselves, the Sage repeats his words over and over again. If the Old Version of the Great Learning were divided into sections, [as is the case with the version currently in use],[2] the meaning which the Sage desired to communicate would be lost. That is why not making the intention sincere, and merely investigating things, results in fragmentation; neglecting investigation of things and merely seeking sincerity of

[1] A discussion of the Great Learning, ch. 1. A part of this first paragraph is quoted in chapter 3.

[2] Reference to the version corrected and commented upon by Chu Hsi.

intention, brings about emptiness; while not being rooted in the extension of knowledge, but merely investigating things and making the intention sincere, leads to falsehood. Fragmentation [of knowledge], emptiness [of mind] and falsehood are far from the highest good.

The more one tries to interpret the text as a whole in terms of reverence,[3] the more artificial appears the resultant unity. The more one seeks to amend it by adding a commentary, the more fragmented its meaning becomes.

Fearing that the tradition of learning removes itself daily further from the highest good, I myself have abolished the chapter divisions and restored the Old Version, while providing it with some side explanations, to clarify the meaning. This enables the reader to see again the mind of the Sage and grasp the essentials of his teachings. Indeed, extension [and realization] of knowledge lies in the awakening (*wu*) of the mind. It really includes everything.

WWKC 7: 241a–b

---

[3] Reference again to Chu Hsi's version, and to Chu's effort to interpret the text by the notion of reverence (*ching*). See *Ta-hsüeh hou-wen*, 1: 1b–3a. See also, for Yang-ming's fuller reaction, chapter 3.

3. PREFACE TO THE ANNOTATED EDITION OF THE BOOK OF RITES (1520)

Rites (*li*$_2$) belong to the [realm of] principles (*li*$_1$). Such principles are discovered in nature (*hsing*). Nature is ordained (*ming*) [by Heaven]. "The ordinances of Heaven are profound and unceasing."[1] They are called nature in man. They are called rites in the rules organizing external decorum. They are called humanity (*jen*) under the form of pure virtue and goodness. They are called righteousness (*yi*) as direct, decisive norms. They are called knowledge (*chih*) as a clear form of consciousness. All these permeate the whole of human nature and make up, in their totality, the one, only Principle (*li*$_1$) For humanity is the substance (*t'i*) of the rites, rightoeusness their proper attribute, and knowledge their comprehension.

There are three hundred rules of canonical rites (*ching-li*) and three thousand additional rules of demeanour (*ch'ü-li*).[2] Not one of them is not based on humanity, not one of them is not based on human nature. Such are the directives and arrangements of Heaven. What [other] mind has the Sage himself? Every one of them is therefore [in accord with] the ordinances [of Heaven]. That is why self-conquest and the recovery of propriety is called humanity.[3] The exhaustive investigation of principles leads to the completion of nature and then to the achievement of destiny (*ming*). The completion of nature implies that activity, demeanor and interactions with others shall all be in accord with propriety.[4]

The later teachings on the rites, however, perplex me. These include arguments over the articles and numbers [of sacrificial vessels] and over minor items of the criminal codes. [The persons who spread

---

[1] Book of Odes, Legge, *Classics*, v. 4, 570. It is cited in Doctrine of the Mean, ch. 26. Legge, *Classics*, v. 1, 421.

[2] Book of Rites, *Li-chi cheng-yi*, 23: 12b. See Legge, tr. *Li-Ki*, SBE series, 404. It is alluded to in Doctrine of the Mean, ch. 27.

[3] Analects 12: 1; Legge, *Classics*, v. 1, 250.

[4] Book of Mencius, 7B: 33; Legge, *Classics*, v. 2, 475.

such interpretations] work very hard, year after year. They use up their energy, learning about the dregs of wine and rice, left over by the sacrificial officials, and forget the great law that regulates all under Heaven and the great foundation that supports the universe. After all, "Do rites refer merely to jade and silk?"[5] And, "if a man is lacking in the virtue of humanity, what can the rites do for him?"[6]

For these reasons, the followers of Lao-tzu and Chuang-tzu abandoned the rites to speak of nature. They say that rites emerge with decline of real virtue,[7] and with the loss of humanity and righteousness. They have already drifted into emptiness and the void. And the scholars of this world continue to abandon nature and seek ritual observance. They say that ritual observance consists merely in the knowledge of sacrificial utensils—of their numbers, and of regulation governing their use. They discuss the sounds and shadows of ritual observance, as though these comprehend its whole meaning. This shows that if the ritual laws of the ancient sage kings have been obscured by smoke and even reduced to ashes, the disaster cannot be attributed solely to the fires of the Ch'in dynasty.[8]

Foolhardy and without considering my limitations, I had wanted to make an exposition of the great law and foundation of the Book of Rites, to explain its contents and reasonings, and so make manifest the unity of *ch'i* (concrete details, sacrificial utensils) and *Tao* (spiritual meaning), of the roots and branches. But my lack of virtue and my fear that time was not yet ripe, inhibited me. What I often say is: "Rites are to the ceremonies what compass and quadrant are to the shapes of circles and squares. Without circles and squares there can be no use for compass and quadrant. Without ceremonies there can be nothing visible called rites. Yet circles and squares are made by compasses and quadrants, and without being themselves compass or quadrant. When compass and quadrant are applied to make circles

[5] Analects 17: 11; Legge, *Classics*, v. 1, 324.

[6] Analects 3: 3; Legge, *Classics*, v. 1, 155.

[7] *Lao-tzu*, ch. 18, SPPY ed., 10a; Chan *Source Book*, 148. *Chuang-tzu* 9, SPPY ed., 4: 7a–b, Watson, tr., 105.

[8] See *Shih-chi* 6: 25 for the account of the burning of books by the Ch'in emperor.

and squares, they can be used indefinitely. But when compass and quadrant are not used to make circles and squares, and the shapes of these circles and squares are used as though they were themselves compasses and quadrants, then the real compass and quadrant would have no more usefulness. For compass and quadrant are not limited to making certain definite circles and squares, while circles and squares are [in their turn] ruled by definite compasses and quadrants."[9] This explains the essential meaning of ritual observance—how men of abundant virtue remain in accord with the Mean in their action and demeanor, and in their relationship with one another.

The Sung scholar, Chu Chung-hui (Chu Hsi), lamenting the confused state of the canonical ritual texts, wanted to examine, correct, and revise them. He took Yi-li (Ceremonials) to be the canonical book, and the Book of Rites to be its commentary.[10] But he was unable to finish his work. After him, came Wu Yu-ch'ing (Wu Ch'eng), who decided to compile an annotated edition,[11] without repeating anything that Chu had already said. He explained many important points, discerning between questions of precedence and of gravity. Both men, Chu and Wu, based their indications and directives on the instructions left behind by the Han scholars. I only regret that I was born too late to be able to hear what they said about seeking the organic unity of the ritual laws, in order to act according to the original intentions of the ceremonies. True, if a later sage had written on the subject, there would be no need now to say anything more. But since no later sage wrote on the subject, Wu Ch'eng's book, the Annotated Edition of the Book of Rites, (Li-chi ts'uan-yen), remains the necessary "sieve and fur coat"[12] and "'fish-trap and bait"[13] for every student of the rites.

---

[9] Part of this paragraph is quoted in chapter 3.

[10] Chu's unfinished work was entitled Yi-li ching-chuan t'ung-chieh (Complete Explanations of the Classic and Commentaries of Yi-li). See the description given in SK 22: 26.

[11] See the description of Wu's book in SK 21: 4.

[12] Allusion to the Book of Rites. See Li-chi cheng-yi, SPPY ed., 11: 5b–6a. Eng. tr. in Legge, Li-Ki v. 2, 90. This reference is to sons who learn their fathers' trades.

[13] Allusion to Chuang-tzu, 26, SPPY ed., 9: 6a; Eng. tr. by Watson, 302.

My friend and relation by marriage, Hu Ju-teng, a faithful man and fond of rites, is going to Ning-kuo [Kiangsi] and intends to reprint the *Li-chi ts'uan-yen* for publication, giving some words of explanation of his purpose. He has asked me to write a preface for it. I wish to help realize Ju-teng's intentions by going back to the roots of the question. And so I have written this preface.

WWKC 7: 241b–242b

4. PREFACE TO THE COLLECTED WRITTINGS OF
LU CHIU-YÜAN (1520)

———————————

The teaching of the sages is the teaching of the Mind. Yao passed it to Shun, and Shun to Yü, saying: "Man's Mind is prone to error, [while] the Mind of the Way (*Tao-hsin*) is subtle. Remain discerning and single-minded; keep steadfastly to the Mean."[1] This was the beginning of the teaching of the Mind. The Mean refers to the Mind of the Way. For the discerning quality and singleness of purpose of the Mind of the Way is called humanity (*jen*), which is the same as the Mean. The teachings of Confucius and Mencius were centered on the quest for humanity. It was their transmission of the doctrine of discernment and single-mindedness. However, already at their times, certain people made the mistake of seeking the Way in externals. Tzu-kung, for example, asked [Confucius] if the Way resided in abundant learning,[2] and if humanity was identical to the practice of "procuring extensive benefits for the people."[3] The Master taught him to seek an "all-pervading unity,"[4] and to learn to judge others by what is near one-self,[5] that is, to seek that Way in one's own mind. At the time of Mencius, disciples of Mo-tzu taught of the virtue of humanity as that which brings one to the point of "rubbing his head and wearing out his heels"[6] while Kao-tzu's disciples said that humanity was internal, but righteousness (*yi*) was external.[7] The school of the Mind was much injured by such teachings. Mencius attacked the opinion of righteousness being external. He said: "The virtue of humanity belongs to man's mind,"[8] and: "There is naught else in

[1] Book of Documents, "Counsels of Great Yü." Legge, *Classics*, v. 3, 61.

[2] Analects 15: 2; Legge, *Classics*, v. 1, 195.

[3] Analects 6: 28; Legge, *Classics*, v. 194.

[4] Analects 15: 2; Legge, *Classics*, v. 1, 295.

[5] Analects 6: 28; Legge, *Classics*, v. 194.

[6] Book of Mencius 7A: 26; Legge, *Classics*, v. 2, 464–65.

[7] Book of Mencius 6A: 4–5; Legge, *Classics*, v. 2, 397–400.

[8] Book of Mencius 6A: 11; Legge, *Classics*, v. 2, 414.

learning except the recovery of the lost mind."[9] He also said: "Humanity, righteousness, propriety and wisdom are not infused into us from outside. We possessed them from the beginning, but we do not think [enough] of this fact."[10]

For when the Way of the sage-kings disappeared, the art of the despots flourished. Those who sought after fame and profit pretended to act according to the heavenly principle (*T'ien-li*) but only fulfill their selfish desires. They deceived others by saying: "Such is the heavenly principle." But how can he who no longer has the [right] mind possess the heavenly principle? From then on mind and principle (*li*) became two different things, and the teaching of discernment and singleness was lost. Scholars of the world became fragmented in their learning, seeking external information on criminal codes, [sacrificial utensils] and their numbers, in order to understand what they call the principles of things (*wu-li*). They did not know that the mind contains the principles of things, which need not be sought outside. As for Buddhists and Taoists, they taught emptiness and the void, they abandoned the constant principles of human relationships and of worldly affairs, in order to seek the understanding of the mind. They did not know that the principles of things reside in the mind, which cannot be understood if things are abandoned. During the Sung dynasty, the two masters, Chou [Tun-yi] and Ch'eng [Hao] attempted once more to return to the sources of inspiratoin in Confucius and Yen-tzu. They taught of *Wu-chi* (Limitless) and *T'ai-chi* (Ultimate), and confirmed these teachings with explanations of humanity and righteousness, of remaining in accord with the Mean, and of the importance of stillness. They said that the mind is always the same, whether active or still, there being no division between the inner and the outer, between following after or going forward to meet external events.[11] In this way they nearly recovered the message of discernment and single-mindedness.

After them came Lu Hsiang-shan (Lu Chiu-yüan). Although his teaching might not appear to have as much purity and harmony as

---

[9] Book of Mencius 6A: 11; Legge, *Classics*, v. 2, 414.

[10] Book of Mencius 6A: 4–5; Legge, *Classics*, v. 2, 397–4c0.

[11] Allusion to *Chuang-tzu* 6, 3: 7b.

Chou's and Ch'eng's, it was nevertheless simple and direct, genuinely going back to the teaching transmitted by Mencius. If certain features of his doctrines also opened new vistas, and differed somewhat from Mencius, these were due to particular differences of temperament and opinion. He remained one [with Mencius] in teaching others to seek the Way in the mind. For this reason, I decided that Lu's teaching was the very teaching of Mencius.[12] But the critics of the world attacked him for having Ch'an Buddhist [sympathies], on account of his disagreements with Hui-an (Chu Hsi). Now, since Ch'an Buddhists advocated the abandonment of moral relationships and of the principles of things, their aim was not the service of the country and the world. If Lu's teaching was really such, he would be a Ch'an Buddhist too. But books exist today that explain both Ch'an Buddhist teachings and Lu's teachings. Scholars need only to read them, to find out the truth for themselves. And then right and wrong. similarities and differences, need no more debate to become known. But it takes only one man to say something for others to follow in chorus, and people act like a dwarf following the crowd in an open-air theater, reacting as do others, without knowing why they are laughing or weeping. Is this not a case of honoring the ears too much and neglecting the eyes? Are they not committing the fault of "not seeing in the mind what is not attained in words"?[13] Talks of right and wrong, similarities and differences, arise often from the fact that people desire to excel, to justify themselves— their deep-seated habits and their own opinions. For this reason even worthy men are not entirely free from the desire to excel and from certain deep-seated habits.

Li Mao-yüan, Prefect of Fu-chou, wishes to republish the Collected Writings of Lu Chiu-yüan (*Hsiang-shan wen-chi*), and has asked me to write a preface for it. And what need I do say? May the readers of Lu's writings seek the truth in the mind, and not be hindered by deep-seated habits and personal opinions! Then will differences between coarse husks and fine rice naturally become known to the mouths of those who taste them.

WWKC 7: 242b–243a

[12] This is quoted in chapter 4.

[13] Reference to Kao-tzu's teaching. See Book of Mencius 2A: 2; Legge, *Classics*, v. 2, 188.

5. On the "Love the People" Pavilion (1525)

When Nan Yüan-shan (Nan Ta-chi) was appointed Prefect of Yüeh (Shao-hsing), he came to me, Yang-ming, for counsel on government. I said: "Government means loving the people." He asked: "How does one love the people?" I answered: "By making manifest clear virtue." He asked: "How does one make manifest clear virtue?" My answer was: "By loving the people." He pursued: "Are 'making manifest clear virtue' and 'loving the people' the same thing?" I replied: "Yes, they are. Making manifest clear virtue means allowing the nature of the Heavenly ordinance (*T'ien-ming*) to manifest its brilliance and spirituality. The Heavenly ordinance is the source of all reality (*li*). All men know what it entails to be filial to their fathers or fraternal to their elder brothers. All possess a natural understanding of how to respond to events and things. This comes from the spiritual clarity of their minds, which continues through past and present without changing and without becoming obscured. This is what we call 'clear virtue.' If, at times, it suffers hindrance from unruly desires (*wu-yü*), the man who understands this removes the hindrance and restores intact the clarity of his *pen-t'i* (mind-in-itself). But it does not mean that anything can be added to this *pen-t'i*."[1]

[Nan] continued: "But why should all this consist in loving the people?" I answered: "Virtue cannot make itself manifest. The man who wishes to make manifest his virtue of filial piety, must love his father. Only then will this virtue become manifest. The man who wishes to make manifest his virtue of fraternal respect, must love his elder brother. Only then will this virtue of fraternal respect become manifest. The same is true of [loyalty] between sovereign and subject, [harmony] between husband and wife, and [reciprocity] between friends. This is why making manifest clear virtue must consist in loving the people, while loving the people is the way by which clear virtue can be made manifest. And so they refer to the same thing." He asked: "I can see how loving the people makes manifest clear

---

[1] The discussion revolves around the main themes of the Great Learning.

virtue and advances self-cultivation. But what has it to do with the family, the country, and the world?" I answered; "Man is the heart (*hsin*) of Heaven and Earth. The word 'people' refers to oneself. With people [Man] the way of the Three Powers (*san-ts'ai*) becomes complete.[2] When I extend affection for my father to other people's fathers, there will be affection between all the fathers and sons of the world. When I extend love for my elder brother to other people's elder brothers, there will be affection between all elder and younger brothers of the world. The same can be said about sovereign and subject, husband and wife, friend and friend, and even about birds and beasts and trees and grass. One can have affection for all. And this affection will always develop more completely one's mind-and-heart, and make manifest its clear virtue. This is the meaning of making manifest clear virtue in the world, giving order to the family, good government to the country, and peace to the world."[3]

He said: "But then, what is 'resting in the highest good' "?

I said: "In the past, some men really wanted to make manifest their clear virtue. But they made the mistake of falling into [the state of] emptiness and void, neglecting the service of family, country and world, because they did not know that 'making manifest clear virtue' meant 'loving the people'. These were Buddhists and Taoists. Others wanted to love the people but made the mistake of relying on power politics and crafty dealings, without practicing sincere benevolence and commiseration. They did not know that 'loving the people' is the way of 'making manifest clear virtue.' These were disciples of the Five Despots, who looked for fame and profit. Neither knew the meaning of 'resting in the highest good'. Now the highest good is the ultimate in clear virtue and in loving the people. The heavenly ordinance is full of pure goodness. Its spiritual clarity reveals this highest good. This is the *pen-t'i* of clear virtue, which is also called *liang-chih*. The highest good reveals right and wrong clearly. It is the discerning principle (*li*) with which the mind (*hsin*) is naturally

---

[2] See *Chou-yi cheng-yi*, 9: 2a–b; Legge, *Yi King*, 423–24. The reference is to the Way of Heaven, which is of *yin* and *yang*, the Way of Earth, which is of softness and hardness, and the Way of Man, which is of humanity and righteousness.

[3] Part of the preceding paragraph is quoted in chapter 5.

endowed, and cannot be increased or diminished. Increase or diminution comes through selfishness and petty cleverness, which have nothing to do with the highest good. But since people do not know that the highest good resides in the mind, they apply their own cleverness to look for it outside, obscuring the principle of right and wrong to the point of confusing these. And so, unruly desires are let loose and the heavenly principle is lost. The teaching of manifesting virtue and of loving the people is distorted. For 'resting in the highest good' stands in relation to 'manifesting virtue' and 'loving the people' as the compass and quadrant to circles and squares, the ruler and measure to length, and the scale to weight. If circles and squares are not ruled by compass and quadrant, they would lose their functions. If length is not governed by ruler and measure, it would lose its usefulness. If weight is not controlled by the scale, it would lose its criterion. And if 'manifesting virtue' and 'loving the people' do not reach the point of resting in the highest good, they would also lose their governing principles. This is the teaching of the Great Man. For the Great Man is he who regards Heaven and Earth and all things as one body, and who can therefore become one body with Heaven and Earth and all things."

Yüan-shan sighed and said: "How very simple and easy is this teaching of the Great Man. Now I know that Heaven and Earth and all things make up one body. Now I know that all under Heaven is one family, and the whole Middle Kingdom is one person. So long as there is yet one man who has not received the benefit [of good government], it will be as though I myself pushed him into a ditch.[4] The sage Yi-yin must have had the same insights as my own mind."

So he named his official hall, the "Love the People Pavilion" (Ch'in-min-t'ang), saying: "My official duty is to love the people. I must love my people and so make manifest my clear virtue." He had these words engraved on the wall as a record for all to see.

WWKC 7: 247a–248b

---

[4] Book of Mencius 5A: 7; Legge, *Classics*, v. 2, 363–64. The allusion is to the words of Yi-yin, explaining his reasons for accepting the invitation of King T'ang, founder of the Shang dynasty, to serve in T'ang's government.

6. On the "Respect the Classics Pavilion" of Chi-Shan Academy (1525)

The Classics give us the constant Way. In Heaven, this is called ordinance or destiny (*ming*). Bestowed on man, this is called human nature (*hsing*).[1] As that which is alive and vital in the person, this is called mind (*hsin*). The mind is one with nature and destiny. It penetrates persons and things, reaching the four seas, filling up Heaven and Earth, going through past and present, comprehending, embracing all that exists, one with all that exists, without changing anything. This is the constant Way. When responding to events, it becomes compassion, sense of shame, modesty in yielding to others, and discernment of right and wrong. When expressed in affairs, it becomes affection between father and son, righteousness between sovereign and subject, differentiation between husband and wife, order between elders and juniors, and fidelity between friends.[2] And so, compassion, sense of shame, modesty, moral discernment, intimate affection, righteousness, order and differentiation and fidelity, all refer to the same thing and express the same mind. And so too, nature, destiny, penetration of persons and things, extension to the four seas, filling Heaven and Earth, continuity between past and present, as well as comprehension of all that exists and oneness with all that exists, but without changing anything—all refer to the constant Way.

This constant Way explains the movements of increase and diminution of *yin* and *yang* in the Book of Changes, presents the execution of laws, regulations and government in the Book of Documents, gives musical and lyrical expression to human nature and emotions in the Book of Odes, and lays down rules of deportment and propriety in the ritual texts. It also expresses movements of joy and peace in the Classic of Music, discerns between sincerity and hypocrisy, perversity and correctness in the Spring-Autumn Annals. For all is one—from the movements of *yin* and *yang*, to the discerning of sincerity and

---

[1] Reference to the Doctrine of the Mean, ch. 1.

[2] Part of this paragraph is quoted in chapter 3.

hypocrisy, perversity and correctness. All express the same mind, the same nature and destiny—penetrating persons and things, reaching the four seas, filling up Heaven and Earth, joining past and present, embracing all, one with all that exists, but without changing anything. Such are the Six Classics. They are nothing other than the constant Way in my mind. And so, the Book of Changes gives the movements of *yin* and *yang* of my mind. The Book of Documents gives the laws, regulations, and government of my mind. The Book of Odes gives the musical and lyrical expressions of my mind. The Book of Rites gives the rules of deportment of my mind. The Classic of Music gives the joy and peace of my mind. The Spring-Autumn Annals give the distinction between sincerity and hypocrisy, perversity and correctness of my mind.

In [using] the Six Classics, the gentleman seeks the movements of *yin* and *yang* of the mind, in order to act according to them, by his respect for the Book of Changes. He seeks the laws and regulations and government of the mind, in order to practice them, by his respect for the Book of Documents. He seeks the musical and lyrical expressions of nature and emotions of the mind, in order to develop them, by his respect for the Book of Odes. He seeks the rules of deportment and propriety of the mind, in order to pay attention to them, by his respect for the Book of Rites. He seeks the joy and peace of the mind, in order to give expression to them, by his respect for the Classic of Music. He seeks the distinctions between sincerity and hypocrisy, perversity and orthodoxy of the mind, in order to discern their differences, by his respect for the Spring-Autumn Annals.[3]

In the past, the sages upheld the criteria of human morality (human ultimate: *jen-chi*), and made a written record of the Six Classics for the benefit of posterity. They acted in the same way as the ancestors of a rich clan, who, fearing that descendants might forget and scatter the mass of wealth, and become poor and destitute, committed to writing an inventory of their porperty for their descendants, telling them to keep and make good use of this wealth, and avoid poverty and destitution. In the same way, the Six Classics present a "record" of my mind. The reality of the Six Classics resides in my mind, just as all kinds of amassed wealth and each little item of these, are preserved in the rich family, while the inventory book merely gives an

[3] Part of this paragraph is quoted in chapter 3.

account of names, kinds and numbers. The scholars of the world, however, do not know how to find the reality of the Six Classics in the mind, and look for it in shadows and sounds, becoming hindered by details of words and meanings, which they proudly consider to be the Six Classics. Their behavior resembles that of the descendants of the rich clan, who have been careless in their management of the inherited property, gradually forgetting and losing it till they themselves become poor beggars. And yet they still point to the inventory books, saying: "Here is our amassed wealth!" What difference is there between the two courses of action?

Alas, the teachings of the Six Classics have been lost to the world for more than just one day or night! To esteem fame and profit and perverse teachings is to distort the Classics. To follow textual exegesis and study by rote, to become attached to superficial knowledge and petty opinions, using these to cover the ears and eyes of the world, is to insult the Classics. To indulge in extravagant and sensuous language, resort to cunning debates, cover up treacherous motives, perform wicked deed, and yet occupy important positions, monopolizing knowledge and claiming to be classical scholars, is to pilfer the Classics. Such people are even ready to tear up and discard the inventory books of their wealth and property! How can they retain any respect for the Classics?

The city, Yüeh, used to have a school called Chi-shan Academy, which was situated on the Wo-lung Hill in the west. This place had long been neglected. The Prefect, Nan Ta-chi (Nan Yüan-shan), native of Wei-nan, given the charge of the government, lamenting the fragmented state of learning, and wishing to advance the Way of the Sages, ordered the magistrate of Shan-yin, Wu Ying to restore this Academy, and add to it a building called Tsun-ching (Respect the Classics) Pavilion. He said: "When the Classics are respected, the people will prosper; when the people prosper, there can be no wickedness." As the Pavilion is now constructed, he requested me to say a few words to serve as a notice to other scholars. I was unable to decline this offer, and have written this record. Alas, may the scholars of the world hear my words and seek the Way in their minds! Then will they know the meaning of Respect for the Classics.

WWKC 7: 250a–251b

7. ON THE RECONSTRUCTION OF THE
SHAN-YIN PREFECTURAL SCHOOL (1525)

On account of age, the Shan-yin Prefectural School has been in a dilapidated condition. The Education Officer, Wang Han and others, requested the magistrate, Ku Tu, to renovate it. They asked me then to write an essay to serve as notice to the students. As I was then in mourning,[1] I declined the invitation. Afterwards, Mr. Ku went to the capital to serve as junior minister of Justice, and Wu Ying of Loyang replaced him as Prefect. He further provided for the School, and renewed the request for an essay. At an earlier time, when I was serving on an official post in Nanking, I once responded to the request of the metropolitan Prefect, and wrote an essay for his school. My general message was then: "In promoting scholarship, the desire of the Court is not specifically to have students pass civil examinations, but rather to dispose them to the teaching of the Sages. Now, by enlarging and restoring the school buildings, providing boarding facilities and introducing regulations, the authorities desire to encourage learning. They seek [as students] those persons who regard the entire world as their large house[2] and peaceful dwelling,[3] to offer them the opportunity of cultivating and perfecting their characters. This is the way by which both teachers and students can promote learning." All those who read these words then were moved to reflection. But I did not say much then about how learning is to be pursued. I shall do so now, for our students of Yüeh.

The teaching of the sages is that of the Mind (*hsin*). The goal of learning is the complete fulfillment of mind and character. What Yao passed to Shun, and Shun to Yü was: "Man's Mind is prone to error;

---

[1] Yang-ming's father died in 1522, so he refers here to the period of mourning spent in his native place after this event.

[2] Book of Mencius 7A: 36; Legge, *Classics*, v. 2, 471.

[3] Book of Mencius 2A: 7; 4A: 10; Legge, *Classics*, v. 2, 204, 302. The allusion is to the virtue of humanity (*jen*) which Mencius considers to be the gentleman's "Peaceful dwelling."

the Mind of the Way (*Tao-hsin*) is subtle. Remain discerning and single-minded; Keep steadfastly to the Mean."[4] This *Tao-hsin* refers to the spontaneous manifestation of [human nature.][5] It is not tainted by human [passions]. It is beyond sound and odor, most subtle and yet clear, the very source of sincerity.[6] But man's mind (*jen-hsin*) is tainted by selfishness and prone to error. It contains the beginnings of hypocrisy. For example, while commiserating an infant falling into the well is to manifest spontaneously one's nature, rescuing him and bringing him back to his parents in order to gain their favor and obtain a good name in the village comes from this *jen-hsin,* man's mind.[7] Also, to eat when hungry, to drink when thirsty, is to manifest nature spontaneously.[8] But to seek the best in taste, to indulge one's mouth and belly, is to follow man's mind.

The word single-mindedness (*yi*) refers to the intensive quest for *Tao-hsin,* while the word discernment (*ching*) refers to the effort of keeping oneself in singleness of purpose without becoming tainted with *jen-hsin.* The Way is in accord with the Mean. To remain singly and constantly intent on the Mind of the Way is to hold steadfastly to the Mean. When one is intent on the Way, one is always in accord with the Mean, while in the state of rest, and one always attains harmony of disposition when stirred [by emotions].[9] And so, when this Mind of the Way is expressed in the father-son relationship, there is always affection; when it is expressed in the sovereign-subject relationship, there is always righteousness; when it is expressed in the relationships between husband and wife, elders and juniors, friend and friend, there is always differentiation of duty, order, and fidelity. Such is the

---

[4] Book of Documents, "Counsels of Great Yü." Legge, *Classics*, v. 3, 61.

[5] Doctrine of the Mean, ch. 1; Legge, *Classics*, v. 1, 383. I am translating *sui-hsing,* following nature completely, as manifesting nature spontaneously, to show the movement from the latent to the manifest, and emphasize the aspect of spontaneity.

[6] Book of Odes, Legge, *Classics*, v. 4, 431. This is alluded to in the Doctrine of the Mean, ch. 33, Legge, *Classics*, v. 1, 434. It is a clear reference to the *Tao-hsin* as the absolute. See also Introduction, n. 39.

[7] Book of Mencius 2A: 6, Legge, *Classics*, v. 2, 78.

[8] See one of the poems translated: Answers to Questions on the Tao. (*WWKC* 20: 630a).

[9] Doctrine of the Mean, ch. 1; Legge, *Classics*, v. 1, 248.

harmony of due degree, the universal path of all under Heaven. It reaches the four seas without going astray, joins past and present without becoming exhausted. All under Heaven, people have this same mind, this same [human] nature, this same universal path. Shun asked Hsieh to be Grand Tutor, to teach the people the moral principles governing human relationships, which is nothing other than this universal path.[10] At that time, all were gentlemen, all qualified for enfeoffment.[11] For those who taught, taught only this doctrine of the Mind, and those who studied, studied only this doctrine.

However, with the passing of the sages, the teaching of the Mind became obscure, and hypocrisy was rampant. Many arose who aimed at fame and profit, applied their efforts to textual exegesis, rote learning, and writing artful prose. Learning was fragmented. With each passing month and year, scholars copied from one another, seeking to make their mistakes appear correct. The Mind of Man became daily more prominent, and no longer knows the subtlety of the Mind of the Way. If, at times, certain persons perceived these errors, and sought to return to the roots and sources, they were criticized and accused by the crowds as disciples of Ch'an Buddhism. Alas, how will the doctrine of the Mind become evident again?

The teachings of Ch'an Buddhism and those of the sages both seek the complete fulfillment of the mind. There is only a slight difference between the two. The sage seeks to fulfill his mind (*ching-hsin*) completely, by regarding Heaven and Earth and all things as one body. When he finds affection in his own father-son relationship, but knows it to be lacking for others in the world, he will not consider his mind to be completely fulfilled. When he finds righteousness in his own sovereign-subject relationship, but knows it to be lacking for others, he will not consider his mind to be completely fulfilled. When he finds the proper differentiation of duty in his own conjugal relationship, when he finds order in his own elder-junior relationship, and fidelity in his relationship with friends, but knows these to be lacking for others he will not consider his mind to be completely fulfilled. When

[10] Book of Documents, "Canon of Shun." Legge, *Classics*, v. 3, 44.

[11] Reference to certain words which Wang Mang, the usurper, (r. A.D. 6–23) used, speaking of the days of the sage-kings. See *Han-shu*, ESWS ed., 99A: 35.

his own family is well fed and warmly clad, with leisure to enjoy themselves, but he knows there are others who lack the essentials of life and advantages of leisure, can he expect them to have affection, righteousness, differentiation of duty and fidelity in their human relationships? This shows that his own mind is not fully fulfilled. And so, he sets up laws and government, dispenses rites, music and education, in order to provide for what is lacking, perfect himself and others, and bring to fulfillment his own mind. When his mind is fulfilled, his family will [naturally] be in good order, his country will be well governed, and all under Heaven will enjoy peace. That is why the teaching of the sages is nothing other than the fulfillment of mind and [realization of self].

On the other hand, although Ch'an Buddhist teachings also speak of the mind, they consider it to be the universal path only in the sense of keeping it free interiorly, without having at all to seek for external fulfillment, And when there is something irregular without, they do not consider it necessary to trouble themselves within on this account. This is what they mean by fulfilling the mind. They hardly realize that they have fallen into the pit of self-interest. And so the abandonment of human morality, of worldly affairs and things, may perhaps contribute to self-perfection, but cannot help the government of family, country, and world.

For the teaching of the sages makes no distinction between self and others, the inner and the outer. It considers Heaven and Earth and the myriad things as the Mind. But the Ch'an Buddhist teachings are rooted in self-interest and cannot avoid the division between the inner and the outer. This is the difference between the two. If the scholars of today who devote themselves to the teaching of mind and nature abandon human morality and concern for affairs and things, they would certainly be disciples of Ch'an Buddhism. But if they do not abandon human morality or concern for affairs and things, but concentrate on fulfilling the mind and nurturing nature, theirs would certainly be the teaching of discernment and single-mindedness of the school of sages. How then, can these persons be called Ch'an Buddhists? [Unfortunately], the scholars of the world have inherited the practice of preparing for civil examinations by writing artful prose, injuring their minds by such indulgence and frivolity. They depart daily further from what the sages teach of the fulfillment of the mind, until it looks as though there are two extremes. When they are asked to return to teachings of mind and nature, they show astonishment and accuse their benefactors of Ch'an Buddhism and regard them as enemies. Is this not very sad?

To be ignorant of one's wrong, and yet accuse others of being wrong, may be due to hindrances of old habits, and should not be regarded as a crime. But there are people who know what is wrong, despise others for their faults, and yet refrain from telling them. This is plain selfishness. There are also those who are told of their wrong, but remain blind to their faults without making any self-examen. These have given themselves up. In our city Yüeh, there are many courageous scholars, many who have emerged and prospered without need of encouragement. But there may also be a few who are yet hindered by old habits. For this reason, I respond to the invitation extended to me to say a few words. Besides, I am addressing these few words to many others, not just to our scholars of Yüeh.

WWKC 7: 251b–253b

SECTION B

THE POEMS

1. POEMS WRITTEN IN THE COMPANY OF CHAN JO-SHUI ON MY DEPARTURE FOR THE SOUTH[1]

The currents of Chu and Ssu[2] have weakened,
The waters of Yi and Lo[3] appear to be only a thread.
As to the three or four later gentlemen—
Their merits cannot adequately make up for their defects.
    Alas, that I should refrain from measuring my own weakness:
    Limping in my walk, yet I desire to go so far.
    So many times, I fall down and I rise up again,
    Breathing heavily, often near the point of breaking.
On the way I met a man with the same mind.
Together, we dare to proclaim the greatness of virtue,
We fight for the important differences which exist between nuances,
And encourage each other to go forward ten thousand *li*.
The winds and waves are rising; I suddenly lose sight of you—
As I utter these words, my tears are vainly falling.

WWKC 19: 572b

---

[1] The poems translated here are the third, fourth, fifth, and sixth of the group, all of which were written in 1507. The first of these is quoted in chapter 1.

[2] The rivers flowing through Shantung, the region belonging to the former state of Lu, where Confucius was born.

[3] The rivers flowing through Honan, and representing the teachings of the Ch'eng brothers, natives of Lo-yang.

This same *hsin* and this same *li* we both share,[4]
What need is there to discern between self and other?
Whose sigh has been immortalized throughout the ages,
Lamenting his separation from the others?[5]
    Between the vastness of Heaven and Earth,
    Is there some one who does not share the same Spring?
    Our thoughts of each other should serve as mutual encourage-
      ment—
    We must not let worldly affairs separate us.
Do not allow our minds to be separated by any distance,
Then will ten thousand *li* only serve to strengthen our friendship.
                                WWKC 19: 572b–573a

Ch'i and *Tao* are inseparable,[6]
To make two out of one is against nature (*hsing*),
Confucius, the Sage, preferred to remain wordless:[7]
Inferior learning can only lead to flippant responses.
    The gentleman is assiduous in little things:
    Their accumulation builds up his conduct.
      I recited the chapters of ceaseless searching,
    And heard, with you, the meaning of destiny.
    How can the solitary scholar
    Find stillness in an empty valley?
                                  WWKC 19: 573a

Tranquil emptiness is not empty nothingness:
It contains within itself, the prestirred equilibrium.
What does it possess within itself,
Without which one would be really empty?

---

[4] Allusion to *HSCC* 34:8a.

[5] Allusion to the words of Tzu-hsia, a disciple of Confucius. See *Li-chi Cheng-chu*, "T'an-kung," pt. 1, 2:10a; Legge, *Li Ki*, v. 1, 135–136.

[6] Allusion to the Appendix of the *Book of Changes*. See *Chou-yi cheng-yi*, 7:18b; Legge, *Yi King*, 377.

[7] Analects 17:19; Leegge, *Classics*, v. 1, 326.

When passions are absent, the True Self[8] may be seen.
"Not forgetting" and "not assisting"[9] are not genuine efforts.
How perfect is the secret of mysterious transformation,
With whom else can I probe it, if not with you?

WWKC 19: 573a

---

[8] The words used here are *chen-t'i*, which refer to "metaphysical reality."
[9] Book of Mencius 2A:2; Legge, *Classics*, v. 2, 190.

2. Two Poems for Ch'u Ch'ai-hsü[1]

Once we decided: you and I
To probe into the Book of Changes and seek its mysteries.
You had to travel to the Western Mountains,
Only after one entire year did you return.
And then, on the point of this endless quest,
We had to utter new farewells again.
Separated by a distance of over ten thousand *li*
How can we count on a future reunion?
You ask me about the secret of long life:
I don't wish to deceive you.
Hidden behind growths and declines,
How perfect are the secret springs of Heaven and Earth!
A divine abyss separates madness (*k'uang*) and sagehood—
Truth and error diverge on an infinitesimal point.[2]

To discern an infinitesimal error:
Look into the mind—does one seek Self, or the Others?
The Unselfish differs from the Selfish
As the action of Heaven from that of Man.
How precious is this body of ours, received from parents:[3]
The fulfillment of character[4] can bring it no loss.
May you excel in respect of moral nature,[5]
And avoid fragmenting your learning.
Let not temperament lead you astray,
And do not allow things to deceive you.

WWKC 19: 573b–74a

[1] He was also known as Ch'u Huan.

[2] The three last lines are quoted at the beginning of chapter 7. And, for reference to an "infinitesimal error," see chapter 3, n. 7.

[3] Allusion to the Classic of Filial Piety. See *Hsiao-ching chu-shu*, with Commentary by Emperor Hsüan-tsung (r. 712–56), SPPY ed., 1:2a.

[4] Book of Mencius 7A:38; Legge, *Classics*, v. 2, 472. The words refer literally to "satisfying the desires of one's physical form."

[5] Doctrine of the Mean, ch. 27; Legge, *Classics*, v. 1, 422.

3. CROSSING THE SEA[1]

Thoughts of danger and safety do not disturb my heart
But pass, as floating clouds, across the infinite space above.
On a quiet night, over thirty thousand *li* of roaring ocean waves,
The boat travels, under a bright moon, pushed by heavenly winds.

WWKC 19: 575b

4. IN THE WU-YI MOUNTAINS[1]

A sedan-chair flies through the clouds between ten thousand peaks,
Turning behind, I hear the roaring waves under the moon.
Having been envoy of the blue ocean waters,
I meet Prince Wu-yi[2] in the Mountains.

WWKC 19: 576a

[1] This poem, as well as the one following, were allegedly written in 1507 during Yang-ming's travel to Kweichow, the place of his exile, although Chan Jo-shui claims that they were written in an effort to feign madness and escape the notice of Liu Chin and so should not be understood as representing any factual happening. See chapter 1, n. 26.

[1] The Wu-yi Mountains are in Fukien.

[2] The god of these Mountains. See *Shih-chih*, 28:116.

5. ON THE DEPARTURE HOME OF MY DISCIPLES,
WANG CHIA-HSIU AND HSIAO CH'I,
I WRITE THIS POEM, TO BE SENT ALSO TO
MY WORTHY STUDENTS IN CH'EN-CHOU[1]

Student Wang wishes also to cultivate life,
Student Hsiao is an admirer of Ch'an Buddhism.
From several thousand *li* away,
They come to Ch'u-chou,[2] to pay respects:

    My Way is neither Buddhist nor Taoist—simple, direct, and open,
    It gives nothing deep and mysterious.
    Listening first with mixed doubt and belief,
    [My students] find their hearts (*hsin*) finally revealed.

[Their hearts] are like mirrors in the mud,
Enclosing the light within the darkness.
Dust and dirt, once removed,
The mirror will reflect the beautiful and the ugly.[3]

    The world's learning is like festoons:
    They serve as decorations; they curl over extended lengths;
    Leaves and branches are all present, entwined
    Yet they are powerless to give life.[4]

[1] Part of the second and the whole of the third stanzas of this poem are quoted in chapter 2.

[2] Since mention is made here of Ch'u-yang, the poem was probably written in 1513 or 1514, during Yang-ming's sojourn there.

[3] Allusion here again is to the *gathas* of Shen-hsiu and Hui-neng. Yang-ming makes use of a known Buddhist—and also Taoist—imagery to describe his Way, which he claims to be "neither Buddhist nor Taoist."

[4] Reference is to the study of classical exegesis.

The gentleman's learning, on the other hand—
Digs for itself roots, deep and firm.
Sprouts come forth gradually,
Strength and prosperity will come from Heaven.

WWKC 20: 600a

6. On the Departure of Luan Tzu-jen[1]

If our Master Confucius desired to remain silent and wordless,[2]
We ought to believe that wordlessness expresses great joy.
When one wakes to the hidden meaning of hawk flying and fish leaping[3]
One knows that moral striving does not lie in expounding texts.
Self-cultivation and mind-culture are not Ch'an practices.
In attempting to correct errors, one may go to the opposite.

Under the influence of hearsay and rumor,
True learning has long been interrupted.
I need to sit in silence in the woods,
Green mountains understand well my unspoken words.

WWKC 20: 605b

---

[1] This poem, written around 1514 or 1515, is quoted in chapter 2.

[2] Analects 22:19; Legge, *Classics*, v. 1, 326.

[3] Book of Odes, Legge, *Classics*, v. 4, 445. The Doctrine of the Mean, ch. 12 (Legge, *Classics*, v. 1, 392) refers to it too. The expression represents the way of nature, which reveals the operations of *T'ien-li*, and occurs frequently in the writings of the Sung-Ming philosophers.

7.   In the Wang-yen Cave
An Answer to Tsou Ch'ien-chih[1]

In inspiration one forgets words,
In great pleasure one forgets food.
As I sit in this rocky mountain cave,
I wonder who created order out of primeval chaos.
Confucius desired to become silent and wordless;[2]
The perfect man attained a glimpse of reality's foundations.
Is this past Tao different from today's
Though this man has gone so far away?
In this empty mountain cave, no man can be seen,
It is as though I am really "facing the wall."[3]
Even rain drops cannot penetrate this deep mountain,
Although flowers grow moist with the return of the clouds.

WWKC 20: 607b

[1] The name of the Cave, "Wang-yen" means "to forget words." The poem was written around 1519.

[2] Analects 17:19; Legge, *Classics*, v. 1, 326.

[3] Reference to Bodhidharma's (fl. 6th cent. A.D.) manner of meditation. See *Ching-te ch'uan-teng lu, TSD* No. 2076, LI, 3:219. But it contains also an allusion to Analects 17:10; Legge, *Classics*, v. 1, 323.

8. For the Scholars and Officials of Kiangsi[1]

Four years in armor galloping here and there,
In the autumn winds, bent homeward, my mind remains a blank.
Ashamed as I am, to know no skills to cure the people's ills,
Possessing mere empty titles for which I receive undeserved recompense.

> The lakes and seas are calmer; the winds and sand have settled.
> But the regions around Yang-tze and River Hsiang still suffer floods and droughts one after another.
> As I write this poem, the lines from the Ping-chou [song][2] come suddenly to my mind:
> Looking back, I know well that Kiangsi is my second home.
>
> *WWKC* 20: 611a

[1] This poem was written in 1519 after Yang-ming's capture of Prince Ch'en-hao.

[2] Reference is to the Ping-chou Song, which sings of the predicament of a scholar who was made a general. See *Yüeh-fu shih-chi* compiled by Kuo Mao-ch'ien (Peking, 1955), 85:7a.

9. On the Joy of Returning Home[1]

Not the least merit have I gained in the service of his sage and august
  Majesty,
Helplessly I watch the graying of hair on my temples.
Han Hsin[2] was surely never a true credit to his country,
While Shao Yung[3] was truly a hero among men.

  The times are hard, and allow no ease:
  No longer able to improve the state of affairs, I wish to keep
    my knife intact.[4]
  I go to seek my old place of retirement east of the Yüeh waters,
  In a thatched hut, high above the mountains, in the company of
    clouds.

WWKC 20: 611b

[1] This poem was written in 1519 after Yang-ming's capture of the rebel, Prince Ch'en-hao. It is quoted in chapter 1.

[2] Han Hsin (d. 196 B.C.) helped to found the Han dynasty but was later killed by Empress Lü with the connivance of Emperor Kao-tsu (r. 206–195 B.C.). See *Shih-chi*, ESWS series, K'ai-ming ed., 92: 221–3.

[3] Shao Yung (1011–77) was the Sung philosopher who spent most of his life in retirement. See *Sung-shih*, 427:1098–99.

[4] Keeping the knife intact refers to cultivation of life. See *Chuang-tzu*, 3, SPPY ed., 2: 1b–2a.

10. ON THE WU-CHEN P'IEN
TWO POEMS WRITTEN IN ANSWER TO CHANG
OF THE COURT OF IMPERIAL SACRIFICES

"On Awakening to Truth" is nothing other than "On Mistaken
    Truth,"[1]
The Three Commentaries came originally from the same hand.
[How I hate] the monstrous demons who, for sake of profit,
Spread deceit and falsehood, far and wide.
Chang P'ing-shu could not have escaped the blame of being the first
    culprit—
Who was the one who falsely attributed it to Hsüeh Tzu-hsien?[2]
Let me tell you my friend, quite frankly:
Look carefully, from head to toe, at "Wild-cat Ch'an"![3]
Was "On Awakening to Truth" no other than "On Mistaken Truth"?
Already, in the time of Chang [P'ing-shu], this has been said.
And yet the deep attachment [to life] of worldly men.
Gave rise to *karma*, in their feelings and desires.
How can dreams be discussed in front of a silly man?
What more mystery is there beyond one's genuine nature?
Men still have eyes, for the search for Tao—
Oh look and see, where is the blue sky?

WWKC 20: 606a

---

[1] A play on words. For a textual discussion of *Wu-chen p'ien*, its three commentaries, and their authors, see Liu Ts'un-yan, "Tao-tsang Wu-chen p'ien san-chu pien-wu," in *Tung-hsi wen-hua*, XV (1968), 33–41.

[2] His other name was Hsüeh Tao-kuang (fl. 1106). He was the alleged author of one of the three commentaries on the *Wu-chen p'ien*. Chang P'ing-shu was the other name of Chang Po-tuan. See chapter 6, n. 28.

[3] Ch'an Buddhists spoke of *fake* Ch'an Buddhists as "Wild-cat Ch'an," alluding to the story of the punishment inflicted on a monk who had given an incorrect answer to his Master and was obliged to undergo a series of transmigrations, becoming a wild-cat after 500 such lives, before finally liberating himself. See Wuming, *Lien-teng hui-yao*, 4, *Zokuzōkyō*, 1st coll., pt. 2B case 9, 248a. The name was frequently given to the T'ai-chou branch of the Yang-ming school of late Ming times, for their overt Buddhist sympathies and to signify contempt.

11. ON CLIMBING MOUNT LOTUS[1]

On Mount Lotus' Peak lives an old monk,
Treading on lotus flowers without touching mud.
At midnight the flower's heart gives forth a bright moon:[2]
Alone, suspended, a pearl-like grain in the sky.[3]

WWKC 20: 619a

[1] The exact location of this Mount Lotus is not known, as mountains bearing this name exist in Anhwei, Kiangsi, and Fukien. The one in Anhwei resembles a lotus in shape, and the climber must wind his way up to the top. The Sung philosopher Chou Tun-yi made his dwelling at the foot of the one in Kiangsi. He was known to be a lover of lotus. See *SS* 427: 1096.

In the Buddhist sutras, the lotus is a symbol of purity, and also of the Pure-land of the Buddha. See *Avataṁsaka sutra (Hua-yen ching) TSD* No. 278, IX, 411–12.

[2] Allusion to the enlightenment-experience (*bodhi*). The so-called Buddhist "moon-contemplation" applies the sixteen nights of the waxing of the moon before it reaches fullness to the development of the *bodhi* within, especially to the "sixteen kinds" of bodhisattva-hood. The idea is that the pure mind is comparable to the full moon, and contemplation of the moon may help one to attain *bodhi*. See *Chu-fo ching-chieh she chen -shih ching, TSD* No. 868, XVIII, 274.

[3] While this line can be understood as a continuation of the Buddhist symbolism expressed in the preceding line, it contains also an allusion to a Taoist classic, and the story concerning the Taoist god of primeval times who preached a sermon to all the gods and immortals in a precious pearl, which looked like a grain suspended in the sky. See *Lin-pao wu-liang tu-jen shang-p'ing miao-ching, TT* No. 1, 1:2b–3a.

12. ON THE T'AI-CHI CAVE, WRITTEN FOR WANG CHIN-SHIH[1]

Who made an opening for primeval chaos,
To give Tao-chou[2] its thousand-year-old form?
To believe that the mind is no bright mirror:
Know well that the *T'ai-chi* (Ultimate) was originally the *Wu-chi* (Limitless).
To believe that the mind is no bright mirror[3]
Know well that the bright mirror is besmirched with dust.
Every man carries his own little circle:
Do not sit on the rush mat till your mind turns to dead ashes.[4]

WWKC 26 : 620a

---

[1] His other name was Wang Hsün.

[2] A place in Hunan, home of Chou Tun-yi. Here it refers to the philosopher himself.

[3] An allusion again to the gathas of Hui-neng and Shen-hsiu.

[4] *Chuang-tzu* 2, SPPY ed., 1 : 10a; Eng. tr. by Burton Watson, 36.

13. On a Moonlit Night[1]

The whole world is drowned in sleep.
But the lonely man—who is he?—by chance still sober
Cries aloud but cannot stir the others,
Who stare at him in great astonishment.
Calling him mad, they rise up
Only to surround him and belabor him.
The waters of Chu and Ssu covered the sounds of the Golden Bell,[2]
The rivers Lien and Lo carried faint echoes.[3]
Who is sounding the poison-painted drum,[4]
While the hearers remain dull and unresponsive?
Alas, what are you all intent on doing,
Going about, toiling so restlessly?
How can you be made to hear this drum,
Which can open your Heaven-endowed intelligence?

WWKC 20: 625a

[1] This poem is quoted in chapter 6.

[2] The Golden Bell is an allusion to the Chou-li, where it describes the official post of a teacher of music. Yang-ming refers here to the teachings of Confucius, a native of the state of Lu, through which the waters of Chu and Ssu flow. See *Chou-li Cheng-chu*, SPPY ed. 12: 8a–9b.

[3] Reference is to Chou Tun-yi and the two Ch'engs.

[4] In the *Mahaparinirvāna sutra*, there is a parable regarding a "poison-painted" drum, the sound of which killed all but one of the hearers. It represents the teachings of the sutra itself, which can extinguish all covetous desires in men's hearts. [*TSD* No. 375, XII, 611.] In Chih-yi's (530–97) Commentaries on the *Saddharma pundarīka*, there are references to two drums, the heavenly one which is productive of good, and the poisoned one, which is productive of evil. See *Maio-fa lien-hua ching hsuan-yi*, *TSD* No. 1716, XXXIII, 758, 761. In Chih-yi's *Miao-fa lien-hua ching wen-chü*, he refers to the "poisoned drum" as the symbol of the Buddha-nature, which brings good to those who hear it. [*TSD* No. 1718, XXXIV, 141.]

14. MURMURING TUNES[1]

The wise have no doubts, the humane no worries,[2]
Why are you sad, and why do you frown?
Pass on, and you will find the road wide and even.
Put your trust in Heaven's judgments, not in man's cunning.
To serve, when called upon; to retire, when set aside[3] : Such is my
    desire.
Keeping myself free, as a light vessel floating on open waters.
Man is made for lifting up Heaven and Earth,
Can he regard his bonds as those of a poor prisoner's?
The pearl worth a thousand gold pieces is not meant for shooting birds,
The precious, carved sword is not made for digging ground.[4]
Don't you know how the old man, our eastern neighbor, after all his
    precautions,
Lost his head to the tiger that jumped into his room at night,
While our western neighbor's little child, without knowledge or fear,
    not knowing the beast,
Chased it away with a bamboo, as if driving a bull?
To prevent choking, a crazy man stops eating,
To avoid drowning [in a sinking ship], a fool jumps first into the water.
Stay free and natural, above life's worries,
Fear of slander leads merely to vain murmuring.

WWKC 20: 626a–b

---

[1] These poems were written around or after 1520.

[2] Analects 9:29; Legge, *Classics*, v. 1, 225.

[3] Analects 7:10; Legge, *Classics*, v. 1, 197.

[4] Allusion is to the precious sword given by the king of the state of Wu, to his faithful minister Wu Tzu-hsü with which he committed suicide. See Annals of Tso, 11th year of Duke Ai of Lu (789 B.C.), Legge, *Classics*, v. 5, 823–26.

15. SITTING AT NIGHT AT THE PI-HSIA POND[1]

An autumn rain brings in the newness of a cool night:
Sitting on the pond's edge, I find my spirit brightened by the solitary
    moon.
Swimming in the depths, the fish are passing on words of power;
Perched on the branches, birds are uttering the true Tao.[2]
Do not say that instinctive desires are not mysteries of Heaven:[3]
I know that my body is one with the ten thousand things.
People talk endlessly about rites and music;[4]
But who will sweep away the heaps of dust from the blue sky?

[1] This poem was written in 1524, during Yang-ming's period of retirement to his native place. See again *WWKC* 34:962. It is quoted in chapter 3.

[2] Allusion to Book of Odes. See Legge, *Classics,* v. 4, 445. It is cited in Doctrine of the mean, ch. 12. (Legge, *Classics,* v. 1, 392.)

[3] Allusion to *Chuang-tzu,* 6; see *SPPY* ed., 3:2a; Burton Watson, tr., 78, where the "True Man" is described as one who is "deep in his passions and desires, and shallow in the workings of Heaven."

[4] Allusion to the controversy regarding posthumous honors, to be given to the deceased father of the emperor, Shih-tsung (r. 1522–66). See *WWKC* 34:962. See also the articles by Amada Takeo, "Tairei no gi to Ōyōmei," *Chūgoku tetsugaku* I (February 1961), 1–9, and Nakayama Hachiro, "Futatabi 'Kasei' chō tairei mondai no hotan ni tsuite," *Mindai shi ronsō,* ed. by the Editorial Committee of Ming Studies, in Honor of the Memory of Dr. Shimizu (Tokyo, 1962), 61–78.

16. Two Poems on a Moonlit Night While Singing with My Disciples on T'ien-ch'üan Bridge[1]

The bright midautumn moon shines high above ten thousand *li*
The fair clouds appear suddenly over the four mountains
A momentary fog disperses quickly with the winds,
Leaving the sky again blue and the moon bright.
If you believe that *liang-chih* was originally unobscured,
How can external objects interfere?
Old as I am, I sing wild songs tonight,
To be transformed into heavenly music, filling up the Great Purity.[2]

Everywhere brightly shines the midautumn moon,
Where else can you find another assembly of such talents?
Alas, that learning should already have been interrupted for a thousand
    years!
Waste not your one life, men born to greatness!
Whether our influence will outreach Chu Hsi's is a matter of doubt.
Yet in no wise shall we imitate Cheng Hsüan's quest for details and
    fragments[3]
Setting aside the lute while the notes are still vibrating in the spring
    breeze,
Tseng Tien,[4] the ardent and eccentric, understands my mind best.

WWKC 20: 627b

---

[1] These poems were written in 1524, on the occasion of a banquet that Yang-ming prepared for his disciples on the night of the midautumn festival, which was attended by over 100 persons. See *WWKC* 34:961. They are quoted in chapter 1.

[2] The Chinese words, *T'ai-ch'ing*, refer to the sky.

[3] For Cheng Hsuan (127–200), the great Han classical exegete, see *Hou Han-shu*, ESWS series, K'ai-ming ed., 65:132–33.

[4] For Tseng Tien, the disciple of Confucius, see Analects 5-21; Legge, *Classics*, v. 1, 181.

17. Sitting at Night[1]

Under the new autumn moon, I sit alone in the courtyard,
Where else between Heaven and Earth has man more freedom and
    ease?
My loud songs move away with the fresh breeze
My quiet feelings follow the stream and turn to spring.

The thousand sages have no secret outside *hsin*,
The Six Classics exist only to wipe away the mirror's dust.[2]
Alas for those disturbed by dreams of Duke Chou[3]
They have not tasted the joys of a quiet life in a poor alley.[4]

WWKC 20: 628a

---

[1] This poem was written around 1524.

[2] Allusion again to the *gathas* of Hui-neng and Shen-hsiu.

[3] Allusion to Analects 7:5; Legge, *Classics*, v. 1, 196.

[4] Allusion to Analects 6:9; Legge, *Classics*, v. 1, 188, and the descriptions of Confucius' favorite disciple, Yen Hui, who was content with a life of poverty.

18. A Poem Written on the New Name of Ch'ien Hsi-ming: Hsin-yü[1]

A fisherman sings:
    The art of fishing depends not on the eye, but on the mind (*hsin*).
    The mind is not on the fish. but on something more profound.
    The whales of the Northern Oceen are all very small.[2]
    It is not enough to catch six sea turtles at one cast of the net.[3]

May I ask then, how do you fish?
    Yes—My net is the Way (*Tao*)
    My ropes are my knowledge of the good (*liang-chih*)
    My bait is the Great Harmony (*T'ai-ho*)
    My boats are Heaven and Earth.
    I adjust the net without thinking,
    And cast it without considering the direction.
    So I cannot glory in my gains,
    Nor need I fear lest anything be forgotten.

WWKC 20: 628a

[1] Ch'ien Hsi-ming was the father of Yang-ming's disciple Ch'ien Te-hung. He was blind since early childhood. The new name, Hsin-yü, means "fishing with the mind." The dialogue form of this poem, as well as the theme of fishing, recalls to mind the conversation that supposedly took place between Ch'ü Yüan (340?–278 B.C.) and a fisherman, some time before the poet committed suicide by drowning himself in the River Mi-lo. See *Shih-chi*, 84:210; *Ch'u-tz'u pu-chu* (amended and Annotated Edition of the Songs of Ch'u), ed. by Wang Yi (Taipei, 1966), 7:1b.

[2] Allusion to *Chuang-tzu* 1, SPPY ed., 1:1a; Eng. tr. by Burton Watson, 29.

[3] Allusion to *Lieh-tzu*, SPPY ed., 5:5a.

19. ON THE DEPARTURE OF LIN JU-HUAN[1]

Every man can emulate Yao and Shun[2]
This saying of the ancient worthy is no deception.
Henceforth, you can go forward a thousand *li* in one day,
Remember that I too, was once lost and led satray.

The myriad principles have always resided in my nature.
The Six Classics serve merely as steps of the ladder.
The rustic life offers its own joy and leisure:
When will you come back to River Yüeh in your solitary boat?

WWKC 20: 627b

[1] This poem was written some time after 1521.
[2] Book of Mencius 6B:2; Legge, *Classics*, v. 6, 424.

20. FOUR POEMS ON LIANG-CHIH WRITTEN FOR MY STUDENTS[1]

Confucius resides in every man's heart,[2]
Hidden by distractions of ears and eyes.
The real image being now discovered,
Doubt no longer [your] *liang-chih*.

Why, sir, are you always agitated:
Wasting efforts in the world of sorrows—
Know you not the sages' occult word,
Liang-chih is your *Ts'an-t'ung ch'i*.

In every man there is a [mariner's] compass,
His mind-and-heart is the seat of a thousand changes.
Foolishly, I once saw things in reverse:
Leaves and branches sought I outside.

The soundless, odorless[3] moment of solitary self-knowledge[4]
Contains the ground of Heaven, Earth, and all beings.
Foolish is he who leaves his inexhaustible treasure,[5]
With a bowl,[6] moving from door to door, imitating the beggar.

WWKC 20: 629a–b

---

[1] These poems, written in 1524, are quoted in chapter 6. See p. xxx.

[2] This appears to echo the Ch'an Buddhist belief in universal Buddhahood.

[3] In Chinese, the words used are *Wu-sheng wu-ch'ou*. See chapter 7, 17.

[4] Allusion to *Huai-nan-tzu*, SPPY ed., 15:16a. Together, the line alludes to the moment of enlightenment ,which, as the next line reveals, is concerned with the insight into the ultimate reality of the universe. For this interpretation, see Ch'en, *Hsueh-pu t'ung-pien*, 9B:5b.

[5] Allusion to *Ching-te ch'uan-teng lu*, *TSD* No. 2076, II, 6:246.

[6] In Chinese, *t'o-po*, in Sanskrit, *paindapātika*, which alludes to the mendicant Buddhist monk. See *Hsu-ch'uan-teng-lu*, ch. 10, *TSD* No. 2076, LI, 527.

21. TWO POEMS: ANSWERS TO QUESTIONS ON LIANG-CHIH[1]

Knowledge of the good is knowledge of self,
Outside of this there is no knowledge.
Who is there without this knowledge?
Yet who is there that understands it?

Who is there that understands this knowledge?
One's pain and irritation is known only to oneself.
Should one ask others what is pain and irritation,
They will answer: what else is it?[2]

WWKC 20: 629 b

[1] These poems were written around 1524.

[2] By giving the example of pain or irritation—especially related to the sense of touch—Yang-ming sought to emphasize the experiential character of the knowledge of the good.

22. THREE POEMS FOR MY STUDENTS[1]

You, students, have each your genuine nature,
You need not ask or beg of others.
Waste not your efforts on old texts
Merely extend your *liang-chih* to accomplish good works.
Ch'ien [Heaven] and K'un [Earth] are transformations, not dia-
grams.
The Mind and Nature can collect no dust, since they have no shape.[2]
Say not that your teacher speaks the language of Ch'an Buddhism,
He offers these words sincerely for your reflection.
Every man has a road that leads to Ch'ang-an,
It stretches ahead, level and wide.
Yet, thinking that sages have secret formulas,
People abandon the simple and direct way, to seek the more
difficult.
Imitate Yao and Shun by filial piety and fraternal devotion,
Do not copy Liu [Tsung-yüan][3] and Han [Yü] by the writing
of artful prose!
Reflect upon yourself in every daily affair,
If you do not believe that you have everything you need.

The road to Ch'ang-an is quite clearly known,
Why do recluses in the wilderness abandon it,
Making a waste of idleness with their straw huts,
Where deers gallop at ease without fear of capture?
Having heard of a dangerous path, their imaginations wander,
Show them the road and they are greatly disturbed:
Taking great risks, they cast themselves into the vipers' pit,
Or lose their lives in dashing over the cliffs.

WWKC 20: 629b

[1] These poems were written around 1524.

[2] Allusion to the gathas of Shen-hsiu and Hui-neng. Note that Yang-ming expresses preference here for Hui-neng's interpretation.

[3] For Liu Tsung-yüan (773–819), see *Chiu T'ang-shu* 160:442.

23. ANSWERS TO QUESTIONS ON THE TAO[1]

To eat when hungry,
> To sleep when weary:[2]
Such is cultivation—
> The mystery of mystery.[3]
The world cannot believe when it hears this,
It seeks immortality outside of the body.

> *WWKC* 20: 630a

24. BIDDING MY STUDENTS FAREWELL[1]

The sages' instruction lasted a thousand years:[2]
Liang-chih is its oral transmission.[3]
Compasses give circles and quadrants squares,
To discover pristine unity, do not wield an axe.
Without leaving the ordinary realm of actions and movements,[4]
Go straight to the primeval moment, before any diagram was made.[5]

> *WWKC* 20: 630a

[1] This poem was written around 1524.

[2] See *Ching-te ch'uan-teng lu, TSD* No. 2076, LI, 6:247.

[3] *Lao-tzu*, ch. 1; see *SPTK* ed., la. In the SPPY ed., the word used is *yüan* rather than *hsüan*, which is given here in the poem. Wing-tsit Chan translates it as 'deep" and "profound." See *Source Book*, 139.

[1] This poem, written around 1524, is quoted in chapter 4.

[2] Probably referring to the thousand years that preceded the death of Mencius, which supposedly interrupted the "orthodox transmission."

[3] This does not necessarily mean that the words *liang-chih* were handed down *verbatim* by the sages, but that they express the core of the sacred message.

[4] Allusion to the Appendix to the Book of Changes. See *Chou-yi cheng-yi*, SPPY ed., Legge, tr. *Yi King* SBE series, v. 1, 356.

[5] Allusion to Chou Tun-yi's *T'ai-chi-t'u*.

25. ON IMMORTALITY[1]

Immortality—I covet in vain
Lacking pills and money
Famous mountains I have combed,
Till my temples yield silken hairs.
My light body fettered by *smṛti*[2]
Daily move I farther from *Tao*,
Awakened suddenly, in middle age, I find
The Pill of Nine Returns.[3]
No need for oven, nor for tripod.
Why seek I *k'an* and why *li*?[4]
No end is there, nor beginning.
So too, for birth and death—
The magicians' wise words
Only increase my doubts;
Confusedly these old men
Transmit arts difficult and complex,
In me is *Ch'ien* (Heaven), in me *K'un* (Earth)
I need not seek elsewhere—
The thousand sages pass as shadows,
Liang-chih alone is my guide.

WWKC 20: 632b

[1] This poem is quoted in chapter 6. See pp.

[2] *Smṛti* is the Sanskrit word for recollection or thought.

[3] Reference to Taoist elixirs, which bring about different degrees of physical immortality. The *Ts'an-t'ung ch'i* speaks of the *huan-tan* (Pill of Return). See Chu Hsi's *Ts'an-t'ung ch'i k'ao-yi*, SPPY ed., 12a. See also an English translation of the *Ts'an-t'ung ch'i* by L.C. Wu and T.L. Davis, "An ancient Chinese Treatise on Alchemy entitled *Ts'an-t'ung-ch'i*," *Isis* XVIII (1932), 240–41.

[4] These words as *k'an*, *li*, taken from the Book of Changes, had specific meanings in Taoist methods of self-cultivation, referring to alchemy related to the quest for the "external" "internal" pill. See Liu, "Taoist Self-cultivation in Ming Thought," in de Bary, ed., *Self and Society*, 293.

APPENDICES

APPENDICES

APPENDIX I

THE WANG YANG-MING SCHOOL IN JAPAN: A BRIEF SURVEY

Was he the sage of Ōmi, or was he the sage of Japan? Was he the sage of the East, or was he also the sage of the whole world?
But a sage is a sage in the same way in the past and the present, in the East and in the West.
As the sage of Ōmi, he was also the sage of the world.[1]

THE WANG YANG-MING school was allegedly introduced to Japan by the Buddhist monk Ryōan Keigo (1425–1514), who claimed to have met Yang-ming in China—a claim that is not always accepted by Chinese scholars.[2] In any case, there was no independent development of the Yōmeigaku until the Tokugawa period, and then only after the rise to power and dominance of the officially supported Shushigaku. Nakae Tōju (1608–48), "the sage of Ōmi," is usually considered as the first important figure in the Japanese Yōmeigaku movement, and he had come to Wang Yang-ming's thought after having first evinced interest in that of Chu Hsi. His reputation as a sage remains a tribute to Yang-ming's doctrine of sagehood, based on the "universal virtue" (t'ung-te)[3] present in men's minds-and-hearts. This man, known also as "Master Yōmei of Japan," devoted his life to teaching disciples, and manifested an extraordinary filial piety toward his mother. He added

to the religious dimension in Yang-ming's legacy through his efforts
to integrate it with Shinto beliefs, and especially through his reverence
for the Supreme Being, called *Taotogami*, whom he regarded as Creator
and Ruler of 'Heaven and Earth and all things.[4]

Understandably, of course, the development of the Yōmeigaku in
Japan should show similarities as well as differences when compared
to that of the parent movement in China. Its early advocates, including
Nakae Tōju himself, were semirecluses or low-ranking *samurai*. It
manifested strongly contrasting attractions for "inner contemplation"
or "outer activity," as exemplified by the two disciples of Nakae
Tōju: the retiring Fuchī Kōzan (1617–86), who had an absolute faith
in the teaching of Nakae, and remained himself a teacher all his life,
and the active Kumazawa Banzan (1619–91), a *samurai* in the service
of Ikeda Mitsumasa, feudal lord of Okayama, and engaged in political
and economic activities.[5] These tendencies continued to manifest
themselves in the later disciples of the Japanese Yōmei school, sometimes described as having had a "rightist" and a "leftist" branch.[6]
But the school or movement as a whole certainly provided a high moral
idealism for the political movement leading to the Meiji Restoration
of 1868, which appealed to the "restoration" of the Golden Past, but
looked forward to Westernization and modernization.

A JAPANESE "ORTHODOXY"?

The establishment of a self-assertive Ch'eng-Chu "orthodoxy" in
seventeenth-century Tokugawa Japan appeared as a contradiction to
the very origin of the history of this school, which had been introduced
into the country by Zen (Ch'an) monks returning from China, who had
absorbed neo-Confucian teachings from their experiences and contacts
with Buddhist monks and members of the Confucian gentry in China.[7]
It seemed to have been partly the result of a conscious imitation of
"things Chinese," and partly the response to the felt need of an ideology
more conducive to peace and orderly government. But the Japanese had
much less reason than the Chinese to discriminate rigidly between
a Ch'eng-Chu orthodoxy and a Lu-Wang heresy. Thus, the Yang-ming
school, considered heretical in China, could find its way more easily

in Japan to a position of dominance in men's minds, once it demonstrated its adequacy in fulfilling certain intellectual and social needs. On the other hand, whatever anxiety the Tokugawa government showed in its defence of the Ch'eng-Chu ideology only offered additional reasons to the followers of the Yōmei philosophy to work arduously for an Imperial Restoration, to which their names would become associated.

Compared to their Chinese counterparts, however, the Japanese disciples of Ō Yōmei usually kept a greater esteem for the philosophy of Ch'eng Yi and Chu Hsi even when their manifest preference was for that of Yang-ming. In the eighteenth century, Miwa Shissai (1669–1744) renewed the scholarly interest in the Yang-ming philosophy, and attempted further to merge it with the Shinto tradition.[8] He was followed in this work by Satō Issai (1772–1859), the philosopher whose thinking exercised a great influence on the Meiji period. Satō explained the First of Yang-ming's Four Maxims according to the teaching of self-cultivation given in the Great Learning, and even according to Chou Tun-yi's and Chu Hsi's description of *T'ai-chi*, effecting thereby a certain reconciliation between the two schools. He had actually studied at the official Confucian school conducted by the descendants of Hayashi Razan (1583–1619), and declared himself to be a teacher of Chu Hsi's philosophy. But most of his disciples were known as adherents of the Yang-ming school.[9]

This greater flexibility of the Yōmei school in Japan was extended, first to Shinto ideas, by Nakae Tōju and Kumazawa Banzan, each in his own way, and then to Westernizing influences. Hayashi Shihei (1738–93) suffered imprisonment for his interest in and discussion of naval affairs.[10] Satō's famous disciple, Sakuma Shōzan (1811–64), raised the cry of "Eastern Ethics and Western Science" (*Tōyō no dōtoku, Seiyō no gakugei*),[11] the counterpart, in China, of the slogan "Old [Chinese] learning as [moral] basis, Western learning for functional use." (*Chiu-hsüeh wei-t'i, Hsin-hsüeh wei-yung*).[12] However, he attributed his interest in Western science and technology, less to Satō's teaching, and more to the doctrine of "investigation of things" of the Ch'eng-Chu school.[13]

THE HEROIC LEGACY

The Tokugawa government had sought to transform, in some ways, the Japanese *samurai* into a Confucian gentleman. Wang Yang-ming's career as a gentleman-soldier fired the enthusiasm of those who were responsive to the Japanese *bushido* tradition as well as to Confucian ethical teachings. In the nineteenth century especially, the reconciliation of the "inner-outer" tensions resulted in the quasi-religious exaltation of "faith" in *ryōchi* (*liang-chih*), the realization of which was frequently sought for in attempted social reform or political action, frequently directed against the shogunate. In this way, the Japanese united the courageous spirit of Yang-ming the soldier, which flowed from his "transcendence" of questions of life and death, achieved first in exile and then in the midst of many battles, with their own discovery, through *ryōchi*, of the need for social and political change, which they sought to fulfill by individual protest or organized revolt. The feudal structure which prevailed under Tokugawa rule permitted them to appeal to the virtue of loyalty in different forms: Ōshio Chusai (1793–1837), a scholar of high calibre, sold all his books to help the needy of Osaka during the famine, but was led to rebellion by the attitudes of the local authorities who had refused to open the granaries. He carried out this action in the name of the sage kings of China who had founded the Shang and Chou dynasties, and of the legendary Emperor Jimmu of Japan.[14] This revolt was doomed to failure, but his heroic spirit can be discerned in these stirring words:

> In face of a crisis, a hero certainly transcends considerations of fortune or disaster, life or death. But even when [the crisis is over and] the work is accomplished, he should still question [the importance of] fortune or disaster, life or death, This is the same with the gentleman whose learning has become refined and genuine.[15]

As a thinker, Ōshio Chusai leaned especially toward the "left-wing" branch of the Yang-ming school, in following Wang Chi's interpretation of the Four Maxims. His revolt has remained a subject of controversy, but his solid scholarship remains useful, as is shown in his extant writings.[16]

The courage that defied death itself was also manifest in Sakuma Shōzan's disciple, the celebrated Yoshida Shōin (1830–59). This fiery young warrior was a believer in the ability and destiny of the common man, in facing the crisis of the superior military and technological challenges coming from the West. He had attempted, without success, to leave Japan for Europe or the United States, in order to learn military technology. He was finally killed at the age of thirty for organizing an assassination plot, thus becoming a heror to generations of his countrymen, and giving inspiration also to the Chinese reformers and martyrs of 1898.[17]

Another important figure in the movement leading to Imperial Restoration was the Yōmei follower Saigō Takamori (1827–77), the chief of staff of the imperial armies at Edo. After the successful accomplishment of the Restoration, he displayed the same independence of mind and *samurai* spirit by his opposition to Westernizers, which led to his violent death in 1877.[18]

In each case, *ryōchi* was the source of their courage and the authority to which they appealed for their convictions.

"RESTORATION" OR "MODERNIZATION"?

The practical, sociopolitical orientations of the Yang-ming school in Japan, combined with a high ideal of self-sacrifice acquired in meditation, prepared its adherents for an important role in the final Meiji Reforms. The restoration of rightful authority to the Emperor was hailed as a glorious return to the Golden Past, not merely to the Taika Reform of 645 or to the time of Prince Shōtoku and Emprèss Suiko (r. 592–628), when Japan first embarked on modeling its government and institutions on the Chinese pattern, but even earlier still, to the legendary past of Emperor Jimmu.[19] The pragmatic needs of government and of technological knowledge were not overlooked. Sakuma Shōzan and Yoshida Shōin were both interested in "Dutch Learning," particularly in the casting of cannons and other weapons. Sakuma's other disciple, Katsu Kaishu (1823–99), became known later as "Father of the Japanese navy.[20] Other Yōmei scholars were more concerned with "enriching the country" than with "strengthening the army." Another pupil of Satō Issai, Yamada Hōkoku (1805–77)[21] and his friend Kasuga Senan (1811–78), offered ideas of economic reform to the Shogunate government.[22] But Kasuga's anti-Shogunate activities brought him imprisonment, and but for the intervention of Yamada, possible execution. A common friend of Yamada and Kasuga, Ikeda Sowan (1813–78), preferred a life of retirement and of education to political activities.[23]

The young, low-ranking *samurai* who had contributed so much to the success of the Imperial Restoration drew up the Charter Oath of 1868, a vague statement of general principles that were derived in great part from the ideas of Saigō Takamori.[24] These vague egalitarian principles, enshrined in the Constitution of the same year, were balanced by the Imperial Rescript on Education of 1890, with its emphasis on the Confucian virtues of loyalty to the Imperial House, of filial piety, conjugal harmony, brotherly love and friendship, which recall the more orthodox influences of Chu Hsi's school. Its conclusion stated:

> The Way (Tao) here set forth is indeed the teaching bequethed by our Imperial Ancestors, to be observed alike by their Descendants and subjects, as infallible [doctrine] for all ages . . . .[25]

This Confucian moral Way, so strongly reasserted in a time of institutional changes and adaptations to Westernizing influences, gave inspiration to the political activities of Itō Hirobumi (1841–1909), a disciple of Yoshida Shōin, whose statesmanly leadership assured the establishment of a constitutional government for his country the victorious outcome of the Sino-Japanese War of 1894, and the successful revision of the "unequal treaties" imposed upon Japan by Western powers a few decades earlier.[26] The success of Japan's effort of modernization, cannot, of course, be entirely attributed to the Yōmei school. It appears quite clearly that the "radicals" of the late Tokugawa period, who were often attached to the Yang-ming teaching as it was interpreted in Japan, turned "conservative" after the Meiji Restoration, and pleaded rather for the preservation of traditional Confucian values against the rapid tide of continued Westernization. Itō Hirobumi himself is known today more as a Westernizer than as a Confucian traditionalist.

And so, Japan entered the twentieth century, dynamic and re-juvenated, ready to confront events and affairs as they arise. The development of an ultranationalism can also be associated in part with the Japanese Yōmei school. Yasuoka Masaatsu (b. 1898), the well-known Yōmei scholar, was one of Japan's most respected in-tellectuals in the pre-War Nationalist movement.[27] Subsequently, the events of the Second World War provided a traumatic experience to the modern, military nation, and all the more to the deeper thinkers, as they reflected in their *ryōchi* on the significance of the victories and defeats. The heroic spirit of the Yōmei philosophy was made manifest by the bravery of the soldiers. But was such heroism the result of blind obedience to military commands, or the manifestation of an adherence to an inner light, to an authority higher than that of the state? Had the true spirit of Ō Yōmei been lost in the formation of an ideology, with its exaltation of the antiintellectual tendencies of the new Shintoist nationalism? Some of these questions gradually emerged in the postwar years,[28] which witnessed the rise of a capitalist society, with clearly pluralist values. Studies on the philosophy of Ō Yōmei continued, with the application of more Western, scientific techniques, and philosophical categories. Even the "Materialist" *versus* "Idealist" dichotomy, which prevails in mainland China, affected the examination of Ō Yōmei's thought in Japan, particularly in the case of the debate regarding the T'ai-chou branch of the Yang-ming school and the later decline of Ming and Ch'ing thought. The debate between the two scholars, Shimada Kenji and Yamashita Ryuji, focused on this subject and went on in a series of published articles.[29]

The inherent heroic legacy of Yang-ming's thought, as well as certain of its tendencies, with potential for a "philosophy of revolution," was explored by the famous novelist, Mishima Yukio (1925–70), in an article published shortly before he committed suicide. He lamented the rise of postwar Marxism, which sought to fill in the spiritual vacuum created by military defeat and nurtured by capitalist materialism. He located the "revolutionary potential" in certain "nihilist" and "mystical" tendencies of the Yang-ming philosophy, which contrib-uted to the fall of the Tokugawa regime. Yet, in true Japanese style, the revolutionary awareness which he desired was directed less against an established political order than against certain prevalent social

and economic values, which threatened to destroy the authentic
Japanese spirit—a courage that transcended the fear of death.[30]

   While Mishima's understanding of Yang-ming's philosophy was
more on the level of ideology than of truth, scholars are not lacking
in today's Japan who seek to present to a wider public an understanding
of Yang-ming's insights. The fifth centenary of Yang-ming's birth
(1973) has witnessed the birth of the project to publish the *Yōmeigaku
taikei* (A Compendium of the Philosophy of Wang Yang-ming),
which is to consist of twelve volumes, including both translations from
Chinese into modern Japanese of Yang-ming's writings, as well as
monograph articles on various aspects of Wang Yang-ming, the man
and the thinker, as well as the development of his school in both China
and Japan, and even beyond.[31]

APPENDIX II

THE WANG YANG-MING SCHOOL IN KOREA: A SUMMARY REPORT[1]

T IS USUALLY taken for granted that the history of Confucianism in Yi Korea (1393–1910) is the history of the school of Chu Hsi— a rigid state orthodoxy that withstood the tensions of hair-splitting, scholastic debates regarding human nature and the emotions, as well as the tragedies of political factionalism that so weakened the nation and government from within. But the truth is somewhat more complex. The great representatives of Korean Confucianism still await full and impartial studies, especially outside of Korea. As to the Wang Yang-ming school in Korea, the time has come for a better appraisal of its existence and evolution, particularly at this moment with the recent publication of the Collected Writings of Chong Che-du more popularly known as Chong Hagok (1649–1736), Yang-ming's greatest follower in Korea.

True, with only a few exceptions, the great figures of Korean Confucianism remained faithful to the tenets of Chu Hsi's philosophy, as they had learned them, especially since the introduction from Ming China in the mid-fifteenth century of the various official compendia, the *Ssu-shu ta-ch'üan*, *Wu-ching ta-ch'üan*, and *Hsing-li ta-ch'üan*.[2] The introduction afterward of the thought of Wang Yang-ming met with stiff resistance, so much so that till our own days, the very existence of the Wang Yang-ming school in Korea has remained little known, not only in the West, but also in China and Japan, and perhaps in Korea itself.

But it would be an exaggeration to depict Korean Confucianism as a monolithic orthodoxy excluding all dissent. A careful examination of facts shows quite otherwise. The esteemed philosopher, So Kyong-tok (Hwadam, 1489–1546), was an exponent of Chang Tsai's philosophy of *ch'i*, and presaged in this way the whole emphasis that many Korean Confucians would give to this aspect of Sung thought, particularly after the spreading into Korea of the works of So Kyongtok's —and Wang Yang-ming's—contemporary, Lo Ch'in-shun.³ The best-known Korean Confucian thinker, Yi Hwang (T'oegye, 1501–70), a staunch follower of Chu Hsi, upheld the dualism of *li* and *ch'i*, and attacked Yang-ming for criticizing Chu Hsi, neglecting the role of study (*hsüeh*) in the quest of sagehood, and showing Buddhist influences.⁴ But his younger contemporary, the great Yi Yi (Yulgtok, 1527–72), displayed more reserve, even while referring to Ch'en Chien's polemics against Lu Chiu-yüan and Wang Yang-ming. He pointed out that Ch'en could not be followed unquestioningly, since the exact depth of his learning and virtue was unknown. He also said that Korean loyalty to Chu Hsi's thought in contrast to Ming Chinese sympathies for Lu and Wang was no indication of greater "correctness of heart," since many Koreans simply paid lip service to Chu Hsi and did not live up to his teachings.⁵

Yet Korean loyalty to Chu Hsi was such that the inclusion of Wang Yang-ming in the official Confucian cult in Ming China (1584) could not change the attitude of the scholars and Court in a country which had demonstrated, in so many other ways, its eagerness to imitate the Chinese. Sung Ying-ch'ang, a Vice Minister of War and follower of the Yang-ming school, came with the Ming forces to the help of Korea during Hideyoshi's invasion. He organized a series of discussions on the Great Learning to which he invited several prominent Korean scholars, hoping thereby to give them an opportunity to discern more clearly the differences and similarities between the views of Chu Hsi and Wang Yang-ming (1593). Those chosen were lecturers-in-waiting to the Crown Prince, and all of them remained unmoved in their adherence to the views of Chu Hsi.⁶ Later, the Ming imperial envoy, Wan Shih-te, who was in Korea from 1598 to 1600, attempted to persuade the Korean government to follow the Ming example and include Lu Chiu-yüan and Wang Yang-ming in the Confucian cult. But he left Korea without having been able to accomplish this aim on account of the strong resistance of Korean scholars.[7]

And yet, even in those times, the teachings of Wang Yang-ming were not entirely unknown or unappreciated in Korea. Yi Yao, a royal clansman and a known follower of the Yang-ming philosophy, discussed this philosophy in an interview (1594) with King Sonjo (r. 1567–1607) himself.[8] The scholar Chang Yu (Kyegok, 1647–98), criticised his fellow countrymen for their stubborn adherence to Chu Hsi's orthodox system, praised the Chinese for allowing more pluralism, and voiced his own appreciation of Yang-ming's teaching of *liang-chih*.[9] His friend and contemporary, Ch'ae Myong-gil (Chich'on), was also known for his sympathies with the Yang-ming school.[10] But the best known follower of Yang-ming in Korea was the scholar and statesman, Chong Hagok.

Chong Hagok was born in 1649 in the capital (Seoul), to a distinguished family, which traced its descent from Chong Mong-ju (P'uon, 1320–92), the great Confucian scholar-patriot, honored in Yi Korea as the first thinker of the Songni (*Hsing-li*) philosophy. His grandfather was a Third State Councillor. Chong Hagok himself passed his first civil examination, but then obtained his widow mother's permission to forego further, formal preparations for an official career, so as to be able to devote himself entirely to the quest of sagehood. His ardor affected his health and he nearly met an early death at the age of thirty-four. Thereafter he took better care of himself and gained in health. In spite of his preference for a quiet life, he was recommended to official service and served in various local posts as governor, and then became chancellor of the National University, a Fifth State Councillor, and Special Mentor to the Crown Prince, during the reign of the great King Yongjo (r. 1725–76), whose confidence he kept despite repeated attempts by his enemies to discredit him because of his attachment to the thought of Wang Yang-ming. He finally died at the ripe old age of eighty-seven, and was accorded various posthumous honors.[11]

Chong Hagok had been a student of the scholar Yon Myongjae, a follower of Chu Hsi. He seemed to have acquired independently his knowledge of and sympathies for Wang Yang-ming, and he showed some familiarity with Wang's Complete Works. In letters to various friends he explained his reasons for preferring Yang-ming to Chu Hsi. He claimed that Yang-ming had found the real road to sage-hood, and with it the meaning of life.[12] He defended Yang-ming against Yi T'oegye's criticisms, saying that Yang-ming had been faithful to Confucius by keeping to the Old Version of the Great Learning, and by explaining the investigation of *li* (truth, principles) in terms of understanding mind, nature, and Heaven.[13] In a poem to which he has given no title, he says:

> [Without going] outside of my mind and my nature, I know that Heaven and Man come from the same beginning.
> Why seek for things, and for their principles?
> [They] will only make you lose your real source![14]

Chong Hagok lived at a time when political factionalism caused sad divisions among the Confucian scholars, and took its tool of victims. He himself belonged to the *soron* group, which has lost its power. It was from this group that he drew his own disciples. One of them, Yi Kanch'ang, a royal clansman from the K'anghwa island, continued to transmit this teaching to the members of his own family. The descendants of Chong Hagok moved residence also to that island, where they allegedly still live, devoted to Yang-ming's thought in a piety that is almost religious.[15]

The philosophy of Wang Yang-ming also gained certain adherents among members of another political group, which remained mostly out of power, the *namin*. Among these, Kwon Ch'ol-sin (1738–1801), disciple and son-in-law of the famous historian, An Chong-bok (Sun'-am, 1712–91), deserves special mention. An remained a faithful follower of Chu Hsi, and Kwon himself became later a Catholic. However, save for some poems and an essay on the Great Learning, Kwon's writings are lost to posterity.[16]

In our own days, Chong In-bo, (b. 1892) a well-known scholar and descendant of Chong Hagok, had argued for the strong if hidden influence of Wang Yang-ming's thought in the history of Korean Confucianism. He asserted that many more of the Confucian scholars of Yi Korea had been followers at heart of Wang Yang-ming, even though they were obliged to profess external adherence to Chu Hsi.

Chong In-bo himself disappeared around 1950, having probably gone over to North Korea.[17]

Hitherto, the Collected Writings of Chong Hagok had remained available only in hand-copied versions. The risks of being condemned for heresy were such that the author himself had even instructed his descendants to delete certain passages discussing the philosophy of Wang Yang-ming. It is our good fortune today that they are coming out in print for the first time. This has been possible on account of the devotion and foresight of contemporary Korean scholars, eager to make known to their own countrymen as well as to others, the legacy of the Yang-ming school in Korea. They have also seen to it—for the benefit of young Koreans today—that a Hangul translation to the Chinese text be provided. The Yang-ming school in Korea has not only a past but also a future.[18]

APPENDIX III

THE SCHOOLS OF MING THOUGHT ACCORDING TO HUANG TSUNG-HSI

A. Till Wang Shou-jen (Yang-ming)

Ts'ung-jen (Kiangsi) 崇仁	Po-sha (Kwangtung) 白沙	Ho-tung (Shansi/Shensi) 河東	San-yüan (Shensi) 三原	Yao-ching (Chekiang) 姚江
Wu Yü-pi (1392–1469) 吳與弼		Hsüeh Hsüan 薛瑄 (1389–1464)		
Lou Liang (1422–91)—Hu Chü-jen (1434–84) 婁諒 胡居仁	—Ch'en Hsien-chang 陳獻章 (1428–1500)	Lü Nan 呂柟 (1479–1542)	Wang Shu 王恕 (1416–1508)	
			Wang Ch'eng-yü 王承裕 (d. 1538)	Wang Shou-jen 王守仁 (1472–1529)

B. Wang Shou-jen's Disciples

Che-chung (Chekiang) 浙中	Chiang-yu (Kiangsi) 江右	Nan-chung (South Kiangsi) 南中	Ch'u-chung (Hunan/Hupei) 楚中	Pei-fang (Shantung/Honan) 北方	Yüeh-Min (Kwang-tung/ Fukien) 粵閩
Wang Chi 王畿 (1498–1583)	Tsou Shou-yi 鄒守益 (1491–1562)	Huang Hsing-tseng 黃省曾 (1490–1540)	Chiang Hsin 蔣信 (1483–1559) (also a disciple of Chan Jo-shui)	Mu K'ung-hui 穆孔暉 (1479–1539)	Hsüeh K'an 薛侃 (fl. 1517)
Ch'ien Te-hung 錢德洪 (1497–1574)	Ou-yang Te 歐陽德 (1496–1554)	T'ang Shun-chih 唐順之 (1507–60)			
	Hu Chih 胡直 (1517–85)				

Tsou Yüan-piao

Chih-hsiu 止修	T'ai-chou (Kiangsu) 泰州	Kan-ch'üan 甘泉	Chu-ju* 諸儒	Tung-lin 東林	Chi-shan 蕺山
			Fang Hsiao-ju 方孝孺 (1357–1402)		
	(Ch'en Hsien-chang)		T'sao Tuan 曹端 (1376–1434)		
(Tsou Shou-yi)	(Wang Shou-jen)	Chan Jo-shui 湛若水 (1466–1560)	Lo Ch'in-shun 羅欽順 (1465–1547)	(Ou-yang Te)	
Li Ts'ai 李材 (fl. 1562)	Wang Ken 王艮 (1483–1541)	T'ang Shu 唐樞 (fl. 1526)	Wang T'ing-hsiang 王廷相 (1474–1544)	(Hsüeh Ying-ch'i)	
	Hsüeh Yüeh 徐樾 (fl. 1532)	Hsü Fu-yüan 許孚遠 (1535–1604)		Ku Hsien-ch'eng 顧憲成 (1550–1612)	
	Yen Chün 顏鈞	Feng Ts'ung-wu 馮從吾 (fl. 1589)		Kao P'an-lung 高攀龍 (1562–1626)	
	Lo Ju-fang 羅汝芳 (1515–88) Ho Hsin-yin 何心隱 (1517–79)	Li Chih 李贄 (1527–1602)		Ch'en Lung-chang 陳龍正 (1585–1645)	Liu Tsung-chou 劉宗周 (1578–1645)
	Chao Hung—Chou Ju-teng 焦竑 (1540–1620) 周汝登 (1547–1629?)				Huang Tsung-hsi 黃宗羲 (1610–95)

*The scholars grouped here are independent, and not disciples of one another.

APPENDIX IV

ON THE
INTERPRETATION
OF CERTAIN
TECHNICAL TERMS

T HE FOLLOWING TERMS, both single words and expressions, have been selected for discussion because of their frequent occurrence in this study, and also because—with the exception of the historical terms—they often illustrate the *unitary* character of the thought of Wang Yang-ming. Very often, they manifest the different dimensions of the same truth that persistently preoccupied Yang-ming's mind. That this truth pertains both to the ontological and methodological orders is a fact that should emerge from the reading of his works and from this discussion. The words and expressions are given roughly in the order of their occurrence in this work, alphabetically whenever possible, and are grouped together according to the associations of meanings to which they are attached.

A. THE HISTORICAL TERMS

Tao-hsüeh 道學	The movement of thought heralded by Han Yü and Li Ao, developed by Chou Tun-yi, Chang Tsai, the Ch'engs and Chu Hsi, and continued through the Yüan, Ming and Ch'ing dynasties, translated into English as "Neo-Confucianism." It is synonymous with *Hsing-li hsüeh*, although it refers sometimes to the earlier stages of development of that movement.
Tao-t'ung 道統	The line of orthodox transmission of the Tao or of the meaning of ultimate reality in the Confucian school.

Hsing-li hsüeh 性理學	The movement of thought which concentrated its interest in the investigation into the meanings of *hsing* and *li*, the Confucian philosophy as reinterpreted by thinkers of Sung and Ming times who gave it a much more metaphysical dimension. It is usually translated into English by the word "Neo-Confucianism."
Li-hsüeh 理學	The movement of thought which concentrated its investigation on the meaning of *li*. It refers sometimes to the whole *hsing-li* movement, and sometimes to that particular school of thought connected with the names of Ch'eng Yi and Chu Hsi.
Hsin-hsüeh 心學	The movement of thought which concentrated its investigation on the meaning of *hsin*. The term refers sometimes to the whole *hsing-li* movement, but more often to that particular school of thought connected with the names of Lu Chiu-yüan and Wang Yang-ming, also known as the School of the Mind.

B. The Philosophical Terms

Chih 知	Literally knowledge, wisdom. For Wang Yang-ming: moral knowledge, wisdom, the mind-and-heart itself, the knowledge that is united to action and experience.
Hsing 行	Literally, to walk, to act. For Wang Yang-ming: every conscious and voluntary human act, which proceeds from the mind-and-heart, and is united to the knowledge of the morality of the act in question.
Chih-hsing ho-yi 知行合一	The Unity of Knowledge and Action, according to the way Yang-ming himself understood knowledge and action.
Ko-wu 格物	a) Usually translated as "the investigation of things." b) For Chu Hsi, it refers essentially to "investigating the meanings (*li*) of things." c) For Wang Yang-ming, it refers to "rectifying the mind-and-heart," *i.e.*, especially through the acts in which man's mind-and-heart is engaged. Thus, Chu understood the word *ko* mainly as "reaching" while Yang-ming understood it to mean "rectifying." Chu also understood *wu* as "things," while Yang-ming meant it primarily as that to which our intention directs itself, *e.g.*, "affairs" (*shih*).
Chih-chih 致知	a) usually translated as "the extension of knowledge." b) For Chu Hsi, knowledge is extended especially through the investigation of the meanings (*li*) of things. c) For Yang-ming, the only "knowledge" to be "extended"

is *liang-chih*, "knowledge of the good" or wisdom. And since this knowledge is regarded as being somehow both innate and acquired, this "extension" involves not merely development and increase, but also realization—the passing from potentiality to actualization.

Ch'eng-yi
誠意

Usually translated as "making the intention sincere." The word *yi* refers to both thought and intertion.

Cheng-hsin
正心

Usually translated as "rectifying the mind-[and-heart]."

These four expressions all come from the Great Learning. It may be said that, whereas Chu Hsi gives greater importance to the first two: *ko-wu* and *chih-chih*, Yang-ming prefers the second two, and indeed, explains all four in terms of *ch'eng-yi*.

Chung
中

Literally, the middle, the Mean.

In the Doctrine of the Mean it refers to the state of "equilibrium," which governs the person's dispositions before his emotions have been stirred or aroused.

Chu Hsi speaks much of the importance of "equilibrium" as the characteristic of *hsing chih pen-t'i*, i.e. of "pure nature" as such.

Ho
和

Literally, harmony, peace.

In the Doctrine of the Mean, it refers to the state of "harmony", that, ideally speaking, should govern the person's dispositions after his emotions have been stirred or aroused.

Chu Hsi emphasizes the importance of acquiring a "harmonious" disposition, as close as possible to that of one's prestirred "equilibrium." He later developed the doctrine of uniting "activity" (*tung*) and "stillness" (*ching*) by permeating one's life with the spirit of "reverence" (*ching*).

Yang-ming makes no distinctions between "equilibrium" and "harmony," or even between "activity" (*tung*) and "stillness" (*ching*), since he says that the work of extending *liang-chih* unites these states of the mind.

Wei-fa/yi-fa
末發已發

In the Doctrine of the Mean, the words refer to the two successive states of consciousness which prevail before and after the emotions are aroused.

Chu Hsi speaks of *wei-fa* in terms of *chung* (equilibrium) and recommends that it be restored and preserved.

Yang-ming regards them as referring to two aspects under which *liang-chih*, always active and yet always the same, can be understood.

Hsing
性

Literally, nature, the natural, human nature.

a) Mencius speaks of human nature as being originally good.

b) Chu Hsi regards *hsing* as the source and principle of moral and ontological goodness in man and the universe, that which is full of *li*, while he takes *hsing* to be that which contains both *li* and *ch'i* and so morally ambivalent.

c) Lu Chiu-yuan and Yang-ming understand *hsing* and *hsin* to represent one and the same reality, considered in its source and principle, as that by which man shares in *Tien-li* and, considered in its more dynamic aspect, as that which directs all human activity, that is, the "given" nature of man as well as that which is to be acquired, through experience and action.

Hsin
心

Literally, the mind, the heart, the seat of consciousness and the source of all human activity.

a) Mencius considers *hsin* to be the principle of all human activity. "He who completely develops his heart knows his nature."

b) In Ch'an Buddhism, it refers to the undifferentiated First Principle.

c) For Chu Hsi, it is composed of both *li* and *ch'i*, and is inferior in importance to *hsing* (nature), which is full of *li*. It is the active principle which controls both *hsing* (nature) and *ch'ing* (emotions), but is less important to *hsing*, the tranquil principle, full of *li* (being and goodness).

d) For Lu Chiu-yüan, *hsin* and *hsing* are identical. There is only one principle of both activity and stillness. It is full of *li*, and possesses the capacity of transcending itself, because it is somehow greater than itself, one with the universe.
In this regard, he speaks also of *pen-hsin*

e) Yang-ming adopts Lu's understanding of *hsin*. More clearly than Lu, he explains that *hsin* is the principle in man that is capable of self-determination and self-perfection, which hides, within itself, that greater than itself, the Absolute. It is also identical with *liang-chih*.

Liang-chih
良知

Literally, good knowledge, knowing the good.
The word *liang* contains also the meaning of "innateness."

a) In the Book of Mencius 7A:15, the expression refers to man's inborn capacity to know the good.

b) For Yang-ming, it is that in man which enables him to discern between right and wrong, an inborn capacity to know and do the good, a capacity to be developed as well as a goal to be attained, since the perfect development of *liang-chih* signifies sagehood.
He places the word *chih* (extend, develop), taken from *chih-chih*, from the Great Learning, before the term *liang-chih* to express his "Way" of acquiring wisdom and sagehood.

Yang-ming also speaks of *liang-chih* as the principle of vital consciousness in man. He identifies it to *hsin*, especially by speaking interchangeably of *hsin chih pen-t'i* and of *liang-chih pen-t'i*, *i.e.* the mind-in-itself, and *liang-chih* in-itself. In this context, he gives it certain metaphysical importance, as being-in-itself, identifying it to *T'ai-shü* (Great Void), which for him signifies in negative terms, the Absolute.

Yang-ming also makes of *liang-chih* in man, as that which possesses the ultimate authority for its own decisions, intentions, and acts.

In the "Four Maxims," he speaks of *hsin chih t'i* also as being "without good and evil," another negative manner of attributing to it absolute qualities (First Maxim). And yet, he returns in the Third Maxim, to *liang-chih* as that which discerns between good and evil.

Li

理

Etymologically, the viens in jade, or polishing jade.

Literally, it signifies meaning, pattern, reason, truth, discernment, analysis.

a) It is found in Book of Mencius, the Book of Rites, and the Appendix to the Book of Changes, where it assumes greater importance.

b) In Hua-yen Buddhism, *li* refers to the realm of noumena as opposed to *shih*, which refers to the realm of phenomena, *Li* refers frequently to ultimate reality, *tathatā*. But *li* and *shih* are also said to interpenetrate each other.

c) For Chu Hsi, it is being, reality, the principle of organization, that which is full of truth and goodness, the transcendent and normative principle of moral action.

d) Lu Chiu-yüan and Wang Yang-ming both consider *li* as being and goodness, perhaps stressing the latter. They regard *hsin* to be full of *li*, and so depart from Chu's views.

Ch'i

気

Literally, breath, ether, vital force, matter-energy.

a) It is found in the Appendix to the Book of Changes, and especially in Wang Ch'ung's *Lun-heng*.

b) Chu Hsi considers it to be the concrete, material, differentiating principle of things, that which together with *li* constitutes all beings, that which gives life to things.

c) For Yang-ming, *li* and *ch'i* represent, not disitnct principles, but the rational and moral versus the irrational, and vital manifestations of the same human nature or of nature at large.

Jen

仁

Literally, kindness, benevolence, humanity, goodness, love.

In Confucian philosophy, the perfect and universal virtue. Ch'eng Hao and other Sung philosophers gave this word a cosmic, life-giving connotation, making it that power or virtue by which man becomes one with Heaven-and-Earth and all things and shares in the creative processes of the universe.

Wang Yang-ming also identified *jen* with the *pen-t'i* of *hsin*, that is, with the mind-in-itself, the Absolute.

T'ai-Chi
太極

Literally, the Great and Ultimate, or the Supreme and Ultimate. For Chou Tun-yi, it represents the source and principle of all being and goodness, the Ground of Being, the One behind the Many, the Fullness of *li*. Chu Hsi identified it with the Ch'engs' *T'ien-li*, the embodiment of all truth, wisdom, and virtue. He thus internalized Chou's *T'ai-chi*, describing it as immanent not only in the whole of the cosmos, but in each individual being as well.

Yang-ming seldom referred to it, and then usually as the source and pripciple of moral goodness.

T'ai-ho
太和

Literally, the Great Harmony.

For Chang Tsai, it is synonymous with Chou Tun-yi's *T'ai-chi*, that is, the undifferentiated First Principle, the fullness of *li*.

Wang Yang-ming spoke little of *T'ai-ho* and much more of *T'ai-hsü*.

T'ai-hsü
太虛

Literally, the Great Void.

For Chang Tsai, it is full of *ch'i* (ether), the shapeless stuff that makes up the universe.

Wang Yang-ming spoke of *liang-chih* as being somehow one with *T'ai-hsü*, thus endowing the latter not only with life and vitality but also with consciousness and a certain intelligence and spirituality. He spoke, for example, of *liang-chih pen-t'i* as *T'ai-hsü*, describing it as a self-transcending state of mind-and-heart.

Tao
道

a) Literal meaning: the "way" by which one travels.

b) Extended meaning: "reason."

c) In Taoist philosophy: ultimate reality, nameless and ineffable.

d) In Taoist occultism: the secret of life, and of the art of prolonging life.

e) In Buddhism: the meaning of life, ultimate reality, Buddhahood.

f) In Confucianism: the way of life—especially the observance of the five relationships, the meaning of life, ultimate reality.

—Chu Hsi: all the above, and also knowledge of ultimate reality or of the Absolute, which was being transmitted to posterity by the Ch'engs and himself after the interruption that occurred with the death of Mencius.

—Wang Yang-ming: all the above, including the meaning given to it by Chu Hsi, but as identified to *hsin*.

Tao-hsin
道心

Literally, "the Mind of *Tao*," or the "moral mind."

In the movement of thought called *Tao-hsüeh*, it refers to the sacred legacy which is transmitted by the sages. As such, it is opposed to *jen-hsin*, literally, "man's mind."

Ch'eng Yi explained *jen-hsin* as the mind-and-heart which is affected by *jen-yü* (passions of selfish desires) and *Tao-hsin* as the mind-and-heart which is full of *T'ien-li*.

Chu Hsi explained *jen-hsin* as man's mind-and-heart, considered as the seat of consciousness, composed of blood and "ether," and *Tao-hsin* as the same mind-and-heart, considered as the source of moral discernment.

Yang-ming regarded *jen-hsin* as the mind-and-heart contaminated by passions and so become prone to error, and *Tao-hsin* as the pure mind-and-heart, without passions or selfish desires, and identical with *liang-chih*.

T'ien
天

a) Literally, "Heaven," "sky",
b) In the Book of Documents, it is synonymous with "Shang-ti" or the "Lord-on-High," *i.e.*, God.
c) For Confucius, it refers especially to the Supreme Being.
d) For Mencius, it refers sometimes to the Supreme Being, sometimes to the ultimate truth of the universe, or to the fullness of goodness, and sometimes to Fate.
e) For Hsün-tzu, it refers especially to the physical heaven, or nature.
f) For Tung Chung-shu, it refers sometimes to nature at large, to which he attributes qualities of intelligence and spirituality.
g) The Sung and Ming thinkers mometimes speak of *T'ien-ti*, *i.e.*, Heaven-and-Earth, as representing the whole universe, and sometimes speak of *T'ien* alone, as representing the whole universe, or of the fullness of being and goodness.
h) Yang-ming identified *T'ien* with *Tao*, with *Hsin*, and with *Liang-chih*.

T'ien-li
天理

Literally, heavenly reason, principle of Heaven.

a) It is found in the Book of Rites, in the chapter on Music, where it refers to the moral law of Heaven, in which all men share by their reason, and is opposed to *jen-yü* (passions).
b) The two Ch'engs speak of *T'ien-li* as the fullness of being and goodness, innate in human nature (*hsing*) as well as in all things, and also oppose it to *jen-yü*.
c) Chu Hsi follows this interpretation, and identifies *T'ai-chi*, a term derived from the Book of Changes and given importance especially by Chou Tun-yi, as source and principle of being and goodness, to *T'ien-li*. He thus internalizes this concept of

T'ai-chi, describing it as immanent not only in the whole cosmos but also in each individual being.

Tung/ching
動靜

Literally, activity and stillness, movement and quiescence.

a) The Great Learning mentions *ching*; the Appendix to the Book of Changes mentions both *tung/ching*, as also does the Book of Rites' chapter on Music.

b) The Sung and Ming thinkers often identify *tung* to *yi-fa* and *ching* to *wei-fa*
They may refer also to action and contemplation.

T'i/yung
體用

Usually translated as substance and function.

a) The words come from Wang Pi's commentary on *Lao-tzu*, ch. 4 and refer to two cosmic states: the latent (*t'i*) and the manifest (*yung*).

b) Seng-chao (384–414) describes the cosmos in terms of *hsin* (Mind) which refers to *t'i*, the "within" (*nei*) and its manifestations, *yung*, or the "without" (*wai*). Through meditative trance (*samādhi*) one can unite with the Mind and so acquire wisdom (*prajña*)

c) T'ien-t'ai Buddhism regards the Absolute, *chen-ju* (*Bhūtatathatā*) or *Tathāgata-garbha* as *t'i* and its manifestations as *yung*.

d) Among the Sung and Ming thinkers, *t'i-yung* sometimes retains its metaphysical meanings, inherited from Neo-Taoism and Buddhism, and sometimes takes on a simpler meaning, as the "essential" or "basis" or the "theory" (*t'i*) and the "function," "application," or "practice" (*yung*).

e) Yang-ming follows the Sung and Ming thinkers' usage, but more frequently refers to the metaphysical meaning. He often speaks of *t'i/yung* in terms of *pen-t'i* and *kung-fu*.

Pen-t'i
本體

Usually translated as "original substance."

a) Wang Pi explains ultimate reality, called (*pen-wu*) or original nothingness, in terms of *pen-t'i* in which *t'i* and *yung* are united.

b) In Ch'an Buddhism, it refers to the Absolute, which is usually described in negative terms, *e.g.*, of emptiness (*sunyāta*).

c) The Sung and Ming thinkers speak often of *pen-t'i*. Chu Hsi speaks especially of *hsing chih pen-t'i*, *i.e.*, nature-in-itself.

d) Yang-ming speaks interchangeably of *pen-t'i*, *i.e.*, ultimate reality, and of nature-in-itself, mind-in-itself, and *liang-chih*. It refers to the "true" self, or the true mind, as opposed to the self or mind which is affected by selfishness or passion.

Kung-fu
工夫

Literally, work and effort.

a) In Ch'an Buddhism, it refers to self-exertion, effort, including that of trying to resolve a riddle (*Kung-an*).

b) Yang-ming speaks frequently of *pen-t'i* and *kung-fu*, explaining the latter as the simple effort of being always attentive and watchful over one's self, *i.e.*, of extending *liang-chih*.

He equates *pen-t'i* and *kung-fu*, signifying that wisdom is to be discovered in its own quest, and especially, that, for the enlightened, this quest is characterized by spontaneity.

Wu/hsiu
悟修

Usually translated as enlightenment and cultivation.

a) The idea of enlightenment or illumination is especially prominent in Chuang-tzu.

The teaching of sudden enlightenment (*tun-wu*) is especially attributed to Tao-sheng (c. 360–434), and to the Ch'an Patriarch, Hui-neng (638–713).

Gradually, discussion evolved regarding the relationship between enlightenment and cultivation (*hsiu*).

b) The word cultivation (*hsiu*) is found in the Great Learning, where it refers to self-cultivation. In this context, it is frequently spoken of by Sung and Ming thinkers. Chu Hsi's teaching contains elements suggesting the importance of enlightenment. Yang-ming speaks of it openly, especially in explaining the Four Maxims.

Nei/wai
內外

Literally, "inner"/"outer"; or "within"/"without."

It has the same metaphysical meaning as *t'i-yung*, referring thereby to the One Reality and its external manifestations. It can also refer in practice to the opposing attractions of contemplation and of activity.

T'ien-jen ho-yi
天人合一

Literally, the "Unity between Heaven and Man."

It refers in particular to the teaching of the Confucian school, developed especially by Mencius and Tung Chung-shu, each in his own way, that Heaven and Man make up a certain continuum.

Wan-wu yi-t'i
萬物一體

Literally, the myriad things form one body.

It refers to the doctrine of the "Unity of All Things," the central doctrine of the Sung and Ming thinkers of the *hsing-li* movement. As such, this formula represents a development of the earlier doctrine of *T'ien-jen ho-yi*, with certain shifts in words and meanings, giving more emphasis to "All Things" rather than to "Heaven" and "Man." Those shifts manifest the incorporation of Taoist and Buddhist ideas into a new "Confucian" world view.

NOTES

PREFACE

[1] I refer to the *Yōmeigaku taikei*, undertaken by the best Japanese scholars on Chinese thought, including Uno Tetsujin, Yasuoka Masaatsu, Okada Takehiko, Araki Kengo, Yamashita Ryūji and Yamanoi Yū (Tokyo, 1971–73). The celebration of the fifth centenary has also led to the holding of a forum on Wang Yang-ming at the annual meeting of the Association of Asian Studies in late March 1972, and to another meeting called by the Philosophy Department of the University of Hawaii, Honolulu, in June 1972. In Taiwan, it has led to the publication of *Yang-ming hsüeh lun-wen chi*, compiled by Chang Ch'i-yün and containing twelve articles, mostly by Chinese scholars but including three articles translated from Japanese (Yang-ming shan: The China Academy, 1972).

[2] *Instructions for Practical Living and Other Neo-Confucian Writings* (New York, 1963).

[3] See J. M. Bocheński, *The Methods of Contemporary Thought* (New York, 1968), 33–51.

[4] The importance of an accurate interpretation of the terms obliges me to take account of the historical evolution of the meanings involved. I have relied for help in this matter especially on two Chinese writers: Tai Chen (1724–77), author of *Meng-tzu tzu-yi shu-cheng*, and Liu Shih-p'ei (1884–1919), author of *Li-hsüeh tzu-yi t'ung-shih*. I have also consulted contemporary works in both Chinese and English, especially those of T'ang Chün-i and Wing-tsit Chan. In the case of providing English translations, whether of terms or of long citations, I have usually given my own translations, after having read the translations which are available, be these for the Classical texts or for Yang-ming's writings.

[5] Some parallels in European thought will be pointed out in footnotes marked by an asterisk, while the numbered notes following the Appendices usually have reference only to problems within the Chinese tradition, or give simple bibliographical indications. Notes to the translations in Part II have been set as footnotes.

[6] I have previously published (1971) a selection of Yang-ming's letters in English translation: *The Philosophical Letters of Wang Yang-ming*.

7 See my article, "Confucius and His Modern Critics, 1916 to present," *Papers on Far Eastern History X* (September, 1974), 117–46.

HISTORICAL SUMMARY

1 Several works on Ming history are now avaiable in English, including the recently published *Chinese Government in Ming Times. Seven Studies*, ed. by Charles O. Hucker (New York, 1969). Thire is no complete biography of Wang Yang-ming in English, although there are many in Chinese and Japanese. There is, however, a good summary of Yang-ming's life "Wang Yang-ming: A Biography," by Prof. Wing-tsit Chan in *Philsophy East and West* [abbrev. as *PEW*] XXII (1972), 63–73. There is also an unpublished doctoral thesis by Tu Wei-ming, entitled *The Quest for Self-realization: A Study of Wang Yang-ming's Formative Years, 1472–1509* (Harvard University, 1968). See also Wing-tsit Chan, "'Wang Yang-ming: Western Studies and an Annotated Bibliography," *PEW* XXII (1972) 75–92.

2There is only one full-length study of Sung-Ming philosophy in English: Carsun Chang's *The Development of Neo-Confucian Thought* (New Haven, 1957–62), which leaves much to be desired. But both Chu Hsi's anthology, *Chin-ssu lu*, and Wang Yang-ming's *Ch'uan-hsi lu* have been translated into English by Wing-tsit Chan. The best available account in English of this philosophical movement remains the chapters in Fung Yu-lan's *A History of Chinese Philosophy*, vol. 2, translated by Derk Bodde (Princeton, 1952–3). For Ming thought, there is now *Self and Society in Ming thought*, ed. by W. T. de Bary (New York, 1970)

3 See the studies by Tilemann Grimm: *Erziehung und Politik im konfuzianischen China der Ming-Zeit, 1368–1600* (Hamburg, 1960), 36–55, and "War das China der Ming-Zeit totalitär?", *Nachrichten der Gesellschaft für Natur und Völkerkunde* LXXIX/LXXX (1956), 30–36, for a complete account of the Ming education system and for an enquiry into Ming despotism. There is a Chinese work by [Yeh] Ting-yi, *Ming-tai te t'e-wu cheng-chih* (Peking, 1950) which treats of the Ming "secret police" system. The "form of expression" refers to the so-called eight-legged essay.

4 See Chao Yi, *Erh-shih-erh shih cha-chi*, SPPY ed., 32:5b–6a.

5 Early Ming scholars who refrained from taking government service included Wu Yü-pi (1392–1469), and his three disciples, Hu Chü-jen (1434–84), Lou Liang and Ch'en Hsien-chang. See *Ming-ju hsüeh-an* [abbrev. as *MJHA*], SPPY ed., 1:1a–2b, 2:1a–2a, 8a–9a, 5:1a–3b.

6 This engagement in a search for a single, all-inclusive method for the attainment of sagehood is also affirmed by Ku Yen-wu (1613–82), who was no admirer of Ming philosophy. See his letter to a friend, in *T'ing-lin wen-chi*, SPTK ed., 3:1a–2a.

7 See the accounts given in his chronological biography: "Nien-p'u," *Wang Wen-ch'eng kung ch'üan-shu* (abbrev. as *WWKC*), SPTK double-page lithograph ed., 19:570, 32:904. See also the two chapters, "Ō Yōmei to Mindai no Dōkyō," by Liu Ts'un-yan, and "Yōmei gaku to Mindai no Bukkyō," by Prof. Araki Kengo, in *Yōmeigaku nyūmon*, which is vol. 1 of *Yōmeigaku taikei*, Tokyo, 1971), 257–90,

291–320. For the English language publications, see Prof. Liu's article, "Taoist Self-cultivation in Ming Thought," in *Self and Society in Ming Thought*, 307–21. While there is difference of opinion regarding Taoist or Buddhist influence on Yang-ming's thought, it was quite obvious that Yang-ming had Taoist and Buddhist associations.

[8] "Nien-p'u," *WWKC* 32:905. See also the epitaph written by Chan Jo-shui, given in *WWKC* 37:1053, and Araki Kengo's article, "Tan Kansen to Ō Yōmei," *Tetsugaku nenpo* XXVII (1968), 301.

[9] "Nien-p'u," *WWKC* 32:909.

[10] See *Ming-shih* [abbrev. as *MS*] *Erh-shih-wu shih* [abbrev. as *ESWS*] series, K'ai-ming ed., 16:31. "Nien-p'u." *WWKC* 33:933–43. The emperor had hoped that the expedition which he personally commanded might have won the victory.

[11] "Nien-p'u," *WWKC* 34:973–4

[12] *Ibid.*, 35:1016–17; *MS* 195:464

[13] See my article "Wang Yang-ming (1472–1529): A Study in 'Mad Ardour'," *Papers on Far Eastern History* III (Canberra, March 1971), 85–130. See also chapter 1 of this book.

[14] *Ibid.*, 88. The reference is to Analects 13:21. See J. Legge, *The Chinese Classics* (Oxford, 1895 ed., reprinted in Hong Kong, 1960), I, 272, for the English translation. [Legge's work will be abbreviated as *Classics*.]

[15] See *Chu-tzu yü-lei* [abbrev. as *CTYL*] (1473 ed., Taipei reprint, 1962), 40:2b, and *WWKC* 34:958–9.

[16] See W. T. de Bary, "Individualism and Humanitarianism in Late Ming Thought," in *Self and Society*, 171–225.

[17] See Abe Yoshio, "Chōsen no Yōmeigaku," in *Yōmeigaku nyūmon op. cit.*, 407–25. See also Appendix 2, "The Wang Yang-ming School in Korea: A Summary Report."

[18] See Appendix 1 in this book, and also Yamashita Ryūji, "Nihon no Yōmeigaku," *Yōmeigaku nyūmon*, 427–67.

[19] See Epilogue to this book.

[20] Ku Yen-wu, *Jih-chih-lu chi-shih*, ed. by Huang Ju-ch'eng. SPPY ed., 18:28a. Wang Yi-fu's other name was Wang Yen (256–311) and Wang Chieh-fu's other name was Wang An-shih (1021–86)

INTRODUCTION

[1] Liang Ch'i-ch'ao, *Yin-ping-shih ho-chi, Wen-chi* (Shanghai, 1941), 9:55–56. This passage is taken from an essay written as an argument against the proposition made in 1908 to establish Confucianism as the official religion of China. Liang makes an appeal for freedom of thought. Han Ch'ang-li refers to Han Yü (786–824), Ou-yang Yung-shu to Ou-yang Hsiu (1007–70), Ch'eng Yi-ch'uan to Ch'eng Yi and Chu Hui-an to Chu Hsi.

2 Kenneth K. S. Ch'en, *Buddhism in China* (Princeton, 1964), 472.

3 For the history of Chinese Buddhism, see especially T'ang Yung-t'ung, *Han-Wei liang-Chin Nan-pei ch'ao Fo-chiao shih* (Changsha, 1938), especially pp. 18·34, 87–120. See also Kenneth K. S. Ch'en, 147–51, 187–271, 610–72. For the interactions between Confucianism, Taoism and Buddhism, see Tokiwa Daijō, *Shina ni okeru Bukkyō to Jukyō Dōkyō* (Tokyo, 1930), 45–120, 627–64.

4 For Taoist philosphy, see Fung Yu-lan, *Chung-kuo che-hsüeh shih* [abbrev. as *che-hsüeh shih*] (Shanghai, 1935), 602–60; Eng. tr. by Derk Bodde, *History of Chinese Philosophy* (Princeton, 1952–53), v. 2., 168–75.

5 For religious Taoism, see Fung, *che-hsüeh shih*, 813–19 [Eng. tr. *History*, v. 2, 424–33] Henry Maspéro, *Les religions chinoises: Mélanges posthumes sur les religions et l'histoire de la Chine: le Taoisme* (Paris, 1950), 25–36, 43–57, 85–116, 179–89, Homes Welch, *The Parting of the Way: Lao-tzu and the Taoist Movement* (London, 1957), 88–97, 105–22, 141–51.

6 For Ch'an Buddhism, see Fung, *che-hsüeh shih*, 772–99 [Eng. tr. *History*, v. 2, 386–406], H. Dumoulin, *A History of Zen Buddhism* (London, 1963), 67–105, and Daisetz T. Suzuki, *Essays in Zen Buddhism*, published in three series (London, 1926, 1950, 1953). There are also good introductory chapters to the various sections of the *Ching-te ch'uan-teng lu* selected for translation by Chang Chung-yuan. See *The Original Teachings of Ch'an Buddhism* (New York, 1969), 3–16, 41–57, 85–101, 129–47.

7 The Five Classics include the *Yi-ching* (Book of Changes), *Shih-ching* (Book of Odes), *Shu-ching* (Book of Documents), *Ch'un-ch'iu* (Spring-Autumn Annals) and the ritual texts, particularly the *Li-chi* (Book of Rites). The work undertaken during the T'ang dynasty was entitled, *Wu-ching cheng-yi*, that is, the "Correct Meaning of the Five Classics," and was done under the supervision of the scholar K'ung Ying-ta (574–648). Since this series included the three commentaries on the Spring-Autumn Annals—The Annals of Tso, and the *Kung-yang* and *Ku-liang*— as well as three distinct ritual texts, there were really Nine Classics involved. Later, these were all engraved in stone together with the Classics of Filial Piety (*Hsiao-ching*), the Analects *(Lun-yü)*, and the ancient glossary, called the *Erh-ya*, thus making up Twelve Classics. During the Sung dynasty, the Book of Mencius was also raised to the status of a classic, giving a total of Thirteen Classics. See *Chiu T'ang-shu* in *ESWS* series, 73:270, see also P'i Hsi-jui, *Ching-hsüeh li-shih*, annotated by Chou Yü-t'ung (Shanghai, 1929), 197–211.

8 Han Yü wrote several treatises that had bearing on the later development of Confucian thought. These were the *Yüan-tao*, *Yüan-jen*, and the *Shih-shuo*. See *Han Ch'ang-li ch'üan-shi*, SPPY ed., 11:1a–b, 9a–b, 5a–7b, 12:1b–2b. For English translations of the first and the last treatises, see W. T. de Bary et al., ed., *Sources of Chinese Tradition* [abbrev. as *Sources*], (New York, 1964), v. 1, 374–75, 376–79.

9 Mencius had regarded Mo Ti (fl. 5th cent. B.C.) and Yang Chu (440–360 B.C.) as teachers of "perverse doctrines." See The Book of Mencius, 3B:9, in J. Jegge, *The Chinese Classics* (Oxford, 1893; Hongkong reprint, 1960) [abbrev. as *Classics*], v. 1, 284.

10 Li Ao's thought is given especially in his treatise, *Fu-hsing shu*. See *Li Wen-*

kung chi, SPTK ed., 2:5a–13b, Fung Yu-lan points out that what Li calls nature (*hsing*) approaches what the Ch'an Buddhists call original mind (*pen-hsin*), while what Li calls emotions (*ch'ing*) resembles what the Buddhists call passions (*yü,* Sanskrit, *kleśa*). See *che-hsüeh shih,* 805–06 [Eng. tr., *History,* v. 2, 414].

11 These scholars included Hu Yüan (993–1059), a famous teacher who transmitted to thousands of students an intensely personal faith in Confucianism, Sun Fu (992–1057), and Shih Chieh (1005–45) the independent interpreters of the Spring-Autumn Annals and the Book of Changes respectively and Ch'en Hsiang (1017–80), who was particularly interested in the Hsing-li philosophy. See Huang Tsung-hsi and Ch'üan Tsu-wang, *Tseng-pu Sung - Yüan hsüeh-an* [abbrev. as *SYHA*], SPPY ed., 1:1a–2b, 2:1a–2a, 21a–b, 5:1a–3b.

12 *SYHA* 1:17. See also de Bary, *Sources,* v. 1, 384. For further explanations of *t'i-yung.* see Appendix 4.

13 For the New Text and Old Text scholars, see Fung, *che-hsüeh shih* 587 (Eng. tr., *History,* v. 2, 150), Chou Yü-t'ung, *Ching chin-ku wen* (Shanghai, 1926), 14–22. The official T'ang-Sung exegesis favored a philological approach that was closer to the New Text tradition than to that of the Old Text scholars.

14 See *Chou-tzu T'ung-shu* (abbrev. as *T'ung-shu*), SPPY ed., 28:5a, for Chou Tun-yi's plea that literature (*wen*) serve merely as a vehicle for the Tao, which contributed to the Sung-Ming philosophers' reluctance to embellish their written expression. In the Lu-Wang school, this tendency led almost to the abandonment of all writing.

15 The *Chin-ssu lu* is the basic text for the study of Sung philosophy. It is a forerunner of the *Hsing-li ta-ch'üan,* compiled by Hu Kuang (1370–1418) and others under imperial command, which gives an expanded form of Chu's anthology. See Chi Yun (1724–1805) et al., *Ssu-k'u ch'üan-shu tsung-mu t'i-yao* (abbrev. as *SK*)(Shanghai, 1933), 18.29–30. The *Chin-ssu lu* has many editions, including those of Chiang Yung (1681–1762), Yeh Ts'ai (fl. 1248), and Chang Po-hsing (1651–1725). The English translation by Wing-tsit Chan, *Reflections on Things at Hand* (New York: 1967) is based on Chiang Yung's edition; the German translation by Olaf Graf, *Djin-si lu* (Tokyo, 1953), in 3 mimeographed volumes, is based on Yeh Ts'ai's edition.

16 The fifth Master was Shao Yung (1011–77), whom Chu Hsi omitted from the line of orthodox transmission, but who is included in the *Sung-shih* [abbrev. as *SS*] as a teacher of *Tao-hsüeh.* See *SS, ESWS* series, 427:1098–99.

17 "T'ai-chi-t'u shuo," *SYHA* 12: 1a–b; Eng. tr. in de Bary, *Sources* 458–59. The notion *T'ai-chi* can be traced to the Great Appendix of the Book of Changes, see *Chou-yi cheng-yi,* 7:17a, Legge, *Yi King,* 373, where it refers to the First Principle and Source of all things, and the "Ground of Being." [Legge translates it as the "Grand Terminus".] Joseph Needham translates *T'ai-chi* as "Supreme Pole," a kind of "organization-center" for the entire universe, viewed as a single organism. See *Science and Civilisation,* v. 2, 460–3.

18 The term, *Wu-chi,* literally comes from *Lao-tzu.* ch. and connotes "that which is without limit." Chou mentioned in the same treatise that T'ai-chi is fundamentally *Wu-chi.*

Chou spoke of *Wu-chi erh T'ai-chi*, a sentence that occasioned much controversy, provoking the famous debate between Chu Hsi and Lu Chiu-yüan. See also Fung, *che-hsüeh shih*, 942–43 [Eng. tr., *History*, 437–38].

[19] The treatise is a commentary on the "Diagram" itself, which purports to show, in a series of circles, the whole cosmic process beginning from *T'ai-chi* and resulting in the production of all things. See *SYHA* 12:1a. The origin of this Diagram has been much discussed. It bears remarkable similarities to the *T'ai-chi Hsien-T'ien-t'u*, which the Taoist Ch'en T'uan (c. 906–89) allegedly transmitted to Ch'ung Fang (d. 1014), who passed it on to Mu Hsiu (979–1032), who in turn passed it to Li Chih-ts'ai (d. 1045), who transmitted it to Shao Yung. See *SS* 427:1098. See also Fung, *che-hsüeh shih*, 822–24 [Eng. tr., *History*, v. 2, 438–42]. This is especially interesting since it refers to a Taoist line of transmission. See also A. Forke, *Geschichte der neueren chinesischen Philosophie* (Hamburg, 1938), 21; Chow Yi-ching, *La Philosophie Morale dans le Néo-Confucianisme (Tcheou Touen-yi)* (Paris, 1953), 47–52.

[20] Chow Yi-ching, 53–54. The interrelationship between the One and the Many indicates a deeper Buddhist influence, coming from T'ien-t'ai and Hua-yen sources, which have penetrated Ch'an.

[21] *SYHA* 12:1a–b.

[22] *T'ung-shu*, ch. 1, p. 1a; ch. 4, p. 1b; ch. 10, p. 5a. Chou's description of the sage alludes to the Great Appendix of the Book of Changes. See *Chou-yi cheng-yi*, SPPY ed. 7:14a, Legge, *Yi King*, Sacred Books of the East [abbrev. as SBE series (Oxford, 1882; Delhi reprint, 1966), 370.

[23] *CTYL* 1 1a–b, 94:4a–6b, 12a, 20b, 35a–b.

Chu Hsi gives emphasis to the ethical dimensions of Chou's *T'ai-chi* by interpreting it in terms of his other book, *T'ung-shu*. He understands it to be the Ultimate, the fullness of being and goodness, present in the universe and in every person and thing. I therefore disagree with the interpretation of Stanislas le Gall, who adhered to the opinion of many Jesuits since the time of Matteo Ricci, in explaining *T'ai-chi* as a materialist principle. See *Tchou-Hi, sa Doctrine, son Influence* (Shanghai, 1925), Preface, p. i, also pp. 32–36.

[24] *Cheng-meng*, in *Chang-tzu ch'üan-shu* (abbrev. as *CTCS*), 2:1b–3b, Eng. tr. in de Bary, *Sources*, 466–69.

[25] *CTCS* 1:1a–3b. Eng. tr., de Bary, *Sources*, 469.

[26] *Cheng-meng*, ch. 7, *CTRS* 21a–22b. In another famous passage Chang Tsai describes the work of the sage thus: "To give heart (*li-hsin*) to Heaven and Earth, to give life to living peoples, to continue the interrupted teaching of the former sages, and to open a new era jo peace for coming generations". See *CTCS*, 14:3b. This had come down to us from Chu Hsi's *Chin-ssu lu*. See Chiang Yung ed., *Chin-ssu lu chi-chu*, SPPY ed., 2:22b. Wing-tsit Chan, tr., *Reflections on Things at Hand*, 83. Chan relates the explanation of Yeh Ts'ai that the sage "gives heart" to Heaven and Earth by participating in their creative processes [through the practice of life-giving *jen*]; he "gives the Way" to the people by the maintenance of moral order, he "continues the interrupted learning" by resuming the "orthodox transmission" (*Tao-t'ung*), and he "gives peace" to the coming generations because his virtue prepares the way for a true and ideal "King" (wang).

[27] See *Cheng-meng*, ch. 6, *CTCS* 2:17a–b. Chang's reference to *liang-chih* [Book of Mencius 7B:15] is important, because of its repercussions on Lu Chiu-yüan's and Wang Yang-ming's thought. Chang was also the first philosopher to make a clear distinction between *T'ien-li* (Principle of Heaven) and *jen-yü* (selfish desires). [*CTCS* 2:18a], a distinction which assumed so much importance in the thought of the Ch'engs and of Chu Hsi. Wang Yang-ming would also make use of this distinction, although Lu Chiu-yüan objected to the excessive dichotomy made by the Ch'engs and Chu. See Fung, *che-hsüeh shih*, 861–66 [Eng. tr., *History*, v. 2, 488–94a]; see also Tokiwa Daijo, 219–44, for the Buddhist influences manifested by Chang Tsai.

[28] *Erh-Ch'eng ch'üan-shu* [abbrev. as *ECCS*] *Yi-shu*, 24:3a–b; [Eng. tr. in de Bary, *Sources*, v. 1, 504–5]. Ch'eng refers in this essay to Chang Tsai's "Western Inscription," and also to the Book of Mencius 7A–15, with the mention of *liang-chih* and *liang-neng*, concepts which were to become so important in the philosophy of Wang Yang-ming.

[29] *ECCS, Yi-shu*, 15:14b–15a. The expressions, *hsing-erh-shang* and *hsing-erh-hsia* also come from the Great Appendix of the Book of Changes. See *Chou-yi cheng-yi*, 7:18b; Legge, *Yi King*, 377.

Outside the Four Books, the appendices to the Book of Changes gave most inspiration to the Sung philosophers, contribuitng to Chou Tun-yi's *T'ai-chi* and Chang Tsai's *T'ai-ho* theories, the Ch'engs' idea of a life-giving *jen* and their method of self-cultivation.

[30] *ECCS, Yi-shu*, 18:5b; de Bary, *Sources*, v. 1, 476. See also Wing-tsit Chan, "Neo-Confucian Solution of the Problem of Evil," first published in *Studies Presented to Hu Shih on his Sixty-fifth Birthday* (The Bulletin of the Institute of History and Philology, Academica Sinica, v. 28, 1957), reprinted in *Neo-Confucianism, etc., Essays by Wing-tsit Chan*, compiled by Charles K. H. Chen (New Haven, 1969), 99–112.

[31] *CTYL* 4:8a–19b.

[32] *Ssu-shu chi-chu* [abbrev. as *SSCC*] *Meng-tzu chi-chu*, 3:1a–b; 2:11a–12a; 6:4b–5b; 7: 1a–2a.

[33] *SSCC, Ta-hsüeh chang-chü*, 4b–5a. This represents Chu's effort to supply a "missing chapter" to the text of the Great Learning. See *CTYL* 15:1a–14b. See also William E. Hocking, "Chu Hsi's Theory of Knowledge," *Harvard Journal of Asiatic Studies* [abbrev. as *HJAS*] I (1936), 109–27. For closer analysis of the meaning of *ko-wu*, see also D. C. Lau, "A Note on Ke Wu," *Bulletin of the School of Oriental and Africa Studies* [abbrev. as *BSOAS*] XXX (1967), 353–57.

[34] Chu speaks about restoring the brightness of man's nature, bestowed by Heaven, and originally full of goodness, but later obscured by passions. See *Ta-hsüeh chang-chü, SSCC*, 1a–b; *CTYL* 4:10a–15b. See also his first letter to friends in Hunan, written in 1169, on the subject of *chung-ho* (equilibrium and harmony) of the Doctrine of the Mean in *CWWC, SPPY* ed., 64:30b–31b, [Chan, *Source Book*, 600–02]. This was considered by Liu Tsung-chou (1578–1645) as the embodiment of Chu's final doctrine on moral cultivation. See his comment in *SYHA* 48:8b–9b. It emphasizes the importance of keeping peace in one's mind and heart. This can

be achieved through the practice of quiet-sitting, as recommended in *CTYL* 12: 15a–18b. See also G. E. Sargent, "Les Débats personnels de Tchou Hi," 222; P. C. Hsü, *Ethical Realism in Neo-Confucian Thought*, (Ph. D. Thesis, Columbia University, 1933, microfilm copy fo 1969 typescript) 136–38; Araki Kengo, *Bukkyō to Jukyō*, 359–67.

35 He did it in his preface to the commentary on the Doctrine of the Mean (*Chung-yung chang-chü*), dated 1189. See Wing-tsit Chan, "Chu-tzu tao-t'ung kuan chih che-hsüeh hsing," *Tung-hsi wen-hua* XV (1968), 25–32' See also Chan's article in English, "Chu Hsi's Completion of Neo-Confucianism," *Etudes Song. Sung Studies. In Memoriam Etienne Balazs*, ed. F. Aubin, Ser. 2, No. 1, 1973, pp. 60–87.

36 See Wang Mou-hung, ed., *Chu-tzu nien-p'u TSCC* ed., 1:13–15.

37 See *SSCC*, SPPY ed., 1a–3a. He also referred to the two Ch'engs as having discovered the lost Way of Confucius and Mencius. Chu established the "line" definitively, especially by preparing, with the help of his friend Lu Tsu-ch'ien (1137–81), the *Chin-ssu lu*, an anthology of quotations from Chou, the Ch'engs, and Chang. He dismissed the pre-Sung exegetes from the "line," giving as his reason their failure to discover the intended meaning of the sages. But he ignored Han Yü, whom he regarded as a man of letters rather than a follower of the Way. *CTYL* 137:13a–18a.

38 These were the Analects, Book of Mencius, the Great Learning and the Doctrine of the Mean (*Chung-yung*), the two later books being chapters taken from the Book of Rites.

39 See Chu's letter to Lu, in *RWWC* 36: 10a–b. "Without sound or smell" (*Wu-sheng wu-ch'ou*) came to signify the metaphysical First Principle. The expression is originally derived from the Book of Odes [Legge, *Classics*, v. 4, 431] and cited in the Doctrine of the Mean, ch. 33 [Legge, *Classics*, v. 1, 433–34].

40 See Lu's first letter to Chu, as well as his answer to Chu's letter cited above in *Hsiang-shan ch'üan-chi*, SPPY ed., 2:5b–11b. This work will be abbreviated as *HSCC*.

41 This was really a teaching of Ch'eng Yi's. See *Yi-shu*, 22A:11a. Chu made frequent references to it. See *CTYL* 65:9b. Chu objects to Ch'eng Yi's explanation of Kao-tzu's contention that "what is born is called nature" [Book of Mencius 6A:3], saying that it is not clear enough and does not explain why nature is totally good.

42 See Lu's letter to Tseng Chai-chih, in *HSCC* 1:3b.

43 See Lu's Chronological Biography in *HSCC* 36:3b. Lu said this at the age of twelve. Like Chu Hsi, he manifested very early an interest in philosophy. The saying is also given in *HSCC* 22:5a.

44 *HSCC* 32:4a. See also Huang Siu-chi, *Lu Hsiang-shan, A Twelfth-Century Chinese Idealist Philosopher* (New Haven, 1944), 51–74. Unlike the Ch'engs and Chu Hsi, Lu lacks an interest in the metaphysical concept of *ch'i*, by which they had explained the rise of evil.

45 See *HSCC* 36:3b, and *HSCC* 22:5a. See also Fung, *che-hsüeh shih*, 939–41; Eng. tr., *History*, v. 2, 585–89. While both Chu and Lu started out speaking of the "mind-and-heart," Lu finished by giving it an absolute quality, seeing in it some-

thing greater than itself. Chu failed to agree. His viewpoint was better expressed by his disciple Ch'en Ch'un (1153–1217) in *Pei-hsi tzu-yi*, a lexicon of some thirty words and expressions that form the core of *Hsing-li* philosophical vocabulary. Appearing at the time of continuing conflict between the two schools of Chu and Lu, as did the lexicon of Hsü Shen at the time of the New Text-Old Text controversy, this work, of a much smaller scale and quite polemic in character, clarified to a certain extent the meanings of the words used by Chu's school. It referred to the Chu-Lu debate without mentioning their names, but compared Lu's notion of *hsin* to the Buddhist idea of consciousness. See *Pei-hsi tzu-yi*, TSCC ed., 1:9–10. In *Hsüeh-pu t'ung-pien*, Ch'en Chien also discussed at length the Buddhist influence displayed by Lu's philosophy. See 4:1a–6–14b. He also quoted from Chen Ch'un in his criticism of Yang-ming. See 7:10a–b.

46 *HSCC* 34:24b. Lu made the remark: "Before the time of Yao and Shun, were there any books that people must study?" to emphasize that the development of *hsin* alone is sufficient for the attainment of sagehood. See his "Nien-p'u," *HSCC* 36:9b.

47 *HSCC* 34:24b. The words "easy and simple" (*yi-chien*) allude to the Great Appendix to the Book of Changes, to be found in *Chou-yi cheng-yi*, SPPY ed., 7:2a–3a; see James Legge, tr., *Yi King*, SBE series, p. 349. On this question, see also my article, "The Goose Lake Monastery Debate (1175)," *Journal of Chinese Philosophy* I (1973), 76–93.

48 See *HSCC* 36:10b. The text of the discourse is given in *HSCC* 23:1a–2a. This appears to be the second meeting of the two men.

49 *CTYL* 126:5b–17a. See Tokiwa Daijō, 185–89, 367–84. Chu's chief concern was that the Buddhist teaching made nature (*hsing*) empty, whereas he considered it to be "full" of *li*. His criticism of Hua-yen philosophy shows that Buddhist influence on his thought is more superificial than real.

50 See Lu's two letters to a friend, *HSCC* 2:1b–4b; Fung, *che-hsüeh shih*, 932–33; Eng. tr., *History*, v. 2, 577–78. In his second letter, Lu attacks Buddhism for not subscribing to the Confucian teaching that Heaven and Earth and Man form "Three Ultimates," in other words, that Buddhism is not a humanism. However, the monk Tsung-mi (d. 841) had spoken explicitly of the "Three Ultimates." Lu was probably aware of this. He could mean either that Tsung-mi's teaching was not thoroughgoing enough, or that he was an exception. In criticizing Buddhism, *Hsing-li* philosophers usually attacked those aspects of it that were most uncongenial to the "Confucian" mind, whether the issue concerned was speculative as regarding an "illusory" view of the world, or practical, as regarding the tendency to minimize the importance of social responsibility. See also Tokiwa Daijō, 385–97.

51 See Chu's preface to *Ta-hsüeh chang-chü*, in *SSCC*, 1a–2b.

52 The famous chapter on the "Evolution of Rites" (*Li-yün*) in the Book of Rites, describes the two ages of "Great Unity" (*ta-t'ung*) and "Lesser Tranquillity" (*hsiao-k'ang*). See *Li-chi cheng-yi* [Correct Meaning of the Book of Rites] SPPY ed., 21:1a–4b. See also Engl. tr. in de Bary, *Sources*, v. 1, 175–76.

53 *CWWC* 36:22b. The Three Dynasties refer to Hsia, Shang (c. 1751–1112 B.C.) and Chou (1111–249 B.C.).

[54] *Ibid.*

[55] Chu Hsi had learned from his father Chu Sung (1097–1143) a strong aversion to the policy of appeasing the Jurchens. See Chu Sung's biography, written by Chu Hsi himself, in *CWWC* 97:18b–28b.

For Ch'en Liang and his ideas, see *SYHA* 56:1a–2b; *Lung-ch'uan wen-chi*, SPPY ed., 20:6b; Carsun Chang, *The Development of Neo-Confucian Thought* (New Haven, 1957), v. 1, 309–31; Hellmut Wilhelm, "The Heresies of Ch'en Liang (1143–94)," *Asiatische Studien* XI, 3/4 (1958), 102–11.

[56] Chu's debate with Ch'en was carried out in a series of letters. For Chu's answer to Ch'en, see especially *CWWC* 36:22b, 24b–28b.

[57] *CWWC* 36:22b. According to Chu, the sovereign's *hsin* or mind-and-heart was the "foundation of the state." Hence the emperor had the strict duty of making sure that his *hsin* was upright. However, Chu did not neglect practical statecraft. His memorials contained also practical proposals related to the reform of taxation, the employment of civil personnel, and other such issues.

[58] See Book of Mencius 1B.9; 2B.2; 5B.9; Legge, *Classics*, v. 1, 167, 210–15, 392–93, for the sage's independent manners toward the ruler, and his teachings regarding regicide and the right of rebellion.

[59] See Ssu-ma Kuang's criticisms of Mencius for disrespect to authority, in *Weng-kuo Wen-cheng Ssu-ma Kung wen-chi*, SPTK ed., 73:10b–11a, 12a–b, and *Lin-ch'uan chi*, SPTK ed., 67:6a–7a.

[60] Wang Mou-hung, ed., *Chu-tzu nien-p'u*, 164; Li Hsin-ch'uan (1126–1243), "Hui-an hsien-sheng fei su-yin" [Master Chu was not a recluse.]; in *Ch'en-yen yi-lai cha'o-yeh tsa-chi*, TSCC ed., pt. 2, pp. 445 f.; and Conrad M. Shirokauer, "Chu Hsi's Political Career: A Study in Ambivalence," in Arthur F. Wright and Denis Twitchett, ed., *Confucian Personalities* (Stanford, 1962), pp. 162–88. Chu Hsi offended the government by his direct criticisms and by his preference for a life of semiretirement, chosen as a protest against policies of which he did not approve.

[61] *CTYL* 78:2a–3a. In the early Ch'ing dynasty (1644–1912), the scholar Hsien Jo-chü (1636–1704) definitively proved that this chapter, together with twenty-four others "preserved" in the old text or script, were all forgeries. See Hsien's *Ku-wen Shang-shu shu-cheng* in *Huang-ch'ing ching-chieh hsü-p'ien*, comp. by Wang Hsien-ch'ien (1842–1918), contracted lithograph ed. (Preface 1889), 13:1a, 10a–b.

[62] See Book of Documents, Legge, *Classics*, v. 3, p. 61. The first three sentences come from *Hsün-tzu* 21, where the philosopher cites a lost classic, and the last from Analects 20:1, which cites a counsel given allegedly by Yao to Shun. The Sung thinkers display an ambivalent attitude toward the authority of the Classics, by quoting from a known forgery to find support for their teachings. See *Hsün-tzu*, SPPY ed., 15:7a, Eng. tr. by B. Watson, *Hsün-tzu: Basic Writings* (New York, 1963), 131; P'i Hsi-jui, *Ching-hsüeh t'ung-lun* (Shanghai, 1929), 51a–52a. The Mean (*chung*) refers to the state of equilibrium which characterises the mind and heart before it is aroused by emotions, as described in the Doctrine of the Mean, ch. 1, in Legge, *Classics*, v. 1, 384. See also *CTYL* 62:1b–2b.

[63] *HSCC* 34:1b.

[64] *CTYL* 78:26b–34a.

65 This idea underlies the entire *Platform Sutra*, attributed to Hui-neng, and to the *Transmission of the Lamp*, the title of which connotes already the notion of an "inner light." See *Ching-te ch'uan-teng lu*, Preface by Yang Yi (974–1030), *TSD*, No. 2076, LI, 196, and also in the text itself, 3:219, 9:274–74.

66 *Yüan-shih, ESWS* series, 81:206.

67 *Sung-shih* [abbrev. as *SS*], *ESWS* series, 427:1096.

68 Let it be noted that under the Sung emperor, Li-tsung (r. 1252–64), the philosophers Chou Tun-yi, Chang Tsai, Shao Yung, the two Ch'engs, and Chu Hsi were officially recognized as true heirs of the Confucian orthodoxy, although the examination system remained unchanged. See the account in *SS* 45:91, 94. See also James T. C. Liu, "How Did a Neo-Confucian School Become the State Orthodoxy?" *PEW* XXIII (1973), 483–506.

69 *MS* 70:155.

70 See Ku Yen-wu, *Jih-chih lu chi-shih*, 18:10b–11b.

71 See Historical Summary.

CHAPTER I   WANG YANG-MING:
THE MAN AND THE PHILOSOPHER

1 English translation adapted from Legge, *Classics*, v. I, 272.

2 Analects 17:13 Legge, *Classics*, v. I, 324. Confucius even calls the *hsiang-yüan* or "Pharisaic" the "thief of virtue."

3 Book of Mencius 7B:37. See Legge, *Classics*, v. 7, 499–500. Tseng Tien, father of Tseng Shen, was characterized as *k'uang* by Ch'eng Hao and Chu Hsi for his carefree reply to Confucius regarding his ambition in life [Analects 11:25; Legge, *Classics*, v. 1. 246–499] See *Yi-shu* 12:1b; *CTYL* 40:2b. Ch'in-chang is often identified with Tzu-chang, a disciple of Confucius, See *Chuang-tzu SPPY* ed., 6 3:10a. See also Burton Watson, Eng. trans., p. 86. Nothing is known of Mu-p'i.

4 Analects, V, 21. Adapted from Legge, trans., v. 1, p. 181. Mou Jun-sun, in his article, "Shih *Lun-yü* 'k'uang-chien' chang," *Hsin-ya hsüeh-pao*, II, (1957), pp. 79–86, explains that this passage of the Analects should not be interpreted as referring to conduct, but that the two words here refer to writing. He therefore objects to Mencius' interpretation of the words, as well as to Chu Hsi's comments.

5 *SSCC*, 3:6b, 7:24b.

6 *CTYL*, 29:11a–13b.

7 Analects 17:16, Legge, *Classics*, v. 1, 325.

8 Analects 18:5. See Legge, *Classics*, v. 1, 332–33. Chieh-yü of course, was only feigning madness to mock Confucius.

9 These seven men included Hsi K'ang (223–62) Juan Chi (210–63) Shan T'ao (205–83), Hsiang Hsiu (c. 221–c. 300), Wang Jung (234–305), Liu Lin (c. 221–

c. 300) and Juan Chi's son Juan Hsien. See Donald Holzman, "Les Sept Sages de Forêt des Bambous," *T'oung-pao* XLIV, (1967), pp. 317–46.

[10] See *Li T'ai-po shih-chi*, SPPY ed., 36:32b.

[11] *MJHA* 32:1a–4b.

[12] "Nien-p'u," *WWKC* 32:094a–b.

[13] This story comes from the novel by Feng Meng-lung (d. 1645), who wrote under the name of Mo Han-chai. The book is entitled, *Wang-Yang-ming ch'u-sheng ching-luan lu* (Wang Yang-ming's Life and Pacification Campaigns). See the copy reprinted in Taipei, 1968, pp. 7–8. It was referred to by Shimada Kenji, *Shushigaku to Yōmeigaku* (Tokyo, 1967), 123.

[14] See above, n. 13.

[15] See Wang Hua's epitaph, written by Yang Yi-ch'ing ,in *WWKC* 37:1042b.

[16] *WWKC* 32:904b.

[16] *WWKC* 32:904b–905a.

[18] *Ibid.*

[19] For Lou Liang, see *MJHA* 2:8a–9a.

[20] *WWKC* 32:905b.

[21] *Ibid.* See also "Ch'uan-hsi lu," *WWKC* 3:153a. English translation adapted from Wing-tsit Chan, *Instructions*, 249.

[22] *WWKC* 32:905b–906b.

[23] For example, compare Mao Ch'i-ling's Draft Biography of Yang-ming, *Wang Wen-ch'eng chuan-pen*, in *Hsi-ho ho-chi* (Preface 1685), v. 1, 1b–2a, with Feng Meng-lung's account, pt. 1, 12a.

[24] *WWKC* 32:907b. Tu Wei-ming gives much importance to this change of mind. See *The Quest for Self-realization: A Study of Wang Yang-ming's Formative Years 1472–1509* (unpublished Ph. D. thesis, Harvard University, 1968), microfilm copy, p. 55.

[25] The memorial is given in *WWKC* 9:276–77.

[26] Some traditional accounts speak of Yang-ming going south to Ch'ien-t'ang River where he pretended to have committed suicide, but then took a boat which was blown off course to Fukien. Supposedly, he stayed for a while in a Taoist monastery on Mount Wu-yi, and then went to Kuang-hsin (Kiangsi), crossed the P'o-yang Lake to Nanking to visit his father, went south again to sail up the Ch'ien-t'ang River to Nanchang (Kiangsi), and from there traveled by boat along the Yüan and Hsiang rivers to his final destination. See *WWKC* 32:908b, 37:1053b, 1057a–b. See also Chan, *Instructions*, Introduction, xxiv.

[27] *WWKC* 32:909a–b; *MS* 195:463. Yamane Yukio alleges that Yang-ming learned how to handle rough men during his exile. See *Mindai yōeki no tenkai* (Tokyo, 1966), 73f.

[28] *WWKC* 32:909b.

[29] *WWKC* 32:911a–b.

[30] *WWKC* 32:917b.

31 *MS* 195:463; *WWKC* 32:917b–925b, 38:1109–11. For Yang-ming's career as a soldier and statesman, see also Chang Yü-ch'üan, "Wang Shou-jen as a Statesman," *Chinese Social and Political Science Review* (abbrev. as *CSPSR*), XXIII (1939–40), 230–35. Yang-ming did not, however, like war; he wept for having had to give orders to kill. See *WWKC* 32:924a.

32 *WWKC* 33:933–43; *MS* 195:463.

33 *WWKC* 33:944; *MS* 16:31; Mao Ch'i-ling, *Ming Wu-tsung wai-chi* (Taipei: 1964), 11–29; Wolfgang Seuberlich, "Kaisertreue oder Auflehnung? Eine Episode aus der Ming-Zeit," *Deutsche Morganlandliche Gesellschaft Zeitschrift* 102 (1952), 304–13.

34 *WWKC* 33:945–52.

35 For this poem, see Part II, p. xxx

36 *WWKC* 33:954b.

37 *WWKC* 34:962, 20:627; *MS* 17:31–32, Hsia Hsieh (fl. 1850), *Ming T"ung-chien*, (Peking: 1959), 50:1851–56; 51:1895–1932. See also the following articles on this controversy over ritual: Amada Takeo, "Tairei no gi to O Yōmei," *Chūgoku Tetsugaku* I (February 1961), 1–9; Nakayama Hachirō, "Futatabi Kasei chō tairei mondai no hotan ni tsuite," in *Mindai shi ronsō*, ed. by Shimizu Hakase tsuitō kinen Mindaishi ronsō hensaniinkai, (Tokyo, 1962), 61–78.

38 See the account by Huang Wan, *WWKC* 37:1071a–b.

39 *Ibid.*

40 *WWKC* 34:973b–81a; *MS* 195:464.

41 *WWKC* 34:976b.

42 *WWKC* 37:976a–81a.

43 *WWKC* 34:990a–91b.

44 *WWKC* 37:1074.

45 *WWKC* 35:1017a.

46 *Ibid.*

47 *WWKC* 37:1074b.

48 *WWKC* 37:1052b–53a.

49 *WWKC* 34:958b.

50 *WWKC* 32:904a.

51 *WWKC* 32:904b, 34:988b.

52 *WWKC* 32:906a–907b; Yü Ch'ung-yao, *Yang-ming hsien-sheng chuan-ts'uan* (Shanghai, 1923), 5.

53 *WWKC* 32:943b.

54 *WWKC* 37:1057a. See also Sung P'ei-wei, *Ming wen-hsüeh shih* (Shanghai, 1934), 89–106.

55 *WWKC* 32:907a.

56 See his letter to a friend, *WWKC* 21:638a–b.

57 *WWKC* 32:904a.

58 *Pao-p'u-tzu*, SPPY ed., 18:1a.

59 See Wang Wen-lu, *T'ai-hsi ching-shu*, in *Po-tzu ch'üan-shu* (Shanghai, 1927), part 1, 1a–3a; Liu Ts'un-yan, "Taoist Self-cultivation in Ming Thought," in W. T. de Bary, ed., *Self and Society in Ming Thought,* 293–96.

60 Liu Ts'un-yan, ibid., 304.

61 For the *Yin-fu* Canon, see *Po-tzu ch'üan-shu*, pt. 1, 1a–3a. For the *Ts'an-t'ung ch'i*, especially Chu's work, see *SK* 36:45, *WWKC* 21:640. According to *SK*, Chu's studies resemble commentaries, but are called textual studies because the texts concerned were Taoist, not Confucian.

62 *WWKC* 20:609; Suzuki Takashi, "Mindai sanjin ko," *Mindaishi ronsō*, 375–88. The term *Shan-jen* was frequently used by Ming scholars and pseudoscholars in the literary names they gave themselves. See *SK* 36:45.

63 *WWKR* 20:609a.

64 Kusumoto Fumio, *Ō Yōmei no Zen no shisō no kenkyū* (Nagoya, 1958), 65–82, *passim*.

65 *WWKC* 19:570b.

66 *WWKC* 31B:876a, 902a.

67 *WWKC* 37:1053, 1057. See Araki Kengo, *Mindai shisō kenkyū* (Tokyo, 1972), 51. See also Wing-tsit Chan, "Chan Jo-shiu's Influence on Wang Yang-ming," *PEW* XXIII (1973), 12–30.

68 *Yi-shu* 3:2a.

69 *WWKC* 32:905a.

70 Nelson I. Wu, "Tung Ch'i-ch'ang ,1555–1636: Apathy in Government and Fervour in Art, " in A. F. Wright and D. Twitchett, eds., *Confucian Personalities*, 277.

71 *WWKC* 32:905b.

72 See T'ang Yung-t'ung, *Wei-Chin hsüan-hsüeh lun-kao* (Peking: 1957), 72–83; Jung Chao-tsu, *Wei Chin te tzu-jan chu-yi* (Peking, 1934), 24–25.

73 *WWKC* 32:906a–b.

74 *WWKC* 32:907b.

75 *WWKC* 37:1053, 1057.

76 *Yi-shu* 2A:3a.

77 *WWKC* 37:1053a.

78 *WWKC* 19:572b. See annotations given in Part II, p. xxx

79 *WWKC* Prefaces, p. 13. See also Yamashita Ryūji, "Ō Yōmei no shisō no hensen," *Nippon Chūgoku gakkaihō* X (1958), 119–33.

80 *MJHA* 10:3b–4a.

81 *Yi-shu* 18:5b.; *RTYL* 15; 4b–8a. See Wing-tsit Chan, *Source Book*, 561.

82 *WWKC* 32:909a–910b; 1: 58a–b; Chan, *Instructions* 11.

83 Book of Mencius 4B:32; Legge, *Classics,* v. 2, 340.

84 *WWKC* Prefaces, p. 13a–b.

85 See above, Introduction, p. xx; Okada Takehiko, *Zazen to seiza* (Nagasaki: 1965), 19–20.

86 The Chinese word, *ting,* can also refer to the Sanskrit *samādhi.*

87 *WWKC* 4:170.

88 *WWKC* 33:951a–b.

89 *WWKC* 26:739a, Chan, *Instructions,* 278. Yang-ming refers to Book of Mencius 7A: 15.

90 *WWKC* Prefaces, 13b.

91 *WWKC* 34:958a.

92 *WWKC* 34:958b.

93 *WWKC* 34:958b–59a.

94 Doctrine of the Mean, ch. 14; Legge, *Classics,* v. 1, 395.

95 *WWKC* 1:66b, 3:140a; Chan, *Instructions,* 31, 215. He refers to Analects 2:12. See Legge, *Classics,* v. 1, 150.

96 *WWKC* Prefaces, p, 8b.

97 *WWKC* 20:627b. The "Great Purity" refers to the sky.

98 *Ibid.* See also Part II.

99 Analects 5:21; Legge, *Classics,* v. 1, 181.

100 *WWKC* 34:961a–b.

101 *WWKC* 1:55b; Chan, *Instructions,* 4.

CHAPTER II   THE STARTING POINT: HSIN

1 *WWKC* 1:79b. [Chan, *Instructions,* 66]. The English translation is my own.

2 Allusion to *Chuang-tzu,* 26, SPPY ed., 9:6a; Eng. tr. by Burton Watson, 302. See also Hsieh Lin-yün's (385–433) "Yü chu tao-jen pien-tsung lun" in Tao-hsüan (596–666) ed., *Kuang hung-ming chi,* SPPY ed., 20:9b–10a. In discussing the question of gradual and sudden enlightenment, he alluded to the fishing rod and the rabbit's traces as representing the Confucian Classics and the Buddhist *Tripitaka* both of which may help one to attain enlightenment. The doctrine of sudden enlightenment discussed therein is attributed to Hsieh's friend, the monk Tao-sheng (c. 360–434).

3 *WWKC* 22:668b. The expression "worthy [scholars] of the past" (*hsien-hsien*) obviously refers to scholars such as Ch'eng Yi and Chu Hsi.

4 *HSCC* 22:5a.

5 *WWKC* 1:79, Chan, *Instructions,* 66. Hiroyuki Iki indicates the importance

Yang-ming placed on a correct "starting-point" in his article, "Wang Yang-ming's Doctrine of Innate Knowledge of the Good," *PEW* XI (1961–2), 27.

6 See Legge, *Classics*, v. 6, 1. Tung Chung-shu had also said much on this first line of the Spring-Autumn Annals, particularly regarding the word *yüan* (first, origin, source). See *Ch'un-ch'iu fan-lu*, SPPY ed., 4:1a. Both Tung and Yang-ming manifest the characteristically Chinese "correlative" thingking by their manners of reading different levels of meanings into words.

7 *WWKC* 26:742b. This document was salvaged by Ch'ien Te-hung from Yang-ming, who had committed much of the manuscript to fire, saying that the doctrine of *liang-chih* hardly needed the support of classical proofs. See Ch'ien's note, *WWKC* 26:742a.

8 Great Learning, ch. 1. Legge, *Classics*, v. 1, 356. See Hsü Fu-kuan, *Chung-kuo jen-hsing lun shih*, *Hsien-Ch'in-p'ien* (Taichung, 1963), 65–74. See also Yasuoka Masaatsu, *Ō Yōmei kenkyū* (Tokyo, 1967), 240.

9 *WWKC* 26:745a Yang-ming was fond of comparing *hsin* to the clear sky or to the bright sun which may be hidden by dark clouds. See also *WWKC* 3:146a–b; 20:627b.

10 Book of Mencius, 7A:1–2, 4. Legge, *Classics*, I. 448–49, 450–51.

11 This idea permeates the *Lankavatāra-sūtra* (*Leng-chia ching*), *TSD*, No. 670, XVI, 480–514. See the English translation by Daisetz T. Suzuki (London, 1959), Introduction, xxi–xxiii, and pp. 36, 44. See also Chang Chung-yüan, tr., *Original Teachings of Ch'an Buddhism, Selected from the Transmission of The Lamp*. Introduction, 4–14.

12 See Wing-tsit Chan, "The Evolution of the Neo-Confucian Concept *li* as Principle," in Chan, *Neo-Confucianism, etc.* (New Haven, 1969), 45–87.

13 *WWKC* 1:56a; Chan, *Instructions*, 6–7. The reference is to Chu's *Ta-hsüeh chang-chü*, 1a–b.

14 *WWKC* 1:56b–57a; Chan, *Instructions*, 7. Wang and Hsü were discussing the the passage from the Great Learning, Ch. 1, regarding the "highest good," which Chu Hsi considered as belonging to the text containing Confucius' words as noted down by his disciple Tseng Shen. See Legge, *Classics*, v. 1, 356.

15 *WWKC* 1:56b; Chan, *Instructions*, 7.

16 *WWKC* 1:57a; Chan, *Instructions*, 8.

17 *Li-chi cheng-yi*, SPPY ed., 47:5b, Legge, *Li Chi* (Oxford, Clarendon, 1885; reprinted in New York, 1967), 215–16.

18 *WWKC* 1:57b; Chan, *Instructions*, 8.

19 Letter to Wang Tao, *WWKC* 4:179b–179a. In *Yang-ming ch'uan-hsin lu* Liu Tsung-chou praised Yang-ming's recovery of *hsin* as an event which achieved as much as Mencius' teaching on the original goodness of human nature. See *Liu-tzu ch'üan-shu yi-p'ien* 11:4a.

20 The Five Despots were Dukes Huan of Ch'i (r. 685–643 B.C.) Wen of Chin (r. 636–628 B.C.) Mu of Ch'in (r. 659–621 B.C.) Hsiang of Sung (d. 637 B.C.) and King Chuang of Ch'u (r. 613–589 B.C.) See *Shih-chi*, *ESWS* series, K'ai-ming ed., 40:

15–16; 18–19; 40:142.

21 *WWKC* 3:155a; English translation adapted from Chan, *Instructions*, 252. See T'ang Chün-i, "Yang-ming-hsüeh yü Chu-Lu yi-t'ung ch'ung pien, "in *Hsin-ya hsüeh-pao*, VIII (August 1968), 67.

22 *WWKC* 1:60a; Chan, *Instructions*, 15. Yang-ming is referring here to the Book of Mencius. 2A:6. See Legge, *Classics*, v. 2, 201–02.

23 Letter to Ku Lin, *WWKC* 2:90a; Chan, *Instructions*, 94.

24 Mencius used the word *li* several times without attaching to it much philosophical meaning. Book of Mencius 5B:1, 6A:7, 7B:19. See Tai Chen, *Meng-tzu tzu-yi su-cheng* in *Tai Tung-yüan te che-hsüeh*, 40–72. See also Chan, "The Evolution of the Neo-Confucian Concept *li*," 50.

25 The feelings of commiseration, shame and modesty, together with the moral intuition, are the beginnings of the virtues of *jen* (humanity), *yi* (righteousness), *li* (propriety), and *chih* (wisdom). See Book of Mencius 2A, 6; Legge, *Classics*, v. 2, 203.

26 See Book of Mencius 6A: 1–6 [Legge, *Classics*, v. 2, 394–403] for Mencius' debate with Kao-tzu, regarding whether righteousness is a virtue external to the self.

27 Letter to Ku Lin, *WWKC* 2: 90a–b; Chan, *Instructions* 95. Note the explicit declaration that the teaching of *hsin chi li* implies an acceptance of the "unity of knowledge and action". It is interesting that Yang-ming should criticize Chu Hsi's teaching of *hsin* and *li* as that which makes of righteousness an external thing. He must have known that Chu had criticized Lu Chiu-yüan's identification of *hsing* and *hsin* as a return to Kao-tzu's view that "what is inborn is called nature" (Book of Mencius 6A:3) See *CTYL* 124: 10b; 126: 11b.

28 Wing-tsit Chan, "Chinese Theory and Practice with Specific Reference to Humanism", in *The Chinese Mind, Essentials of Chinese Philosophy and Culture*, ed. by Charles A. Moore, (Honolulu, 1967), 82. On this point, Wang was in agreement with Chu Hsi.

29 In "Wang Yang-ming and Existential Phenomenology," *International Philosophical Quarterly* V, (1965), 621. Jung Hwa Yol says of this "unity of knowledge and action": "Not withdrawal, but involvement, is the essence of Wang's philosophy . . . The mind is of centrifugal character: it extends or directs itself toward the world."

30 *WWKC* 3: 134b; Chan, *Instructions*, 201. See also Shimada Kenji, "Yomeigaku ni okeru ningen-gainen jiga ishiki no tenkai to ki igi" *Tōyoshi kenkyū* VIII, (July 1943), 155–56.

31 Analects 3: 15; Legge, *Classics*, v. 1, 160.

32 Letter to His Younger Brothers, (1518), *WWKC* 4: 189b; Shimada Kenji, "Yomeigaku ni okeru," 156–57.

33 *WWKR* 1: 65a; 2: 112b–113a; Chan, *Instructions*, 27: 148–49. The parable recalls to mind the *gathas* of the 7th cent. Ch'an monks Shen-hsiu and Hui-neng recorded in *Liu-tsu ta-shih fa-pao t'an-ching*, TSD No. 2007; XLVIII, 337–38. Eng. tr., in Yampolsky, 130–32; Wing-tsit Chan, *Platform Scripture*, 35–41. Yang-ming prefers here the position of Shen-hsiu to that of Hui-neng.

[34] *WWKC* 2: 112b; Chan, *Instructions*, 148. The reference is to Ch'eng Hao, *Wen-chi*, 3: 1a, but Yang-ming was quoting from Lu's letter.

[35] Letter to Huang Wan and Ying Liang (1511) *WWKC* 4: 171b. By using the image, Yang-ming was continuing a long tradition.

[36] Poem written as farewell to his students Wang Chia-hsiu and Hsiao Ch'i, *WWKC* 20: 600a. For fuller understanding, see the annotations given in Part II.

[37] *WWKR* 1: 71b; Chan, *Instructions*, 45. Wing-tsit Chan remarks that this is the only independent saying by a disciple of Yang-ming's that is recorded in the *Ch'uan-hsi lu*.

[38] *WWKC* 1: 60a; Chan, *Instructions*, 14–15.

[39] *WWKC* 1: 71b; Chan, *Instructions*, 44. In an essay addressed to Wang Chia-hsiu, Yang-ming develops at some length the work of self-mastery, saying that its aim is complete selflessness. See *WWKC* 8: 262.

[40] Book of Mencius 4A: 4, Legge, *Classics*, v, 2, 294.

[41] *Ibid.*

[42] Letter to Huang Wan (1513), *WWKC* 4: 176a, Liu Tsung-chou remarked that Yang-ming gave a certain priority to "Establishing sincerity," even over the doctrine of *liang-chih*. See *Yang-ming ch'uan-hsin lu* 1: 3b.

[43] According to *Shih-chi*, Po-yi was the scion of a feudal house who chose to live in retirement as a hermit, in order to yield his position to a younger brother. He opposed the expedition of King Wu of Chou against the Shang dynasty and starved to death after the King's victory through his refusal to live on the grains of Chou. Yi-yin belonged to an earlier period. He was a minister of King T'ang, founder of the dynasty Shang, whom he helped in the task of bringing peace and prosperity to the country. The fact that Po-yi, the hermit, and Yi-yin, the minister, were both venerated as sages had always given room in Confucian doctrine to the teaching that both the eremitical and active lives could lead to sagehood, with the choice of one or the other being dependent on varying needs and circumstances. Confucius, however, was the sage who sought for an opportunity of active service but was obliged to live in retirement. For this reason, he was considered greater than Po-yi and Yi-yin. See Book of Mencius 6B: 1, [Legge, v. 2, 369–72;] *Shih-chi* 61: 179 –b; 3: 11a–b.

[44] *WWKC* 1: 77b; Chan, *Instructions*, 60. For the importance of this passage and of what follows, to Yang-ming's doctrine of sagehood, see Takahashi Koji, "Yōmei Kyōgaku no mujun-seijinkan chūshin to shite," *Chūgoku Tetsugaku*, III (1965), 2. Takahashi also considers this doctrine as the natural consequence of the doctrine of the identity of *hsin* and *li*.

[45] One *yi* contains twenty taels weight.

[46] *WWKC* 1: 77b–78a; Chan, *Instructions*, 61. The citation is from the Book of Mencius 6B: 2; Legge, *Classics*, v. 424.

[47] *WWKC* 1: 78a–80b; Chan, *Instructions*, 61–69.

[48] *Ibid.*

[49] *Ibid.* Professor de Bary compares the development of Yang-ming's ideal of

sagehood to the proclamation of universal Buddhahood through the Mahayana in China, Japan, and Korea centuries earlier, and especially to those forms which emphasized the attainment of Buddhahood in this life and this body. But he points out the difference between Yang-ming's ideal and that of Mahayana Buddhism: where the latter identifies life with suffering and illusion, the former consistently exalts life, creativity, and the potentialities of the human individual. See *Self and Society*. Introduction, 14–15.

[50] *WWKC* 3: 151a; Chan, *Instructions*, 240.

[51] *WWKC* 32: 910a–b.

[52] *WWKC* 1: 57b: Chan, *Instructions*, 10.

[53] Leterally, "in their *pen-t'i*."

[54] Referring to a sentence in the Great Learning, ch. 6 which describes how a gentleman ought to make his intention sincere. See Legge, *Classics*, v. 1, 366.

[55] *WWKC* 1: 58a; Chan, *Instructions*, 10.

[56] Jung Hwa Yol, 633.

[57] *WWKC* 1: 58b; Chan, *Instructions*, 11.

[58] *Ibid*. For a general discussion of the ethical aspects of this teaching, see also Liang Ch'i-ch'ao, *Wang Yang-ming chih-hsing ho-yi chih chiao* (1926), in *Yin-ping shih wen-chi*, 43: 46–49. Ch'ien Mu, *Yang-ming hsüeh shu-yao* (Taipei: 1963), 57–60; Okada Takehiko, *Ō Yōmei to Minmatsu no jugaku* (Tokyo: 1970), 57–59.

[59] *WWKC* 1: 58; Chan, *Instructions*, 11–12.

[60] *WWKC* 1: 58–59; Chan, *Instructions*, 12.

[61] *WWKC* 3: 134a–b; Chan, *Instructions*, 201.

[62] *WWKC* 2: 89b–90a; Chan, *Instructions*, 92–94.

[63] *Ibid*.

[64] *WWKC* 6: 215a. In Liang Ch'i-ch'ao's words, "The entire *Complete Works of Wang Yang-ming (WWKC)* serves merely as a footnote to the words concerning the unity of knowledge and action." See *Yin-ping shih wen-chi*, 43: 27–28, n. 2.

[65] Of the Ming thinkers who preceded Yang-ming, Ch'en Hsien-chang (1428–1500) was the best known for his practice of quiet-sitting and for the discovery of an interior world of vital activity through such contemplation. See *MJHA* 5: 2a–3a, 6a, Jen Yu-wen, *Po-sha-tzu yen-chiu* (Hongkong: 1970), 157–64. See also Jen's English article, "Ch'en Hsien-chang's Philosophy," in de Bary, ed., *Self and Society*, 53–57, 75–78.

[66] This poem was written by Yang-ming in honor of a friend, Luan Tzu-jen. See See *WWKC* 20: 605b. See also the annotations given in Part II.

[67] *Chuang-tzu* ch. 2, *SPPY* ed., 1: 18a.

[68] *WWKC* 1: 64b; Chan, *Instructions*, 26. See Kusumoto Masatsugu, "Conflicts between the Thoughts of the Sung Dynasty and the Ming Dyansty," *Philosophical Studies of Japan*, 54–57. Later on, in seeking to correct the abuses of the T'ai-chou branch of the Yang-ming school, Nieh Pao and others after him would again emphasize quiet-sitting and tranquility and thus effect a certain return to Chu's

teachings. See also Kusumoto Masatsugu, *Sō-Min jidai jugaku shisō no kenkyū*; (Chiba-ken, 1963), 173–84, 327, Okada Takehiko, Ō *Yōmei to Minmatsu no jugaku,* 21, 173–74. 256–8.

69 *WWKC* 1: 68a; Chan, *Instructions*, 35. Note that Yang-ming would also comment on the relative easiness of the work of suppressing bandits when compared to that of removing "the bandits of *hsin*." See Okada Takehiko, Ō *Yōmei to Minmatsu no jugaku*, 60–62.

70 *WWKC* 1: 68a; Chan, *Instructions*, 35. The example given of the cat was taken from Ch'an sources. Chu Hsi had made reference to it also in teaching the need of concentration. See *CWWC* 71: 7a–b. Yet Ch'en Chien argued that Chu merely used *Chian* parables to teach Confucian truths whereas Yang-ming, like Lu Chiu-yüan, was a "Buddhist." See *Hsüeh-pu t'ung-pien* 7: 15b–16a. For the Ch'an source, see Wu-ming (fl. 1189) *Lien-teng hui-yao*, 15, *Zokuzokyo* 1st coll., pt. 2, B, case 9, 339b. Even after he had begun teaching the doctrine of *liang-chih* Yang-ming continued to insist on the need of discovering and eliminating selfish desires through the practice of sitting in meditation. The fact that he developed the later doctrine did not imply his discarding this practice, although he gave it less emphasis. *WWKC* 3: 144a–b; Chan, *Instructions*, 223–4.2

71 *WWKC* 3: 144a–b; Chan, *Instructions*, 223–24.

72 *WWKC* 3: 130b; Chan, *Instructions*, 190–91. The incident concerning Ch'eng Yi is given in *ECCS*, *Yi-shu*, 3: 5a.

73 *WWKC* 3: 140a; Chan, *Instructions*, 214. See also Yang-ming's letter to Liu, in *WWKC* 5: 202.

74 *WWKC* 32: 907.

75 *WWKC* 3: 130b, 141a; Chan, *Instructions*, 191, 216–17.

76 *WWKC* 4: 172b

77 See his essay addresed to Meng Yüan, *WWKC* 8: 263b.

78 *WWKC* 3: 141a; Chan, *Instructions*, 217.

CHAPTER III   THE CONTROVERSIES: KO-WU

1 From a letter to Yang-ming by Chan Jo-shiu, in *Kan-ch'üan wen-chi* (1866 ed.), 14: 36a.

2 Chu Hsi's teachings can be found in his *Meng-tzu chi-chu*, where he sought to explain the beginning lines of The Book of Mencius 7A in terms of the first chapter of the Great Learning, and *vice versa*. See *SSCC* 7: 1a–b.

3 For other references to the importance of a "firm determination" and "single-mindedness" emphasized by the Ch'eng-Chu school as well but made into the essential component of self-realization in the Lu-Wang school, see *WWKC* 1: 82; 7: 230, 254.

4 *WWKC* 1: 59b; Chan, *Instructions*, 12–14. The same subject came back in the

letter Yang-ming wrote to Ku Lin, before 1524. See *WWKC* 2: 90a–92b. Chan, *Instructions*, 95–97. Yang-ming gave the same exposition as he did to Hsü Ai.

5 *WWKC* 1: 59b–60a; Chan, *Instructions*, 14–15.

6 *Ibid.* See also Yang-ming's letter to Wang Tao, *WWKC* 4: 178b–179a.

7 *WWKC* 2: 118b; Chan, *Instructions*, 162. This is a variant of a frequently cited sentence: "To make a mistake of a hair's breadth may lead [a person] one thousand *li* astray." See *Shih-chi, op. cit.*, 130: 279. This quotation, often given as from the Book of Changes, actually comes from the *apocryphal* Book of Changes. See Tjan, v. 1, 102. Tjan cites as his authority a commentary of P'ei Yin (5th cent. A.D.). See also Takigawa Kametaro, *Shiki kaichu kosho* (Tokyo, 1956–60), 130: 24.

8 *WWKC* 1: 87a–b; Chan, *Instructions*, 86–87. See Chang Lieh's criticism of Yang-ming's argument, *Wang-hsüeh chih-yi*, CYTC ed., 2: 4b–6b. The story concerning drawing the snake's feet comes from Liu Hsiang (c. 77–76 B.C.) ed., *Chan-kuo ts'e*. See *Chan-kuo ts'e chao-chu*, SPTK ed., 1st series, 4: 17b–18a. Eng. tr. by J.I. Clump, Jr. (Oxford, 1970), 167. The Warring States period lasted from c. 300–22% B.C.

9 To Wang Ch'eng-yü, *WWKC* 4: 183b–184a.

10 The name "Po-lu tung" means "White Deer Cave." See *CWWC* 73: 18a–19a.

11 *WWKC* 7: 238b.

12 The preface is in *WWKC* 3: 160a–b; Eng. tr., Chan, *Instructions*, 264–67. One version of this work can be found in the *Han-hai* collection, comp. by Li Tiao-yüan, (Preface 1782, Taipei reprint, 1967), v. 13, 8165–74. But Wing-tsit Chan has expressed doubt regarding its authenticity. See *Instructions*, 103, n. 27. Yang-ming's side commentaries were based on the commentaries of Cheng Hsüan and of K'ung Yin-ta. The work has been praised by Chu Yi-tsun (1629–1709) in *Ching-yi k'ao*, SPPY ed., 159: 3a. The two works were published in 1518, a particularly busy year for Yang-ming. During the first five months, he was engaged in military compaigns against bandits in southern Kiangsi. On concluding these successfully, he initiated measures of rehabilitation for the population. He also mourned the premature death of Hsü Ai, his brother-in-law and most promising disciple. that had occurred shortly after Hsü's publication of certain recorded conversations between himself and Wang, which now make up the first part of *Ch'uan-hsi lu*.

13 See above, Introduction, n. 33.

14 *WWKC* 3: 168b–169a. Wu Ch'eng was one of the two best-known philosophers of Yüan times, the other being Hsü Heng (1209–81). But where Hsü remained an adherent of the Ch'eng-Chu school, Wu showed a greater fondness for Lu Chiu-yüan. See *SYHA* 90 1b–2a for Hsü, and 92: 1a–b for Wu. It is therefore not astonishing that Yang-ming should criticize Hsü [*WWKC* 1: 73; Chan, *Instructions*, 44] and single out Wu for praise. See also below, his praise of Wu's commentary on the Book of Rites.

15 *WWKC* 3: 160a–b; Chan, *Instructions*, 264–67.

16 See criticisms of Yang-ming by Kao P'an-lung, in *Kao-tzu yi-shu*, (1631) 1: 3a–4b; 3: 46b–51a; 4: 51a–b; and by Ku Yen-wu, in *Jih-chih lu chi-shih*, 18: 2a–b; 8a–9a; 11b–14b; Feng K'o, *Chiu-shih p'ien* 3: 3a–4a, 14a–1tb; 4: 1a–2b,

and Lu Lung-ch'i, in *Lu Chia-shu chi, CYTC* ed., 1: 1a–17b.

But Yang-ming also had his supporters, including Liu Tsung-chou and Huang Tsung-hsi. See *MJHA*, "Shih-shuo," 4a–b, 10: 1a–b.

[17] The Preface, given in *WWKC* 7: 241a–b, is dated 1518. But we know that it was first written in 1515, and then published in 1518. According to Lo Ch'in-shun however, the preface dated 1518 and sent to him by Yang-ming in 1520, was later amended and expanded before being finally published by Yang-ming's students in 1536. See *K'un-chih chi, CYTC* ed., 4: 9a–10a. A comparison of the texts as quoted by Lo and as given in *WWKC* shows that the latter represents the final version of the preface. See also Yang-ming's letter to Hsüeh K'an (1523), for mention of changes made in the preface. *WWKC* 5: 208b.

[18] *WWKC* 7: 241a–b.

[19] *MJHA* 47: 1a–2b. Lo has been hailed as "the first important thinker who opened the way to modern thought" by his support of a rational, objective approach to reality and by his independent emphasis of *ch'i* (matter-energy). See Abe Yoshio's article in *Chūgoku no shisōka* (Tokyo; 1963), 571–83. See also his article, "The Development of neo-Confucianism in Japan, Korea and China: A Comparative Study," *Acta Asiatica* XIX (1970), 16–39.

[20] *Lo Cheng-an chi ts'un-kao*, CYTC ed., 1: 6a–7b.

[21] *Ibid.*, 1: 9b.

[22] Lo Ch'in-shun, *K'un-chih chi*, CYTC ed., 1: 1a–b, 2: 2a–b, 3: 7a–b.

[23] He is referring to the Great Learning, ch. 1.

[24] *WWKC* 2: 117a–b; Chan, *Instructions*, 160–61.

[25] *WWKC* 2: 118a–b; Chan, *Instructions*, 161. He speaks here of acquiring *li*.

[26] *ECCS, Yi-shu*, 18: 17a.

[27] *WWKC* 3: 154b–55a; Chan, *Instructions*, 251. Kao P'an-lung would say that Chu Hsi had neither separated *hsin* and *li*, or knowledge and action, but had rather reconciled them. According to him, Yang-ming had misinterpreted Chu Hsi's thought. See *Kao-tzu yi-shu*, 1: 3a; 3: 49a–51a. While taking into consideration the fact that the abuses Yang-ming attacked were attributable more to the latter-day disciples of Ch'eng Yi and Chu Hsi than to the philosophers themselves, one can also recall Huang Tsung-hsi's judgment, that Kao himself was very close in his thinking to Yang-ming, without having acknowledged it. See *MJHA* 58: 18b–19a.

[28] *WWKC* 3: 155a; Chan, *Instructions*, 251–52. The example of the Despots has been used before. Here Yang-ming clearly enunciates the practical purpose of his philosophy.

[29] *WWKC* 3: 155a; Chan, *Instructions*, 252.

[30] From an essay written in Chan's honor (1511) when he was sent as envoy to Annam. See *WWKC* 7: 232a–b. Yang-ming's intellectual debt to Chan implies also a certain debt to Chan's teacher, Ch'en Hsien-chang, whom he never met, but whose spontaneous and dynamic approach to sagehood and consciousness of the unity of all things are reflected in his philosophy. While Yang-ming himself never

acknowledged this debt, his disciple Wang Chi mentioned it. See *Wang Lung-hsi ch'üan-chi*, (1822 ed., Taipei reprint, 1970) [abbrev. as *WLRR*], 10: 31b–32a. See also *MJHA* 5: 1a–3b; Jung Chao-tsu ,*Ming-tai ssu-hsiang shih*, 78–79.

31 *WWKC* 7: 232b. See Okada Takehiko, *Ō Yōmei to Minmatsu no jugaku*, 72–73; 87–94. See also Lo Ch'in-shun's criticism of Chan's understanding of *hsin* and *T'ien-li*, which, according to Lo, required merely "awakening" (*wu*) to the power of consciousness in *hsin*. [*K'un-chih chi*, 4: 11a–b.]

32 *ECCS, Wai-shu*, 12: 4a.

33 *WWKC* 3: 129; Chan, *Instructions*, 186.

34 *Kan-ch'uan wen-chi*, 7: 1a.

35 *MJHA* 37: 2b–3a.

36 *Ibid.*

37 *WWKC* 3: 129b; Chan, *Instructions*, 188–89.

38 *WWKC* 3: 130a; Chan, *Instructions*, 190.

39 *Kan-ch'üan wen-chi*, 7: 18a.

40 *WWKC* 2: 94a; Chan, *Instructions*, 105.

41 *WWKC* 2: 94b–95a; Chan, *Instructions*, 105–6. Chan Jo-shui had followed Chu Hsi in interpreting *ko* as "reach." See *SSCC Ta-hsüeh chang-chü*, 2a; *Kan-ch'üan wen-chi*, 7: 1a.

42 I have consulted the edition published in Yang-chou, with a preface dated 1533.

43 *WWKC* 1: 77b; Chan, *Instructions*, 59–60.

44 *WWKC* 1: 78b; Chan, *Instructions*, 62–63.

45 *WWKC* 7: 239a–b; Chan, *Instructions*, 264–66.

46 *Lo Cheng-an chi ts'un-kao* 1: 7b–9b. Ku Yen-wu pointed out that the repercussions raised by the controversial question of Chu Hsi's "mature views" were still going on in his own time. For himself, however, he considered Lo Ch'in-shun's refutations as already adequate. See *Jih-chih lu chi-shih*, 18: 23a.

47 *Lo Cheng-an chi ts'un-kao* 1: 9a–b.

48 *WWKC* 2: 119a–b; Chan, *Instructions*, 164.

49 *WWKC* 2: 119b; Chan, *Instructions*, 164. In his letter to Ku Lin, Yang-ming avoided giving a direct answer to Ku's charge of his having made arbitrary selection from Chu Hsi's writings for the publication. He merely argued on the problem of "investigation of things." See *WWKC* 2: 91b–92a; Chan, *Instructions*, 98–99.

50 Yang-ming's critic, Ch'en Chien, carefully compared the chronology given in Chu Hsi's *Nien-p'u*, his biography, and his *Collected Writings* and *Recorded Conversations* with Yang-ming's work itself, giving the necessary details of Chu's activities year by year in his refutation of Yang-ming. See *Hsüeh-pu t'ung-pien*, 11: 2a–14b.

See also Kusumoto Masatsugu, *Sō-Min jidai jugaku shisō no kenkyū*, 241–43 on Chu Hsi's doctrine of "reverence," especially as given in those letters he wrote which were included by Yang-ming in his publication. Kusumoto noted that if this development brought Chu nearer to Lu Chiu-yüan and Wang Yang-ming in their method of cultivation in one way, it also brought him further from them in another way, by Chu's increased emphasis on the investigation of things and of *li*.

In his *Ethical Realism in Neo-Confucian Thought*, 135–38, Hsü Pao-ch'ien remarked also that Chu Hsi's "spiritual crisis" occurred in middle age rather than in his later life, and resulted in his greater emphasis on the practice of "reverence," as that which united the inner development of the mind and the outer investigation of things.

51 *WWKC* 1: 61a–63b; Chan, *Instructions*, 17–24. This was probably in 1513.

52 *WWKC* 1: 64b; Chan, *Instructions*, 26–27.

53 *WWKC* 1:62a; Chan, *Instructions*, 20.

54 *WWKC* 7: 250–51.

55 *WWKC* 7: 250.

56 *WWKC* 7: 250b–51a.

57 *WWKC* 7: 251a.

58 For *hsin*-in-itself (*hsin-chih-pen-t'i*), see ch. 4, p. XXX.

59 *WWKC* 1: 67a; Chan, *Instructions*, 32.

60 *WWKC* 7: 250b–51a. The Classic of Music is no longer extant. Liu Tsung-chou remarked that to regard the Classics as footnotes to one's personal insight is to respect the Classics rather than to disregard them. See *Yang-ming ch'uan-hsin lu*, 2: 17a.

61 See *WWKC* 7: 241b–42a. The preface was dated 1520.

62 Book of Rites (*Li-chi cheng-yi* SPPY ed., 23: 12b) See Legge, *Li Ki*, v. 1 p. 404.

63 *WWKC* 7: 241b.

64 Analects 17: 11; Legge, *Classics*, v. 1, 324.

65 Analects 3: 3; Legge, *Classics*, v. 1, 155.

66 See Lao-tzu, ch. 18, SPPY ed., 10a, where the rise of *jen* (humanity) and of *yi* (righteousness) is described as that which follows the abolition of the Great Way. Chan, *Source Book*, 148.

67 See *Chuang-tzu* 9, SPPY ed., 4: 7a–b. Eng. tr. by Burton Watson, 105. This idea is also in the Book of Rites. See *Li-chi cheng-yi* 21: 1a–13a.

68 *WWKC* 7: 242a. Yang-ming also used the parable of "compass and quadrant" to describe man's *liang-chih* or capacity to know the good. See letter to Ku Lin, *WWKC* 2: 96; Chan, *Instructions*, 109.

69 Addressed to Ho Meng-ch'un (1512), and to Tsou Shou-yi (1526). See *WWKC* 21: 646a–b; 210a–211b.

70 *MS* 17: 31–32. See also ch. I, n. 37.

71 For Yang-ming's attitude toward this controversy, see "Nien-p'u," *WWKC* 34: 962b.

72 "Sitting at Night at the Pi-hsia Pond," *WWKC* 20: 627a. For fuller understanding of the poem, see the annotations given in Part II.

73 *Kan-ch'üan-wen-chi* 7: 25b. The citation was from the *Varjacchedikā* or Diamond Sutra, *TSG* No. 235, VIII, 749; Eng. tr. by E. Bonze, *Buddhist Wisdom Books* (London, 1958); 47–48. The Ch'an Patriarch Hui-neng allegedly attained enlightenment through meditation on this passage. It should be pointed out that Yang-ming himself cited this sentence with approval in a letter to his disciple Lu Ch'eng (1524); see *WWKC* 2: 112–13; Chan, *Instructions*, 148–49.

74 *Kan-ch'üan wen-chi* 7: 25b.

75 Analects 2: 4; Legge, *Classics*, v. 1, 147.

76 *Kan-ch'üan wen-chi* 7: 25b.

77 The "Nine Items" refer generally to various practices associated with intellectual inquiry as a means of self-cultivation. They are enumerated in Chu Hsi's *Ta-hsüeh huo-wen*. See the text given in *Chu-tzu yi-shu*, Ch'ing ed., ch. 2, 6a–9b. See also Chan, *Instructions*, 162, n. 11.

78 *WWKC* 2: 118b; Chan, *Instructions*, 162. Yang-ming was not attacking Chu Hsi himself, but Chu's latter-day disciples. It was thus unfair to criticize Yang-ming for having called Chu Hsi a "heretic," comparable to Yang Chu and Mo Ti, as did Lu Lung-ch'i in a ltter to a friend. See *Lu Chia-shu chi*, 1: 23a.

79 *WWKC* 2: 118b–19a; Chan, *Instructions*, 163–64.

80 *WWKC* 3: 155b; Chan, *Instructions*, 253. The reference is to the Doctrine of the Mean, ch. 1.

81 *WWKC* 3: 137a; Chan, *Instructions*, 207.

82 *WWKC* 3: 148a–b; Chan, *Instructions*, 233–35.

83 *WWKC* 3: 137a–b; Chan, *Instructions*, 207–08.

84 *Ibid.*

85 *Ibid.*

86 Letter to Chi Pen (1526), *WWKC* 6: 218b.

87 Letter to Lu Ch'eng, *WWKC* 2: 111a; Chan, *Instructions*, 146.

88 Letter to Chi Pen, *WWKC* 6: 218b.

89 *WWKC* 2: 117a; Chan, *Instructions*, 159.

90 *Ibid.* Yang-ming had been criticized many times for "belittling Confucius." Ku Hsien-ch'eng considered it impossible that one's *hsin* might find incorrect the words of the sages. Like Chan Jo-shui, he also objected to the identification of *hsin* and *li*, recalling that even Confucius did not attain the state of being able to follow the desires of his heart without transgressing the Mean till old. *MJHA* 58: 14a; see also Ch'en Chien, *Hsüeh-pu t'ung-pien* 12: 4b, and T'ang Chen (1930–1704), *Ch'ien-shu* (Peking, 1955). 11. An ardent admirer of Yang-ming's learning and ability, T'ang remarked that Yang-ming did not attain the virtue of sagehood, since he lacked esteem for Confucius, having once compared himself favorably with Confucius when speaking of the knowledge of warfare.

91 *WWKC* 2: 117a; Chan, *Instructions*, 159.

92 *WWKC* 3: 147b; Chan, *Instructions*, 230.

93 *WWKC* 3: 147b–148a; Chan, *Instructions*, 231–32.
94 *WWKC* 20: 629a.
95 "Sitting at Night," *WWKC* 20: 628a.

CHAPTER IV The "Way" Discovered: CHIH LIANG-CHIH

1 *WWKC* 3: 150a; Chan, *Instructions*, 237. Although this chapter discusses Yang-ming's practical philosophy in terms of a "method," I wish to indicate at the outset that the Chinese words *kung-fu* refer more to self-exertion or ascesis, which disposes the person to inner enlightenment.

2 After his victory over the rebellious forces of Prince Ch'en-hao, Yang-ming proposed various practical measures for the alleviation of the difficulties of the people of Kiangsi, such as reduction of taxation, and increase of emolument to the impoverished officials in the lower ranks of local bureaucracy. In the meantime, Emperor Wu-tsung was enjoying himself south of the Yangtze. Instead of submitting moral lectures to the throne as did Ch'eng Yi and Chu Hsi, Yang-ming took the occasion of flood and famine in Kiangsi to rebuke himself for these natural calamities, begging for removal from office. Enumerating four cirmes of which he regarded himself as being guilty, including that of failure to persuade the emperor to mend his ways, he concluded a memorial by saying: "Even if your servant should be executed as an example to the world, he would consider himself fortunate."

An expression of irony and protest, this document certainly was. But it represented a futile effort, a desperate act undertaken with the hope of moving the heart of the sovereign, the really guilty party.

See *WWKC* 33: 949b–951b; Mao Ch'i-ling, *Ming Wu-tsung wai-chi*, Yang-ming's memorial is found in *WWKC* 13: 390–91a. See its English translation by Chang Yü-ch'uan in his article, "Wang Shou-jen as a Statesman," *CSPSR* XXIII (1930–40), 221–22.

3 See *WWKC* 33: 949–50a; Mao Ch'i-ling, *Wang Wen-ch'eng chuan-pen*, 2: 4a–5b as well as ch. 3 of thesis.

4 *WWKC* 33: 950b. We have two extant letters written by Yang-ming to T'ang Lung. In the first, written in 1520, Yang-ming explained the reasons why he was willing to take disciples, including those who were less bright, for instruction in his philosophy. In the second, written the next year, he discussed "the study of the instructions of the ancients." See *WWKC* 4: 192–93, 5: 196–97.

5 *WWKC* 33: 951a.

6 *Ibid.* In 'a letter to Hsüeh K'an (1518) there was already a hint of *liang-chih*, described as "this little thing" (*che-hsieh-tzu*) *WWKC* 4: 188b.

7 *WWKC*, Prefaces, 13b–14a.

8 *WWKC* 6: 214a–b.

[9] Great Learning, ch. 1; Legge, v. 1, 358. The text says that "the extension of knowledge is in the investigation of things." It may also be said that Yang-ming simply put the word *chih* (extend) in front of the words *liang-chih*. See the following note.

[10] Book of Mencius 7A, 15; Legge, v. 2, 456. The text says, "The ability man has without having to acquire by learning is *liang-neng ;* the knowledge man has without having to acquire by reflection is *liang-chih*." '

[11] *MJHA* 37: 2b; Jung Chao-tsu, *Ming-tai ssu-hsiang shih*, 52.

[12] Huang Wan, *Ming-tao p'ien*, 20. *MJHA* 13: 5b; Jung Chao-tsu, *Ming-tai ssu-hsiang shih*, 174–77. The two Chinese words literally mean, to limit and to stop. The expression is taken from the Book of Changes. The word *ken* represents the fourth trigram, and has also the meaning of "mountain." It also represents the fifty-second hexagram. See *Chou-yi cheng-yi*, 5: 15b–16a; Legge, *Yi King*, 256, where the metaphysical meaning is "when one's movements and restings all take place at the proper time for them, his way [of proceeding] is brilliant and intelligent." I have simplified it by saying "[acting] and reposing harmoniously." It refers especially to keeping one's spirit always recollected in both activity and stillness.

[13] *MJHA* 62: 4b; Jung Chao-tsu, *Ming-tai ssu-hsiang shih*, 329–31.

[14] *CTYL* 5: 1b–3b. The idea that *hsin* controls both *hsing* and *ch'ing* came from Chang Tsai. Yet Chu Hsi continued to consider *hsin* as somehow "less good" than *hsing* because he considered the former, more dynamic principle to be affected by *ch'i*, and the latter, more passive principle to be full of *li*, with no admixture of *ch'i*.

[15] Letter to Ku Lin, *WWKC* 2: 94a; [Chan, *Instructions*, 103]. Letter to Ou-yang Te, *WWKC* 2: 114b; [Chan, *Instructions*, 152]. See Mou Tsung-san, *Wang Yang-ming chih-liang-chih chiao* (Taipei: 1954); '2–4.

[16] Letter to Ku Lin, *WWKC* 2. 94a, Chan, *Instructions*, 103.

[17] Letter to Ou-yang Te, *WWKC* 2: 113b; Chang, *Instructions*, 150.

[18] *Ibid.*, *WWKC* 2: 116a; Chan *Instructions*, 156.

[19] Book of Mencius 7A: 15; Legge, Classics, v. 2, 456.

[20] *Chou-yi cheng-yi*, 8: 13b; Legge, *Yi King*, 404.

[21] Book of Mencius 7A: 15; Legge, *Rlassics*, v. 2, 456.

[22] Book of Changes, Appended Remarks, pt. 2. See *Chou-yi cheng-yi*, 8: 13b; Legge, *Yi King*, 404.

[23] Book of Mencius 2A: 6. Legge *Classics*, v. 2, 202. Mencius says that this "innate" feeling arises spontaneously, before the man has time to consider other reasons for which he may wish to save the child, for example, to gain the favor of the child's parents, the praise of friends and neighbors, or to avoid criticism for not showing compassion. Chu Hsi also commented on the "prereflective" nature of such feeling. See *CTYL* 53: 4a–5b. Yang-ming made reference to this parable in the Book of Mencius in his essay, "Ta-hsüeh wen" [Inquiry into the Great Learning], *WWKC* 26: 736a; Chan, *Instructions*, 272.

[24] Letter to Nieh Pao, *WWKC* 2: 124b; Chan, *Instructions*, 176. This letter was

written in 1528, not long before Wang's death.

[25] *Iibd.*

[26] Letter to Ou-yang Te, *WWKC* 2: 113b; Chan, *Instructions*, 150.

[27] *WWKC* 3: 131a; Chan, *Instructions*, 193. According to Ch'en Wei-chün (1405–1562), this was in 1520. The accent placed on making intention sincere is clearly given.

[28] *WWKC* 3: 131b; Chan, *Instructions*, 194. For the allusions to Taoist alchemy, see Arthur Waley, "Notes on Chinese Alchemy," *Bulletin of the School of Oriental Studies* VI (1930), 12–13.

[29] *Ibid.*

[30] *WWKC* 3: 145a–b; Chan, *Instructions*, 226.

[31] Letter to Ku Lin, *WWKC* 2: 97b; Chan, *Instructions*, 112–13.

[32] Letter to Ku Lin, *WWKC* 2: 96b; Chan, *Instructions*, 109–10. This letter was written some time before 1524. Shun was supposedly the filial son of a blind and foolish father and a wicked stepmother who hated him but spoilt her own son, his stepbrother. Shun distinguished himself in the service of Emperor Yao, who offered his own [two] daughters to Shun in marriage. To prevent any obstacle his own father and stepmother might place in his way, Shun married them without first asking for his parents' consent. Shun was a figure of legend. King Wu, on the other hand, was a figure of history, the founder of the dynasty of Chou, who undertook to fight against his tyrannical overlord before the burial of his own father, King Wen, was properly accomplished. He successfully defeated the forces of King Chou of Shang and established a new dynasty. See Book of Mencius 5A: 2, Legge, *Classics*, v. 2, 345–46, for the question of Shun's marriage. See also *Shih-chi* 4: 73; 61: 179.

[33] Letter to Ku Lin, *WWKC* 2: 96b; Chan, *Instructions*, 110. See also Yamada Jun, 121–25.

[34] *Ibid.* See T'ang Chün-i; "Yang-ming-hsüeh yü Chu-Lu yi-t'ung ch'ung-pien," 39–43.

[35] *Ibid. WWKC* 2: 96a; Chan, *Instructions*, 109. Yamada Jun, 130.

[36] *Ibid.*, *WWKC* 2: 97b; Chan, *Instructions*, 112.

[37] *Ibid.*, *WWKC* 2: 99a–b; Chan, *Instructions*, 116–17.

[38] *Ibid.*

[39] *WWKC* 3: 146b; Chan, *Instructions*, 229–30.

[40] *WWKC* 3: 146a; Chan, *Instructions*, 228

[41] This teaching of Chu's, based on the Doctrine of the Mean, ch. 1, evolved after much thought and discussion, and is considered to lie at the core of his philosophy and method of cultivation. Ch'eng Yi had identified *hsing* with mind-and-heart (*hsin*) before the rise of emotions (*wei-fa*, unstirred), when it was in a state of "equilibrium" or "stillness," and *hsin* with mind-and-heart after the rise of emotions (*yi-fa*, stirred). If the emotions were "in due proportion," *hsin* would be in a state of "harmony," or harmonious "activity." [*Yi-shu*, 18: 15a–17a; Chan, *Source Book*, 566–67.] Chu Hsi explained this by emphasing on the oneness of *hsin*,

and by pointing out that one should seek to unite "stillness" and "activity" by permeating life with the spirit of reverence (*ching*). See *Chung-yung chang-chü*, *SSCC*, 2a; Letter to his friends in Hunan, *CWWC* 64: 30b–31b; Chan, *Source Book*, 600–02. See also *Chin-ssu-lu chi-chu*, 2: 19b–20a, Chan, *Reflections*, 79–80, for the comment by Yeh Ts'ai.

[42] Letter to Lu Ch'eng, *WWKC* 2: 106b.

[43] Letter to Lu Ch'eng, *WWKC* 2: 107b–08b; Chan, *Instructions*, 137.

[44] *Ibid.*

[45] *WWKC* 3: 103b; Chan, *Instructions*, 192. See also T'ang Chün-i, "Yang-ming hsüeh yü Chu-Lu yi-t'ung ch'ung-pien," 16.

[46] *WWKC* 3: 150a; Chan, *Instructions*, 237.

[47] Letter to Lu Ch'eng, *WWKC* 2: 107b; Chan, *Instructions*, 136. See also Wang Tchang-tche, *La Philosophie Morale*, 127–631.

[48] *Ibid. WWKC* 2: 110b–111a; Chan, *Instructions*, 143–44. The reference is to the Book of Mencius, 2A: a; Legge, *Classics*, v. 2, 190.

[49] *Ibid. WWKC* 2: 109a; Chan, *Instructions*. 139–40. Note the "mirror image" again. See Wang Tchang-tche, *La Philosophie Morale*, 131–34. Wang Tchang-tche noted that *hsin* refers both to the principle of action and the act itself. Hence the adjective "shining" can also refer to the object reflected in *hsin*, to *hsin* itself as that which reflects, or to the action of reflecting light.

[50] *Ibid., WWKC* 2: 112b–113a; Chan, *Instructions*, 148–49. '

[51] Letter to Ou-yang Te, *WWKC* 2: 114b; Chan, *Instructions*, 152. T'ang Chün-i, *Chung-kuo che-hsüeh yüan-lun, Yüan-hsing p'ien* (Hongkong, 1968), 433–34.

[52] *WWKC* 3: 145a; Chan, Instructions, 225.

[53] Letter to Ku Lin, *WWKC* 2: 96a; Chan, *Instructions*, 108; Okada Takehiko, *Ō Yōmei to Minmatsu no jugaku*, 75–76.

[54] "Shu Wei Shih-meng chüan" (1525), *WWKC* 8: 268b.

[55] Letter to Ch'en Wei-chün (1527), *WWKC* 6: 225a. See Kusumoto Masatsugu, *Sō-Min jidai jugaku*, 436–37; Okada Takehiko, *Ō Yōmei to Minmatsu no jugaku*, 76.

[56] Book of Mencius 6A: 6; Legge, Classics, v. 2, 402.

[57] Book of Changes, Commentary on the Hexagram *Ch'ien*; see *Chou-yi cheng-yi*, 1: 8a; Legge, *Yi King*, 410.

[58] Letter to Lu Ch'eng (1529), *WWKC* 5: 201a.

[59] Liang ch'i-ch'ao, *Wang Yang-ming chih-hsing ho-yi chih chiao, Yin-ping shih wen-chi*, 43: 50; T'ang Chün-i, "Yang-ming-hsüeh yü Chu-Lu yi-t'ung ch'ung-pien," 13–15.

[60] The term *wu-yü* (literally, desire for things) recalls to mind Lu Chiu-yüan's teaching, which also attributed evil to *wu-yü*. In Yang-ming's case, however, the word used by the Ch'engs and Chu Hsi, *jen-yü* (selfish, human desires) occurs even more frequently. See *WWKC* 1: 62a–b, 81a–b; 2: 109a–b; Chan, *Instructions*, 20–21, 60–62, 140–41.

[61] Letter to Lu Ch'eng, *WWKC* 2: 109b; Chan, *Instructions*, 140–41.

[62] *WWKC* 3: 136b; Chan, *Instructions*, 206.

[63] *WWKC* 3: 158a; Chan, *Instructions*, 259.

[64] *WWKC* 3: 144a; Chan, *Instructions*, 223. The subject of single-mindedness and indifference to life or death is treated in Book of Mencius 7A: 1.

[65] *WWKC* 3: 144a–b; Chan, *Instructions*, 223–24. As this occurred in 1520 or after, it shows Yang-ming's mature attitude toward "quiet sitting."

[66] The reference is to *Lao-tzu*, ch. 55, SPPY ed., 12a. See Eng. tr. in Chan, *Source Book*, 165.

[67] Letter to Hsü Hsiang-ch'ing, *WWKC* 27: 769b.

[68] Letter to Wang Chün (1511) *WWKC* 4: 172b. Kusumoto Masatsugu spoke of the influence of the Ts'ao-tung [Japanese: *Sōtō*] sect of Ch'an Buddhism with its quietist tendency, on Chu Hsi, and that of the more active Lin-chi [Japanese: *Rinzai*] sect, on Wang Yang-ming. See *Sō-Min jidai jugaku*, 238–41.

[69] *WWKC* 3: 136a; Chan, *Instructions*, 204–5.

[70] *WWKC* 3: 146a–147b; Chan, *Instructions*, 230.

[71] See above, n. 48.

[72] Book of Mencius 2A: 2; Legge, *Classics*, v. 2, 190. See also the discussion on *chi-yi* in Yang-ming's letter to Tung Yün (1515), *WWKC* 5: 207–08. See Kusumoto Masatsugu, *Sō-Min jidai jugaku*, 441–42.

[73] Letter to Nieh Pao, (1528), *WWKC* 2: 123a–124a; Chan, *Instructions*, 173–75. A disciple of Yang-ming's, Nieh Pao, would later develop a more quietist tendency, and would be helped in this by Lo Hung-hsien (1504–64) in an effort to counteract the excesses of the T'ai-chou branch. See *MJHA* 17: 10a–13b; 18: 4b–11b.

[74] *WWKC* 1: 83b; 2: 108b; Chan, *Instructions*, 77:139–40, Such watchfulness over one's least interior movements would be emphasized by those of his disciples who have been considered as his rightful heirs. They included Ch'ien Te-hung, Tsou Shou-yi, and Ou-yang Te and, still later, Liu Tsung-chou. See *MJHA* 11: 6a;'16: 5a; 17: 2a; 62: 7a–b. See also Yamada Jun, 170; Okada Takehiko, *Ō Yōmei to Minmatsu no jugaku*, 170–73.

[75] Letter to Shu Kuo-yung (1523), *WWKC* 5: 201b.

[76] *Ibid.*, *WWKC* 5: 202a.

[77] See *CTYL* 62: 17b–23b; see also T'ang Chün-i, "Yang-ming-hsüeh yü Chu-Lu yi-t'ung ch'ung-pien," 21–27.

[78] *WWKC* 3: 138a; Chan, *Instructions*, 209.

[79] Letter to Nieh Pao, *WWKC* 2: 120b; Chan, *Instructions*, 167.

[80] *Ibid.* Allusion made is to the Book of Documents. Legge, *Classics*, v. 3, 262.

[81] The Three Kings were T'ang of Shang, and Wen and Wu of Chou. See also above, n. 33.

[82] Letter to Nieh Pao, *WWKC* 2: 120b; Chan, *Instructions*, 167.

83 Book of Mencius 6b: 2; Legge, *Classics*, v. 2, 424.

84 Letter to Nieh Pao (1528) *WWKC* 2: 124b; Chan, *Instructions*, 176.

85 Doctrine of the Mean, ch. 21; Legge, *Classics*, v. 1, Li Ao had quoted this sentence earlier. See "Fu-hsing shu," *Li Wen Kung chi*, 1: 8a.

86 Letter to Ou-yang Te, *WWKC* 2: 115a; Chan, *Instructions*, 153.

87 *Yi-shu*, 18: 5a. Ch'eng Yi alludes here to the Doctrine of the Mean ch. 31.

88 Letter to Chou Heng (1524), *WWKC* 2: 103b–104a; Chan, *Instructions*, 127–28.

89 See Ch'ien, *WWKC* Prefaces, 13b–14a; see also *WWKC* 33: 951a–b.

90 Allusion to the Buddhist story regarding the origin of Ch'an according to which Siddharta once showed his listeners a flower while preaching a sermon. The only person who understood his meaning was his disciple Mahākāsyapa, who smiled. So Siddharta gave him the "orthodox treasure" of the "dharma-eye," that is, the heart of his message, which is not transmitted by the written texts. "Dharma-eye" (*fa-yen*) is literally, that which looks into the depths of truth. The story, however, is of very late origin, to be found in the Ch'an collection compiled by Wu-ming (fl 1189) (*Lien-teng hui-yao* 1, *Zokuzōkyo* 1st coll., pt. 2B, case 9, 220b–221a and is also alluded to in the Preface to the *Liu-tsu ta-shih fa-pao t'an ching*, *TSD* No. 2008, XLVIII, 345c and *Ching-te ch'uan-teng lu* 1, *TSD* No. 2076, No. I, 205b–c. For this reason Mahākāsyapa was considered to be the first Ch'an patriarch. See also Daisetz T. Suzuki, *Studies in Zen* (London, 1955), 12, 21.

91 Letter to Yang Shih-ming (1521), *WWKC* 5: 198a. Allusion is to Doctrine of the Mean, ch. 29; Legge, *Classics*, v. 1, 425–526.

92 This was done in his Preface to the new edition of *Hsiang-shan wen-chi* which Yang-ming published. *WWKC* 7: 242b–243a. Earlier, in 1511, in a preface written in honor of Chan Jo-shui, Yang-ming had spoken of the transmission of Confucian doctrine to Yen Hui, Tseng-tzu, and Mencius, with whose death it was lost. But he made no mention then of Lu. See *WWKC* 7: 242a–243b.

93 *WWKC* 7: 242b. This shows a continuity of the emphasis made earlier by Ch'eng Hao on *jen*.

94 Analects 6: 28; Legge, *Classics*, v. 1, 194.

95 A description given in the Book of Mencius, 7A: 26; Legge, *Classics*, v. 2, 464–65.

96 Book of Mencius 6A: 4–5; Legge, *Classics*, v. 2, 397–400.

97 Book of Mencius 6A: 11; Legge, *Classics*, v. 2, 414.

98 "Ta-hsüeh wen," *WWKC* 26: 737b; Chan, *Instructions*, 274–75.

99 *WWKC* 7: 243a. Note that Yang-ming explicitly mentioned both *Wu-chi* and *T'ai-chi*.

100 *WWKC* 7: 243a–b. Earlier, Yang-ming had praised Lu Chiu-yüan as the only great thinker who had appeared since the time of Chou and of the Ch'engs, but remarked that his teaching lacked precision. See *WWKC* 3: 130–31a; Chan, *Instructions*, 192.

101 *CYTL* 78: 2b–3a. See above, Introduction.

[102] *WWKC* 1: 60b; 2: 106a; 3: 139a; 4: 189b. Chan, *Instructions*, 16–17; 132–33; 212.

[103] Letter to Ku Lin, *WWKC* 2: 97b; Chan, *Instructions*, 112. See also Araki Kengo, *Bukkyō to Jukyō*, 401.

[104] *WWKC* 1: 70; 74; Chan, *Instructions*, 42, 52. For Chu Hsi, the Mean refers to the state of equilibrium, although he also said that it can be understood—in the context of the Book of Documents—as meaning "to go to no excess." See *CTYL* 62: 2a–b, 78: 104a.

[105] *WWKC* 2: 117b; 3: 134a. Chan, *Instructions*, 160, 200.

[106] *WWKC* 33: 951a. Allegedly, if the descent was not genuine, the bones would not absorb the blood. On this point, see the biography of Hsiao Tsung—second son of Emperor Wu of Liang (r. 502–49)—who had doubts regarding his paternity. *Nan-shih, ESWS* series, K'ai-ming ed., 53: 128a. Kusumoto Masatsugu points out that Yang-ming attributes to *liang-chih* the power of instinctive consciousness which such "warm blood" was supposed to possess, and so gives to ethical awareness a certain *vital* quality. See *So-Min jidai jugaku*, 415.

[107] *WWKC* 20: 630a. The diagram is an allusion to Chou Tun-yi's *T'ai-chi t'u.* See the annotations given in Part II.

[108] See Letter to Tsou Shou-yi (1525), *WWKC* 6: 212. In Chinese, the question and answer are phrased in identical words.

Chapter v   The Culmination:
Liang-chih pen-t'i

[1] *WWKC* 1: 72a–b; Chan, *Instructions*, 47. See also *WWKC* 2: 126a; 3: 146a; Chan, *Instructions*, 180, 228.

[2] *Ibid.* See also *WWKC* 34: 958a–62b. Yang-ming wrote several of his most important letters dealing with his philosophical teaching during this period.

[3] *WWKC* 3: 152a; Chan, *Instructions*, 245. See also *WWKC* 34: 960b.

[4] *WWKC* 34: 960b; Yamada Jun, *Yomeigaku seigi*, 187–89.

[5] *WWKC* 3: 152a–b; Chan, *Instructions*, 245.

[6] *WWKC* 3: 152b; Chan, *Instructions*, 245–46.

[7] See letter to Ku Lin, *WWKC* 2: 97; Chan, *Instructions*, 111–12.

[8] See his letter to Hsüeh K'an (1518), *WWKC* 4: 188. These Buddhist ideas can traced especially to the *Avatamsaka sūtra* (*Hua-yen ching*), ch. a. See for example the poem in *TSD* No. 279, IX, 4, 9; 453–58.

[9] The expression, "Pulling out the Roots and Stopping the Source" (*Po-pen sai-yüan*), is found in the Annals of Tso, 9th year of Duke Chao, See Legge, *Classics*, v. 5, 624–25. Ou-yang Hsiu (1007–70) took it up in his "Essay on Fundamentals" (*Pen-lun*), *Ou-yang Wen-chung kung wen-chi*, SPTK ed., 17: 1a–6b.

Eng. tr. in de Bary, *Sources*, 387–90. It was from Ou-yang Hsiu's famous call for social renovation that the idea came of the physician treating a disease, and of the need of healing the source of the infection by "strengthening the patient's vitality."

[10] See his preface to the *Ta-hsüeh chang-chü*, 1a–b; *CTYL* 14: 3b.

[11] He does so by explaining the Great Learning, ch. 1, in terms of the Book of Mencius, 2A: 6, and of the teaching of the T'ien-t'ai patriarch, Ch'an-jan (d. 779) concerning the universal presence of the Buddha-nature, even in plants and stones. This Buddhist teaching had already entered the Ch'eng-Chu interpretation of the universal presence of *hsing* (nature). See Fung, *Che-hsüeh-shih*, 770–11, Eng. tr., *History*, v. 2, 385–86.

[12] *WWKC* 26: 736a–b; Chan, *Instructions*, 272–73.

[13] Doctrine of the Mean, ch. 1; Legge, *Classics*, v. 1, 385.

[14] Allusion to the Book of Changes, Commentary on Hexagram *Ch'ien*. See *Chou-yi cheng-yi*, 1: 12a–b; Legge, *Yi-King*, 417.

[15] *WWKC* 26: 736b; Chan, *Instructions*, 272–73.

[16] See his letter to Lu Ch'eng, *WWKC* 2: 107b; Chan, *Instructions*, 137. Wang Tchang-tche, *La Philosophie Morale*, 135–36.

[17] *WWKC* 1: 76a; Chan, *Instructions*, 56–57.

[18] *WWKC* 1: 76b; Chan, *Instructions*, 57. Fung, *che-hsüeh-shih*, 960–62. Eng. tr., *History*, v. 2, 612–14.

[19] *WWKC* 5: 205a.

[20] *Han Ch'ang-li chi*, 11: 1a.

[21] *Chou-tzu T'ung-shu*, 1: 1a.

[22] Allusion to Ch'eng Yi's criticism of Han Yü. See *Yi-shu*, 18: 1a.

[23] *WWKC* 5. 205a–b.

[24] Analects 12: 22; Legge, *Classics*, v. 1, 260.

[25] *WWKC* 3: 143b; Chan, *Instructions*, 222. The questioner was probably Huang Hsing-tseng, who recorded this section. The reference is to the Great Learning, ch. 1; Legge, *Classics*, v. 1, 359.

[26] *WWKC* 3: 144a; Chan, *Instructions*, 223.

[27] *WWKC* 26: 736b; Chan, *Instructions*, 273.

[28] *WWKC* 26: 737a; Chan, *Instructions*, 273.

[29] *WWKC* 2: 99b; Chan, *Instructions*, 118. The oneness between self and others can be understood either as a state of consciousness attained through genuine sympathy with all, or as a gross form of egoism, by which the ruler identifies the interests of the state with his own interests. It is interesting that in Sung and Ming China, under a strongly centralized and authoritarian government, the political ideal was always for the ruler to forget and transcend himself in the service of his people, while in actual practice it was frequently the contrary notion of an inflated egoism that prevailed.

[30] *WWKC* 2: 100b; Chan, *Instructions*, 121. See also Liang Ch'i-ch'ao, *Wang*

Yang-ming chih-hsing ho-yi chih-chiao, in *Yin-ping-shih wen-chi,* 43: 59–61. Liang points out Yang-ming's ideal as being diametrically opposed to the pursuit of personal profit. It was thus a development of Lu Chiu-yüan's polarization of righteousness (*yi*) and profit (*li*).

31 "Ch'in-min-t'ang chi," *WWKC* 7: 247b.

32 *WWKC* 13: 388b. This memorial was written in 1521 after his suppression of Ch'en-hao's rebellion. It requested a thorough investigation into the wealth which the rebel prince had appropriated, in order to make suitable compensation to the victims.

33 *WWKC* 26: 738a–b; Chan, *Instructions,* 276. Although the name of Chu Hsi was not explicitly mentioned, there is no doubt that the reference was to him, as the Great Learning. See *SSCC, Ta-hsüeh chang-chü,* 1a–b.

34 *WWKC* 1: 85a; Chan, *Instructions,* 80.

35 *WWKC* 26: 738b–739a; Chan, *Instructions,* 277–78.

36 *WWKC* 26: 740a; Chan, *Instructions,* 279.

37 See *Chih-ssu-lu chi-chu,* 2: 8a–b; Eng. tr. in Chan, *Reflections,* 50.

38 *WWKC* 2: 112a–b; Chan, *Instructions,* 147–48. See *Ching-te ch'uan-teng lu. TSD* No. 2076, XLIX, 267 for a parable regarding "riding on an ox and looking for it."

39 Letter to Huang Mien-chih (1524), *WWKC* 5: 204b–205a. "Joy in-itself" or the *pen-t'i* of joy.

40 Book of Mencius 7A: 4; Legge, *Classics,* v. 1, 450–51.

41 *WWKC* 3: 155a; Chan, *Instructions,* 252. See also *WWKC* 1: 85a; Chan, *Instructions,* 80.

42 *WWKC* 1: 84b–85a; Chan, *Instructions,* 80.

43 *WWKC* 1: 84b; Chan, *Instructions,* 80. Allusion is here made to *Lao-tzu* ch. 12 [See Chan, *Source Book,* 145].

44 *WWKC* 1: 85a; Chan, *Instructions,* 80.

45 *WWKC* 3: 144a; Chan, *Instructions,* 223. Allusion is to Analects 12: 1; Legge, *Classics,* v. 1, 250.

46 Legge, *Classics,* v. 1, 385–85.

47 Letter to Nan Ta-chi (1526), *WWKC* 6: 217.

The context of the letter supports the interpretation that Yang-ming was speaking of "scholars of virtue" who despise considerations of wealth, honor, profit, and position. Kusumoto Masatsugu remarks that Nan was Chang Tsai's fellow countryman. See *Sō-Min jidai jugaku,* 427.

48 *WWKC* 3: 142; Chan, *Instructions,* 220.

49 Kusumoto Masatsugu, 426–27.

50 See Letter to Lu Ch'eng, *WWKC* 2: 106a; Chan, *Instructions,* 132 for the one known isolated instance of Yang-ming's discussion of *li* and *ch'i,* where he makes a conceptual distinction between the two in the same manner as he had done between *hsing* and *ch'i,* while carefully asserting their necessary existential unity:

"*Li* is that which gives a pattern of organization (*t'iao-li*) to *ch'i*, and *ch'i* is that through which *li* functions. Without the pattern of organization, there can be no functioning; without functioning, there can be no way of discerning any pattern of organization."

The difficulty with this passage is the obscurity surrounding its context. While it appears quite evident that the answer was to a question posed by Lu Ch'eng on the line, "Be discerning and single-minded" of the Book of Documents, "Counsels of Great Yü," the question itself is missing in all editions of *WWKC* that I have consulted.

51 Letter to Lu Ch'eng, *WWKC* 2: 106–8, Chan, *Instructions*, 134–38.

52 *CTCS* 2: 2a–3b. See also ch. I, Yang-ming's fondness for the use of negative language in describing *liang-chih* recalls also Chu Hsi's insistence on *T'ai-chi* being described also as *Wu-chi*, as well as Ch'an Buddhist descriptions of the Absolute Mind. See, for example, Hsi Yün's (fl. 850). *Wan-ling lu, TSD* No. 2012B, XLVIII, 386b, where he spoke of the "Mind-ground" as being like empty-space, with neither form nor shape, direction nor location. See also Eng. tr. by John Blofeld, *The Zen Teaching of Huang Po* (London, 1958), 93.

53 *WWKC* 3: 142; Chan, *Instructions*, 219.

54 *WWKC* 3: 157b; Chan, *Instructions*, 258. For the Chinese words given:
"Yu-hsin chü shih shih, wu-hsin chü shih huang,
Wu-hsin chü shih shih, yu-hsin chü shih huang,"
see the glossary.

55 This negative logic can be traced back to *Chuang-tzu* 2 and to the Middle Way of Mādhyamika's philosophy, originally formulated by Nāgārjuna (1st–2nd cent. A.D.) and brought to China in the 5th cent. by Kumārajiva. .It became expecially important in the Three Treatises (*San-lun*) school, and was reformulated by Chi-tsang (5th–7th cents.) as the "Double Truth on Three Levels." It was further developed in the 8th century by the monk Yung-chia. See Chang Chung-yüan, *The Transmission of the Lamp*, 2–16.

56 *WWKC* 3: 157b; Chan, *Instructions*, 258.

57 *Ibid.*

58 *Ibid.* See also *Wang Lung-hsi ch'üan-chi* (abbrev. as *WLCC*) 1–1a–3b.

59 *WWKC* 3: 157b; Chan, *Instructions*, 258.

60 *WWKC* 3: 143a–b; Chan, *Instructions*, 221–22.

61 *WWKC* 3: 143b; Chan, *Instructions*, 222.

62 *WWKC* 3: 157b; Chan, *Instructions*, 158. Certainly then, for those who are alive, there is yet a Heaven-and-Earth and all things which they may call "theirs."

63 *WWKC* 3: 142a; Chan, *Instructions*, 219.

64 *WWKC* 3: 137b–138a; Chan, *Instructions*, 209.

65 *WWKC* 1: 85a; Chan, *Instructions*, 80–81.

66 *WWKC* 1: 85a; Chan, *Instructions*, 81.

67 *WWKC* 3: 143b; Chan, *Instructions*, 222. I agree with Ch'ien Mu: *Sung-Ming li-hsüeh kai-shu*, (Taipei, 1962), 67–68, and Yasuoka Masaatsu, *Ō Yōmei kenkyū*,

134, that Yang-ming was then speaking of the experience of consciousness, not of the reality of the flower.

[68] Reference to Ch'eng Hao, *ECCS*, *Yi-shu*, 2A: 3b. This quotation has been interpreted out of its context as meaning [*Liang-chih*] can have [or, put up with] nothing contradictory to it [or, no "antitheses"] and even given as evidence of Yang-mings' disapproval of "class struggles" and of the Marxist dialectical method. See Hou Wai-lu, *Chung-kuo ssu-hsiang tiung-shih*, v. 4, pt. 2, 890–91.

[69] Letter to Nieh Pao, *WWKC* 2: 120a; Chan, *Instructions*, 166. See Kusumoto Masatsugu, *Sō-Min jidai jugaku*, 419–24.

[70] *WWKC* 3: 157a–b; Chan, *Instructions*, 257.

CHAPTER VI   THE CULMINATION: WU-SHAN WU-Ô

[1] *WWKC* 3: 142b; Chan, *Instructions*, 220. The allusion is to the Book of Mencius 6A: 8, regarding how men's hearts agree in approving of virtue, and going on to say: "The sages only apprehended before me that which my *hsin* shares with other men." See Legge, *Classics*, v. 2, 406–7.

[2] *WWKC* 1: 79a; Chan, *Instructions*, 63.

[3] Chu Hsi preferred to distinguish between *hsing* and *ts'ai*, *li*, and *ch'i*, calling *li* all that is good, while making *ch'i* somehow responsible for the rise of evil through excess of emotions. See Fung, *che-hsüeh shih*, 942–44; Eng. tr., *History* v. 2, 614–18.

[4] *WWKC* 3: 134b–135a; Chan, *Instructions*, 202.

[5] Takahashi Koji discussed the problem of this contradiction in Yang-ming's philosophy n an article, "O Yōmei ni okeru aku no seritsu," *Daitō Bunka Daigaku Kangaku-kai shi* IV (1961), 19–25. See also Nomura Keiji, "Ō Yōmei dokirun ni tsuite no ichi kosatsu," *Osaka Furitsu Daigaku Kiyō* XI (1963), 83–93.

[6] *WWKC* 3: 149–50; Chan, *Instructions*, 236–37. See also Homer Dubs, "Mencius and Sündz on Human Nature," *PEW* VI (1956), 213–22. Dubs regards Chu Hsi as continuing Hsün-tzu's belief in human nature being evil, in spite of his declarations in favor of Mencius' ideas.

[7] *WWKC* 1: 79b; Chan, *Instructions*, 65.

[8] *WWKC* 2: 110a–b; Chan, *Instructions*, 140–43. The special effort would refer particularly to an arduous practice of meditation for the sake of inducing a certain state of mind.

[9] *Liu-tsu ta-shih fa-pao t'an-ching*, *TSD* No. 2008, XLVIII, 349. The *pen-lai mien-mu* refers to ultimate reality. The version of the *t'an-ching* (Platform Scripture) which refers to it has no English translation although Yampolsky mentions this line in his work. See 134, n. 48.

[10] *WWKC* 2: 110a; Chan, *Instructions*, 141.

[11] *Ibid.* For the story about the hare, see *Han Fei Tzu*, ch. 49, SPTK ed., 19: 1a. Eng. tr. by W. K. Liao, *The Complete Works of Han Fei Tzu* (London, 1959), v. 2, 276.

[12] *WWKC* 3: 151a–b; Chan, *Instructions*, 243. There are other versions of the Four Maxims, usually giving the teaching in a slightly different form, as *MJHA* 16: 3b–4a. But as the accounts of both Ch'ien and Wang Chi coincide—which indeed resulted in their disagreement over the interpretation of the First Maxim— it is better to accept that version of the Maxims.

[13] This was essentially the interpretation of Huang Tsung-hsi [*MJHA* 10: 1b] who remarked that *wu-shan wu-ô* referred to the absence of *thoughts* which maybe called good or evil, rather than a description of human nature itself. The mistake would be to take *yi-fa* [which belongs to the realm of thoughts, intentions, and emotions] to be *wei-fa* [the state prior to the rise of thoughts, intentions, and emotions]. Kao P'an-lung expressed a similar opinion, saying that Yang-ming's doctrine did not affect the truth of the goodness of human nature, although it had other undesirable consequences. *MJHA* 58: 29b.

[14] *WWKC* 3: 151b; Chan, *Instructions* 243; *WLCC* "T'ien-ch'üan cheng-tao chi," 1, 1a–b. For more on Wang Chi's philosophy, see Chang Chung-yüan, "The Essential Source of Identity in Wang Lung-ch'i's Philosophy," *PEW* XXIII (1973), 31–48; Mou Tsung-san, "The Immediate Successor of Wang Yang-ming: Wang Lung-hsi and His Theory of *ssu-wu*," *PEW* XXIII (1973), 103–20.

[15] *WWKC* 3: 151b; Chan, *Instructions*, 244. See also *WLCC*, 1: 1b–2a; *MJHA* 11: 6a–b.

[16] *WWKC* 3: 151b–152a; Chan, *Instructions*, 244–45. Wang Chi's account affirmed that for those of superior perceptivity, Yang-ming favored "sudden enlightenment" but delayed saying so for fear that listeners might be tempted to forgo systematic self-cultivation for an easy shortcut. See *WLCC* 1: 2a–b; and a letter he wrote to a friend, in 12: 8a–b, where he also mentioned that inner enlightenment cannot be induced, although he regarded such enlightenment to be the key to wisdom.

[17] *WWKC* 3: 151b–152a; Chan, *Instructions*, 244–45. See also *WLCC* 1: 2b. Wang Chi added that Yang-ming recommended even for the "already enlightened" the practice of gradual cultivation in order to enter sagehood. For a discussion of the Four Maxims see also Takahashi Koji, "Ō Yōmei no 'shiku ketsu' ni tsuite," *Chūgoku Tetsugaku*, I, (1961) 10–18.

[18] *Ibid.* Yang-ming's teaching of the Four Maxims have frequently been cited as evidence of Buddhist influence on his thinking. The differences between Ch'ien Te-hung and Wang Chi have been said to resemble those between the Ch'an Buddhist monks, Hui-neng and Shen-hsiu. See Wang Fu-chih, *Ssu-chieh*, in *Ssu-wen lu/Ssu-chieh* (Peking, 1956), p. 13.

[19] For the conscious amalgamation of the "Three Ways" on the part of later scholars under Yang-ming's influence, see Sakai Tadao, *Chūgoku zensho no kenkyū* (Tokyo, 1960), 226–304, *passim*, and Araki Kengo, "Minmatsu ni okeru Ju Butsu chōwaron no seikaku," *Nippon Chūgoku gakkaihō* XVIII (1966), 210–24.

[20] *WWKC* 1: 70a; Chan, *Instructions*, 40–41.

[21] *WWKC* 1: 70b; Chan, *Instructions*, 41–42. Yang-ming was citing from the

Appendix to the Book of Changes. See *Chou-yi cheng-yi*, 7: 7b; Legge, tr., *Yi King*, 355–56. See also Yang-ming's letter to Tsou Shou-yi (1526), *WWKC* 6: 212b.

22 *WWKC* 34: 958a–960a.

23 *WWKC* 34: 960a. See also *WLCC* 1: 19a–b.

24 This letter to T'ung chen is in *WWKC* 21: 634b–635a. Yang-ming's own prayer for rain on this occasion is given in *WWKC* 25: 723. He chose to pray at Nan-chen, a place east of K'uai-chi, probably on account of the temple there dedicated to the sage emperor, Yu. See *Chechiang t'ung-chih* (1899 ed.; Shanghai reprint, 1934), 1: 210–14.

25 *WWKC* 21: 638a–b. Note that these are Yang-ming's earliest extant letters and that 1508 was the year of his enlightenment.

26 A legendary immortal who supposedly lived in the K'ung-t'ung mountain and whose advice was sought by the Yellow Emperor. See *Chuang-tzu*, 4: 18a, Eng. tr. by Burton Watson, 118–20.

27 *WWKC* 21: 638.

28 Dated 1078, this was written by Chang Po-tuan (983–1082) and is included in *Tao-tsang* [abbrev. as *TT*] ,64, Epilogue, 1b. See also Liu Ts'un-yan, "Taoist Self-cultivation in Ming Thought", in de Bary, ed., *Self and Society in Ming Thought*, 311–15.

29 *WWKC* 5: 199b. See *SKTY*, 28: 88.

30 *Ibid.* See Ch'en Chien's criticism, *Hsüeh-pu t'ung-pien*, 9: 4a–b.

31 *WWKC* 5: 199a–b. The references regarding caution and apprehension are to the Doctrine of the Mean, ch. 1.

32 Letter to Lu Ch'eng, *WWKC* 2: 106a–b; Chan, *Instructions*, 133.

33 See *WWKC* 20: 632b for the poem. See also the annotations given in Part II.

34 See pp. 3–5.

35 See Ch'en Chien, *Hsüeh-pu t'ung pien*, 9: 4b, P. C. Hsü, *Ethical Realism in Neo-Confucian Thought*, 145–48. Possibly, such wide knowledge of Buddhist literature was typical of many Ming scholars and might not necessarily indicate deep research into Buddhist thought. But this fact alone would support the extent of Buddhist penetration into Confucian lives.

36 He alluded to the sayings of Tsung-mi, Ch'eng-kuan (c. 760–838), Yüan-wu (fl. 1125) and others. See *WWKC* 1: 85b, Chan, *Instructions*, 33, 82.

37 *WWKC* 1: 84a–b; Chan, *Instructions*, 79. Hui-k'o had said to Seng-ts'an: "Give me your sins, and I shall do penance for you." See *Ching-te ch'uan-teng lu*, in *TSD* No. 2076, LI, 3: 220. For a fuller discussion of Buddhist influences on Yang-ming, see Tokiwa Daijō, 461–66.

38 *WWKC* 3: 151b–152a; Chan, *Instructions*, 243–44.

39 See Bodde, *History*, v. 2, 402–6. This section was rewritten by Fung Yu-lan for the English translation and is not to be found in his Chinese original.

40 See *Wu-men kuan*, *TSD* No. 2005, XLVIII, 295; German tr. by H. Dumoulin, p. 32. See also Araki Kengo, *Bukkyō to Junkyō*, p. 390.

41 Bodde, *History*, v. 2, 392–99, *passim*. See n. 39.

42 See *WWKC* 20: 600a, 605b.

43 *WWKC* 20: 626a–b, 629a–b, 630a.

44 *Hsüeh-pu t'ung-pien*, 9B: 4a–6a.

45 *WWKC* 20: 625a. For fuller understanding, see the annotations given in Part II.

46 Bodde, *History*, v. 2. 406.

47 *WWKC* 3: 136a–b; Chan, *Instructions*, 205.

48 Letter to Lo Ch'in-shun, *WWKC* 2: 119a; Chan, *Instructions*, 163.

49 See Yang-ming's preface to *Chu-tzu wan-nien ting-lun, WWKC* 3: 160a–b; Chan, *Instructions*, 165.

50 Letter to Tsuo Shou-yi (1526), *WWKC* 6: 212b–213a. There are five extant letters to Tsou, all dated 1526. This is the fourth one.

51 Letter to Ku Lin, *WWKC* 2: 101b; Chan, *Instructions*, 123.

52 Preface to *Ch'uan-hsi lu*, pt. 2, in *WWKC* 2: 88a; Chan, *Instructions*, 90.

53 *WWKC* 3: 142a–b; Chan, *Instructions*, 220.

54 *WWKC* 2: 113a; Chan, *Instructions*, 149.

55 *WWKC* 2: 121b; Chan, *Instructions*, 169–70. The references are to Analects 14: 41–42; 6: 26 (Legge, *Classics*, v. 1, 290–91; 193).

56 *WWKC* 2: 121a–b; Chan, *Instructions*, 169.

57 *WWKC* 2: 121b–22a; Chan, *Instructions*, 171. The word "mad" in Chinese is *k'uang*.

58 This is the literal meaning of the book's title.

59 *WWKC* 20: 629a. See also the annotations given in Part II.

CHAPTER VII   CONCLUSION

1 *WWKC* 19: 573b–574a. For a translation of the entire poem, see Part II.

2 I wish to point out that I have found Benjamin Schwartz' article, "Some Polarities in Confucian Thought," in *Confucianism in Action*, ed. by David S. Nivison and Arthur F. Wright (Stanford, 1959), 50–62, very stimulating.

3 Kusumoto Masatsugu, *Sō-Min jidai Jugaku shisō no kenkyū*, 237–39; 341–46.

4 For Chu Hsi, see ch. 1. For Lu Chiu-yüan, see *SS* 434: 1114.

5 See Yang-ming's preface to *Chu-tzu wan-nien ting-lun*, in *WWKC* 3: 160; Chan, Instructions, 265.

6 *Chuang-tzu* 33, SPPY ed., 10: 14a; Eng. tr. in Burton Watson, 364.

7 In this respect, I have found stimulation in W. T. de Bary's "Spiritual Cultivation and Intellectual Enlightenment in Neo-Confucian Thought," in *The Unfolding of Neo-Confucianism*, ed. by himself (New York, 1975), 141–215.

[8] *HSCC* 34: 14b. Lu himself is a good example of an "enlightened" man, who acquired profound insights into the meaning of *hsin* during early youth. But his judgment of Chu should not be regarded as expressive of conceit. To a disciple who suggested that both he and Chu should publish books, in order to allow posterity to choose between the two of them, Lu had replied severely that neither his own presence nor that of Chu could make the universe a better or greater place. See also *HSCC* 36: 3b. On my own part, I wish to point out that I am not denying Chu's wisdom, nor the possibility of attaining enlightenment and sagehood by following his method of cultivation.

[9] Yang-ming's critics, especially Ch'en Chien, referred especially to his teaching of inner enlightenment as a proof of his Ch'an Buddhist affiliations. 9B: 6a–b.

[10] See the article by Ho Lin, "Sung-ju te ssu-hsiang fang-fa," in *Sung-shih yen-chiu chi*, comp. by the Study Committee on Sung History (Taipei, 1964), 54. See also Jung Chao-tsu, *Ming-tai ssu-hsiang shih*, 92–94.

[11] See chapter 2.

[12] Joseph Levenson, *Confucian China and Its Modern Fate*, v. 2: *The Problem of Monarchical Decay* (London, 1964), 65–66.

[13] See Introduction, n. 68.

[14] *WWKC* 33: 951. See also Wang Tchang-tche, *La Philosophie Morale de Wang Yang-ming*, 68–71.

[15] He would also formulate the so-called Four Negative (*ssu-wu*), declaring that
"The-mind-without-mind hides depth,
   The intention-without-intending responds with perfection,
   The knowledge-without-knowing realizes silence,
   The thing-without-thing (act-without-acting) works wonders."
See *WLCC* 1: 1a–2b. See also the Glossary-index for the Chinese characters.

[16] For Li Chih, see Okada Takehiko, *Ō Yōmei to Minmatsu no jugaku*, 249–55; de Bary," Individualism and Humanitarianism in late Ming," in de Bary, ed., *Self and Society*, 191–99. See also Preface, p. XX.

[17] See Introduction, n. 39. In criticizing Wang Yang-ming for using the other expression, *wu-shan wu-ô*, Ku Hsien-ch'eng says: "*Wu-sheng wu-ch'ou* refers to what we Conducian scholars consider to be emptiness (*k'ung*). *Wu-shan wu-ô* refers to what the Buddhists and Taoists consider to be emptiness. The expressions appear to resemble each other, but the realities designated are very different." *MJHA* 58: 7a.

[18] Ku Yen-wu, *Jih-chih-lu chi-shih*, 8: 14b–17b.

[19] For the use of negation as a means of reaching and of affirming the Absolute, both in Ch'an Buddhism and in the Christian mystics, see Suzuki, *Essays in Zen Buddhism*, 1st series (London, 1927), 267–77.

[20] See chapter 6.

[21] The expression *yi-chien* comes from the Appendix to the Book of Changes, and has been used especially by Lu Chiu-yüan to describe his own teaching in contradistinction to Chu Hsi's. See Introduction, no. 47. (Legge translates it as "ease and freedom.") See *Yi King*, SBE series, v. 1, p. 349.)

22 Wing-tsit Chan says that Yang-ming confuses reality with value, and lacks in analytical depth. Carsun Chang, however, calls Yang-ming "the greatest thinker of China", and "comparable to the greatest thinkers of the West." See Chan, *Source Book*, 655, *Instructions*, Introduction, xxxiii; Chang, *The Development of Neo-Confucian Thought*, v. 2, 71.

23 *WWKC* 3: 158a–b.

24 *Ibid.*

25 *Ibid.*

26 *WWKC* 3: 147, Chan, *Instructions*, 230.

27 That the doctrine of the unity of all things does not preclude all distinction between self and the other is borne out even in Ch'an Buddhism. The lay Buddhist, P'an Yün, gave expression to it after hearing a lecture on the Diamond Sutra. See *Ching-te ch'uan-teng lu, TSD* No. 2076, LI, 263; Eng. tr. in Chang Chung-yüan, *Original Teachings of Ch'an Buddhism*, 175–76.

28 *MJHA* 12: 1a–2b, 32: 1a–4b; Okada Takehiko, *Ō Yōmei to Minmatsu no Jugaku*, 122–37, 183–255. These men belonged to the so-called "leftist" Yang-ming school.

29 *MJHA* 16: 1a–4a, 17: 1a–2b; Okada Takehiko, *Ō Yōmei to Minmatsu no Jugaku*, 138–82. See Appendix 1.

30 *WWKC* 20: 607b.

EPILOGUE: NOTES ON THE "YANG-MING CONTROVERSY"

1 See Ch'en Chien, *Hsüeh-pu t'ung-pien* (Preface 1548), bk. 4, pt. 3; Feng K'ao, *Ch'iu-shih p'ien*, ch. 4; Lu Lung-ch'i, *Lu Chia-shu chi*, ch. 2; Chang Lieh, *Wang-hsüeh chih-yi* (Preface 1681).

2 See the preface he wrote to his own book, the *Cheng-meng chu*, in *Chang-tzu Cheng-meng chu* (Peking, 1956), 8–9.

3 See *Shun-shui yi-shu* (Hangchow, 1913), 6–7b.

4 *Jih-chih-lu chi-shih* 7: 6a.

5 *Ch'ing Hsüeh-an hsiao-shih* (Preface 1845; Taipei reprint, 1969), Introduction, p. 5. See also Liang Ch'i-ch'ao, *Chung-kuo chin san-pai-nien hsüeh-shu shih*, in *Yin-ping shih ho-chi, chuan-chi* 75: 6–14, 79–80; Hsü Shih-ch'ang (1858–1939), *Ch'ing-ju hsüeh-an* (Taipei, 1967), 8: 1–2; Ch'ien Mu, *Chung-kuo chin san-pai-nien hsüeh-shih shih* (Shanghai, 1937), 18–21.

6 *MJHA* ch. 58; Jung Chao-tsu, *Ming-tai ssu-hsiang shih*, 284–314; Okada Take-kiho. *Ō Yōmei to Minmatsu no Jugaku*, 399–438, *passim*.

7 *MJHA* 58: 32a.

8 For Huang's life, see *MJHA* 13: 5b–6b and his own *Ming-tao p'ien* (1st published, 1547; reprinted in Peking, 1959), especially the Introduction by Hou Wai-lu.

9 Ch'eng Hao, *ECCS*, *Yi-shu*, 2A: 3a–b.

10 Huang Wan, *Ming-tao-p'ien*, 1: 11–13.

11 *Ibid.*, 1: 12–14.

12 *Ibid.*, 1: 12.

13 It is my opinion that those who argue from ideology frequently know the inadequacies of their preassumptions, but do so for specific aims, such as to correct practical abuses, and they often refrain from questioning their own preassumptions, for fear of shaking the foundations of belief accepted by the masses who cannot clearly discern between truth and ideology. I believe this was the case in the Confucian *versus* Ch'an Buddhist controversy over Yang-ming's thought.

14 See the references given above in n. 5.

15 For K'ang Yu-wei, see his biography, in Liang Ch'i-ch'ao, *Yin-ping-shih ho-chi, wen-chi*, 6: 58–64.

16 T'an recommended the reading of Chou Tun-yi, Chang Tsai, Lu Chiu-yüan, Wang Yang-ming and Huang Tsung-hsi, but not of Ch'eng Yi and Chu Hsi. See his "Jen-hsüeh," in *T'an Ssu-t'ung ch'üan-chi* (Peking reprint, 1954), v. 1, pt. 1, 6–9.

17 See his *Wang Yang-ming chih-hsing ho-yi chih chiao*.

18 *Geschichte der neueren chinesischen Philosophie* (Hamburg, 1938), 380–99.

19 *Science and Civilization in China*, v. 2, 506–10.

20 Chang's book was entitled *Wang Yang-ming: Idealist Philosopher of Sixteeth-Century China* (New York, 1962). See especially p. 30.

21 See Preface, p. XXX.

22 *Chung-kuo ssu-hsiang t'ung-shih*, ed. by Hou Wai-lu (Peking, 1960), v. 4, pt. 2, 875. Hou Wai-lu lost official favor during the Cultural Revolution. See my paper, "Confucius and His Modern Critics, 1916 to Present," *Papers on Far Eastern History* X (September, 1974), 141.

23 *Ibid.*, ch. 22, 23, 24 (pp. 958–1095).

24 *Chung-kuo che-hsüeh-shih lun-wen ch'u-chi*, 1st series (Shanghai, 1957), pp. 90–93, 122–23.

25 *Chung-kuo che-hsüeh-shih lun-wen chi* (Shanghai, 1958), 108–9.

26 *Ibid.*, I realize that Fung Yu-lan has publicly announced his intention to rewrite all his books according to what he purported to have learnt during the Anti-Confucius Campaign, but I shall make no comment on this subject here. See my article, "Confucius and His Modern Critics, 1916 to Present," *Papers on Far Eastern History* X (September, 1974), 137.

Appendix I   The Wang Yang-ming School in Japan: A Brief Survey

[1] The praise of Nakae Tōju, by Sugiura Jūgō, who had been tutor to Emperor Taishō (r. 1912–26). It is cited in Chang Chün-mai, *Pi-chiao Chung-Jih Yang-ming hsüeh* (Taipei, 1970), 61. Eng. tr. in R. Tsunoda, W. T. de Bary and D. Keene, ed., *Sources of Japanese Tradition* (New York, 1964), v. 1, 370.

[2] See Chu Ch'ien-chih, *Jih-pen te ku-hsüeh chi Yang-ming hsüeh* (Shanghai, 1962), 220–21.

[3] *WWKC* 3: 142b; Chan, *Instructions*, 220. This is quoted above in chapter 6, n. 1.

[4] See Inoue Tetsujirō et al., *Nihon rinri ihen: Yōmeigakuha no bu* (Tokyo, 1970), v. 1, 1–6.

[5] For Fuchi Kōzan, see Inoue Tetsujirō, *Nihon Yōmeigakuha no tetsugaku* (Tokyo, 1936), 167–71; Chu Ch'ien-chih, *Jih-pen te ku-hsüeh chi Yang-ming hsüeh*, 262. For Kumazawa Banzan, see Inoue, *Nihon rinri ihen: Yōmeigakuha no bu*, v. 1, 6–8; Chu Ch'ien-chih, 260–61.

[6] Chu Ch'ien-chih, 2201, 383–87.

[7] See Inoue Tetsujirō, *Nihon Shushi gakuha no tetsugaku* (Tokyo, 1945), 605–15; Chu Ch'ien-chih, *Jih-pen te Chu-tzu hsüeh* (Peking, 1958), 31–78, *passim*.

[8] Inoue Tetsujirō, *Nihon rinri*, v. 2, 2–5; Chu Ch'ien-chih, *Jih-pen te ku-hsüeh chi Yang-ming hsüeh*, 276–79.

[9] Inoue Tetsujirō, *Nihon rinri*, v. 3, 1–6; Chu Ch'ien-chih, *Jih-pen te ku-hsüeh chi Yang-ming hsüeh*, 294–379. Okada Takehiko, "The Chu Hsi and Wang Yang-ming Schools at the End of the Ming and Tokugawa Periods," *PEW* XXIII (1973), 150.

[10] Chu Ch'ien-chih, *Jih-pen te ku-hsüeh chi Yang-ming hsüeh*, 288–91.

[11] See especially his "Seiken roku" (Examination of Conscience), in *Shōzan zenshu* (Tokyo, 1913), v. 2, p. 6.

[12] Chang Chih-tung (1837–1909), "Ch'üan-hsüeh p'ien," *Chang Wen-hsiang-kung ch'üan-chi* (Taipei reprint, 1963), 203: 9b. See on this subject, Hellmut Wilhelm, "The Problem of Within and Without: A Confucian Attempt in Syncretism," *Journal of the History of Ideas* XII (1951), 48–60, and Joseph R. Levenson, *Confucian China and Its Modern Fate. v. 1: The Problem of Intellectual Continuity* (Berkeley, 1968), 59–79.

[13] Inoue Tetsujirō, *Nihon no Yōmeigakuha*, 515–20; Chu Ch'ien-chih, *Jih-pen te ku-hsüeh chi Yang-ming hsüeh*, 314–19. Sakuma is sometimes classified as a follower of the school of Chu Hsi. Interestingly, he is included in Inoue's *Yōmeigakuha no tetsugaku* (first published, 1900), but not in the *Nihon rinri ihen* (first published, 1901–3), as a member of the Yōmei school.

[14] Inoue Tetsujirō, *Nihon rinri*, v. 3, 6–11; Chu Ch'ien-chih, *Jih-pen te ku-hsüeh chi Yang-ming hsüeh*, 337–65, *passim*.

[15] "Senshindō Sakki," (Notes of Senshindō), in Inoue Tetsujirō et al., *Yōmeigakuha* (Tokyo, 1936), v. 3, 15.

[16] Ōshio's *Kohon Daigaku katsumuku* is a collection of all the commentaries on the Great Learning by Hang, T'ang, Sung, Ming, and Ch'ing scholars, especially those written by the disciples of the Yang-ming school, It is included in the *Nihon rinri ihen*, v. 3, 143–442, together with one version of Yang-ming's "Side Commentaries on the Great Learning" (pp. 194–98), which is different from that given in the *Han-hai* collection.

[17] Chu Ch'ien-chih, *Jih-pen te ku-hsüeh chi Yang-ming hsüeh*, 371–73.

[18] *Ibid.*

[19] See also Motoyama Yukihiko, *Meiji shisō no keisei* (Tokyo, 1969), 47–67.

[20] For Katsu, see his autobiography, *Katsu Kaishu jiden : Hikawa seiwa* (Chibaken, 1968), especially his praise of Ō Yōmei on p. 105.

[21] Inoue Tetsujirō, *Nihon no Yōmeigakuha*, 497–503; Chu Ch'ien-chih, *Jih-pen te ku-hsüeh chi Yang-ming hsüeh*, 320–23.

[22] Inoue Tetsujirō, *Nihon no Yōmeigakuha*, 521–36; Chu Ch'ien-chih, *Jih-pen te ku-hsüeh chi Yang-ming hsüeh*, 323–25. See also Yasuoka Masaatsu, "Ming-chih wei-hsin yü Yang-ming hsüeh," tr. into Chinese by Ching-chia in *Tung-hsi wen-hua*, XXV (1969), 10–15.

[23] Inoue Tetsujirō, *Nihon no Yōmeigakuha*, 537–43; Chu Ch'ien-chih, *Jih-pen te ku-hsüeh chi Yang-ming hsüeh*, 325–27.

[24] Yoshida Sakuzō et al., comp., *Meiji bunka zenshū* (v. 2) *Seishihen* pt. 1, (Tokyo, 1927–30), 33.

[25] Yoshida Sakuzō et al., comp., *Meiji bunka zenshū* (v. 3), *Seishihen*, pt. 2, p. 275. Eng. tr. in de Bary, et al., *Sources of Japanese Tradition*, v. 2, 140.

[26] Kimura Ki, ed., *Meiji jinbutsu ronshū* (*Meiji bunka zenshū*, v. 92) (Tokyo, 1970), 3–25.

[27] Maruyama Masao, *Thought and Behaviour in Modern Japanese Politics* (London, 1963), 1–23: 135–54; 332.

[28] Gotō Motomi, "Studies in Chinese Philosophy in Postwar Japan," *Monumenta Serica* XIV (1949–55), 164–48.

[29] See especially Shimada Kenji, *Chūgoku ni okeru kindai shi no zasetsu* (Tokyo, 1949), and Yamashita Ryuji, "Yōmeigaku kenkyū no rekishi kara," *Rekishi kyoiku* III (1955), 71–77.

[30] See Mishima's article, "Kakumei tetsugaku to shite no Yōmeigaku," in *Shokun* (Sept. 1970), 22–45.

[31] See Preface, n. 1.

APPENDIX II THE WANG YANG-MING SCHOOL IN KOREA:
A SUMMARY REPORT

1 There are available three articles, in Chinese and Japanese, giving a survey history of the Yang-ming school in Korea. They are: Yi Nung-hwa, "Chōsōn Yuhak chi Yang-myŏng hak-pa," *Seikyūgakusō* XXV (1936), 105–42; Takahashi Tōru, "Chōsen no Yōmeigakuha," *Chōsen gakuho* IV (1953), 131–56; Abe Yoshio, "Chōsen no Yōmeigakuha," *Yōmeigaku nyūmon* (*Yōmeigaku taikei*, v. 1), 407–25.

2 *MS* 320: 816a. This happened in 1433.

3 Yi Pyŏng-do, *Charyo Han'guk Yuhak sa ch'ogo* (A Draft History of Confucianism in Korea), Seoul National University, 1959, mimeographed copy. Part 3, p. 94. I am grateful to Fang Chao-ying for lending me his copy of this book, probably the only one in the United States. See also Takahashi Tōru, "Richo Jugaku-shi ni okeru Shuriha Shugiha no hattatsu" (The Development of the Schools of *li* and *ch'i* during the Yi Dynasty), *Chōsen Shina bunka no kenkyū* (Tokyo, 1929), 262–63. For a general account of Korean Confucianism in English, see K. P. Yang and G. Henderson, "An Outline History of Korean Confucianism," *Journal of Asian Studies*, XVIII (1958), 81–102, (1959), 259–76.

4 *T'oegye sonsaeng munjip* (Collected Writings of Yi Hwang) (Seoul, 1959), 41: 23a–30b.

5 *Yulgok chonso* (Complete Works of Yi Yi) (Seoul, 1958), 13: 32a–33b.

6 Yi Nung-hwa, 112–13.

7 *Ibid.*, 115–6.

8 *Ibid.*, 116.

9 *Kyegok manp'il* (Random Notes by Chang Yu), 24–25, quoted in Yi Nung-hwa, 119.

10 *Chich'on jip* (Collected Writings of Ch'ae Myong-gi), 17: 23–25, quoted in Yi Nung-hwa, 121–22.

11 "Hagok sŏnsaeng yŏnbo" (Chronological Biography of Chong Hagok), in *Hagok sonsaeng munjip*, unpublished edition, 1–25. I wish to thank Lew Seung-kook of the Songyungwan University for providing me with a xerox copy of this chronological biography.

12 See *Hagok jip* (Seoul, 1972), v. 1, 7–40, *passim*.

13 *Ibid.*, 29, 33.

14 *Ibid.*, 69.

15 Yi Nung-hwa, 139.

16 Yi Pyŏng-do, Part 4, 60.

17 Chŏng In-bo speaks of the Yang-ming school in *Tamwon kukhak san'go* (Random Writings on Korean Learning) (Seoul, 1955), Part 4. He discusses Chong Hagok

and other Yang-ming followers after him in pp. 274–93. The book is written in Korean.

18 I wish to thank Lew Seung-kook of Songyungwan University for introducing me to the Yang-ming school in Korea. I wish also to thank G. Ledyard of Columbia University for giving me various bibliographical references on this subject. It was from Prof. Lew that I learned about and acquired the *Collected Writings of Chong Hagok* (Seoul, 1972), 2 volumes.

GLOSSARY

A. TECHNICAL TERMS IN CHINESE AND JAPANESE

ai	愛	*ching*	經
		ching-hsin	盡心
Ch'an	禪	*ch'ing*	情
che-hsieh-tzu	這些子	*ch'ing-li*	經禮
chen-ju	真如	*ching-tso*	靜坐
chen-t'i	真體	*Chiu-hsueh wei-t'i*	舊學爲體
chen-wo	真我	*ch'ü-li*	曲禮
cheng-hsin	正心	*chüan*	狷
cheng-nien-t'ou	正念頭	*chün-tzu*	君子
ch'eng	誠	*chung*	中
ch'eng-yi	誠意	chung	忠
ch'i	氣	*chung-ho*	中和
ch'i	器		
ch'i-yi	集義	*fa-yen*	法眼
chien	簡	*fo-hsing*	佛性
chien-ai	兼愛	*fu-sao*	賦騷
Ch'ien	乾	*hao-man pu-chü*	豪邁不羈
chih, chih₁	知		
chih, chih₂	致	*ho*	和
chih-chih	致知	*Hsi-hsüeh wei-yung*	西學爲用
chih-hsing ho-yi	知行合一	*hsiang*	相
chih-liang-chih	致良知	*hsiao-jen*	小人
chih-shan chih-o	知善知惡	*hsiao-k'ang*	小康
ch'in	親	*hsien-hsien*	先賢
ch'in-min	親民	*hsin*	心
ching	敬	*hsin*	新
ching	靜	*hsin chi li*	心即理
ching	精	*hsin chih pen-t'i*	心之本體

hsin chih t'i	心之體	*ming*	明
Hsin-hsüeh	心學	*ming*	命
hsin-min	新民	*ming ming-te*	明明德
hsing	性	*ming-te*	明德
hsing	行		
hsing-chih-pen-t'i	性之本體	*nei*	內
hsing-erh-hsia	形而下	*nei/wai, nei-wai*	內外
hsing-erh-shang	形而上	*pa*	霸
Hsing-li, hsing-li	性理	*pen-hsin*	本心
Hsing-li hsüeh	性理學	*pen-lai mien-mu*	本來面目
hsüan	玄	*pen-t'i*	本體
hsüeh	學	*pen-wu*	本無
huan-tan	還丹	*p'ing-ch'ang-hsin*	平常心
		po	博
jen	仁	*po-pen sai-yüan*	拔本塞源
jen-hsin	人心		
jen-yü	人欲	*ryōchi*	良知
K'an	坎	*san-ts'ai*	三才
ken-chih	艮止	*Seiyō no gakugei*	西洋の學藝
ko	格	*Shan-jen*	山人
ko-wu/ke-wu	格物	*Shang-ti*	上帝
k'ung	狂	*shen-tu*	慎獨
K'uang-Ch'an	狂禪	*sheng*	聖
K'un	坤	*sheng*	身
		shih	事
kung-fu	工夫	*shih-hsien*	詩仙
k'ung	空	*shih-she*	詩社
		sui-ch'u-ti'-jen T'ien-li	隨處體認天理
*li*₁	理	*sui-hsing*	隨性
*li*₂	禮		
li	離	*ta-t'ung*	大同
li	利	*T'ai-chi*	太極
li-ch'eng	立誠	*T'ai-ho*	太和
li-ch'i	理氣	*T'ai-hsü*	太虛
li-hsin	立心	*Tao, tao*	道
Li-hsüeh	理學	*Tao-hsin, tao-shin*	道心
li-ming	立命	*Tao-hsüeh*	道學
liang	良	*Tao-t'ung*	道統
liang-chih	良知	*Taotogami*	太乙神
liang-chih pen-t'i	良知本體	*te*	德
liang-neng	良能	*t'i*	體
		t'i/yung, t'i-yung	體用
min	民	*t'iao-li*	條理

T'ien	天	*Wu-yi-chih-yi tse ying-yüan*	無意之意則應圓
T'ien-jen ho-yi	天人合一		
T'ien-li	天理	*Wu-chih-chih-chih tse t'i-chi*	無知之知則體寂
T'ien-ming	天命		
t'o-po	托鉢	*Wu-wu-chih-wu tse yung-shen*	無物之物則用神
t'ou-nao	頭腦		
Tōyō no dōtoku	東洋の道德	*wu/hsiu, wu-hsiu*	悟修
ts'ai	才	*wu-li*	物理
Tsun-ching	算經	*wu-shan-wu-o*	無善無惡
tun-wu	頓悟	*wu-cheng wu-ch'ou*	無聲無臭
tung	動	*wu-yü*	無欲，物欲
tung/ching, tung-ching	動靜		
t'ung-te	同德	*yang*	陽
tzu-te	自得	*yi*	義
		yi	意
wai	外	*yi*	藝
Wan-wu yi-t'i	萬物一體	*yi chi yi-ch'ieh*	一即一切
wang	王	*yi-ch'ieh chi yi*	一切即一
Wang-yen	忘言	*yi-chih tung*	意之動
wei-fa	未發	*yi-fa*	己發
wei-fa/yi-fa	未發・己發	*yin*	陰
wei-hsin	唯心	*yin-yang*	陰陽
wei-shan ch'ü-o	爲善去惡	*yu-shan yu-o*	無善無惡
wen	文	*yü*	欲
wu	物	*yü-lu*	語錄
wu	無	*yüan*	元
wu	悟	*Yu-hsin chü shih shih*	有心俱是實
Wu-chi	無極	*wu-hsin chü shih huang*	無心俱是幻
Wu-chi erh T'ai-chi	無極而太極	*wu-hsin chü hsih shih*	無心俱是實
wu-hsin	無心	*yu-hsin chü shih huang*	有心俱是幻
Wu-hsin-chih-hsin tse ts'ang-mi	無心之心則藏密		

B. PERSONAL NAMES IN CHINESE, JAPANESE AND KOREAN

Only such names are included which appear in the main text of the book or in the footnotes.

Abe Yoshio	阿部吉雄
Ai, Duke	哀公
Amada Takeo	天田武夫
An Chong-bok (Sun'am)	安鼎福（順庵）
Araki Kengo	荒木見悟

Ch'ae Myong-gil (Chich'on)	崔鳴吉（遲川）
Chan Jo-shui (Kan-ch'üan)	湛若水（甘泉）
Chan Wing-tsit	陳榮捷
Chan-jan	湛然
Chang Ch'i-yün	張其昀
Chang Chün-mai	張君勱
Chang Chih-tung	張之洞
Chang Chung	張忠
Chang Chung-yüan	張鐘元
Chang Lieh	張烈
Chang Po-hsing	張伯行
Chang Po-tuan (P'ing-shu)	張伯端（平叔）
Chang Shu-ch'ien (Yüan-ch'ung)	張叔謙（元冲）
Chang Tsai	張載
Chang Yu (Kyegok)	張維（谿谷）
Chang Yü-ch'üan	張煜全
Chao, Duke	昭公
Chao T'ai-ting	趙泰定
Chao Yi	趙翼
Ch'en Chien	陳建
Ch'en Ch'un	陳淳
Ch'en Hsiang	陳襄
Ch'en Hsien-chang (Po-sha)	陳獻章（白沙）
Ch'en Liang	陳亮
Ch'en T'uan	陳搏
Ch'en Wei-chün (Chiu-ch'uan)	陳維憻（九川）
Ch'en-hao, Prince of Ning	宸濠（寧王）
Cheng Hsüan	鄭玄
Ch'eng Hao (Ming-tao)	程顥（明道）
Ch'eng Yi (Yi-ch'uan)	程頤（伊川）
Ch'eng-kuan	澄觀
Ch'eng-tsu, Emperor	成祖
Ch'engs, the (see Ch'eng Hao and Ch'eng Yi)	
Chi Pen (Ming-te)	季本（明德）
Chi Yün	紀昀
Ch'i-sung	契嵩
Chiang Kai-shek	蔣介石
Chiang Yung	江永
Chiao Hung	焦竑
Chieh	桀
Chieh-yü	接輿
Ch'ien Hsi-ming (Hsin-yü)	錢希明（心漁）
Ch'ien Mu	錢穆

Ch'ien Te-hung	錢德洪
Chih-yi	智顗
Ch'in-chang	琴張
Chŏng Che-ku (Hagok)	鄭齊斗（霞谷）
Chŏng In-bo	鄭寅普
Chŏng Mong-ju (P'uon)	鄭夢儒（葡隱）
Chou, Duke	周公
Chou Heng (Tao-t'ung)	周衡（道通）
Chou Ju-teng	周汝登
Chou, King	紂壬
Chou Tun-yi	周敦頤
Chou Yü-t'ung	周予同
Chu Ch'ien-chih	朱謙之
Chu Chih-yü (Shun-shui)	朱之瑜（舜水）
Chu Hsi (Chung-hui, Hui-an)	朱熹（仲晦・晦庵）
Chu Sung	朱松
Chu Yi-tsun	朱彝尊
Ch'u Huan (Ch'ai-hsü)	儲瓘（柴墟）
Ch'ü Yüan	屈原
Ch'üan Tsu-wang	全祖望
Chuang-tzu	莊子
Ch'ung Fang	种放
Fa-tsang	法藏
Fang Chao-ying	房兆楹
Fang Hsiao-ju	方孝儒
Feng K'o	馮訶
Feng Meng-lung (Mo Han-chai)	馮夢龍
Fuchi Kōzan	淵岡山
Fung Yu-lan	馮友蘭
Han Hsin	韓信
Han Yü (Ch'ang-li)	韓愈（昌黎）
Hayashi Shihei	林子平
Ho Ching-ming	何景明
Ho Hsin-yin (Liang Ju-yüan)	何心隱（梁汝元）
Ho Lin	賀麟
Ho Meng-ch'un	何孟春
Hou Wai-lu	侯外盧
Hsi K'ang	稽康
Hsi Shu	席書
Hsi Yün (see Huang Po)	希運
Hsia Hsieh	夏燮

Hsiang, Duke	襄公
Hsiang Hsiu	向秀
Hsiao Ch'i	蕭琦
Hsiao Liang-kan	蕭良幹
Hsiao Tsung	蕭綜
Hsieh Ling-yün	謝靈運
Hsien Jo-chü	閻若璩
Hsü Ai	徐愛
Hsü Cheng-ch'ing	徐禎卿
Hsü Fu-kuan	徐復觀
Hsü Heng	許衡
Hsü Hsiang-ch'ing	許相卿
Hsü T'ai	許泰
Hsüan-tsung, Emperor	玄宗
Hsüeh Hsüan	薛瑄
Hsüeh K'an (Shang-ch'ien)	薛侃
Hsüeh Tao-kuang	薛道光
Hsün-tzu	荀子
Hu Chü-jen	胡居仁
Hu Hung	胡宏
Hu Ju-teng	胡汝登
Hu Kuang	胡廣
Hu Shih	胡適
Hu Yüan	胡瑗
Huan, Duke	桓公
Huang Chih	黃直
Huang Hsing-tseng	黃省曾
Huang Mien-chih	黃勉之
Huang Po (see Hsi Yün)	黃檗
Huang Tsung-hsi	黃宗羲
Huang Ju-ch'eng	黃汝成
Huang Wan	黃綰
Hui-k'o	慧可
Hui-neng	惠能
Ikeda Mitsumasa	池田光政
Ikeda Sōwan	池田草庵
Inoue Tetsujirō	井上哲次郎
Itō Hirobumi	伊藤博文
Jen Yu-wen	簡又文
Jimmu, Emperor	神武天皇
Juan Chi	阮籍

Juan Hsien	阮咸
Jung Chao-tsu	容肇祖
K'ang Yu-wei	康有爲
Kao Li-shih	高力士
Kao P'an-lung	高攀龍
Kao-tsu, Emperor	高祖
Kao-tzu	告子
Kasuga Senan	春日潛庵
Katsu Kaishu	勝海舟
Kimura Ki	木村毅
Ko Hung	葛洪
Ku Hsien-ch'eng	顧憲成
Ku Lin (Tung-ch'iao)	顧麟 (東橋)
Ku Tu	顧鐸
Ku Yen-wu	顧炎武
Kui Ô	桂萼
K'ui	夔
Kumazawa Banzan	熊澤蕃山
K'ung Ying-ta	孔穎達
Kuo Mao-ch'ien	郭茂倩
Kusumoto Fumio	久須本文雄
Kusumoto Masatsugu	楠本正繼
Kwon Ch'ol-sin	權哲身
Lao-tzu	老子
Lew Seung-kook	柳承國
Li Ao	李翱
Li Chih	李贄
Li Chih-ts'ai	李之材
Li Ching-te	黎靖德
Li Hsin-ch'uan	李心傳
Li Mao-yüan	李茂元
Li Meng-yang	李夢陽
Li Po	李白
Li T'ung	李侗
Li Yüan-kang	李元綱
Li-tsung	理宗
Liang Ch'i-ch'ao	梁啓超
Lin Ju-huan	林汝桓
Lin An	劉安
Liu Chin	劉瑾
Liu Chün-liang	劉君亮

Liu Hsiang	劉向
Liu Lin	劉伶
Liu Shih-p'ei	劉師培
Liu Ts'un-yan	柳存仁
Liu Tsung-chou	劉宗周
Liu Tsung-yüan	柳宗元
Lo Ch'in-shun (Cheng-an)	羅欽順（整庵）
Lo Hung-hsien	羅洪先
Lo Ju-fang (Chin-hsi)	羅汝芳（近溪）
Lo Ts'ung-yen	羅從彥
Lou Liang	婁諒
Lu Ch'eng	陸澄
Lu Chiu-ling	陸九齡
Lu Chiu-yüan (Hsiang-shan)	陸九淵（象山）
Lu Lung-ch'i (Chia-shu)	陸隴其（稼書）
Lü, Empress	呂后
Lü Tsu-ch'ien	呂祖謙
Luan Tzu-jen	欒子仁
Ma Yüan	馬援
Mao Ch'i-ling	毛奇齡
Mao Tse-tung	毛澤東
Meng Yüan	孟源
Mishima Fuku	三島復
Mishima Yukio	三島由吉夫
Miwa Shissai	三輪執齋
Mo Ti (Mo-tzu)	墨翟（墨子）
Motoyama Yukihiko	本山幸彦
Mou Jen-sun	牟潤孫
Mou Tsung-san	牟宗三
Mu, Duke	穆公
Mu-p'i	牧皮
Mu-tsung	穆宗
Nakae Tōju	中江藤樹
Nakayama Hachirō	中山八郎
Ōshio Chusai	大塩中齋
Shimada Kenji	島田虔次
Shōtoku, Prince	聖德太子
Shu Kuo-yung	舒國用
Shun, Emperor	舜

Sŏ Kyŏng-tŏk (Hwadam)	徐敬德（花潭）
Sŏnjo, King	宣祖
Ssu-ma Kuang	司馬光
Sugiura Jūgō	杉浦重剛
Suiko, Empress	隨古天皇
Sun Ch'i-feng	孫奇逢
Sun Fu	孫復
Sung P'ei-wei	宋佩韋
Sung Ying-ch'ang	宋應昌
Suzuki, Daisetzu T.	鈴木大拙
Suzuki Tadashi	鈴木正
Tai Chen (Tung-yüan)	戴震（東原）
T'ai-tsung, Emperor	太宗
Takahashi Koji	高橋行司
Takahashi Tōru	高橋亨
Tan Kanesen (see Chan Jo-shui)	
T'an Ssu-t'ung	譚嗣同
T'ang Chen	唐震
T'ang Chien	唐鑑
T'ang Chün-i	唐君毅
T'ang, King	湯王
T'ang Lung	唐龍
T'ang Yung-t'ung	湯用彤
Tao-hsüan	道宣
Tao-sheng	道生
Tokiwa Daijō	常盤大定
Ts'ai Tsung-tui (Hsi-yüan)	蔡宗兌（希淵）
Tseng Chai-chih	曾宅之
Tseng Shen (Tseng-tzu)	曾參（曾子）
Tseng Tien	曾點
Tsou Ch'ien-chih (Shou-yi)	鄒謙之（守益）
Tsung-mi	宗密
Tung Chung-shu	董仲舒
Tung Yün	董澐
T'ung Chen	佟珍
Tzu-chang	子張
Tzu-hsia	子夏
Tzu-kung	子貢
Tzu-lu	子路
Tzu-ssu	子思
Uno Tetsujin	宇野哲人

Wan Shih-te	萬世德
Wang An-shih (Chieh-fu)	王安石（介甫）
Wang Ch'eng-yü	王承裕
Wang Chi (Lung-hsi)	王畿（龍溪）
Wang Chia-hsiu	王嘉秀
Wang Ch'iung	王瓊
Wang Chün (Shih-t'an)	汪俊（石潭）
Wang Ch'ung	王充
Wang Fu-chih	王夫之
Wang Han	王瀚
Wang Hsün (Ching-chih)	汪循（景之）
Wang Hua	王華
Wang Jung	王戎
Wang Ken (Hsin-chai)	王艮（心齋）
Wang Mang	王莽
Wang Mou-hung	王懋竑
Wang Pi	王弼
Wang Po-an (see Wang Yang-ming)	王伯安
Wang Shou-jen (see Wang Yang-ming)	王守仁
Wang Wen-lu	王文祿
Wang Yang-ming	王陽明
Wang Yen (Yi-fu)	王衍（夷甫）
Wang Yi	王逸
Wei Han	魏瀚
Wu Ch'eng (Yu-ch'ing)	呉澄（幼清）
Wu Emperor of Liang	梁武帝
Wu, King	武王
Wu-tsung	武宗
Wu Tzu-hsü	伍子胥
Wu Yin	呉瀛
Wu Yü-pi	呉與弼
Wu-ming	悟明
Wu-yi	武夷
Yamada Hōtoku	山田方谷
Yamada Jun	山田準
Yamane Yukio	山根幸夫
Yamanoi Yū	山井湧
Yamashita Ryūji	山下龍一
Yang Chu	陽朱
Yang Shih	楊時
Yang Shih-ming	楊士鳴
Yang Yi	楊億

Yang Yi-ch'ing (Siu-an)	楊一清（邃庵）
Yang-ming (see Wang Yang-ming)	
Yao, Emperor	堯
Yasuoka Masaatsu (Masashiro)	安岡正篤
Yeh Ting-yi	葉丁易
Yeh Ts'ai	葉采
Yen Chün	顏鈞
Yen Hui (Yen-tzu)	顏回（顏子）
Yi Hwang (T'oegye)	李滉（退溪）
Yi Kan-ch'ang	李建昌
Yi Nung-hwa	李能和
Yi Pyong-do	李丙燾
Yi Yao	李瑤
Yi Yi (Yulgok)	李珥（栗谷）
Yi-yin	伊尹
Ying Liang (Yüan-chung)	應良（原忠）
Yŏn Myŏngjae	尹明齋
Yŏngjo	英祖
Yoshida Shōin	吉田松蔭
Yoshino Sakuzō	吉野作造
Yu, Emperor	禹
Yü Ch'ung-yao	余重耀
Yüan-wu	圓悟

SELECTED
BIBLIOGRAPHY

I. Primary Sources and Other Older Works

A. Chinese Works

Ι<small>NCLUDED HERE</small> are the Confucian Classics and their Commentaries, the Buddist sūtras and their Commentaries, the Taoist texts and Commentaries, the Dynastic Histories and Other Historical Sources, the writings of the Sung-Ming philosophers, especially those of Wang Yang-ming himself, and all works that treat of their philosophy which were written before the midnineteenth century. In the case of the important philosophers, the works for which they have become famous are given below usually after their own names, although the titles may indicate certain commentaries that have been added to the original writings, either by their disciples or by other persons.

I wish to give have a brief description of the principal Chinese source, the so-called Complete Works of Wang Yang-ming: *Wang Wen-ch'eng kung ch'üan-shu (WWKC)*. I have especially made use of the standard text, as given in the *SPTK* First series, double-page lithograph edition. In its final form, this work was compiled by Hsieh T'ing-chieh (1572), and includes various groups of writings, which had been published earlier, whether during or after Wang-ming's lifetime. In terms of content, these writings may be described generally as being philosophical, literary, and administrative. In terms of structure, they may be divided into three groups, roughly according to chronological order.

The first three *chüan* make up the first and most important group of writings, the *Ch'uan-hsi lu*, inclnding two *chüan* (1 and 3) of recorded dialogues, and one of important philosophical letters. They were published for the first time before and after 1519, but not always under the supervision of Yang-ming himself. They have appeared in English translation, making up the bulk of Wing-tsit Chan's *Instructions for Practical Living* (1964). They are essential for the study of Wang Yang-ming's philosophy.

The second group is chs. 4–25, published together for the first time in 1535. Within this group, the first five *chüan* (4–8) present letters and other prose writings, frequently with philosophical content. Then follow chs. 9–18, a solid block of administrative documents, including memorials to the throne, and official announcements. Chs. 19–20 give Yang-ming's poems, beginning with prose-poems *(fu)*, and going on to *shih*—in five-or seven-word lines, truncated or regular verse. Most are lyrics, and many have philosophical content. Chs. 21–25 present another collection of prose writings, both letters and essays, some times with philosophical import, sometimes communicating personal messages and sentiments.

The third group, chs. 26–31, contains a miscellaneous collection published previously in 1566. It includes a long and important essay, the *Ta-hsüeh-wen* (Inquiry into the Great Learning), also translated into English in Chan's *Instructions for Practical Living ;* various essays and letters bearing no dates; and a continuation of administrative documents, which are usually dated.

The last group, chs. 32–38, is the Appendices, including the Chronological Biography *(nien-p'u)* (chs. 32–34); accounts of events after Yang-ming's death, such as the erection of academies in his memory; the granting of posthumous honors; and the compilation of the Chronological Biography (chs. 35–36), At the end are short biographical essays of Yang-ming's ancestors and of himself, followed by brief eulogies composed by his friends and disciples.

The *Wang Wen-ch'eng-kung ch'üan-shu* provides an adequate and largely reliable collection for the study of Wang Yang-ming's life and thought. It does not, however, include all of Yang-ming's extant writings. His *Ta-hsüeh ku-pen p'ang-chu* (The Old Version of the Great Learning, with Side Commentaries), for example, is not given. (For further reference, see Wang Tchang-tche, *La Philosophie Morale de Wang Yang-ming*, 36–37, and Wing-tsit Chan, *Instructions for Pracrical Living*, 311–16).

Aśvaghoṣa (fl. 1st cent. A.D.). *Ta-ch'eng ch'i-hsin lun* 大乘起信論 [Awakening of Faith in the Mahayana]. *TSG* No. 1667.

Avataṃsala sura (*Hua-yen ching* 華嚴經). *TSG* No. 279, IX, 395–688.

Chan Jo-shui 湛若水 (1466–1560). *Kan-ch'üan wen-chi* 甘泉文集 [Collected Writings of Chan Jo-shui]. Chih-cheng t'ang 資政堂 ed. [1886]. Microfilm copy.

—— *Sheng-shüeh ko-wu t'ung* 聖學格物通 [A Penetrating Study of the Doctrine of Investigating Things According to the School of Sages]. Yang-chou 揚州 ed., Preface 1533. Microfilm copy.

Chang Hsüeh-ch'eng 章學誠 (1738–1801). *Wen-shih t'ung-y'* 文史通義 [Reflections on Literature and History]. 1922 ed. Reprinted in Taipei; Commercial Press, 1967.

Chang Lieh 張烈 (1622–85). *Wang-hsüeh chih-yi* 王學質疑 [Questions 'on Wang Yang-ming's Philosophy]. CYTC ed.

Chang Po-hsing 張伯行 (1652–1725), comp. *Cheng-yi yi t'ang ch'üan-shu* 正誼堂全書 [Complete Works of Cheng-yi t'ang]. [1866–70].

—— *Lien-Lo Kuan-Min shu* 濂洛關閩書 [Collected Writings of the Philosophers of the Schools of Chou Tun-yi, the Ch'engs, Chang Tsai, and Chu Hsi]. CYTC ed.

—— *Tao-t'ung lu* 道統錄 [On the Orthodox Transmission of the Way]. CYTC ed.

Chang Po-tuan 張伯端 (983–1082). *Wu-chen p'ien chu-su* 悟眞篇注疏 [Commentary on the "On Awakening to Truth"]. *Tao-tsang* 道藏 [Taoist Canon] LXI/LXII.

—— "Tzu-yang chen-jen hou-hsü" 紫陽眞人後序 [Epilogue to the Three Commentaries on "On Awakening to Truth"]. *Tao-tsang* LXIV, 1a–3a.

Chang T'ing-yü 張廷玉 (1672–1755) et. al. comp. *Ming-shih* 明史 [Ming Dynastic History], *Erh-shih-wu shih* 廿五史 [Twenty-five Histories] series. K'ai-ming 開明 ed.

Chang Tsai 張載 (1020–77). *Chang-tzu ch'üan-shu* 張子全書 [Complete Works of Chang Tsai]. SPPY ed.

Chao T'ai-ting 趙泰定 (fl. 1570). *Mai-wang* 脈望 [On Conducting Breath-circulation]. TSCC ed.

Chao Yi 趙翼 (1727–1814). *Erh-shih-erh shih cha-chi* 廿二史劄記 [Study Notes on the Twenty-two Histories]. SPPY ed.

Ch'en Chien 陳建 (1497–1567). *Hsüeh-pu t'ung-pien* 學蔀通辨 [A General Critique of Obscure Learning]. CYTC ed.

Ch'en Ch'un 陳淳 (1153–1217). *Pei-hsi tzu-yi* 北溪字義 [The Neo-Confucian Dictionary of Ch'en Chun]. TSCC ed.

Ch'en, Hsien-chang 陳獻章 (1428–1500). *Po-sha-tzu* 白沙子 [Selected Works of Ch'en Hsien-chang]. SPPY ed.

Ch'eng Hao 程顥 (1032–85) and Ch'eng Yi 程頤 (1033–1107). *Erh-Chieng ch'üan-shu* 二程全書 [Complete Works of the Two Ch'engs], incorportaing *Yi-shu* 遺書 (1–10 attributed to both brothers, 11–14 to Ch'eng Hao, 15–25 to Ch'eng Yi), *Wai-shu* 外書 (attributed to both brothers), *Ts'ui-yen* 粹言 (attributed to Ch'eng Yi), *Ming-tao wen-chi* 明道文集 and *Yi-ch'uan wen-chi* 伊川文集.

SPPY ed.

Ch'en Liang 陳亮 (1143–94). *Lung-ch'uan wen-chi* 龍川文集 [Collected Writings of Ch'en Liang]. SPPY ed.

Chi Tseng-yun 稽曾筠 (1671–1739) et al., comp. *Che-chiang t'ung-chih* 浙江通志 [Chekiang Gazetteer]. Ed. by Shen Yi-chi 沈翼機 (fl. 1706) and others. 4 vol. Shanghai. Commercial Press, 1934.

Chi Yün 紀昀 (1724–1805) et al. *Ssu-k'u ch'üan-shu tsung-mu t'i-yao* 四庫全書總目提要 [Essential Information on the Complete Catalogue of the "Four Libraries" Series]. Shanghai: Commercial Press, 1933.

Chiang Fan 江藩 (1761–1831). *Sung-hsüeh yüan-yüan chi* 宋學淵源記 [The Origins of Sung Learning]. SPPY ed.

Ch'i-sung 契嵩 (fl. 1062). *Ch'uan-fa cheng-tsung chi* 傳法正宗記 [A Record of the Orthodox Transmission of the Buddhist Doctrine]. *TSD* No. 2078, LI, 715–68.

Chih-yi 智顗 (530–97). *Miao-fa lien-hua ching hsüan-yi* 妙法蓮華經玄義 [The Metaphysical Ideas of the *Lotus Sutra*]. *TSD* No. 1716, XXXIII, 681–814.

—— *Miao-fa lien-hua ching wen-chü* 妙法蓮華經文句 [On the Sentences of the *Lotus Sutra*]. *TSD* No. 1718, XXXIV, 1–149.

Chou Ju-teng 周汝登 (1547–1629). *Sheng-hsüeh tsung-chuan* 聖學宗傳 [Orthodox Transmission of the School of Sages], amended by T'ao Wang-ling 陶望齡. Preface 1606.

—— *Wang-men tsung-chih* 王門宗旨 [The Essential Doctrines of the School of Wang Yang-ming]. Preface 1609.

Chou Tun-yi 周敦頤 (1017–73). *Chou-tzu T'ung-shu* 周子通書 [Penetrating into the Book of Changes]. SPPY ed.

Chou-li Cheng-chu 周禮鄭注 [The *Rites of Chou*, with Cheng Hsüan's 鄭玄 (127–200) Commentary]. SPPY ed.

Chou-yi cheng-yi 周易正義 [Correct Meaning of the *Book of Changes*]. Annotated by Wang Pi. Ed. by K'ung Ying-ta. SPPY ed.

Chu Chih-yü 朱之瑜 (1600–82). *Rhu Shun-shui ch'üan-chi* 朱順水全集 [Complete Works of Chu Chih-yu]. Taipei: World Book Shop, 1963.

Chu Hsi 朱熹 (1130–1200). *Chin-ssu lu chi-chieh* 近思錄集解 [Collected Explanations of the *Chin-ssu lu*]. Comp. by Chang Po-hsing. CYTC ed.

—— *Chin-ssu lu chi-chu* 近思錄集注 [Collected Commentary on the *Chin-ssu lu* of Chu Hsi and Lü Tsu-ch'ien 呂祖謙 (1137–81).] Comp. by Chiang Yung 江永 (1681–1762). SPPY ed.

—— *Chu-tzu ch'üan-shu* 朱子全書 [Complete Works of Chu Hsi]. 1714 ed., comp. by Imperial command.

—— *Chu-tzu yü-lei* 朱子語類 [Recorded Conversations]. Comp. by Li Ching te 黎靖德 (1473). Reprinted in Taipei, 1962.

—— *Hui-an hsien-sheng Chu Wen Kung wen-chi* 晦庵先生朱文公文集 [Collected Writings of Chu Hsi]. SPPY ed.

—— *Ssu-shu chi-chu* 四書集注 [Collected Commentary on the Four Books], incorporating *Ta-hsüeh chang-chü* 大學草句, *Chung-yung chang-chü* 中庸草句, *Lun-yü chi-chu* 論語集注, and *Meng-tzu chi-chu* 孟子集注. SPPY ed.

—— *Ta-hsüeh huo-wen* 大學成問 [Questions on the Great Learning] in *Chu-tzu yi-shu* 朱子遺書 [Surviving Works of chu Hsi]. Ch'ing ed.

—— *Ts'an-t'ung ch'i k'ao-yi* 參同契考異 [An Investigation into Wei Po-yang's 魏伯陽 (fl. 147–67) *Tallying Ideas of Taoist Cultivation* with the Book of Changes]. SPPY ed.

Chu Yi-tsun 朱彝尊 (1629–1709). *Ching-yi k'ao* 經義考 [An Investigation into the Classics and their Meanings]. SPPY ed.

Chu-fo ching-chieh she chen-chih ching 諸佛境界攝眞實經 [The Sutra of Collected Truths of the Buddha's Realms]. *TSD* No. 868, XVIII.

Ch'ü Yüan 屈原 (340?–278 B.C.). *Ch'u-tz'u pu-chu* 楚辭補注 [An Amended and Annotated Edition of the Songs of Ch'u]. Ed. by Wang Yi 王逸. Taipei: Chung-hua shu-chü 中華書局, 1966.

Chuang-tzu 莊子. SPPY ed.

Chung-ching 忠經 [Classic of Loyalty], in *Po tzu chiüan-shu* 百子全書 [Complete Works of a Hundred Philosophers]. Shanghai: Shao-yeh shan-fang 金師子章, 1927.

Fa-tsang 法藏 (643–712). *Chin-shih-tzu chang* 掃葉山房 [Treatise on the Golden Lion]. *TSD* No. 1881, XLV, 668–70.

Fan Yeh 范曄 (398–445). *Hou Han-shu* 後漢書 [History of the Latter Han Dynasty]. *Erh-shih-wu shih*. K'ai-ming ed.

Fang Hsüan-ling 房玄齡 (578–648), et al. *Rhin-shu* 晉書 [Chin Dynastic History]. *Erh-shih-wu shih*. K'ai-ming ed.

Feng K'o 馮訶 (fl. 1562). *Ch'iu-shih p'ien* 求是篇 [In Quest of Correct Learning]. CYTC ed.

Han Pei Tzu 韓非子. SPPY ed.

Han Yü 韓愈 (768–824). *Han Ch'ang-li ch'üan-chi* 韓昌黎全集 [Complete Works of Han Yü]. SPPY ed.

Hsi-yün 希運 (fl. A.D. 850). *Huang-po-shan Tuan-chi Ch'an-shih Ch'uan-hsin ga-yao* 黃蘗山斷際禪師傳心法要 [The Essential Teaching of the Transmission of the Mind]. Comp. by P'ei Hsiu 裴休 (767–870). *TSD* No. 2012A, XVIII. XVIII, 379–84.

—— *Huang-po Tuan-chi Ch'an-shih Wan-ling lu* 黃蘗斷際禪師宛陵錄 [The Wan-lin Record of Hsiyün]. Comp. by P'ei Hsiu. *TSG* No. 2014B, XLVIII, 384–87.

Hsia Hsieh 夏燮 (fl. 1850). *Ming T'ung-chien* 明通鑑 [Comprehensive Mirror of the Ming Dynasty]. Peking: Chung-hua shu-chü, 1959.

Hsiao Liang-kan 蕭良幹 et al., comp. *Shao-hsing fu-chih* 紹興府志 [The Shao-hsing Prefecture Gazetteer]. 1586 ed. Microfilm copy.

Hsiao-ching chu-su 孝經注疏 [Classic of Filial Piety with Emperor Hsüan-tsung's Commentary]. SPPY ed.

Hsieh Lin-yün 謝靈運 (385–433). "Yü tao-jen pien-tsung lun" 與諸道人辨宗論

[On the Essentials of Learning, Addressed to the Reverend Gentlemen]. *Kuang Hung-ming chi* 廣弘明集 [Further Collection of Essays on Buddhism]. Comp. by Tao-usüan 道宣 (596–667). SPPY ed., 20: 9a–10b.

Hsien Jo-chü 閻若璩 (1636–1704). *Ku-wen Shang-shu su-cheng* 古文尚書疏證 [A Documented Commentary on the Old Text Version of the *Book of Documents*] in *Huang-Ch'ing ching-chieh hsü p'ien* 皇清經解續編 [Supplement to the Collection of Classical Commentaries of the Ch'ing Dynasty]. Comp. by Wang Hsien-ch'ien 王先謙 (1842–1917). Contracted ed. Preface 1889.

Hsü Ch'uan-teng lu 續傳燈錄 [Supplement to the Transmission of the Lamp]. Comp. by Chü-ting (d. 1404). *TSD* No. 2067, LI, 469–714.

Hsü Shen 許慎 (c. A.D. 30–124). *Shuo-wen chieh-tzu Tuan-chu* 說文解字段注 [The Lexicon of Hsü Shen, with Annotations by Tuan Yü-ts'ai 段玉裁 1735–1815]. Taipei reprint: Yi-wen 藝文, 1964.

Hsüeh Hsüan 薛瑄 (1389–1464). *Tu-shu lu* 讀書錄 [Study Notes]. CYTC ed.

Hsüeh Tao-kuang 薛道光 (fl. 1106) et al. *Tzu-yang chen-jen Wu-chen p'ien san-chu* 紫陽眞人悟眞篇三注 [The Three Commentaries to "On Awakening to Truth"]. *Tao-tsang* LXIII/LXIV.

Hsün-tzu 荀子. SPPY ed.

Hu Hung 胡宏 (1105–55). *Chih-yen* 知言 [Knowledge of Words], in *Po-tzu ch'üan-shu*. Shanghai: Shao-yeh shan-fang, 1927.

Hu Kuang 胡廣 (1370–1418) et al., comp. *Hsing-li ta-ta-ch'üan* 性理大全 [A Great Compendium of *Hsing-li* Philosophy]. 1597 ed.

—— ed. *Ming shih-lu* 明實錄 [True Records of the Ming Dynasty]. Taipei: Academia Sinica, 1962.

Huang Tsung-hsi 黃宗羲 (1610–95). *Ming-ju hsüeh-an* 明儒學案 [Philosophical Records of 'the Ming Dynasty]. SPPY ed.

—— and Ch'üan Tsu-wang 全祖望 (1705–55). *Tseng-pu Sung-Yüan hsüeh-an* 增補宋元學案 [Philosophical Records of the Sung and Yüan Dynasties, Expanded Version]. SPPY ed.

Huang Wan 黃綰 (1477–1551). *Ming-tao p'ien* 明道篇 [An Elucidation of the Way]. With introduction by Hou Wai-lu. Peking: Chung-hua shu-chü, 1959.

Hui-k'ai 慧開 (1184–1260). *Wu-men kuan* 無門關 [The Pass Without Door]. *TDS* No. 2005, LI, 292–99.

Hui-ssu 慧思 (514–77). *Ta-ch'eng chih-kuan fa-men* 大乘止觀法門 [The Method of Concentration and Insight in the Mahayana]. *TDS* No. 1924. XLVI, 642–61.

Kao P'an-lung 高攀龍 (1562–1626). *Kao-tzu yi-shu* 高子遺書 [Surviving Works of Kao P'an-lung]. 1631 ed.

Keng Ting-hsiang 耿定向 (1524–96). *Keng T'ien-t'ai hsien-sheng wen-chi* 耿元台先生文集 [Collected Writings of Keng Ting-hsiang], in Shen Yun-lung's 沈雲龍 *Ming-jen wen-chi ts'ung-k'an* 明人文集叢刊 [Collected Writings of Ming Personalities]. Taipei: Wenhai ch'u-pang-she 文海出版社, 1970.

Ko Hung 葛洪 (253–333?). *Pao-p'u Tzu* 抱朴子 [The Philosopher Who Embraced Simplicity]. SPPY ed.

Ku Hsien-ch'eng 顧憲成 (1550–1612). *Ku Tuan-wen Kung yi-shu* 顧端文公遺書 [Surviving Works of Ku Hsien-ch'eng]. 1877 ed.

Ku Yen-wu 顧炎武 (1613–82). *Jih-chih lu chi-shih* 日知錄集釋 [Record of Daily Knowledge, with Collected Commentary]. Comp. by Huang Ju-ch'eng 黃汝成. SPPY ed.

Lankāvatāra sutra (*Leng-chia ching* 楞伽經). *TSD* No. 670, XVI, 479–514.

Lao-tzu 老子. SSPY ed.

Li Hsin-ch'uan 李心傳 (1166–1243). "Hui-an hsien-sheng fei su-yin" 晦庵先生非索隱 [Master Chu Was Not a Recluse], in *Chien-yen yi-lai ch'ao yeh tsa-chi* 建炎以來朝野雜記 [Miscellaneous Notes on Court and Country since Chien-yen Period (1127–30)]. TSCC ed.

Li Po 李白 (701?–762). *Li Tiai-po chi* 李太白集 [Collected Poems of Li Po], Shanghai: Commercial Press, 1930.

Li Yen-shou 李延壽 (7th cent. A.D.), *Nan-shih* 南史 [History of the Southern Dynasties], *Erh-shih-wu-shih* series, K'ai-ming ed.

Li Yüan-kang 李元綱 (fl. 1190), "Sheng-men shih-yeh t'u" 聖門事業圖 [Diagram of the Transmission of the School of Sages], in *Po-ch'uan hsüeh-hai* 百川學海. Vol. 2, 1001–2.

Li-chi cheng-yi 禮記正義 [Correct Meaning of the *Book of Rites*], with Cheng Hsüan's annotations, Ed. by K'ung Yin-ta 孔穎達. SPPY ed.

Lin-pao wu-liang tu-jen shang-p'ing miao-ching 靈寶無量度人上品妙經 [The Excellent and Wonderful Canon of the Most Precious and Limitless Salvation]. *Tao-tsang* I.

Liu An 劉安 (d. 122 B.C.) et al. *Cuai-nan tzu* 淮南子. SPPY ed.

Liu Hsiang 劉向 (c. 77–6 B.C.). *Chan-kuo tsie ch'ao-chu* 戰國策校注 [Intrigues of the Warring States, Annotated Version], SPPY ed.

—— *Lieh-hsian* 列仙傳 [Biographies of the Taoist Immortals], in *Ku-chin yi-shih* 古今逸史 [Histories of Hermits, Past and Present], Ming ed. Reprinted in Shanghai, 1937.

Liu Hsü 劉昫 (887–947) et al. *Chiu T'ang-shu* 舊唐書 [T'ang Dynastic History, old Version], *Erh-shih-wu shih* series, K'ai-ming ed.

Liu, Tsung-chou 劉宗周 (1578–1645), *Liu-tzu ch'üan-shu* 劉子全書 [The Complete Works of Liu Tsung-chou], 1824 ed.

—— *Yang-ming ch'uan-hsin lu* 陽明傳信錄 [Yang-ming's Transmission of Truth], in *Liu-tzu ch'üan-shu yi-p'ien* 劉子全書遺編 [Supplement to the Complete Works of Liu Tsung-chou], 1850 ed.

Liu-tsu ta-shih fa-pao t'an-ching 六祖大師法寶壇經 [The Platform Scripture of the Sixth Partiarch]. Comp. by Fa--hai [The full title of this version is: Nan-tsung Tun-chiao tsui-shang Ta ch'eng prajña pāramita ching—Liu tsu Hui-neng ta-shih yü shao-chou Ta-fan-shih shih-fa T'an-ching 六祖慧能大師於韶州大梵寺施法壇經 Southern School Sudden Doctrine Supreme Mahayana Great Perfection of Wisdom: The Platform Sutra preached by the Sixth Patriarch Hui-neng at the Ta-fan Temple in Shao-chou]. *TSD* No. 2007,

XLVIII, 337–345.

—— Comp. by Tsung-pao 宗寳. *TSD* No. 2008, XLVIII, 345–65.

Lo Ch'in-shun 羅欽順 (1465–1547). *Lo Cheng-an chi tsiun-kao* 羅整庵集存稿 [Surviving Writings of Lo Ch'in-shun]. CYTC ed.

—— *K'un-chih chi* 困知記 [Record of Assiduous Learning]. CYTC ed.

Lo Hung-hsien 羅洪先 (1504–64). *Nien-an Lo hsien-sheng chi* 念庵羅先生集 [Collected Writings of Lo Hung-hsien]. 1586 ed.

Lo Ju-fang 羅汝芳 (1515–88). *Lo Chin-hsi yü-lu* 羅近溪語錄 [The Recorded Conversations of Lo Ju-fang]. Taipei: Kuang-wen shu-chü 廣文書局, 1960.

Lu Chiu-yüan 陸九淵 (1139–93). *Hsiang-shan ch'üan-chi* 象山全集 [Complete Works of Lu Chiu-yüan]. SPPY ed.

Lu Lung-ch'i 陸隴其 (1630–93). *Lu Chia-shu chi* 陸稼書集 [Collected Works of Lu Lung-ch'i]. CYTC ed.

Mahāparinirvāna sūtra [*Ta-p'an Nieh-p'an ching* 大般涅槃經]. *TSD* No. 375, XII, 1–852.

Mao Ch'i-ling 毛奇齡 (1623–1716). *Ming Wu-tsung Wai-chi* 明武宗外紀 [An Unofficial Account of Emperor Wu-tsung]. Taipei: Kuang-wen shu-chü, 1964.

—— *Wang Wen-ch'eng chuan-pen* 王文成傳本 [Draft Biography of Wang Yang-ming], in *Hsi-ho ho-chi* 西河合集 [Collected Writings of Mao Ch'i-ling]. 2 vols. Preface 1685.

Mo Tzu 墨子. SPTK ed.

Mo Han-chai 墨憨齋 [Feng Meng-lung 馮夢龍] (d. 1645): *Wang Yang-ming ch'u-sheng ching-luan lu* 王陽明出身靖亂錄 [Wang Yang-ming's Life and Pacification Campaigns]. Taipei reprint: Kuang-wen shu-chü 1968.

Nieh Pao 聶豹 (1487–1563). *Shuang-chiang Nich hsien-sheng wen-chi* 雙江聶先生文集 [The Collected Writings of Nieh Pao]. 1572 ed.

Ou-yang Hsiu 歐陽修 (1007–72). *Ou-yang Wen-chung kung wen-chi* 歐陽文忠公文集 works'of Ou-yang Hsiu]. SPTK ed.

Ou-yang Te 歐陽德 (1496–1554). *Ou-yang Nan-yeh hsien-sheng wen-hsüan* 歐陽南野先生文選 [Selected Writings of Ou-yang Te]. Ed. by his disciple Li Ch'un-fang 李春芳, Preface 1569.

Pan Ku 班固 (A.D. 32–92). *Han-shu* 漢書 [History of the Former Han Dynasty]. *Erh-shih-wu shih* series. K'ai-ming ed.

Saddharma puṇḍarīka sūtra (*Maio-fa lien-hua ching* 妙法蓮華經). *TSD* No. 262, IX, 1–62.

Ssu-ma Ch'ien 司馬遷 (c. 145–c. 86 B.C.). *Shih-chi* 史記 [Historical Annals]. *Erh-shih-wu shih* series. K'ai-ming ed.

Ssu-ma Kuang 司馬光 (1019–86). *Wen-kuo wen-cheng Ssu-ma wen-kung wen-chi* 溫國文正司馬文公文集 [Collected Works of Su-ma Kuang]. SPTK ed.

Seng-chao 僧肇 (374–414). *Rhao-lun* 肇論 [Book of Chao]. *TSD* No. 1858, XLV, 150–61.

Sun Ch'i-feng 孫奇逢 (1585–1675). *Li-hsüeh tsung-chuan* 理學宗傳 [The Orthodox Transmission of Neo-Confucian Philosophy]. 5 vol.s 1666 ed. Taipei reprint:

Yi-wen, 1969.

Sung Lien 宋濂 (1310–81) et al. *Yüan-shih* 元史 [Yuan Dynastic History]. *Erh-shih-wu shih* series, K'ai-ming ed.

Surangama sūtra (*Leng-yen ching* 楞嚴經). *TSD* Nol 945, XIX, 105-55.

Tai Chen 戴震 (1724–77). *Meng-tzu tzu-yi su-cheng* 孟子字義疏證 [A Documentary Commentary of the Meanings of Words in the Book of *Mencius*], Appendix to Hu shih's *Tai Tung-yüan to che-hsüeh*. Taipei, 1963, 37–137.

—— *Yüan-shan* 原善 [An Inquiry into Goodness]. Appendix to Hu Shih's *Tai Tung-yüan to che-hsüeh*. Taipei, 1963, 1–36.

T'ang Chen 唐甄 (1630–1704). *Ch'ien-shu* 潛書 [Book of Depth], Peking: Ku-chi ch'u-pan she 古今出版社, 1955.

T'ang Chien 唐鑑 (1778–1861). *Ch'ing hsüeh-an hsiao-chih* 清學案小識 [A few Notes on the Philosophical Records of the Ch'ing Dynasty]. Preface 1845. Taipei reprint: Commercial Press, 1969.

Tao-yüan 道元 (fl. 1004). *Ching-te ch'uan-teng lu* 景德傳燈錄 [Transmission of the Lamp]. *TSD* No. 2076, LI, 196–497.

T'o-[q]-t'o 脫克脫 (fl. 1320) et. al. *Sung-shih* 宋史 [Sung Dynastic History]. *Erh-shih-wu shih* series, K'ai-ming ed.

Tsou Shou-yi 鄒守益 (1491–1562). *Tung-kuo hsien-sheng wen-chi* 東廓先生文集 [Collected Writings of Tsou Shou-yi]. Ming ed. Microfilm copy.

Tsung-mi 宗密 (780–841). *Yüan-jen lun* 原人論 [Inquiry into Man]. *TSD* No. 1886, XLV, 708–10.

Tung Chung-shu 董仲舒. (2nd cent. B.C.). *Ch'un-ch'iu fan-lu* 春秋繁露 [Luxuriant Gems of the *Spring-autumn Annals*]. SPPY ed.

Vajracchedikā (*Chin-kang ching* 金剛經). *TSD* No. 235, VIII, 748–52.

Wang An-shih 王安石 (1021–86). *Lin-ch'uan-chi* 臨川集 [Collected Writings of wang An-shih]. SPTK ed.

Wang Chi 王畿 (1498–1583), *Wang Lung-hsi hsien-sheng ch'üan-chi* 王龍溪先生全集 [Complete Works of Wang Chi]. 1822 ed. Taipei reprint: Hua-wen shu-chu 華文書局, 1970.

Wang Chün 汪俊 (fl. 1494). *Ta Tsung-po Wang Shih-t'an hsien-sheng chuo chiou-kao* 大宗伯汪石潭先生濯舊稿 [Selected Writings of Wang Chun]. Preface of 1529. Handwritten copy of Edo 江戶 kept at the Naikaku Bunkō 內閣文集.

Wang Fu-chih 王夫之 (1619–92). *Chang-tzu Cheng-ment chu* 張子正蒙注 [A Commentary on Chang Tsai's Treatise on the *Correction of Ignorance*]. Peking reprint: Ku-chi ch'u-pang she 古籍出版社, 1956.

—— *Ssu-wen lu/Ssu-chieh* 思問錄俟解 [Reflections on Certain Questions/Awaiting Answers]. Peking, 1956.

—— *Sung-lun* 宋論 [On Sung History]. Peking reprint Chung-hua shu-chü, 1964.

Wang Hung-hsü 王鴻緒 (1645–1723). *Ming-shih kao* 明史稿 [A Draft History of the Ming Dynasty]. 1714 ed. Taiepi reprint: Wen-hai ch'u-pan shê 文海出版社, 1962.

Wang Ken 王艮 (1483–1514). *Wang Hsin-chai hsien-sheng ch'üan-chi* 王心齋先生全集

[Complete Works of Wang ken]. With Additions by Wang Yüan-ting 王元鼎. Ming ed.

Wang Mou-hung 王懋竑 (1668–1741). *Chu-tzu nien-p'u* 朱子年譜 [Chronological Biography of Chu Hsi]. TSCC ed.

Wang Wen-lu 王文祿 (fl. 1531). *T'ai-hsi ching-su* 胎息經疏 [Commentary on the Embryo Breath Canon], in *Po-tzu ch'üan-shu*. Shanghai, 1927.

Wang Yang-ming 王陽明 (1472–1529), *Hsiang-chu Wang Yang-ming ch'üan-shu* 詳注王陽明全書 [A Fully Annotated Version of the Complete Works of Wang Yang-ming]. Annotated by Ni Hsien 倪錫恩, Shanghai: Shou-yehshan-fang 掃葉山房, 1935.

—— *Ta-hsüeh Ku-pen p'ang-chu* 大學古本旁注 [The Old version of the Great Learning with Side Commentaries]. *Han-hai* 函海. Comp. by Li Tiao-yüan 李調元 Taipei: Hung-yeh shu-chü 宏業書局, 1967. Vol. 13, pp. 8155–64.

—— *Wang Wen-ch'eng kung ch'üan-shu* 王文成公全書 [Complete Works of Wang Yang-ming]. Comp. by Hsieh T'ing-cheh 謝廷傑. 1972 SPTK 1st series, double-page lithograph ed.

—— *Yang-ming ch'üan-shu* 陽明全書 [Complete Works of Wang Yang-ming]. SPPY ed.

—— *Yang-ming hsien-sheng chi-yao* 陽明先生集要 [The Essential Writings of Wang Yang-ming]. Comp. by Shih Pang-yao 施邦曜 (1585–1644). SPTK ed.

—— *Yang-ming wen-lu* 陽明文錄 [Collected Writings of Wang Yang-ming] 1536 ed. Library of Congress Microfilm No. 2015.

Wu-ming 悟明 (fl. 1189). *Lien-teng hui-yao* 聯燈會要 [Essentials of the Combined Lamps]. *Zokuzōkyo* 續藏經 [Supplement to the Buddhist Canon], Pt. 2B, Case 9, [v. 136], 208–475.

Yin-fu ching-chu 陰符經注 [Commentary on the Yin-fu Canon]. Attributed to Chang Liang 張艮 (3rd cent. B.C.). *Po-tzu ch'üan-shu*. Shanghai, 1927.

Yü Hsien 俞憲 (fl. 1540). *Huang-Ming chin-ssu teng-k'o k'ao* 皇明進士登科考 [A Record of the Successful Candidates for the *chin-shih* Examinations in the Ming Dynasty], *Ming-tai shih-chi hui-k'an* 明代史籍彙刊 [A Collected Depository of the Historical Records of the Ming Dynasty]. Ed. by Ch'ü Wan-li 屈萬里. Taipei: Hsueh-sheng shu-chu 學生書局, 1969.

Yüan-wu 圓悟 (d. 1135). *Pi-yen lu* 碧巖錄 [Records of the Green cave]. *TSD* No. 2003, XLVIII, 139–225.

Yü-ch'ing wu-chi tsung-chen Wen-ch'ang ta-tung hsien-ching 玉清無極總眞文昌大洞仙經 [The Purest, Limitless, Truest, Wen-ch'ang Classic of Immortality]. *Tao-tsang* LI.

Yüeh-fu shih-chi 樂府詩集 [Collected Ancient Ballads]. Comp. by Kuo Mao-ch'ien 郭茂倩. Peking: Wen-hsüeh ku-chi k'an-hsing she 文學古籍刊行社, 1955.

B. Japanese and Korean Works

The works included here are those of the "makers" of Confucian thought, particularly of the Yang-ming school, in Japan and Korea. The Korean works listed were all written bsfore the mid-eighteenth century, the Japanese works, before 1900. Certain Japanese compendir presenting selections from the collections from the great thinkers are also included.

Chong Che-ku 鄭齊斗. *Hagok jip* 霞谷集 [Collected Writings of Chong Haok]. 2 vols. Seoul: Songgyungwan University Press, 1972.

"Hagok sonsaeng yonbo" 霞谷先生年譜, in *Hagok jip.* Unpublished edition.

Inoue Tetsujirō 井上哲次郎 et al., ed. *Nihon rinri ihen: Yomeigaku no bu* 日本倫理彙編：陽明學の部 [A Compendium of Japanese Ethics: The Section on the Yang-ming School], v. 1, 2, 3. Kyoto: Rinzen shoten 臨川書店 1970.

Kasuga Senan 春日潛庵. *Yomeigaku no shinzui* 陽明學の精髓 [The True Essence of Yang-ming's Teaching]. Related by his son, and recorded by his grandson. n.p. Nishikawa 西川 shōten, 1908.

Katsu Kaishu 勝海舟. *Katsu Kaishu jiden: Hikawa seiwa* 勝海舟自傳・氷川清話 [Autobiography of Katsu Kaishu]. Ed. by Katsube Managa Chiba-ken. Kashiwa shi: Hiroike Gakuen Shuppanbu 千葉縣柏市廣池學園出版部, 1968.

Koyanagi Shigeta 小柳司氣太 et al., ed. *Yōmeigakuha* 陽明學派. 3 vols. Tokyo: Shunyōdō 春陽堂, 1935–36.

Nakae Tōju 中江藤樹. *Tōju sensei zenshu* 中江先生全集 [Complete Works of Nakae Tōju]. Kyoto, 1928.

Okada Takehiko 岡田武彦, ed. *Bakumatsu ishin Yōmeigakusha shokan shu* 幕末維新陽明學者書簡集 [The Letters of Yang-ming Followers of the Late Tokugawa and Early Meiji Times], in *Yōmeigaku taikei* 陽明學大系. Comp. by Araki Kengo 荒木見悟 and others, v. 11. Tokyo: Meitoku shuppansha 明德出版社, 1972.

Sakuma Shōzan 佐久間象山. *Shōzan zenshu* 象山全集 [Complete Works of Sakuma Shōzan]. Tokyo, 1913.

Yamazaki Michio 山崎道夫, ed. *Nihon no Yōmeigaku* 日本の陽明學 [The Yang-ming School in Japan], in *Yōmeigaku taikei*, v. 8, 9, 10.

Yi Hwang 李滉. *T'oegye sonsaeng munjip* 退溪先生文集 [Collected Writings of Yi T'oegye]. Seoul: Songgyungwan University Press, 1959.

Yi Yi 李珥. *Yulgok chonso* 栗谷全書 [Complete Works of Yi Yulgok]. Seoul: Songgyungwan University Press, 1958.

Yoshida Shōin 吉田松陰. *Yoshida Shōin zenshu* 吉田松陰全集 [Complete Works of Yoshida Shōin]. Tokyo: Iwanami 岩波, 1934.

C. Western Translations from Chinese and Japanese Texts

Aśvaghosha. *The Awakening of Faith.* Tr. by Yoshito S. Hakeda. New York: Columbia University Press, 1967.

Book of Changes. (Yi-ching) The Yi King. Tr. by James Legge. *The Sacred Books of the East,* vol. 16, Oxford: Clarendon, 1882. Reprinted in Delhi, 1966.

Book of Historical Documents. (Shu-ching). Tr. by James Legge with introduction, critical and exegetical notes, and indexes. *The Chinese Classics,* vol. 3, parts 1 and 2. Oxford: Clarendon, 1893. Reprinted by the Hong Kong University Press, 1960.

Book of Poetry. (Shih-ching). Tr. by James Legge with introduction, critical and exegetical notes, and indexes. *The Chinese Classics,* vol. 4, parts 1 and 2. Oxford: Clarendon, 1893. Reprinted by the Hong Kong University Press, 1960.

Book of Rites. (Li-chi) The Li Ki, an Encyclopaedia of Ancient Ceremonial Usages, Religious Creeds and Social Institutions. Tr. by James Legge. *The Sacred Books of the East,* vol. 27 and 28. Oxford: Clarendon, 1885. Ed. by Ch'u Chai and Wimberg Chai. New York: University Books, 1967.

Chang Po-tuan. "An Ancient Chinese Treatise on Alchemy entitled *Ts'an T'ung Ch'i.*" Tr. by L. C. Wu and T. L. Davis. *Isis* XVIII (1932), 210–89.

Chu Hsi. *Djin-si lu, die Sungkonfuzianische Summa.* Tr. into German with introduction by Olaf Graf. 3 vols. Tokyo: Sophia University Press, 1953.

—— *The Philosophy of Human Nature.* A translation of Chapters 42–48 of Chu Hsi's *Complete Works* by J. Percy Bruce. London: Probsthain, 1922.

—— *Reflections on Things At Hand.* The Neo-Confucian Anthology Compiled by Chu Hsi and Lu Tsu-ch'ien. Tr. from the Chinese by Wing-tsit Chan with introduction and annotations. New York: Columbia University Press, 1967.

Chuang-tzu. *The Complete Works of Chuang Tzu.* Tr. by Burton Watson, New York: Columbia University Press, 1968.

Confucian Analects. (Lun-yü). Tr. by James Legge with introduction, critical and exegetical notes, and indexes. *The Chinese Classics,* vol. 1. Oxford: Clarendon, 1893. Reprinted by the Hong Kong University Press, 1960.

Doctrine of the Mean. (Chung-yung). Tr. by James Legge. *The Chinese Classics,* vol. 1. Oxford: Clarendon, 1893, Reprinted by the Hong Kong University Press, 1960.

Great Learning. (Ta-hsüeh). Tr. by James Legge. *The Chinese Classics,* vol. 1. Oxford: Clarendon, 1893, Reprinted by the Hong Kong University Press, 1960.

Han Fei Tzu. *The Complete Works of Han Fei Tzu.* Tr. by W. K. Liao. 2 vols. London: Probsthain, 1939 and 1959.

Han Fei Tzu: Basic Writings. Tr. by Burton Watson. New York: Columbia University Press, 1964.

Hsi-yün. *The Zen Teaching of Huang Po on the Transmission of the Mind.* Tr. by

John Blofeld. London: Rider, 1958.

Hsün-tzu. *Hsün-tzu*. Tr. by Hermann Köster with annotations. Kaldenkirchen: Steyler Verlag, 1957.

Hsün Tzu: Basic Writings. Tr. by Burton Watson with annotations. New York: Columbia University Press, 1963.

Hui-k'ai. *Wu-men-kuan, Der Pass ohne Tor*. Tr. by Heinrich Dumoulin, S. J. Tokyo: Sophia University Press, 1953.

Hui-neng. *The Platform Scripture: the Basic Classic of Zen Buddhism*. Tr. with introduction and annotations by Wing-tsit Chan. New York: St. John's University Press, 1963.

The Platform Sutra of the Sixth Patriarch: the Text of the Tun-haung Manuscript. Tr. with introduction and annotations by Philip B. Yampolsky. New York: Columbia University Press, 1967.

The Lankāvatara-sūtra, Mahāyānu Text. Tr. by Daisetz Teitarō Suzuki. London: Routledge, 1932; Reprinted in 1959.

Lao-tzu. *The Way and Its Power*. Tr. by Arthur Waley. London: Allen and Unwin, 1935.

Liu Hsiang, comp. *Chan-kuo ts'e*. Tr. by J. I. Crump, Jr. Oxford: Clarendon, 1970.

Mencius. *The Works of Mencius*. Tr. by James Legge. *The Chinese Classics*, vol. 2. Oxford: Clarendon, 1895. Reprinted by the Hong Kong University Press, 1960.

Mo-tzu. *Mo Zu: Basic Writing*. Tr. by Burton Watson. New York: Columbia University Press, 1963.

Pan Ku, ed. *A History of the Former Han Dynasty*. A critical translation with annotations by H. H. Dubs with the collaboration of Jen T'ai and P'an Lo-chi. Baltimore: Waverly Press, 1938–55.

——— ed. *Po Hu T'ung, the Comprehensive Discussions in the White Tiger Hall*. Tr. by Tjan Tjoe Som with introduction. 2 vols. Leiden: Brill, 1949 and 1952.

Saddharma pundarīka Sūtra. The Lotus of the Wonderful Law. Tr. by William E. Soothill. Oxford: Clarendon, 1930.

Seng-chao. *Chao lun: The Treatises of Seng-chao*. Tr. by Walter Liebenthal. Peiping: Catholic University of Peking, 1948. 2nd rev. ed., Hong Kong University Press, 1968.

Source Book in Chinese Philosophy. Comp. and tr. by Wing-tsit Chan. Princeton: Princeton University Press, 1963.

Sources of Chinese Tradition. Ed. by Wm. Theodore de Bary, Wing-tsit Chan, Burton Watson et al. 2 vols. New York: Columbia University Press, 1960.

Sources of Japanese Tradition. Ed. by Wm. Theodore de Bary, R. Tsunoda, and D. Keene. 2 vols. New York: Columbia University Press, 1964.

Spring-Autumn Annals (Ch'un-ch'iu) and *Annals of Tso (Tso-chuan). The Ch'un Ts'ew, with the Tso Chuan*, parts 1 and 2. Tr. by James Legge with introduction critical and exegetical notes, and indexes. *The Chinese Classics*, vol. 5. Oxford: Clarendon, 1893. Reprinted by the Hong Kong University Press, 1960.

Tao-yüan. *The Transmission of the Lamp: Original Teachings of Ch'an Buddhism, Selected from the Transmission of the Lamp.* Tr. by Chang Chung-yüan. New York: Pantheon, 1969.

Tai Chen. *Yüan Shan. Tai Chen's Inquiry into Original Goodness.* Tr. by Ch'eng Chung-ying with annotations. New Haven: Oriental Society, 1969.

Vajraccjedikā Praj ñāpāramitā. (Buddhist Wisdom Books: The Diamond Sutra and the Heart Sutra). Tr. by Edward Conze. London: Allen and Unwin, 1958.

Wang Yang-ming. *Instructions for Practical Living and Other Neo-Confucian Writings.* Tr. by Wing-tsit Chan. New York: Columbia University Press, 1963.

"Lettres doctrinales de Wang Yang-ming." Tr. into French by Y. Henry, S. J. *Bulletin de l'Université de l'Aurore* IX (1921), 19–41; X (1924–25), 40–77 XIII (1925–27), 50–69.

The Philosophical Letters of Wang Yang-ming. Tr. and annotated by Julia Ching. Canberra: Australian University Press, 1972.

The Philosophy of Wang Yang-ming. Selected translations by Frederick Henke. Chicago: Open Court, 1916.

II. OTHER REFERENCES

A. CHINESE WORKS

Chan Wing-tsit 陳榮捷. "Chu-tzu tao-t'ung kuan chih chehsüeh hsing" 朱子道統觀之哲學性 [The Philosophical Nature of Chu Hsi's Doctrine of the Orthodox Transmission of the Confucian Way], *Tung-hsi wen-hua* 東西文化 XV (1968), 25–32.

Chang Chih-tung 張之洞. "Ch'üan-hsüeh p'ien" 勸學篇, in *Chang Wen-hsiang kung chii üan-chi* 張文襄公全集. Taipei reprint: 1963.

Chang Ch'i-yün 張其昀, ed. *Yang-ming-hsüeh lun-wen chi* 陽明學論文集 [Symposium on Wang Yang-ming's Philosophy]. Yang-ming-shan, Taiwan: The China Academy, 1972.

Chang Chün-mai 張君勱 (1886–1969). *Pi-chiao Chung-Jih Yang-ming hsüeh* 比較中日陽明學 [A Comparative Study of the School of Wang Yang-ming in China and Japan]. Taipei: China Culture Publications, 1956.

Chang Hsi-chih 張希之. *Yang-ming hsüeh-chuan* 陽明學傳 [The Teaching of Wang Yangming]. Taipei: Chung-hua shu-chü, 1961.

Chang Hsit-t'ang 張西堂. *Wang Chiuan-shan hsüeh-p'u* 王船山學譜 [An Intellectual Biography of Wang Fu-chih]. Changsha: Commercial Press, 1938.

Ch'en An-jen 陳安仁. *Ming-tai hsüeh-shu ssu-hsiang* 明代學術思想史 [The Scholarship and Thought of the Ming Dynasty]. Changsha: Commercial Press, 1940.

Ch'en T'ieh-fan 陳鐵凡. "Ssu-shu chang-chü chi-chu k'ao-yüan" 四書章句及其考源 [An Investigation of the Origins of the Collected Commentaries of the Four Books], *K'ung-Meng hsüeh-pao* 孔孟學報 [Journal of the Confucius-Mencius

Society] IV (Taipei, 1962), 206–53.

Ch'en Yüan 陳垣. *Nan-Sung ch'u Hopei hsin Tao-chiao k'ao.* 南宋初河北新道教考 [A Study of the New Taoism of Hopei at the Beginning of the Southern Sung Period, 1127–1279]. Peking: Chung-hua shu-chü, 1957.

Ch'eng Fa-jen 程發靭. "Ch'eng-Chu chi ch'i men-jen chih Li-hsüeh" 程朱及其門人 之理學 [The Philosophy of Ch'eng Yi, Chu Hsi and Their Disciples], *K'ung-Meng hsüeh-pao* XVI (1968), 143–70.

Chia Feng-chih 賈豐臻. *Yang-ming hsüeh* 陽明學 [The Philosophy of Wang Yang-ming]. Shanghai: Commercial Press, 1930.

Chiang Tsu-yen 蔣祖怡, and Chiang Po-ch'ien 蔣伯潛. *Li-hsueh tsuan-yao* [The Essentials of Neo-Confucian Philosophy]. Taipei: Cheng-chung shu-chü 正中書局, 1953.

Chiang Wei-ch' iao 蔣維喬. *Chung-kuo chin-tai san-pai nien che-hsüeh shih* 中國近 代三百年學史 [A History of Chinese Philosophy in the Last Three Hundred Years]. Shanghai: Chung-hua shu-chü, 1936.

Ch'ien Mu 錢穆. *Chu-tzu hsin-hsüeh-an* 朱子新學案 [A New Record of Chu Hsi's Philosophy]. Taipei: San-min shu-chü 三民書局, 1971.

—— *Chung-kuo chin-san-pai-nien hsüeh-shu-shih* 中國近三百年學術史 [The History of Thought and Scholarship in China during the Past Three Hundred Years]. Shanghai: Commercial Press, 1940.

—— *Sung-Ming li-hsüeh kai-shu* 宋明理學概述 [A General Discussion of the Philosophy of the Sung and Ming Dynasties]. 3rd ed. Taipei: Chinese Culture Publications, 1962.

—— *Yang-ming hsüeh shu-yao* 陽明學述要 [The Essentials of Wang Yang-ming's Philosophy]. 3rd ed. Taipei: Cheng-chung shu-chü, 1930.

Chou Yu-t'ung 周予同. *Ching chin-ku wen* 經今古文 [Old and New Text Classical Scholarship]. Shanghai: Commercial Press, 1926.

Chu Ch'ien-chih 朱謙之. *Jih-pen te Chu-tzu hsüeh* 日本的朱子學 [The Chu Hsi School in Japan]. Peking: San-lien shu-chü 三聯書局, 1958.

—— *Jih-pen te ku-hsüeh chi Yang-ming hsüeh* 日本的古學及陽明學 [The School of old Learning and the Yang-ming School in Japan]. Shanghai: Jen-min ch'u-pan shê 人民出版社, 1962.

—— "Shih-pa shih-chi Chung-kuo che-hsüeh tui Ou-chou che-hsüeh te ying-hsiang" 十八世紀中國哲學對歐洲哲學的形響 [The Influence of Chinese Philosophy on European Philosophy in the Eighteenth Century], *Che-hsüeh yen-chiu* 哲學研究 [Philosophical Studies], IV (Peking, 1957), 48–57.

—— *Sung-ju li-hsüeh tui-yü Ou-chou wen-hua chih ying-hsiang* 宋儒理學對於歐洲文 化之影响 [The Influence of the Sung Neo-Confucian Philosophy on European Culture]. Address given at the National Sun Yat-sen University, in December, 1935, n.p. [1937].

Fan Shou-k'ang 范壽康. *Chu-tzu chi ch'i che-hsüeh* 朱子及其哲學 [Chu Hsi and His Philosophy]. Taipei: K'ai-ming, 1964.

Fung Yu-lan 馮友蘭. *Chung-kuo che-hsüeh shih* 中國哲學史 [A History of Chinese

Philosophy]. Shanghai: Commercial Press, 1935.

—— *Chung-kuo che-hsüeh shih lun-wen chi* 中國哲學史論文集 [Collected Essays on the History of Chinese Thought]. Shanghai: Jen-min ch'u-pan shê, 1958.

—— *Chung-kuo che-hsüeh shih lun-wen ch'u-chi* 中國哲學史論文初集 [Collected Essays on the History of Chinese Thought, First Series]. Shanghai: Jen-min ch'u-pan shê, 1958.

Ho Lin 賀麟. "Sung-ju te ssu-hsiang fang-fa" 宋儒的思想方法 [The Method of Thinking of the Sung Philosophers]. *Sung-shih yen-chiu chi* 宋史研究集 [Studies in Sung History]. Second Collection. Ed. by the Committee on Sung History. Taipei: Chung-hua ts'ung-shu 中華叢書, 1964, 39–66.

Ho Shan-ch'ün 郝善群. "Tui Wang Yang-ming chu-kuan wei-hsin chu-yi te p'ing" 對王陽明主觀唯心主義的批評 [A Criticism of Wang Yang-ming's Subjective Idealism], *Hsin Chien-she* 新建設 [New Construction], IV (1957), 30–35.

Hou Wai-lu 侯外盧 et al. *Chung-kuo ssu-hsiang t'ung-shih* 中國思想通史 [A General History of Chinese Thought]. 6 vols. Peking: Jen-min ch'u-pan shê, 1957.

Hsi Wen-fu 嵇文甫. *Tso-p'ai Wang-hsüeh* 左派王學 [The Leftist Branch of the Yang-ming School]. Chungking: Commercial Press, 1944.

Hsiao Kung-ch'üan 蕭公權. *Chung-kuo cheng-chih ssu-hsiang shih* 中國政治思想史 [A History of Political Thought in China]. 6 vols. Taipei: China Culture Publication, 1954.

Hsieh Wu-liang 謝無量. *Yang-ming hsüeh-piai* 陽明學派 [The Philosophical School of Wang Yang-ming]. Shanghai: Chung-hua shu-chü, 1930.

Hsiung Shih-li 熊十力. *Tu-ching shih-yao* 讀經示要 [On Reading the Classics]. First published, 1948. Taipei reprint: Kuang-wen shu-chü, 1960.

Hsü Fu-kuan 徐復觀. *Chung-kuo jen-hsing lun-shih, Hsien-Ch'in p'ien* 中國人性論史先秦編 [The History of the Chinese Philosophy of Human Nature, Pre-Ch'in period]. Taichung: Tung-hai University Press, 1963.

—— *Chung-kuo ssu-hsiang shih lun-chi* 中國思想史論集 [Collected Discussions on the History of Chinese Thought]. Taichung: Tung-hai University Press, 1959.

Hsü Shih-ch'ang 徐世昌 (1858–1939). *Ch'ing-ju hsüeh-an* 清儒學案 [Philosophical Records of the Ch'ing Dynasty]. 5 vols. Taipei: National War College, 1967.

Hu Che-fu 胡哲敷. *Lu-Wang che-hsüeh pien-wei* 陸王哲學辨微 [On the Differences of Nuances in the Philosophies of Lu Chiu-yüan and of Wang Yang-ming]. Shanghai: Chung-hua shu-chü, 1930.

Hu Shih 胡適 (1891–1962). "Chi-ko fan li-hsüeh te ssu-hsiang chia" 幾個反理學的思想家 [Several Anti-Neo-Confucian Thinkers]. *Hu Shih wen-ts'un* 胡適文存 [The Writings of Hu Shih], v. 3. Taipei: Far East Publications, 1953.

—— *Chung-kuo ku-tai che-hsüeh shih* 中國古代哲學史 [History of Ancient Chinese Philosophy]. 3rd ed. Taipei: Commercial Press, 1968.

—— *Tai Tung-yüan te che-hsüeh* 戴東原的哲學 [The Philosophy of Tai Chen]. Taipei: Commercial Press, 1963.

Huang Chang-chien 黃彰健. "Ô-hu chih-hui Chu-Lu yi-t'ung lüeh-shuo" 鵝湖之會朱陸異同略說 [The Goose Lake Meeting and the Differences between Chu

Hsi and Lu Chiu-yuan]. *Sung-shih yen-chiu chi*. Second Collection. Taipei, 1964, 31–38.

Huang Chien-chung 黃建中. "Yang-ming che-hsüeh k'an-wei" 陽明哲學闡微 [Explanations of the Philosophy of Wang Yang-ming]. *Ko-ming ssu-hsiang* 革命思想 [Revolutionary Thought] IV (Taipei, 1958), 4–6.

Huang Kai-chee 黃繼持. "*Wen* yü *tao, ch'ing* yü *hsing*, Li-hsüeh-chia chih wen-yi ssu-hsiang shih-lun" [文] 與 [道] [情] 與 [性] 理學家之文藝思想試論 [The Literary Theory of the Neo-Confucianists: A Preliminary Survey], *Ch'ung-chi hsüeh-pao* 崇基學報 [The Ch'ung-chi Journal] VII (1968), 187–96.

Huang Kung-wei 黃公偉. *Sung-Ming-Ch'ing li-hsüeh t'i-hsi lun-shih* 宋明清理學體系論史 [Neo-Confucianism of Sung, Ming, and Ch'ing Dynasties]. Taipei: Yu-shih 幼獅, 1971.

Huang Tun-han 黃敦涵. *Yang-ming hsüeh-shuo t'i-hsi* 陽明學說體系 [Yang-ming's Thought-system]. Taipei: T'ai-shan ch'u-pan-she 泰山出版社, 1962.

Jen Yu-wen 簡又文. *Po-sha-tzu yen-chiu* 白沙子研究 [A Study of Ch'en Hsien-chang]. Hong Kong: Chi-ch'eng 集成, 1970.

[Jung Chao-tsu] 容肇祖. *Ming-tai ssu-hsiang shih* 明代思想史 [The History of Ming Thought]. First published 1941. Reprinted in Taipei: Kaiming, 1962.

—— *Wei-Chin te tzu-jan chu-yi* 魏晉的自然主義 [The Naturalism of the Wei-Chin Periods]. Peking: Peking University, 1934.

Ku Chieh-kang 顧頡剛. *Han-tai hsüeh-shu shih-lüeh* 漢代學術史略 [A Brief History of Scholarship during the Han Dynasty]. Shanghai: Chung-kuo wen-hua fu-wu shê 中國文化服務社, 1936.

—— "Ming-tai wen-tzu yü k'ao-lüeh" 明代文字獄考略 [A Study of Literary Persecution during the Ming Dynasty], *Tung-fang tsa-chih* 東方雜誌 XXXII (1935), 21–34.

Kuo Ai-ch'un 郭藹春. *Yen Hsi-chai hsüeh-p'u* 顏習齋學譜 [Intellectual Biography of Yen Yüan]. Shanghai: Commercial Press, 1957.

Liang Ch'i-ch'ao 梁啓超 (1873–1929). *Chung-kuo chin-san-pai-nien hsüeh-shih shih* 中國近三百年學術史 [The History of Thought and Scholarship of China during the Past Three Hundred Years], in *Yin-ping-shih ho-chi* 飲冰室合集 *Chuan-chi* 專集 v. 75. (The *ho-chi* or Collected Writings include *Wen-chi* as well as *Chuan-chi*.) Shanghai: Chung-hua shu-chü, 1941.

—— "Nan-hai K'ang hsien-sheng chuan" 南海康先生傳 [Biography of K'ang Yu-wei], in *Yin-ping-shih ho-chi, wen-chi* 6: 57–89.

—— "Pao-chiao fei suo-yi tsun-K'ung lun" 保教非所以尊孔論 [To Defend Ideology Is Not to Respect Confucius] (1902), in *Yin-ping-shih ho-chi, wen-chi* 4: 50–59.

—— "Tai Tung-yüan hsien-sheng chuan" 戴東原先生傳 [Life of Tai Chen], *Yin-ping-shih ho-chi, wen-chi* 40: 41–52.

—— *Wang Yang-ming chih-hsing ho-yi chih-chiao* 王陽明知行合一之敎 [Wang Yang-ming's Doctrine of the Unity of Knowledge and Action] *Yin-ping-shih ho-chi, wen-chi* 43: 23–68.

Liao Yü-jen 廖宇仁. "Lun Yang-ming che-hsüeh yü Sun Wen hsüeh-shuo chih haiang-hu fu-yi" 論學明哲學與孫文學說之相互輔議 [The Interrelationships between Yang-ming's Philosophy and Sun Yat-sen's Theory], *Hsüeh-tsung* 學宗 II (Taipei, 1961), 47–9, 57.

Lin Chi-p'ing 林繼平. "Kan-ch'üan hsüeh t'an-chiao yü Wang-Chan pi-chiao" 甘泉學探究與王湛比較 [A Study of the Philosophy of Chan Jo-shui and the Comparison of Chan with Wang Yang-ming], *Jen-sheng* 人生 XXX (1965), 14–21.

—— "Wang-hsüeh te kung-fu wen-t'i" 王學的工夫問題 [The Problem of Moral Effort in Wang Yang-ming's Philosophy], *Jen-sheng* XXV (1963), 7–13.

Liu Shih-p'ei 劉師培 (1884–1919). "Han-Sung chang-chü hsüeh yi-t'ung lun" 漢宋章句學異同論 [Similarities and Differences between the Exegetical Studies of Han and Sung]. *Han-Sung hsüeh-shu yi-t'ung lun* 漢宋學術異同論, in *Liu Sheng-shu hsien-sheng yi-shu* 劉申叔先生遺書 [Surviving Works of Liu Shih-p'ei], n.p. [1936], [v. 15], 4a–6a.

—— "Han-Sung yi-li hsüeh yi-t'ung lun" 漢宋義理學異同論 [Similarities and Differences between the Moral Philosophy of Han and Sung], *Han-Sung hsüeh-shu yi-t'ung lun*, in *Liu Sheng-shu hsien-sheng yi-shu* [v. 15], 1a–4a.

—— *Li-hsüeh tzu-yi t'ung-shih* 理學字義通釋 [A Survey of the Meanings of Words in Neo-Confucian Philosophy], in *Liu Sheng-shu hsien-sheng yi-shu* [v. 12].

—— "Nan-pei li-hsüeh pu-t'ung lun" 南北理學不同論 [Differences between the Neo-Confucianism of the North and That of the South], *Nan-pei hsüeh-p'ai pu-t'ung lun* 南北學術不同論 [Differences between Northern and Southern Scholarship], in *Liu Sheng-shu hsien-sheng yi-shu* [v. 15], 4b–12b.

Liu Ts'un-yan 柳存仁. "Ming-ju-yü Tao-chiao" 明儒與道教 [Taoism and Neo-Confucianists in Ming Times], *Hsin-ya hsüeh-pao* VIII (February, 1967), 259–96.

—— "Tao-tsang Wu-chen, p'ien san-shu pien-wu" 道藏悟眞篇三注辨誤 [On the Edition of the Combined Three Commentaries on the *Wu-chen p'ien* in the Taoist Canon] *Tung-hsi wen-hua* XV (1968), 33–41.

Lü Ssu-ming 呂思勉. *Li-hsüeh kang-yao* 理學綱要 [The Essentials of Neo-Confucian Philosophy]. Shanghai: Commercial Press, 1931.

Mai Chung-kui 麥仲貴. *Wang-men chu-tzu chih liang-chih hsüeh chih fa-chan* 王門諸子致良知學之發展 [The Development of the Teaching of the Extension of "liang-chih" by the Disciples of Wang Yang-ming's School]. Hong Kong: Chinese University of Hong Kong, 1973.

Mou Jun-sun 牟潤孫. "Shih *Lun-yü* k'uang-chien chang" 釋論語狂簡章 [An Interpretation of the 'k'uang-chien' Chapter of the Analects], *Hsin-ya hsüeh-pao* 新亞學報 II (February, 1957), 79–86.

Mou Tsung-san 牟宗三. *Chung-kuo che-hsüeh te t'e-hsing* 中國哲學的特性 [The Special Characteristics of Chinese Philosophy]. Kowloon, Hong Kong: Jen-sheng ch'u-pan-shê 人生出版社, 1963.

—— *Hsin-t'i yü hsing-t'i* 心體與性體 [Mind-in-itself and Nature-in-itself]. 3 vols.

Taipei: Cheng-chung shu-chü, 1968.

—— *Ts'ai-shing yü hsüan-li* 才性與玄理 [On Capacity, Nature, and Metaphysical Reason]. Kowloon, Hong Kong: Jen-sheng ch'u-pan shê, 1963.

—— "Tsung-lun Chu-tzu san-shih-ch'i sui ch'ien chih ta-t'i ch'in-hsiang yi-chi ch'ih-hou ch'i ch'eng-shu chih yi-li hsi-t'ung chih hsing-t'ai" 總論朱子三十七歲前之大體傾向以及此後成熟之義理系統之形態 [A Study of Chu Hsi's Scholarship Before the Age of Thirty-seven and the Later Mature Form of His Philosophical System], *Hsin-ya hsüeh-pao* X (September, 1969) 37–57.

—— *Wang Yang-ming chih-liang-chih chiao* 王陽明致良知教 [Wang Yang-ming's Teaching on the Extension of *liang-chih*]. Taipei: Chung-yan wenwu kung-ying shê 中央文物供應社, 1954.

P'i Hsi-jui 皮錫瑞 (1850–1910). *Ching-hsüeh li-shih* 經學歷史 [A History of Classical Studies]. Annotated by Chou Yü-t'ung. Shanghai: Commercial Press, 1929.

—— *Ching-hsueh t'ung-lun* 經學通論 [A Discussion of the Five Classics]. 5 vol.s n.p. [1923].

Sun K'e-k'uan 孫克寬. *Sung-Yüan Tao-chiao fa-chan* 宋元道教發展 [The Development of Taoism during the Sung and Yuan Dynasties]. Vol. 1. Taichung: Tunghai University Press, 1965.

Sung P'ei-wei 宋佩韋. *Ming wen-hsüeh shih* 明文學史 [History of Ming Literature]. Shanghai: Commercial Press, 1934.

—— *Wang Yang-ming yü Ming li-hsüeh* 王陽明與明理學 [Wang Yang-ming and the Neo-Confucian Philosophy of Ming Times]. Shanghai: Commercial Press, 1931.

Tai Chün-jen 戴君仁. "Chu-tzu Yang-ming te ko-wu chih-chih shuo ho t'a-men cheng-ko ssu-hsiang te kuan-hsi" 朱子陽明的格物致知說和他們整個思想的關係 [Chu Hsi and Yang-ming: Their Theories on Science and Philosophy within the Context of their Entire Thinking], *K'ung-Meng hsüeh-pao* IX (1965), 77–97.

—— "Chu-tzu yü Lu Hsiang-shan te chiao-yi chi pien-hsüeh te ching-kuo" 朱子與陸象山的交誼及辯學的經過 [The Friendship between Chu Hsi and Lu Chiu-yüan and Their Philosophical Debates]. *Sung-shih yen-chiu chi*. First Collection. Taipei, 1958, 463–71.

T'an Ssu-t'ung 譚嗣同 (1865–98). *T'an Ssu-t'ung ch'üan-chi* 譚嗣同全集 [Complete Works of T'an Ssu-t'ung]. Peking reprint; San-lien shu-chü, 1954.

T'ang Chun-i 唐君毅. *Che-hsüeh kai-lun* 哲學概論 [A General Discussion of Philosophy]. Hong Kong: Mencius Educational Foundation, 1961.

—— "Chu-Lu yi-t'ung t'an-yuan" 朱陸異同探源 [The Origins of the Similarities and Difficulties between Chu's Thought and Lu's Thought]. *Hsin-ya hsüeh-pao* VIII (February, 1967), 1–100.

—— *Chung-kuo che-hsüeh yüan-lun* 中國哲學原論 [An Inquiry into Chinese Philosophy] part 1. Hong Kong: Jen-shen ch'u-pan shê, 1966.

—— *Chung-kuo che-hsüeh yüan-lun, Yüan-hsing p'ien* 中國哲學原論原性篇 [An Inquiry into Chinese Philosophy, Section on Human Nature]. Hong Kong:

New Asia College, 1968.

—— "Yang-ming hsüeh yü Chu-Lu yi-t'ung ch'ung-pien" 陽明學與朱陸異同重辨 [Repeated Discussion Concerning the Similarities and Differences between Wang Yang-ming's Philosophy and That of Chu Hsi and of Lu Chiu-yüan], *Hsin-ya hsüeh-pao* VIII (1968), 53–126; IX (1969), 1–69.

T'ang Yung-t'ung 湯用彤. *Han-wei liang-Chin Nan-pei ch'ao Fo-chiao shih* 漢魏兩晉南北朝佛教史 [History of Buddhism during Han, wei, Chin, and the Northern and Southern Dynasties]. Changsha: Commercial Press, 1938.

—— *Wei-Chin hsüan-hsüeh lun-kao* 魏晉玄學論稿 [A Preliminary Discussion of the Metaphysical Learning of the Wei-Chin Periods]. Peking: Jen-min ch'u-pan she, 1957.

Uno Tetsujin 宇野哲人. *Chung-kuo chin-shih ju-hsüeh shih* 中國近世儒學史 [History of Confucianism in Modern China]. 2 vols. Tr. from the Japanese by Ma Fu-ch'en 馬福辰. Taipei: China Culture Publications, 1957.

Wu K'ang 吳康. "Lu Hsiang-shan hsüeh-shu" 陸象山學述 [The Philosophy of Lu Chiu-yüan]. *Sung-shih yen-chiu chi*. First Collection. Taipei, 1958, 107–30.

Yang Jung-kuo 楊榮國 ed. *Chien-ming Chung-kuo che-hsüeh shih* 簡明中國哲學史 [A Simplified History of Chinese Philosophy]. Peking: Jen-min ch'u-pan she, 1973.

Yang T'ien-shih 楊天石. *Wang Yang-ming*. Peking: Chung-hua shu-chü, 1972.

Yao Ts'ung-wu 姚從吾. *Tung-pei shih lun-ts'ung* 東北史論叢 [On the History of the Northeast]. Taipei: Cheng-chung shu-chü, 1959.

Yasuoka Masashirō 安岡正篤. "Ming-chih wei-hsin yü Yang-ming hsüeh" 明治維新與陽明學 [The Meiji Reforms and the Yang-ming School]. Tr. from the Japanese by Ching-chia 景嘉. *Tung-hsi wen-hua* XXV (July, 1969), 3–19.

[Yeh] Ting-yi 葉丁易. *Ming-tai te t'e-wu cheng-chih* 明代的特務政治 [The Secret Police Politics of the Ming Dynasty]. Peking; Chung-wai ch'u-pan she 中外出版社, 1950.

Yü Ch'ung-yao 余重耀. *Yang-ming hsien-sheng chuan-ts'uan* 陽明先生傳纂 [A Collated Biography of Wang Yang-ming]. Shanghai: Chung-hua shu-chü, 1923.

B. JAPANESE AND KOREAN WORKS

Abe Yoshio 阿部吉雄. "Chosen no Yōmeigakuha" 朝鮮の陽明學派 *Yōmeigaku nyūmon* 陽明學入門, in *Yōmeigaku taikei*, v. 1, 407–25.

—— "Ra Kinjun" 羅欽順, in *Chugoku no shisoka* 中國の思想家 [The Thinkers of China]. Ed. by the Tokyo University Chinese Philosophy Department. Tokyo University Press, 1963, 571–83.

Akisuki Kazutsugu 秋月胤繼. *Riku-Ō kenkyū* 陸王研究 [A Study of Lu Chiu-yuan and Wang Yang-ming]. n.p., Shōbasha 章華社, 1935.

Amada Takeo 天田武夫. "Ō Yōmei ni okeru byōdō no shisō ni tsuite" 王陽明における平等の思想について [Wang Yang-ming's Ideas on Human Equality],

Chūgoku Tetsugaku 中國哲學 II (1962), 1–6.

—— "Tairei no gi to Ō Yōmei" 大禮の議と王陽明 [The Great Ceremonial Dispute and Wang Yang-ming], *Chūgoku Tetsugaku* I (1961), 1–9.

Andō Hideo 安藤英男. *Nihon ni okeru Yōmeigaku no keifu* 日本に於る陽明學の系譜 [The Lineal Transmission of the Yang-ming School in Japan]. Tokyo: Shin Jimbutsu Ōrai sha 新人物往來社, 1971.

Andō Shūichi 安藤州一. *Ō Yōmei no gedatsu-kan* 王陽明の解脱觀 [Wang Yang-ming's Ideas on Salvation], Ōsaka: Shōbunkan 敞文館, 1942.

Araki Kengo 荒木見悟. *Bukkyo to Jukyo: Chūgoku shisō o keisei suru mono* 佛教と儒教—中國思想を形成するもの [Buddhism and Confucianism: The Formation of Chinese Thought]. Kyoto: Heirakuji shoten 平樂寺書店, 1963.

—— "Chikō gōitsu ron no ichi kentō" 知行合一論の一檢討 [An Examination of the Theory of the Unity of knowledge and Action], *Shinagaku kenkyū* 支那學研究 XVII (1957), 23–32; XVIII (1958), 33–42.

—— "Minmatsu ni okeru Ju Butsu chōwaron no seikaku" 明末における儒佛調和論の性格 [On the Thought of the Late Ming Era as Revealed in the Attempts at Harmony between Confucianism and Buddhism], *Nippon Chūgoku gakkai ho* 日本中國學會報 XVIII (1966), 210–24.

—— "Tan Kansen to Ō Yōmei" 湛甘泉と王陽明 [Chan Jo-shui and Wang Yang-ming], *Tetsugaku nenpo* 哲學年報 XXVII (1968), 275–305.

—— "Yōmeigaku to Mindai no Bukkyo" 陽明學と明代の佛教 [The Yang-ming School and Ming Buddhism], *Yōmeigaku nyūmon* 陽明學入門 [Introduction to the Yang-ming School], *Yōmeigaku taikei* 陽明學大系 [A Compendium of the Yang-ming School], v. 1, 291–320.

—— et al., comp. *Yōmeigaku taikei.* 12 vols. Tokyo: Meitoku shuppansha 明德出版社, 1971–73.

Chong In-bo 鄭寅普. *Tamwon kukhak sanigo* 詹園國學散稾 [Random Writings on Korean Learning]. Seoul, 1955.

Fumoto Yasutaka 麓保孝. *Hokusō ni okeru Jūgaku no tenkai* 北宋に於る儒學の展開 [Introduction to the Development of Confucianism in the Northern Sung Period of China]. Tokyo: Shōseki bunbutsu ryūtsū-kai 書籍文物流通會, 1967.

Hirashita Kinji 平下欣二. "Shikukyō hokō—Ō Yōmei no tetsugaku ni tsuite" 四句教法王陽明の哲學について [On the Four Maxims: The Philosophy of Wang Yang-ming], *Tōa kenkyū* 東亞研究 XXIV (1943), 35–39.

Inoue Tetsujirō 井上哲次郎. *Nihon Shushi gakuha no tetsugaku* 日本朱子學派の哲學 [The Philosophy of Chu Hsi's School in Japan]. 28th ed. Tokyo: Fuzanbō 富山房, 1945.

—— *Nihon Yōmeigakuha no tetsugaku* 日本陽明學派の哲學 [The Philosophy of the Yang-ming School in Japan]. 18th rev. ed. Tokyo: Fuzanbō, 1936.

Kimura Eiichi 木村英一. *Chugoku jitsuzai-kan no kenkyū* 中國實在觀の研究 [A Study of Chinese Realism]. Part 1. Tokyo: Kōbundo 弘文堂, 1948.

Kimura Ki 木村毅, ed. *Meiji jimbutsu ronshū* 明治人物論集 [On the Personalities of the Meiji Period]. *Meiji bunka zenshu* 明治文學全集 [Collected Writings on the Literature of the Meiji Period]. Vol. 92. Tokyo: Chikuma 筑摩, 1966.

Kojima Yūma 小島祐馬. *Chūgoku shisō shi* 中國思想史 [A History of Chinese Thought]. Tokyo: Sōbunsha 創文社, 1968.

Kusumoto Fumio 久須本文雄. *Ō Yōmei no zenteki shisō kenkyū* 王陽明の禪的思想研究 [A Study of the Zen Buddhist Elements in Yang-ming's Thought]. Nagoya: Nisshindo Shoten 日進堂書店, 1958.

Kusumoto Masatsugu 楠本正繼. "Ō Yōmei banen no shisō" 王陽明晩年の思想 [Wang Yang-ming's Thought in Later Life], *Josetsu* 敍說 V (1956), 1–45.

—— *Sō-Min jidai Jugaku shisō no kenkyū* 宋明時代儒學思想の研究 [A Study of the Confucian Thought of the Sung and Ming Periods]. 2nd ed. Chiba-ken, Kashiwa-shi Hiroike Gakuin 廣池學園, 1963.

Liu Ts'un-yan. *Ō Yōmei to Mindai no Dōkyo* 王陽明と明代の道教 [Wang Yang-ming and Ming Taoism], *Yōmeigaku nyumon*, in *Yōmeigaku taikei*, v. 1, 257–90.

Mano Senryū 間野潛龍. *Yōmeigaku to Ju-Butsu ronsō: tokuni Choko Shoin o chushin to shite—*" 陽明學と儒佛論爭—特に姚江書院を中心として [The Yang-ming School and the Confucian-Buddhist Debates as Focused in the Yao-chiang Academy], *Shinagakuhō* 支那學報 I (1956), 12–22.

Mekada Makoto 見加田誠. *Yōmeigaku to Mindai no bungei* 陽明學と明代の文藝 [The Yang-ming School and Ming Literature], *Yōmeigaku taikei*, v. 1, 321–39.

Mishima Fuku 三島復. *Ō Yōmei no tetsugaku* 王陽明の哲學 [The Philosophy of Wang Yang-ming]. Tokyo: Ookayama 大岡山, 1934.

Mishima Yukio 三島由起夫. "Kakumei tetsugaku to shite no Yōmeigaku" 革命哲學としての陽明學 [The Yang-ming School as Revolutionary Philosophy], *Shokun* 諸君 (September, 1970), 22–45.

Motoyama Yukihiko 本山幸彦. *Meiji shisō no keisei* 明治思想の形成 [The Formation of Meiji Thought]. Tokyo: Fukumura 福村, 1969.

Murayama Yoshihiro 村山吉廣. "Mingaku kara Shingaku e" 明學から清學へ[From the Learning of Ming to That of Ch'ing], part 1. *Chūgoku koten kenkyū* 中國古典研究 [Journal of Sinology] XII (1964), 15–23.

Nakamura Hajime 中村元 and Uno Seiichi 宇野精一. *Kōza Tōyō shisō* 講座東洋思想 [On the Ways of Thinking of Eastern Peoples]. Vol. 2, 3, 4: *Chūgoku shiso* 中國思想 [Chinese Thought]. Tokyo: Tokyo University Press, 1967.

—— *Kōza Tōyō shisō*. Vol. 5: *Bukkyō shisō* 佛教思想 [Buddhist Thought]. Tokyo: Tokyo University Press, 1967.

Nakayama Hachirō 中山八郎. "Futatabi 'Kasei' chō tairei mondai no hattan ni tsuite" 再び嘉靖朝大禮問題の發端 [Another Discussion on the Origin of the Ceremonial Dispute in the Chia-ching 嘉靖 1522–1567 Period]. *Shimizu Hakase tsuitō kinen Mindaishi ronsō* 清水博士追悼紀念明代史論叢 [Studies on the Ming Period Presented to the Late Taiji Shimizu in Memory of His Achievements in the Field of Ming History]. Tokyo: Daian 大安, 1962, 61–84.

—— *Ō Yōmei to Mindai no seiji gunji* 王陽明と明代の政治軍事 [Wang Yang-ming and Ming Politics and Warfare], *Yōmeigaku nyūmon*, in *Yōmeigaku taikei*, v. 1, 161–99.

Nemoto Makoto 根本誠. *Sensei shakai ni okeru teikō seishin Chūgoku initsu no kenkyū* 専制社會における抵抗精神—中國隱逸の研究 [The Spirit of Resistance in Authoritarian Societies: A Study of Chinese Hermits]. Tokyo: Sōgensha 創元社, 1952.

Nishi Junzō 西順藏. "Sōdai no Jukyō" 宋代の儒教 [The Confucianism of the Sung Dynasty], *Rekishi Kyōiku* 歷史教育 II (1954), 33–38.

Nomura Keiji 野村惠二. "Denshū roku ni okeru jinyō tenrei" 傳習錄に於ける引用典例 [Classics, Similes, and Examples Quoted in *Denshuroku*], *Osaka Furitsu Gaigaku Kiyō* 大阪府立大學 [Bulletin of the University of Osaka Prefecture] XIII (1965), 103–19; XIV (1966), 101–14.

—— "Ō Yōmei dokirun ni tsuite no ichi kōsatsu" 王陽明動機論についての一考察 [A Study of Motivism in Wang Yang-ming's Philosophy], *Ōsaka Furitsu Gaigaku Kiyō* XI (1963), 83–93.

—— "Ō Yōmei ni okeru Kyōiku to Chūyō no kankei" 王陽明に於る教育と中庸の關係 [The Relationship between Wang Yang-ming's Teaching and the Doctrine of the Mean], *Geirin* 藝林 XVIII (1967), 143–50.

—— "Ō Yōmei rinri setsu ni okeru seizen no kenkyū—Mōshi seizen setsu to hikaku ni tsuite" 王陽明倫理說に於ける「性善」の研究—孟子性善說と比較について [A Study of Wang Yang-ming's Doctrine of the Goodness of Human Nature as Compared to That of Mencius], *Osaka Furitsu Daigaku Kiyo* 大阪府立大學紀要 X (1962), 15–25; XI (1963), 83–93.

Okada Takehiko 岡田武彦. *Ō Yōmei to Minmatsu no Jugaku* 王陽明と明末の儒學 [Wang Yang-ming and Late Ming Confucianism]. Tokyo: Meitoku shuppan-sha, 1970.

—— *Zazen to seiza* 坐禪と靜坐 [Ch'an Meditation and Quiet Sitting]. Nagasaki, 1965.

Sakai Tadao 酒井忠夫. *Chūgoku zensho no kenkyū* 中國善書の研究 [A Study of Chinese Morality Books]. Tokyo: Kōbundō 弘文堂, 1960.

—— "Ō gaku no shominsei ni kansuru shakkai teki rekishi teki igi" 王學の庶民性に關する社會的歷史的意義 [Some Social and Historical Meanings in the Popular Doctrine of Wang Yang-ming], *Ryūkoku-shidan* 龍谷史壇 LVI/LVII (1966), 193–203.

Shiga Ichiro 志賀一朗. "Ō Yōmei to Tan Kansen" 王陽明と湛甘泉 [Wang Yang-ming and Chan Jo-shui], *Nippon Chūgoku gakkaiho* XXI (1969), 176–95.

Shimada Kenji 島田虔次. *Chūgoku ni okeru kindai shii no zasetsu* 中國に於る近代思維の挫折 [The Breakdown of Modern Thought in China]. Tokyo: Chikuma shobō, 1949.

—— *Shushi gaku to Yōmei gaku* 朱子學と陽明學 [The Chu Hsi School and the Yang-ming School]. Tokyo: Iwanami 岩波, 1967.

—— "Yōmei gaku ni okeru ningen-gainen jiga ishiki no tenkai to sono igi" 陽明學に於る人間觀念自我意識の展開と其意義 [The Evolutions of the Notion of the

Human and of the Consciousness of Self in the Yang-ming School and the Meaning of This Evolution], *Tōyōshi kenkyū* 東洋史研究 VIII (July, 1943), 143–68, 233–58.

Shimizu Taiji 清水泰次. "Yōmeigaku shōron" 陽明學小論 [A Short Discussion on the Yang-ming Philosophy], *Rekishi kyōiku* 歷史敎育 II (1954), 26–32.

—— "Yōmeigaku no seisei" 陽明學の生成 [The Origin and Development of the Yang-ming Philosophy], *Shakkai kagaku kenkyū* 社會科學研究 [Studies of Social Sciences, Waseda University], III (1958), 59–110.

Shimotomai Akira 下斗米晟. "Yōmeigaku no san kōryō" 陽明學の三綱領 [The Three Themes of Yang-ming's Philosophy], *Daitō Bunka Gaigaku Kiyō* 大東文化大學紀要 I (1963), 55–72.

Suzuki Tadashi 鈴木正. "Mindai sanjin kō" 明代山人考, in *Shimizu Hakase tsuitō kinen Mindaishi ronsō*. Tokyo: Daian, 1962, 357–88.

Takahashi Kōji 高橋行司. "Ō Yōmei ni okeru aku no seiritsu" 王陽明に於ける惡の成立 [The Origin of Evil in the Philosophy of Wang Yang-ming], *Daitō Bunka Daigaku Kangaku-kai shi* 大東文化大學漢學會誌 [Bulletin of the Sinological Society of the Daitō Bunka University] IV (1961), 19–25.

—— "Ō Yōmei no 'shiku ketsu' ni tsuite" 王陽明の四句訣について [On Wang Yang-ming's "Four Maxims"], *Chūgoku tetsugaku* I (1961), 10–18.

—— "Yōmei kyōgaku no mujun—seijin-kan o chūshin to shite" 陽明敎學の矛盾—聖人觀を中心として [The Contradiction in Yang-ming's Teaching: the Notion of Sagehood], *Chūgoku tetsugaku* III (1965), 1–10.

Takahashi Tōru 高橋亨. "Chōsen no Yōmei gakuha" 朝鮮の陽明學 [The Wang Yang-ming School in Korea], *Chosen gakuho* 朝鮮學報 IV (1953), 131–56.

—— "Richo Jugaku-shi ni okeru Shuriha Shugiha no hattatsu" 李朝儒學史に於る主理派主氣派の發達 [The Development of the Schools of *li* and *ch'i* during the Yi Dynasty in Korea], *Chōsen China bunka no kenkyū* 朝鮮支那文化の研究 [Studies in Korean and Chinese Cultures]. Ed. by Tabobashi Kiyoshi 田保橋潔. Tokyo, 1929, 142–281.

Takao Giken 高雄義堅. "Unsei daishi Shukō ni tsuite" 雲棲大師袾宏に就て [On the Master Yün-ch'i Chu-hung], in *Naitō Hakase shojū kinen shigaku ronso* 内藤博士頌壽紀念史學論叢 [Historical Essays Presented to Dr. Naito in Honor of His Birthday], Kyoto: Sōbundo, 1930, 215–72.

Takase Takejirō 高瀬武次郎. *Ō Yōmei shōden* 王陽明詳傳 [A Detailed Biography of Wang Yang-mind]. Tokyo: Bunmeidō 文明堂, 1905.

—— "Yōmeigaku no jinsei kan" 陽明學の人生觀 [The Philosophy of Life of the Yang-ming School], *Zengaku kenkyū* 禪學研究 X (1928), 1–12.

Takeuchi Yoshio 武内義雄. *Chūgoku shisō shi* 中國思想史 [History of Chinese Thought]. Tokyo: Iwanami, 1957.

—— *Shushi Yōmei* 朱子陽明 [Chu Hsi and Wang Yang-ming]. Tokyo: Iwanami, 1936.

Takigawa Kametarō 瀧川龜太郎. *Shiki kaichū kosho* 史記會注考證 [An Investigation into the Collected Commentaries of *Shih-chi*]. Tokyo: Tokyo University, Tōyō bunka kenkyūsho 東洋文化研究所, 1956–60.

Tasaka Kō 田坂昂. "Sono shi no baiwa: Mishima Yukio no nihilism" その死の場合：三島由紀夫のニヒリスム [Mishima Yukio's Nihilism: The Circumstances Surrounding His Death], *Tenbō* 展望 No. 148 (April, 1971), 100–7.

Tokiwa Daijō 常盤大定. *Shina ni okeru Bukkyo to Jukyo Dōkyo* 支那に於る佛敎と儒敎道敎 [Buddhism, Confucianism, and Taoism in China]. Tokyo: Tōyō Bunko 東洋文庫, 1930.

Tomoeda Ryōtarō 友枝龍太郎. "Yōmei no Daigaku kaishaku ni tsuite—seii to chi ryōchi—" 陽明の大學解釋について—誠意と致良知— [Yang-ming's Explanation of the *Great Learning*: The Sincerity of the Will and the Extension of *liang-chih*], *Tetsugaku* 哲學 XIII (Hiroshima, 1961), 116–29.

Uete Michiari 植手通有. "Meiji keimo shisō no keisei—Seiyō kan no tenkai to no kanren ni oite" 明治啓蒙思想の形成—西洋觀の轉回との關連において [The Formation of the Idea of "Enlightenment" of the 'Meiji Period: The Evolution of Japanese Attitudes to the West], *Shisō* 思想 No. 511 (1967), 56–72; No. 512 (1967), 183–201.'

Yamada Jun 山田準. *Yōmeigaku seigi* 陽明學精義 [The Essentials of Yang-ming's Philosophy]. Tokyo: Kinrei sha 金鈴社, 1926.

Yamamoto Makoto 山本命. *Min-jidai jugaku no rinrigaku teki kenkyū* 明時代儒學の倫理學的研究 [A Study of the Confucian Ethics of the Ming Dynasty]. Tokyo: Risō sha 理想社, 1974.

Yamamoto Shōichi 山本正一. " Ōgaku no matsuryū ni tsuite" 王學の末流について [On the Later Degeneration of the Philosophy of Wang Yang-ming], *Daitō bunka gakuhō* 大東文化學報 No. 1/11 (1939), 43–70.

——— *Ō Yōmei* 王陽明 [Wang Yang-ming]. Tokyo: Chūbunkan 中文館, 1946.

Yamane Mitsuyoshi 山根三芳. "Chō Ōkyo no Ten-jin Gōitsu shisō" 張橫渠の天人合一思想 [On the Unity of Heaven and Man in Chang Tsai's Thought], *Nippon Chūgoku gakkaihō* XIX (1967), 144–58.

Yamane Yukio 山根幸夫. *Mindai yōeki seido no tenkai* 明代徭役制度の展開 [The Development of the Corvée System in the Ming Dynasty]. Tokyo: Tokyo joshi daigaku gakkai kenkyū sōsho 東京女子大學學會研究叢書, 1956.

Yamai Yū 山井湧. "Shin soku ri. Chi-gyō gōitsu. Chi-ryōchi no imi: Yōmeigaku no ichi seikaku" 心卽理知行合一致良知の意味：陽明學の一性格 [The Meanings of *hsin chi li, chih-hsing ho-yi,* and *chih laing-chih*: The Peculiarity of the Doctrine of Wang Yang-ming], *Nippon Chūgoku gakkaiho* XXII (1970), 119–40.

Yamashita Ryūji 山下龍二. "Ō Kan no *Mindohen*" 黃綰の明道篇 [Huang Wan's *Ming-tao-pien*], *Chūgokukoten-kenkyū* XII (1964), 1–14.

—— "Ō Ryōkei ron" 王龍溪論 [On Wang Chi], *Nihon Chūgoku gakkaihō* VIII (1956), 85–97.

—— *Yōmeigaku no kenkyū* 陽明學の研究 [A Study of Yang-ming's Philosophy]. 2 vols. Tokyo: Gendai Jōhō sha 現代情報社, 1971.

—— "Yōmeigaku kenkyū no rekishi kara" 陽明學研究の歷史から [On the History of the Study of the Yang-ming School], *Rekishi kyōiku* III (1955), 71–77.

Yasuda Kiyoshi 保田清. *Ō Yōmei.* Tokyo: Kōbundo, 1942.

—— "Tegami yori mitaru Ō Yōmei no shisō daiyō" 手紙より王陽明の思想大要 [The Essentials of Wang Yang-ming's Thought as Seen in His Letters], *Tetsugaku kenkyū* No. 380 (1949), 19–36.

Yasuoka Masaatsu 安岡正篤. *Ō Yōmei kenkyū* 王陽明研究. Tokyo: Meitoku, 1967

Yi Nung-hwa 李能和. "Choson Yuhak chi Yang-myong hak-pa" 朝鮮儒學及陽明學派 [Korean Confucianism and the Yang-ming School], *Seikyūgakuso* 青丘學叢 XXV (1936), 105–42.

Yi Pyong-do 李丙燾. *Charyo Han'guk Yuhak sa ch'ogo* 資料韓國儒學史草稿 [A Draft History of Confucianism in Korea]. Seoul National University, 1959, mimeographed copy.

Yōmeigaku. Nos. 1–193 (1908–28).

Yōmei shugi 陽明主義. Nos. 1–146 (1918–28).

Yoshida Kenkō 吉田賢抗. "Shin soku ri no tetsugaku" 心卽理の哲學 [The Philosophy of *hsin chi li*], *Tōyō gaku* 東洋學 VI (1961), 98–102.

—— *Chūgoku shisōshi* 中國思想史 [A History of Chinese Thought]. Tokyo: Meiji Shoin 明治書院, 1947.

Yoshino Sakuzō 吉野作造 et al., comps. *Meiji bunka zenshū* 明治文化全集 [Collected Writings on the Meiji Period]. Vol. 2–3: *Seishihen* 正史篇 [History Section], Pts. 1–2, Tokyo: Nippon hyōronsha 日本評論社, 1927–30.

C.   WESTERN PHILOSOPHICAL AND RELIGIOUS WORKS CONSULTED

Anscombe, G. E. M. *An Introduction to Wittgenstein's Tractatus.* London: Hutchenson, 1959.

Aristotle. *Selected Works. Translations.* Ed. by Philip Wheelwright. New York: Odyssey, 1951.

Augustinus, Aurelius. *Les Plus Belles Pages de Saint Augustin.* Tr. by L. Bertrand. Paris: A. Fayard, 1916.

Bergson, H. *Creative Evolution.* Tr. by A. Mitchell. New York: Modern Library, 1944.

—— *The Two Sources of Morality and Religion.* Tr. by R. A. Audra and C. Brereton. New York: Henry Holt, 1935.

Berkeley, G. *A Treatise Concerning the Principles of Human Knowledge.* Ed. by Philip Wheelwright. New York: Doubleday, Doran, 1935.

Bočhenski, J. M. *The Methods of Contemporary Thought.* New York: Harper & Row, 1968.

Bonaventura, Saint. *The Mind's Road to God.* Tr. by G. Boas. New York: Liberal Arts Press, 1953.

Bradley, F. H. *Appearance and Reality: A Metaphysical Essay.* Oxford: Clarendon, 1962.

—— *Essays on Truth and Reality*. Oxford: Clarendon, 1962.

Copleston, F. *A History of Philosophy*. 8 vols. New York: Image Books, 1962–67.

Descartes, R. *Philosophical Writings: A Selection,* Tr. and ed. by E. Anscombe and P. T. Geache. London: Nelson, 1964.

Fackenheim, E. L. *The Religious Dimension in Hegel's Thought*. Bloomington: Indiana University Press, 1968.

Hegel, G. W. F. *The Philosophy of History*. Tr. by J. Sibree. New York: Dover, 1956.

Heidegger, M. *Being and Time*. Eng. tr. by J. Macquarrie and E. Robinson. London: SCM Press, 1962.

—— *An Introduction to Metaphysics*. Tr. by R. Manheim. New Haven: Yale University Press, 1959.

James, William. *The Varieties of Religious Experience: A Study in Human Nature*. New York: Modern Library, 1929.

Jaspers, Karl. *The Great Philosophers*. Tr. by R. R. Manheim. 2 vols. New York: Harcourt, Brace & World, 1962–66.

—— *Way to Wisdom: An Introduction to Philosophy*. Tr. by R. Manheim. New Haven: Yale University Press, 1959.

Kant, Immanuel. *Fundamental Principles of the Metaphysics of Ethics*. Tr. by T. K. Abbott. London: Longmans, 1965.

Kierkegaard, S. A. *Either/Or: A Fragment of Life*. Tr. by D. P. and L. M. Swenson. London: Oxford University Press, 1946.

Lach, Donald F., tr. *The Preface to Leibniz' Nobissima Sinica*. Honolulu: University of Hawaii Press, 1957.

Leclerq, J., et al. *Histoire de la Spiritualité chrétienne*. 4 vols. Paris: Aubier, 1941.

Leibniz, G. W. *Selections*. Ed. by Philip P. Winer. New York: Scribner's. 1951.

McKeon, Richard, ed. *Selections from the Medieval Philosophers*. New York: Scribner's, 1929–30.

Masson-Oursel, Paul. "True Philosophy Is Comparative Philosophy," *Philosophy East and West* I (1951), 6–9.

Nietzsche, F. W. *The Philosophy of Nietzsche*. New York: Modern Library, 1964.

—— *Thus Spake Zarathustra*. London: Dent, 1933.

Otto, Rudolf. *The Idea of the Holy*. Eng. tr. by J. W. Harvey. London: Oxford University Press, 1950.

—— *Mysticism East and West*. Eng. tr. by B. L. Bracey and R. C. Payne. New York: Colliers, 1962.

Pascal, B. *Pensées*. Texte établi par L. Lafuma. Paris: Seuil, 1962.

Plato. *The Great Dialogues of Plato,* Tr. by W. H. D. Rouse. New York: New American Library, 1956.

Plotinus. *The Enneads*. Tr. by S. Mackenna. London: Faber and Faber, 1956.

Russell, B. *Mysticism and Logic and Other Essays*. London: Allen and Unwin, 1969.

Spinoza, Benedictus de. *Spinoza: Selections*. Ed. by John Wild. New York: Scribner's, 1930.

Tillich, P. *The Courage to Be*. New Haven: Yale University Press, 1958.

Whitehead, A. N. *Process and Reality*. New York: Free Press, 1969.

Wittgenstein, L. *Philosophical Investigations*. Translated by G. E. M. Anscombe, New York: Macmillan, 1953.

Zaehner, R. C. *At Sundry Times: An Essay in the Comparison of Religions*. London: Faber and Faber, 1958.

—— *Mysticism Sacred and Profane: An Inquiry into Some Varieties of Preternatural Experience*. Oxford: Clarendon, 1957.

D.   OTHER WORKS IN EUROPEAN LANGUAGES

Abe Yoshio. "The Development of Neo-Confucianism in Japan, Korea and China: A Comparative Study," *Acta Asiatica* XIX (1970), 16–39.

Abegg, Lily. *The Mind of East Asia*. Tr. by A. J. Crick and E. E. Thomas, from the German work, *Ostasien Denkt Anders*. London: Thomas and Hudson, 1952.

Balazs, Etienne. *Political Theory and Administrative Reality in Traditional China*. London: School of Oriental and African Studies, University of London, 1965.

Bernard, Henri, S. J. "Chu Hsi's Philosophy and Its Interpretation by Leibniz," *T'ien Hsia Monthly* V (1937), 9–18.

—— *Sagesse chinoise et philosophie chrétienne*. Tientsin: Institut des Hautes Études, 1935.

Bodde, Derk. "Harmony and Conflict in Chinese Philosophy," in *Studies in Chinese Thought*. Ed. by Arthur F. Wright. Chicago: University of Chicago Press, 1953, 19–80.

Brière, O. *Fifty Years of Chinese Philosophy, 1898–1950*. Tr. by Laurence G. Thompson. London: Allen and Unwin, 1956.

Bruce, J. Percy. *Chu Hsi and his Masters: An Introduction to Chu Hsi and the Sung School of Chinese Philosophy*. London: Probsthain, 1923.

Busch, Heinrich. "The Tung-lin Academy and Its Political and Philosophical Singnificance," *Monumenta Serica* XIV (1949–55), 1–163.

Cady, Lyman Van Law, *The Philosophy of Lu Hsiang-shan, a Neo-Confucian Monistic Idealist*. New York: Union Theological Seminary Doctoral Thesis, 1939; University Microfilms, microfilm copy.

—— *Wang Yang-ming's "Intuitive Knowledge,"* Peiping: Privately published, 1936.

Cahill, James F. "Confucian Elements in the Theory of Painting," in *The Confucian Persuasion*. Ed. by Arthur F. Wright. Stanford: Stanford University Press, 1960, 115–40.

Callahan, Paul E. "Chu Hsi and St. Thomas: A Comparison." *Papers on China*, IV. Harvard University Regional Studies Seminar, mimeographed for private distribution by the Committee on International and Regional Studies (1950), 1–23.

Chai, Ch'u. "Neo-Confucianism of the Sung-Ming Period," *Social Research* XVIII (1951), 370–92.

Chan, Wing-tsit. "Chan Jo-shui's Influence on Wang Yang-ming," *Philosophy East and West* XXIII (1973), 12–30.

—— "The Ch'eng-Chu School of Early Ming", in *Self and Society in Ming Thought*. Ed. by W. T. de Bary: New York: Columbia University Press, 1970, 29–52.

—— "Chinese Philosophy in Mainland China 1949–1963," *Philosophy East East and West* XIV (1964), 25–38.

—— "Chinese Theory and Practice, with Specific Reference to Humanism," in *The Chinese Mind*. Ed. by Charles A. Moore. Honolulu: Hawaii University Press, 1967.

—— "Chu Hsi's Completion of Neo-Confucianism," in *Études Song. Sung Studies. In Memoriam Étienne Balazs*. Ed. by Francoise Aubin. Series 2, No. 1 1973, 60–87.

—— "The Evolution of the Confucian Concept *Jen*", *Philosophy East and West* IV (1954–55), 295–319; reprinted in Chan, *Neo-Confucianism, etc.*, 1–44.

—— "The Evolution of the Neo-Confucian Concept *Li* as Principle," *Tsing Hua Journal of Chinese Studies*, n. s., 4, No. 2 (1964), 123 49. Reprinted in Chan, *Neo-Confucianism, etc.*, 45–87.

—— "How Buddhistic Was Wang Yang-ming?" *Philosophy East and West* XII (1962), 203–16.

—— *Neo-Confucianism etc.: Essays by Wing-tsit Chan*. Com. by Charles K. H. Chen. New Haven: Oriental Society, 1969.

—— "Neo-Confucianism: New Ideas in Old Terminology," *Philosophy East and West* XVII (1967), 15–36.

—— "The Neo-Confucian Solution of the Problem of Evil," in *Studies Presented to Hu Shin on His sixty-fifth Birthday (Bulletin of the Institute of History and Philosophy, Academia Sinca, 28)*. Taipei, 1957, 773–92; reprinted in Chan, *Neo-Confucianism, etc.*, 88–116.

—— "The Unity of East and West," in *Radhakkishnan, Comparative Studies in Philosophy Presented in Honour of His 60th Birthday*. Ed. by W. R. Inge *et al.* London: Allen and Unwin, 1951, 104–17.

Chang, Carsun. "Buddhism as a Stimulus to Neo-Confucianism," *Oriens Extremus* II (1955), 157–66.

—— "Chinese Intuitionism: A Reply to Fergl on Intuition," *Philosophy East and West* X (1960), 35–49

—— *The Development of Neo-Confucian Thought*. 2 vols. New Haven: Bookman Associates, 1957–62.

—— "Reason and Intuition in Chinese Philosophy," *Philosophy East and West* IV (1954), 99–112.

—— *Wang Yang-ming, Idealist Philosopher of Sixteenth-Century China.* New York: St. John's University Press, 1962.

—— "Wang Yang-ming's Philosophy," *Philosophy East and West* V (1955–56), 3–18.

Chang, Chung-yüan. *Creativity and Taoism: A Study of Chinese Philosophy, Art and Poetry.* New York: The Julian Press, 1963.

—— "The Essential Source of Identity in Wang Lung-ch'i's Philosophy," *Philosophy East and West* XXIII (1973), 31–48.

Chang, Yü-ch'uan. "Wang Shou-jen as a Statesman", *Chinese Social and Political Science Review* XXIII (1939–40), 30–99, 155–252, 319–75, 473–517.

Ch'en, Kenneth K. S. *Buddhism in China.* Princeton: Princeton University Press, 1964.

Cheng Chung-ying. "Unity and Creativity in Wang Yang-ming's Philosophy of mind", *Philosophy East and West* XXIII (1973), 49–72.

Julia Ching. "Confucius and His Modern Critics", *Papers on Far Eastern History* X (Canberra, 1974), 117–46.

—— "The Goose Lake Monastery Debate (1175)". *Journal of Chinese Philosophy* I (1974), 161–78.

—— "Neo-Confucian Utopian Theories and Political Ethics," *Monumenta Serica* XXX (1972–73), 1–56.

—— "Truth and Ideology: The Confucian Way (Tao) and Its Transmission (Tao-t'ung)," *Journal of the History of Ideas* XXXV (1974), 371–88.

—— "Wang Yang-ming (1472–1529): A Study in 'Mad Ardour,' " *Papers on Far Eastern History* III (March, 1971), 85–130.

Chow, Yi-ching. *La Philosophie Morale dans le Neo-confucianisme (Tcheon Touen-yi).* Paris: Presses Universitaires de France, 1953.

Contag, Victoria. "Erkenntnisse des alter Chu Hsi," *Sinologica* VII (1963), 217–27.

Conze, Edward. *Buddhism, Its Essence and Development.* Oxford: Bruno Cassirer, 1951.

Creel, Herrlee G. *Chinese Thought from Confucius to Mao Tse-tung.* Chicago: University of Chicago Press, 1955.

—— *Confucius, the Man and the Myth.* New York: John Day, 1949.

Dai, Shen-yu. *Mao Tse-tung and Confucianism.* Unpublished Ph. D. Thesis. University of Pennsylvania, 1953. Microfilm copy.

De Bary, Wm. Theodore, "Individualism and Humanitarianism in Late Ming Thought," in *Self and Society in Ming Thought.* Ed. by W. T. de Bary. New York: Columbia University Press, 1970.

—— "A Re-appraisal of Neo-Confucianism," in *Studies in Chinese Thought.* Ed. by Arthur F. Wright. Chicago: University of Chicago Press, 1953, 81–111.

—— ed. *Self and Society in Ming Thought.* New York: Columbia University Press, 1970.

—— "Some Common Tendencies in Neo-Confucianism," in *Confucianism in Action.* Ed. by David S. Nivison and Arthur F. Wright, Stanford: Stanford

University Press, 1959, 25–49.

—— ed. *The Unfolding of Neo-Confucianism.* New York: Columbia University Press, 1975.

De Groot, J. J. M. *Sectarianism and Religious Persecution in China.* 2 vols. Amsterdam: J. Miller, 1903.

—— *Universismus: die Grundlage der Religion und Ethik, des Staatswesens und der Wissenschaften Chinas.* Berlin: Verlag v. Georg Reimer, 1918.

De Harlez, Charles. *L'École Philosophique Moderne de la Chine, ou Systeme de la Nature Sing-li. Mémoires de l'Academie Royale des Sciences, des Letters et des Beaux Arts de Belgique* XLIX (1890–93).

Demiéville, Paul. "Le Mirroir Spirituel," *Sinologica* I (1948), 112–37.

—— "La Pénétration du Bouddhisme dans la Tradition Philosophique Chinoise," *Cahiers d'Histoire Mondiale* I (1956), 19–38.

Drake, David. "Logic of the One-Mind Doctrine," *Philosophy East and West* XVI (1966), 207–20.

Dubs, Homer H. "The Development of Altruism in Confucianism," *Philosophy East and West* I (1951), 48–55.

—— *Hsün-tzu, the Moulder of Ancient Confucianism* London: Probsthain, 1927.

—— "Mencius and Sundz on Human Nature," *Philosophy East and West* VI (1956) 213–22.

Dumoulin, Heinrich, ed. *Buddhismus der Gegenwart.* Freiburg: Herder, 1970.

—— *The Development of Chinese Zen after the Sixth Patriarch in the Light of Mumonkan.* Trans. by Ruth Fuller Sakaki. New York: First Zen Institute of America, 1953

—— *A History of Zen Buddhism.* Trans. by Paul Peachey. London: Faber and Faber, 1963.

—— *Östliche Meditation und Christliche Mystik.* Munich: Verlag Karl Alber, 1966.

Eberhard, Wolfram. *Guilt and Sin in Traditional China.* Los Angeles: University of California Press, 1967.

Erkes, E. "Die Dialektik als Grundlage der chinesischen Weltanschauung," *Sinologica* II (1949), 31–43.

Fairbank, J. K. ed. *Chinese Thought and Institutions.* Chicago: University of Chicago Press, 1957.

Fang, Thomé. "The Essence of Wang Yang-ming's Philosophy in a Historical Perspective," *Philosophy East and West* XXIII (1973), 73–90.

Forke, Alfred. *Geschichte der alten chinesischen Philosophie.* Hamburg: Friederichsen, 1927.

—— *Geschichte der neuren chinesischen Philosophie.* Hanische Universite Abhandlungen B. 46, Hamburg: Friederichsen De Gruyter, 1938.

Franke, Otto. *Li Tschi: Ein Beitrag Zur Geschichte der chinesischen Geisteskampfe im 16 Jahrhundert.* Berlin: Verlag der Akademie der Wissenschaften, 1938.

—— "Die religiöse und politische Bedeutung des Konfuzianismus in Vergangenheit und Gegenwart," *Zeitschrift für Systematische Theologie* VIII (1931), 579–88.

Fung Yu-lan. *A History of Chinese Philosophy*. Tr. by Derk Bodde. 2 vols. Princeton: Princeton University Press, 1952–53.

—— *A Short History of Chinese Philosophy*. Ed. by Derk Bodde. New York: Macmillan, 1948.

—— *The Spirit of Chinese Philosophy*. Tr. by E. R. Hughes. London: Kegan Paul, 1947.

Gotō, Motomi. "Studies in Chinese Philosophy in Post-war Japan," *Monumenta Serica* XIV (1949–55), 164–87.

Gotō, Toshimidzu. "The Ontology of the 'Li' Philosophy of the Sung Dynasty of China," *Philosophical Studies of Japan* II (1960), 119–43.

Graf, Olaf. "Chu Hsi und Spinoza," in *Proceedings of the 10th International Congress of Philosophy* (Amsterdam, August 11–18, 1948). Ed. by E.W. Berth, H. J. Pos, and J. H. A. Hollak. Amsterdam: North-Holland Pub. Co., 1949, 238–42.

—— *Tao und Jen: Sein und Sollen im sungchineschichen Monismus*. Wiesbaden: Otto Harrassowitz, 1970.

Graham, Angus C. *The Problem of Value*. London: Hutchinson, 1961.

—— *Two Chinese Philosophers, Ch'eng Ming-tao and Ch'eng Yi-ch'uan*. London: Lund Humphries, 1958.

Granet, Marcel. *La Pensée Chinoise*. Paris: La Renaissance du Livre, 1934.

Grimm, Tilemann. *Erziehung und Politik im konfuzianischen China der Ming-Zeit, 1368–1600*. Hamburg: Deutsche Gesellschaft für Natur und Volkerkunde Ostasiens, 1960.

—— "Ming Educational Intendants," in *Chinese Government in Ming Times: Seven Studies*. Ed. by Charles O. Hucker. New York: Columbia University Press, 1969, 129–47.

—— "War das China der Ming-Zeit totalitär?" *Gesellschaft für Natur und Völkerkunde Ostasiens Nachrichten* LXXIX/LXXX (1956), 30–36.

Haroutunian, H. D. *Toward Restoration, the Growth of Political Consciousness in Tokugawa Japan*. Berkeley: University of California Press, 1970.

Henthorn, William E. *A History of Korea*. New York: Free Press, 1971.

Hisamatsu, Shinichi. "The Characteristics of Oriental Nothingness," *Philosophical Studies of Japan* II (1960), 65–9.

Hocking, W. E. "Chu Hsi's Theory of Knowledge," *Harvard Journal of Asiatic Studies* I (1936), 109–27.

—— "Value of the Comparative Study of Philosophy," in *Philosophy East and West*. Ed. by Charles A. Moore. Princeton: Princeton University Press, 1949, 1–11.

Holzman, Donald. "The Conversational Tradition in Chinese Philosophy," *Philosophy East and West* VI (1956), 223–30.

—— "Les Sept Sages de Foret de Bambous," *T'oung-Pao* XLIV (1967), 317–46.

Hsieh Yu-wei. "Filial Piety and Chinese Society," in *Philosophy and Culture East and West*. Ed. by Chalres A. Moore. Honolulu: University of Hawaii Press, 1962, 411–27.

Hsü, Pao-ch'ien. *Ethical Realism in Neo-Confucian Thought.* Columbia University Ph. D. Thesis, 1933. Microfilm copy of typescript made in 1969 by Columbia University Libraries.

Hu Shih. *"Ch'an* Buddhism in China: Its History and Method," *Philosophy East and West* III (1953), 3–24.

—— "Chinese Thought," in *China.* Ed. by H. F. MacNair. Berkeley: University of California Press, 1946, 221–30.

—— "Religion and Philosophy in Chinese History," in *Symposium on Chinese Culture.* Ed. by Sophia H. Ch'en Zen. Shanghai: China Institute of Pacific Relations, 1931, 31–58.

—— "The Scientific Spirit and Method in Chinese Philosophy," in *Philosophy and Culture East and West.* Ed. by Charles A. Moore. Honolulu: University of Hawaii Press, 1962, 199–222.

Huang Siu-chi. "Chang Tsai's Concept of *ch'i,*" *Philosophy East and West* XVIII (1968), 247–59.

—— *Lu Hsiang-shan: A Twelfth Century Chinese Idealist Philosopher.* New Haven: American Oriental Society, 1944.

Hucker, Charles O. *The Censorial System of Ming China.* Stanford: Stanford University Press, 1966.

—— ed. *Chinese Government in Ming Times: Seven Studies.* New York: Columbia University Press, 1969.

—— "Confucianism and the Chinese Censorial System," in *Confucianism in Action.* Ed. by Arthur F. Wright. Stanford: Stanford University Press, 1959, 182–208.

—— "Government Organization of the Ming Dynasty," *Harvard Journal of Asiatic Studies* XXI (1958), 1–66.

—— *The Traditional Chinese State in Ming Times (1368–1644).* Tucson: University of Arizona Press, 1961.

Hughes, E. R. *Chinese Philosophy in Classical Times.* Rev. ed. London: Dent, 1954.

Hughes, Margaret. *The Epistomological Foundations of Ethics with Specific Reference to the Views of Wang Yang-ming and Immanuel Kant.* Hong Kong University, unpublished M. A. Thesis, 1965.

Hurvitz, Leon. "Chu-hung's One Mind of Pure Land and Ch'an Buddhism," in *Self and Society in Ming Thought.* Ed. by W. T. de Bary. New York: Columbia University Press, 1970, 451–82.

Iki, Hiroyuki. "Wang Yang-ming's Doctrine of Innate Knowledge of the Good," *Philosophy East and West* XI (1961), 27–33.

Jen, Yu-wen. "Ch'en Hsien-chang's Philosophy of Nature, "in *Self and Society in Ming Thought.* Ed. by W. T. de Bary. New York: Columbia University Press, 1970, 53–86.

Joe, Wanne J. *Traditional Korea: A Cultural History.* Seoul: Chung'ang University Press, 1972.

Jung, Hwa Yol. "Wang Yang-ming and Existential Phenomenology," *International Philosophical Quarterly* V (1965), 612–36.

Kimura, Eiichi. "The New Confucianism and Taoism in China and Japan from the Fourth to the Thirteenth Centuries, A. D.," *Cahiers d'histoire Mondiale* V (1959–60), 801–29.

Kōsaka, Massaki. *Japanese Thought in the Meiji Era* (*Japanese Culture in the Meiji Era*, v. 9). Tr. and adapted by David Abosch. Tokyo: Pacific Press, 1958.

Kusumoto, Masatsugu. "Conflict between the Thoughts of the Sung Dynasty and the Ming Dynasty," *Philosophical Studies of Japan* V (1964), 39–68.

Ku Chieh-kang. "A Study of Literary Persecutions during the Ming." Tr. by L. Carrington Goodrich. *Harvard Journal of Asiatic Studies* III (1938), 254–311.

Lau, D. C. "A Note on Ke Wu," *Bulletin of the School of Oriental and African Studies* XXX (1967), 353–57.

—— "Theories of Human Nature in Mencius and Shyuntzyy," *Bulletin of the School of Oriental and African Studies* XV (1953), 541–658.

Le Gall, Stanislas, S. J. *Tchou Hi, sa Doctrine, son Influence.* Variété Sinologiques, 6. 2nd ed. Shanghai: La Mission Catholique, 1923.

Levenson, Joseph. *Confucian China and Its Modern Fate.* Vol. 1: *The Problem of Intellectual Continuity.* Berkeley: University of California Press, 1958.

—— *Confucian China and Its Modern Fate.* Vol. 2: *The Problem of Monarchical Decay.* London: Routledge and Kegan Paul, 1964.

—— *Confucian China and Its Modern Fate.* Vol. 3: *The Problem of Historical Significance.* London: Routledge and Kegan Paul, 1965.

Levy, Andre. "*Un Document sur la Querelle des Anciens et des Modernes more sinico,*" *T'oung-Pao* LIV (1968), 51–274.

Liu, James T. C. "How Did a Neo-Confucian School Become the State Orthodoxy?" *Philosophy East and West* XXIII (1973), 483–506.

—— *Reform in Sung China: Wang An-shih (1021–86) and His New Policies.* Cambridge, Mass. Harvard University Press, 1959.

Liu Ts'un-yan. "Lin Chao-en (1517–1598), the Master of the Three Teachings," *T'oung-Pao* LIII (1967), 253–78.

—— "Taoist Self-Cultivation in Ming Thought," in *Self and Society in Ming Thought.* Ed. by W. T. de Bary. New York: Columbia University Press, 1970, 291–330.

—— "Yuan Huang and His 'Four Adminitions,' " *Journal of the Oriental Society of Australia* V (1967), 108–32.

McMorran, Ian, "Late Ming Criticism of Wang Yang-ming: The Case of Wang Fu-chih," *Philosophy East and West* XXIII (1973), 91–102.

MacNair, Harley F., ed. *China.* Berkeley and Los Angeles: University of California Press, 1951.

Maruyama Masao. *Thought and Behaviour in Modern Japanese Politics.* Ed. by Ivan Morris. London: Oxford University Press, 1963.

Maspéro, Henri. *Les Religions chinoises, Mélanges posthumes sur les Religions et l'Histoire de la Chine: le Taoisme.* Paris: Civilisations du Sud, 1950.

Mei, Y. P. "The Basis of Social, Ethical, and Spiritual Values in Chinese Philosophy," in *Essays in East-West Philosophy*. Ed. by Charles A. Moore. Honolulu: University of Hawaii Press, 1951, 301–16. Reprinted in *The Chinese Mind*, Ed. by Charles A. Moore, 149–66.

Meskill, John. "Academies and Politics in the Ming Dynasty," in *Chinese Government in Ming Times: Seven Studies*. Ed. by Charles O. Hucker. New York: Columbia University Press, 1969, 147–74.

Miyuki, Mokusen. *An Analysis of Buddhist Influence on the Formation of the Sung Confucian Concept of Li-ch'i*. Unpublished Claremont Graduate School and University Center Thesis, 1965. University Microfilms, Xeroxed copy.

Moore, Charles A., ed. *The Chinese Mind: Essentials of Chinese Philosophy and Culture*. Honolulu: East-West Center Press and University of Hawaii Press, 1967.

—— ed. *Essays in East-West Philosophy*. Honolulu: University of Hawaii Press, 1951.

—— ed. *Philosophy and Culture, East and West*. Honolulu: University of Hawaii Press, 1962.

—— ed. *Philosophy—East and West*. Princeton: Princeton University Press, 1946.

Mou Tsung-san. "The Immediate Successor of Wang Yang-ming: Wang Lung-hsi and His Theory of *ssu-wu*," *Philosophy East and West* XXIII (1973), 103–20.

Nivison, David S. "Moral Decision in Wang Yang-ming: The Problem of Chinese 'Existentialism,' " *Philosophy East and West* XXIII (1973), 121–38.

Okada Takehiko. "The Chu Hsi and Wang Yang-ming Schools at the End of the Ming and Tokugawa Periods," *Philosophy East and West* XXIII (1973), 139–62.

—— "Wang Chi and the Rise of Existentialism", in *Self and Society in Ming Thought*. Ed. by W. T. de Bary. New York: Columbia University Press, 1970.

Politella, Joseph. "Meister Eckhart and Eastern Wisdom," *Philosophy East and West* XV (1965), 117–34.

Pulleyblank, Edwin G. "Neo-Confucianism and Neo-Legalism in T'ang Intellectual Life, 755–805," in *The Confucian Persuasion*. Ed. by Arthur F. Wright. Stanford: Stanford University Press, 1960, 77–114.

Richards, I. A. *Mencius on the Mind: Experiments in Multiple Definition*. London: Kegan Paul, 1932.

Sakai, Tadao. "Confucianism and Popular Educational Works," in *Self and Society in Ming Thought*. Ed. by W. T. de Bary. New York: Columbia University Press, 1970, 331–66.

Sargent, Galen Eugène. "Les débats personnels de Tchou Hi en matière de méthodologie," *Journal Asiatique* 243 (1955), 213–28.

Schwartz, Benjamin. "Some Polarities in Confucian Thought," in *Confucianism in Action*. Ed. by David S. Nivison and Arthur F. Wright. Stanford: Stanford University Press, 1959, 50–62.

Seuberlich, Wolfgang. "Kaisertreu oder Auflehnung? Eine Episode aus der Ming-Zeit," *Deutsche Morgenlandliche Gesellschaft Zeitschrift* 102 (1952), 304–13.

Shih, Vincent Y. C. "The Mind and the Moral Order," *Mélanges chinoises et boudhiques* X (1955), 347–64.

—— "Some Chinese Rebel Ideologies," *T'oung-Pao* XLIV (1956), 151–226.

Shirokauer, Conrad M. "Chu Hsi's Political Career: A Study in Ambivalence," in *Confucian Personalities*. Ed. by Arthur F. Wright. Stanford: Stanford University Press, 1962, 162–88.

Sun, Stanislaus, S. J. "The Doctrine of *Li* in the Philosophy of Chu Hsi," *International Philosophical Quarterly* VI (1966), 155–88.

Suzuki, Daisetz Teitaro. *Essays in Zen Buddhism*. 1st series. London: Rider, 1927.

—— *Essays in Zen Buddhism*. 2nd series. London: Rider, 1950.

—— *Essays in Zen Buddhism*. 3rd series. London: Rider, 1953.

—— "Interpretation of Zen Experience," in *Philosophy—East and West*. Ed. by Charles A. Moore. Princeton: Princeton University Press, 1946, 106–29.

—— *Studies in the Lankavatara Sutra*. London: Routledge, 1930.

—— *Studies in Zen*. London: Rider, 1955.

—— "Zen: A Reply to Hu Shih," *Philosophy East and West* III (1953), 25–46.

—— *The Zen Doctrine of No-Mind*. London: Rider, 1949.

Takakusu, Junjirō. "Buddhism as a Philosophy of Thusness," in *Philosophy—East and West*. Ed. by Charles A. Moore. Princeton: Princeton University Press, 1949, 69–108.

—— *The Essentials of Buddhist Philosophy*. Ed. by Wing-tsit Chan and Charles A. Moore. Honolulu: University of Hawaii Press, 1947.

T'ang Chün-i. "Chang Tsai's Theory of Mind and Its Metaphysical Basis," *Philosophy East and West* VI (1956), 113–36.

—— "The Criticisms of Wang Yang-ming's Teachings as Raised by His Contemporaries," *Philosophy East and West* XXIII (1973), 163–86.

—— "The Development of the Concept of Moral Mind from Wang Yang-ming to Wang Chi," in *Self and Society in Ming Thought*. Ed. by W. T. de Bary. New York: Columbia University Press, 1970.

Tu Wei-ming. "The Development of Ideas of Spiritual Value in Chinese Philosophy," in *Philosophy and Culture East and West*. Ed. by Charles A. Moore. Honolulu: University of Hawaii Press, 1962, 225–44.

—— *The Quest for Self-realization—A Study of Wang Yang-ming's Formative Years 1472–1509*. Unpublished Ph. D. Thesis, Harvard University, 1969. Microfilm copy.

—— "Subjectivity and Ontological Reality—an Interpretation of Wang Yang-ming's Mode of Thinking," *Philosophy East and West* XXIII (1973), 187–206.

Twitchett, Denis, and A. F. Wright, eds. *Confucian Personalities*. Stanford: Stanford University Press, 1962.

Waley, Arthur. "History and Religion: On Suzuki and Hu Shih's Exchange," *Philosophy East and West* V (1955),75–78.

—— "Notes on Chinese Alchemy," *Bulletin of the School of Oriental Studies* VI (1930), 1–24.

—— *Three Ways of Thought in Ancient China*. London: Allen and Unwin, 1939.

Wang Tchang-tche, S. J. *La Philosophie Morale de Wang Yang-ming*. Variété sinologiques, no. 63. Shanghai-Paris: T'ou-se-we and P. Geuthner, 1936.

Weber, Max, *The Religion of China, Confucianism and Taoism*. Tr. by Hans H. Gerth. London: George Allen, 1951.

Welch, Holmes. *The Parting of the Way, Laotzu and the Taoist Movement*. London: Methuen, 1957.

Wen, Hsi-tseng. *The Status of Man in Neo-Confucianism*. Unpublished Ph. D. Thesis, University of Southern California, 1954. Microfilm copy.

Wienpahl, Paul. "Spinoza and Wang Yang-ming," *Religious Studies* V (1969), 19–27.

—— "Wang Yang-ming and Meditation," *Journal of Chinese Philosophy* I (1974), 199–228.

Wilhelm, Hellmut *Change: Eight Lectures on the I Ching*. Trans. by C. F. Baynes. Princeton: Princeton University Press, 1960.

—— "The Heresies of Ch'en Liang (1143–94)," *Asiatische Studien* XI (1958), 102–11.

—— "On Ming Orthodoxy," *Monumenta Serica* XXIX (1970–71), 1–26.

—— "A Reappraisal of Neo-Confucianism," *The China Quarterly* XXIII (1965), 122–39.

—— "The Problem of Within and Without: A Confucian Attempt in Syncretism," *Journal of the History of Ideas* XII (1951), 48–60.

Wright, Arthur F. *Buddhism in Chinese History*. Stanford; Stanford University Press, 1959.

—— and Denis Twitchett, eds. *Confucian Personalities*. Stanford: Stanford University Press, 1962.

—— ed. *The Confucian Persuasion*. Stanford: Stanford University Press, 1960.

—— and D. S. Nivison, eds. *Confucianism in Action*. Stanford · Stanford University Press, 1959.

—— ed. *Studies in Chinese Thought*. Chicago: University of Chicago Press, 1953.

Wu, John C. H. "Chinese Legal and Political Philosophy," in *Philosophy and Culture East and West*. Ed. by Charles A. Moore. Honolulu: University of Hawaii Press, 1962, 611–30.

Wu, Nelson I. "Intellectual Movements and the Teachings of Wang Yang-ming: Parallel but Nonconcurrent Developments," *Philosophy East and West* XXIII (1973), 225–36.

—— "Tung Ch'i-ch'ang, 1555–1636: Apathy in Government and Fervor in Art," in *Confucian Personalities*. Ed. by A. F. Wright and D. Twitchett. Stanford: Stanford University Press, 1962, 260–93.

Yang, K. P., and G. Henderson. "An Outline History of Korean Confucianism," *Journal of Asian Studies* ZVIII (1958), 81–102; (1959), 259–76.

Zenker, E. V. *Histoire de la Philosophie Chinoise*. Paris: Payot, 1932.

Zürcher, E. *The Buddhist Conquest of China*. 2 vols. Leiden: Brill, 1959.

GENERAL INDEX

TRANSLATIONS FROM THE ORIENTAL CLASSICS

STUDIES IN ORIENTAL CULTURE

COMPANIONS TO
ASIAN STUDIES

INTRODUCTION TO
ORIENTAL CIVILIZATIONS

Wm. Theodore de Bary, *Editor*